TESTIMONIALS TO ROBERT H. MICHEL

"Bob Michel loved this institution [the House of Representatives] . . . . He did not just shape events. He shaped people's lives—how they lived and how they treated others. That's what makes a giant a giant. It is the values they instill in us. Those moments that make you say, 'Wow, I will never forget this.' Bob Michel had a lot of those kinds of moments in his good and long life. You wouldn't know it by how humble and genial he was."

—Speaker of the House Paul Ryan (R-WI)

Source: "Memorial Service for Leader Bob Michel," March 9, 2017, www.youtube.com/watch?v=nOTOkx73524

"He showed us that consensus is not weakness, and principled, intelligent compromise is not capitulation—it's how a democracy works."

—Senator Dick Durbin (D-IL)

Source: "Memorial Service for Leader Bob Michel," March 9, 2017, www.youtube.com/watch?v=nOTOkx73524

"Bob Michel was a patriot, a proud immigrant son, a soldier, and a great American statesman. A patriot indeed. . . . He brought the values of the heartland to Washington, and he personified the highest ideals of our nation. . . . We all benefited from his wisdom, his dignity, and his integrity."

—Former Speaker of the House Nancy Pelosi (D-CA)

Source: "Memorial Service for Leader Bob Michel," March 9, 2017, www.youtube.com/watch?v=nOTOkx73524

"Bob was one of the finest men I've ever known. . . . Our leader was never known to make a disagreement personal or let opposition give way to hostility, to show the signs of injured vanity. And forget about holding a grudge. Bob wouldn't know how to acquire a grudge in the first place. He was a straight-up guy through and through. And authentic and devoid of pretense as any man could be. . . . The gentleman from Illinois commanded respect well beyond anything required by title. He was a man of courage, rectitude, and personal kindness—a friend we looked up to and were lucky to have in our lives."

—Former Vice President Richard B. Cheney

Source: "Memorial Service for Leader Bob Michel," March 9, 2017, www.youtube.com/watch?v=nOTOkx73524

"In what now seems to be a long-lost approach to governance, Bob preferred to reach across the aisle than battle across the aisle. He could, and he did, disagree agreeably."

—Former Secretary of State James A. Baker

Source: "Memorial Service for Leader Bob Michel," March 9, 2017, www.youtube.com/watch?v=nOTOkx73524

"As his colleague for the past fifteen years, I have been witness to the central role Bob Michel has played in advancing both Republican and national interests. Without Bob Michel's leadership, Ronald Reagan would never have passed his tax and budget cuts. Without his leadership, George Bush would not have sustained his veto strategy for four years. Indeed, little that Republican Presidents have accomplished would have been possible without Bob Michel's solid leadership."

—Representative Newt Gingrich (R-GA)

Source: "Newt Gingrich Praises Rep. Robert Michel on His Accomplishments for Republican Party," Press Release, The Republican Whip, October 4, 1993, RHM Papers, Personal, f. Retirement.

"Time and again, Bob Michel has provided not only forward-looking leadership, but a center of gravity for the Republican Party and for Congress as a whole. These have been difficult times for America and for Congress. Bob Michel has held the party together while maintaining necessary lines of communications to all elements of Congress."

— Representative Newt Gingrich (R-GA)

Source: "Newt Gingrich Praises Rep. Robert Michel on His Accomplishments for Republican Party," Press Release, The Republican Whip, October 4, 1993, RHM Papers, Personal, f. Retirement.

"Years ago, before taking a show on the road to the nation's heartland, Broadway used to ask, 'Will it play in Peoria?' Were the question to be asked about Bob Michel's contributions to public service, the answer would be a resounding yes. As prevailing political philosophies have changed over the years, Bob Michel remained steadfast in his commitment to consensus in the interest of the nation and the institution of the House of Representatives. His great dignity, his constant professionalism, and his instinct for decency and moderation in the face of extremes have always been proof that politics can be an ennobling profession."

—Speaker of the House Thomas Foley (D-WA)

Source: "Speaker Comments on Republican Leader Michel," Press Release from the Speaker, October 4, 1993, RHM Papers, Personal, f. Retirement.

"Although he has spent much of his life in Washington, D.C., there is no doubt that Peoria is still Bob Michel's home. And the values that define Bob Michel as a man and a leader—values like hard work, honesty, and loyalty—are values that remain important in America's heartland. When Bob retires from Congress, he will have served as Republican leader for 14 years. And no doubt about it, they have been some of the most remarkable years in American history."

—Senator Bob Dole (R-KS)

Source: "Salute to Bob Michel," News Release from the Senate Republican Leader, October 4, 1993, RHM Papers, Personal, f. Retirement.

"Robert Michel has served in the United States House of Representatives since 1957. That is the second longest tenure of any Republican in American history. As minority leader in the House for the last 13 years, he has served his party well, but he has also served our Nation well, choosing the pragmatic but harder course of conciliation more often than the divisive but easier course of confrontation. In the best sense he is a gentleman legislator who, in spite of the great swings in public opinion from year to year, has remained always true to the midwestern values he represents so faithfully in the House. He retires at the end of this year, generally regarded by Democrats and Republicans alike as one of the most decent and respected leaders with which any President has had the privilege to work."

—President William J. Clinton

Source: "Remarks on Presenting the Presidential Medals of Freedom," August 8, 1994, *Public Papers of the President*, American Presidency Project, www.presidency.ucsb.edu/ws/index.php?pid=48956&st=&st1=.

"My colleague, Bob Michel, the minority leader of the House of Representatives, has announced his retirement. I am sorry to see him go. We are on opposite sides of the aisle, we have disagreed many times, but he has always been a gentleman. And most importantly, Bob Michel has been a voice of reason and moderation in an institution which is becoming increasingly shrill, increasingly partisan, and increasingly destined for gridlock. We need his wise counsel. We have needed it over the years."

—Representative Dick Durbin (D-IL)

Source: *Congressional Record*, October 6, 1993, H 7459.

ROBERT H. MICHEL

CONGRESSIONAL LEADERS

Burdett A. Loomis
Series Editor

ROBERT H. MICHEL

LEADING THE REPUBLICAN HOUSE MINORITY

Edited by Frank H. Mackaman
and Sean Q Kelly

University Press of Kansas

Published by the University Press of Kansas (Lawrence, Kansas 66045), which was organized by the Kansas Board of Regents and is operated and funded by Emporia State University, Fort Hays State University, Kansas State University, Pittsburg State University, the University of Kansas, and Wichita State University.

Publication made possible, in part, by funding from
The Dirksen Congressional Center.

Library of Congress Cataloging-in-Publication Data

Names: Mackaman, Frank H., editor. | Kelly, Sean Q, editor.
Title: Robert H. Michel : leading the Republican House minority / edited by Frank H. Mackaman and Sean Q Kelly.
Description: Lawrence, Kansas : University Press of Kansas, [2019] | Series: Congressional leaders | Includes bibliographical references and index.
Identifiers: LCCN 2018058262
ISBN 9780700627592 (cloth : alk. paper)
ISBN 9780700627608 (ebook)
Subjects: LCSH: Michel, Robert H., 1923–2017. | Legislators—United States—Biography. | United States. Congress. House—Minority leaders—Biography. | United States—Politics and government—20th century.
Classification: LCC E840.8.M523 R63 2019 | DDC 328.73/092 [B]—dc23
LC record available at https://lccn.loc.gov/2018058262.

British Library Cataloguing-in-Publication Data is available.

Printed in the United States of America

10 9 8 7 6 5 4 3 2 1

CONTENTS

CONTENTS

ABBREVIATIONS

The Robert H. Michel Papers housed at The Dirksen Congressional Center, Pekin, Illinois, consist of several discrete series. The following abbreviations were used to simplify bibliographical citations to these sources.

RHM   Robert H. Michel
RHM Papers   Robert H. Michel Papers, The Dirksen Congres-
                        sional Center, Pekin, IL

The template for document citations follows this format: RHM Papers, [name of collection series], [document information, such as author and date], f. [to denote the folder within the series]. Examples follow:

RHM Information File
RHM Papers, Audiovisual Series
RHM Papers, Campaigns and Politics, 1956, f. Candidates: Unland, James.
RHM Papers, General Series, f.
RHM Papers, General Series, f. 90th Congress: RHM Personal, A–H.
RHM Papers, Interfile: Personal, f.
RHM Papers, Leadership Series, f.
RHM Papers, Leadership Series, Box 2, f. 96th Congress, 1979–80: Leadership contest, 1980 (1).
RHM Papers, Legislative Series, Special Subjects, Other Special Subjects, Box 4, f. 102nd Congress: Reform.
RHM Papers, Personal, f.
RHM Papers, Personal, f. Memoir Notes, 22–23.
RHM Papers, Post-Congressional Series, f. Subjects: Interviews (2).

RHM Papers, Post-Congressional Series, f.

RHM Papers, Presidential Scrapbooks, f.

RHM Papers, Press Series, f. Subjects: Michel Office General.

RHM Papers, Press Series, f. Remarks and Releases: [date].

RHM Papers, Project Series, 1961–1992, Box 9, f.

RHM Papers, Remarks and Releases, December 5, 1988.

RHM Papers, Scrapbooks, [Box number] f.

RHM Papers, Scrapbooks, President Scrapbooks, f.

RHM Papers, Speech and Trip File, f.

RHM Papers, Staff Series: Bill Gavin, f.

SERIES FOREWORD

With *Robert H. Michel: Leading the Republican House Minority*, the University Press of Kansas offers the inaugural work of its Congressional Leaders series. In some ways, Illinois's long-time US Representative Bob Michel (1923–2017) might seem an unlikely candidate for an initial volume. Despite decades of service in the US House of Representatives (1957–1995) and Republican leadership responsibilities, he never became Speaker. Rather, he served his entire career as part of the minority, given Democratic control of the House from 1955 through 1994. Yet he demonstrated, time and again, an ability to both lead his party and to forge alliances with presidents and Democratic leaders.

This series seeks to address congressional leadership in many forms, from revolutionary Speakers such as Newt Gingrich (R-GA) to informal yet pathbreaking leaders such as Senator Margaret Chase Smith (R-ME). As with other University Press of Kansas series, such as those on presidents and presidential elections, these volumes will concentrate on relatively specific time periods and actions; in short, they will not constitute full biographies but will focus on the nature of leadership within the institution of the Congress. Congressional scholarship, while robust, remains pocketed by gaps and omissions. This series will fill some of these blank spaces, one leader at a time.

Forthcoming volumes will include studies of Speaker Gingrich and Speaker Tom Foley (D-WA). Subsequent subjects will address committee leadership, insurgent leadership, and leadership behind the scenes. The series will feature leaders from all congressional eras, thus encouraging scholars to place leadership within the historical, political, and legislative context of the time.

The studies in this series emphasize an intersection between history, biography, and political science. Indeed, over the past thirty years, it has been political science scholars who have most advanced the study of the institution, especially in its nineteenth-century manifestation. These volumes will build on this scholarship as they examine a single leader, or perhaps a pair of leaders, both from the overall perspective of congressional research and the placement within the historical framework of their times.

Support for this series comes from The Dirksen Congressional Center in Pekin, Illinois, whose support of the study of congressional leadership continues to stimulate new research, important findings, and significant publications.

—Burdett A. Loomis
Lawrence, Kansas
October 2018

PREFACE AND ACKNOWLEDGMENTS

Frank H. Mackaman and Sean Q Kelly

Founded in 1949 by thirteen Republican members of the House of Representatives led by Glenn Davis (R-WI) and Donald Jackson (R-CA), the Chowder and Marching Club (C&M) sprang from traditional Republican fiscal conservatism.[1] John Rankin, the dictatorial Democratic chair of the Veterans Affairs Committee, proposed a $90 a month payment to veterans of World Wars I and II. Appalled by the cost of the bill—$2 billion per year—Jackson brought together the founding members to plot a strategy to defeat the bill.[2] They won by a single vote. Buoyed by their success, C&M began adding members by invitation, determined by a secret ballot vote, and membership in the group carried prestige. Future presidents Richard Nixon and Gerald Ford were among the founding members. Robert H. Michel (R-IL) was one of only two members of his 1956 freshman class admitted to the group.

The Chowder and Marching Club was a way for junior members of the minority to learn the "norms and folkways" of the complex chamber and for all members to collect and exchange intelligence. Junior members such as Bob Michel could find support and encouragement as they learned the ropes in Congress. Michel explained: "Freshmen in the group who are unfamiliar with committee operations received tutoring in parliamentary tactics from more senior members." In the minority—especially in an era when professional staff was in short supply, particularly for the minority—these societies were crucial. Meetings also allowed members to exchange information on the legislative goings-on in the House. Michel continued: "At the same time, senior members who are all tied up with committee work can find out what's been happening on the floor."[3]

In 1953 another group, the Society of Statesmen (SOS), formed. John Rhodes of Arizona, who later became the Republican minority leader (1973–1981), was among SOS's founding members.[4] Though offered membership in C&M, Rhodes declined to the surprise of many.[5] However, the two groups began to meet informally, allowing members to develop personal and professional relationships. On Wednesday mornings, for example, SOS and C&M invited an outside group, a cabinet member, a columnist, or a senior White House official for a jointly held breakfast. Dick Cheney, a member of both groups, insisted to the political scientist William F. Connelly that "one cannot understand House Republicans (in the 1980s) without understanding two member social groups, the Society of Statesmen and the Chowder and Marching Club."[6]

Clubs such as C&M and SOS illustrate the rich social tapestry of the House of Representatives during Bob Michel's era. Members of Congress and their families who moved to Washington built networks that promoted effective legislating and personal camaraderie. It was a time in Congress when committee chairmen were kings (and they were all men—women were a rarity in Congress, especially in the 1950s and 1960s) and legislating proceeded via regular order. Bipartisanship was more common than it is today, and loyalty to the institution was valued.

Of course, Congress was not a Garden of Eden. For the thirty-eight years of Michel's service in the House, the Republicans suffered as the minority. The Democratic majority closely controlled the institution and the resources available to minority members. However, occasional fractures in the Democratic coalition provided Republicans opportunities to influence or kill legislation by uniting with groups of independent-minded Democrats. Success came to those who learned at the knee of more senior members of Congress. They mastered the culture of the House and the rules of the institution. Success came to those who were well prepared.

And Bob Michel was well prepared by temperament and by experience. A prudent, hard-working, pragmatic conservative, Michel personified what has become known as "midwestern values." In terms of experience, he joined the staff of the Republican Congressman Harold H. Velde in 1949 just as the postwar House took shape. Seven years later, he won election to Velde's seat in his own right, the only freshman with experience as a congressional staff

Figure 0.1 In an interview Bob Michel recalled: "[Richard] Nixon was one of the found-ing members [of the Chowder and Marching Club] with [Gerald] Ford. Nixon played the piano, and I sang. There was a community of interest in music, of all things." Nixon (*seated*), Bob Michel, Charlotte Reid, Les Arends, Gerald Ford, and Melvin Laird
RMH Papers, Audiovisual Series, Still Photographs, f. Chowder and Marching Club.

member. As a sign of things to come, Michel's colleagues elected him presi-dent of the 85th Congress Club, the organization formed by the twenty-two Republican freshman members of their first Congress.

Beginning in the late 1970s, the Republican coalition began to shift ideologically and regionally. Previously dominated by members from the Northeast and Midwest, the Republican Party evolved to reflect the electoral coalition that catapulted Ronald Reagan to the presidency—a political alchemist's mixture of fiscal conservatives and religiously inspired social conservatives. The Reagan coalition drew increasing numbers of Republicans from the South and conservative parts of the West. The Chowder and Marching Club sought to reflect the changing complexion of the party. As Michel recalled: "When more southerners began getting themselves elected as Republicans to the Congress we'd take in a few of them and boy I'll tell you they were always right back for new members, getting more members from their state or from the South."[7] New Republican members, however, often bridled at the "collaborationism" of the Chowder and Marching Club and similar groups, even when Michel's tactics resulted in major legislative victories such as the Reagan tax cuts and increases in defense spending.

Despite success in the presidential elections of 1980 and 1984, a Republican House majority was nowhere in sight. In 1983 Newt Gingrich (R-GA) founded the Conservative Opportunity Society—an ideologically motivated group of movement conservatives. Gingrich argued that the philosophy of Republicans associated with C&M and with Bob Michel's leadership obscured the differences between Democrats and Republicans. Vin Weber (R-MN) described Gingrich's strategic approach: "We needed to develop as a party—wedge issues and magnet issues. It's a fairly simple notion with wedge issues, or ideas that really separated the Democratic majority from the public, issues where they were plainly wrong and the public did not support them. But they were, for a variety of reasons, not paying a political price." Weber continued: "In those cases our assignment was to find ways of making clear the differences between the Democratic Party and the public on those issues driving a wedge between the Democrats and their constituencies."[8] By 1994 and the Republican Revolution, the Chowder and Marching Club was a relic of the past, the textbook Congress was dead, and Bob Michel had chosen retirement.

Bob Michel: Learner, Leader

Contemporary political science largely relies on theories drawn either from cognitive psychology or economic theories of expected utility. In these theories, individual member behavior is understood as stimulus-response behavior. If we understand individual motivations, we understand why peo-ple behave as they do.[9] In the study of leadership, these scholars tend to focus on actor-agent models. Congressional leaders (agents) are constrained by the preferences of the members of their party caucuses (actors). (In both cham-bers—House and Senate—the GOP party caucus is referred to as the "Con-ference," and the Democratic party caucus is referred to as the "Caucus.") Congressional institutions—formal institutions such as committees and parliamentary procedures—are mechanisms to overcome collective action problems.[10] Leaders (agents) are transactional. Leadership occurs within a "black box."[11] Followers are strategic.

Social learning theory (SLT) offers an alternative. As expressed by Albert Bandura and others, SLT posits that individual behavior is best understood within a social context, as a reflection of the social fabric in which individuals are embedded. Institutions shape individuals, and in turn individuals shape the institutions to which they belong.[12] Bandura argues that "the environ-ment is only a potentiality, not a fixed property that inevitably impinges upon individuals and to which their behavior eventually adapts. Behavior partly creates the environment and the resultant environment, in turn, influences their behavior."[13] In this two-way causal process, writes Bandura, the envi-ronment is just as influenceable as the behavior it controls. From this point of view, leaders are capable of learning, creating, adapting, and disrupting. Institutions, members of Congress, and rank-and-file members exist in a feedback loop in which they make, and remake, the institution, and the insti-tution remakes them.

The chapters in this book are a testament to the latter conception of the role of congressional leaders, that is to say, folks who are shaping and shaped by their political context. Michel's six years as a congressional staffer followed by his admission to the Chowder and Marching Club pro-vided opportunities to learn about the institution by observing the behav-ior of more senior members. His time on the Appropriations Committee was also formative. As Scott Frisch and Sean Kelly (chapter 2) demon-strate, Michel learned from his initial failures as the minority manager on Labor-H (i.e., Labor, Health, Education, and Welfare/HHS Subcommittee) appropriations bills. His success sprouted from early setbacks. On Appro-priations he learned the hard work of legislating and governing, pursued his fiscally conservative policy goals, and experimented with strategies for policy success. Michel employed his legendary patience, learning to legis-late and preparing himself to become a leader. Proof of Michel's capacity to create and foster personal relationships is highlighted in Burdett Loomis's contribution (chapter 3). Michel and his colleagues in leadership on both sides of the aisle shared personal and political experiences that allowed them to bridge their differences, at least to some extent. Virtually all of them served in the military during World War II, entering congressional service in the late 1950s and early 1960s. Loomis notes that Michel's "store of strong personal ties allowed him to maximize his influence, both for his members and in his role as President Reagan's agent."

Michel's ascent in the ranks of House Republicans is emblematic of his capacity to adapt the party to a changing political environment. Elected to head the National Republican Campaign Committee in 1973 and as minority whip in 1974, Michel replaced men who had served for decades in those positions. Scott Meinke (chapter 4) argues that Michel sought to modernize and professionalize those operations to advance the conservative goals of the Republican Conference. Michel's growing understanding of the chamber—as a member of Appropriations, campaign committee chair, and then whip—prepared him to move into the leader's position in 1981. In their discussion of Michel as minority leader, Douglas Harris and Matthew Green (chapter 5) illustrate his capacity to learn and "adapt to the changing environment, maintaining a delicate balancing act by keeping one foot in the old order while trying to fulfill the leadership roles suggested by the new order."

For Michel, substance mattered. Serving in Congress was about changing policy outcomes. In his discussion of Michel's foreign and domestic policy legacy, Andrew Taylor (chapter 6) argues that Michel "was responsible, in ways both great and small, for most of the landmark laws of the 1980s and early 1990s." Taylor describes Michel's involvement in foreign policies as disparate as the Reagan defense buildup, Iran-Contra, and Operation Desert Storm. On domestic policy, the Reagan agenda benefited mightily from Michel's leadership on taxes and deficit reduction. Taylor argues that it was Michel's mastery of legislative strategy and his grasp of policy that proved the difference.

Michel's capacity to learn and adapt creatively to a changing political environment was on full display when House Republicans achieved the unthinkable: passing the Reagan tax cuts in 1981 despite being outnumbered 244–191. Matthew Mendez (chapter 7) demonstrates how Michel's "gentle persuasion" and ability to unite the House GOP Conference behind the tax cuts—while trading on discord within the House Democratic Caucus—allowed Michel to achieve what he would always consider his signature achievement in the

House. Dan Palazzolo (chapter 8) underscores Michel's "pragmatism and preference for legislating." There is little doubt that these are the values that he developed as a congressional staffer, in the Chowder and Marching Club, through his work on the Appropriations Committee, and in his methodical rise through the formal leadership positions in his party.

In a majoritarian body such as the House of Representatives, the majority exercises considerable control by limiting the power of the minority. An increasingly rambunctious House Republican Conference led Bob Michel to pursue substantive changes to improve the position of his party. Douglas Harris (chapter 9) illustrates how Michel sought to improve majority party accountability and restore the committee-centered focus of the legislative process—he sought to return to a more open and deliberative style of legislating. Colton Campbell (chapter 10) discusses Michel's focus on reforming committees in particular, including provisions for reducing the number of subcommittees, realigning committee jurisdictions, and imposing term limits on committee chairs. Remarking in 1993, Michel noted that "as the House has become more autocratic, it has become more unpopular."[14] Prophetic words. Since the Republican takeover in 1995, and the increasing centralization of power in party leaders, the popularity of Congress has cratered. Like the Ghost of Christmas Present, C. Lawrence Evans (chapter 11) provides a long view of the implications of the changes ushered in by the Republican era in the House.

Although much of this book focuses on Bob Michel's career on the Hill, the voters in his district were always uppermost in his mind. He developed broad support in his district—rarely fearing electoral defeat—yet there is an essential tension between holding a national leadership position and serving the interests of voters back home. The 1982 midterm election brought Bob Michel as close to electoral defeat as he would ever be. Success on the Reagan tax cuts might have been Michel's crowning legislative achievement, but the recession that ravaged the economy in 1981 and 1982 tarnished Republicans. As the leader of his party in the House, Michel was vulnerable to guilt by association if not in fact. Robert David Johnson (chapter 12) recalls the election of 1982 and the balancing act that Michel had to perform to, on the one hand, support a president of his party and, on the other, convince voters that he deserved more time in Congress. He scraped by, winning only 51.5 percent of the vote, well below his average reelection margin of 66 percent.

Michel's political near-death experience caused a fundamental change in his "homestyle." David Parker (chapter 13) describes how Michel and his staff realigned his district strategy to put increasing emphasis on serving the district and reconnecting with voters. In another example of his adaptive prowess, Michel acknowledged the reality of modern politics, the "constant campaign." As Parker notes: "Successful incumbents . . . learn to evolve with their districts and are attentive to the signals sent by their constituents, which requires a re-orientation of their representational styles."

There are limits to what leaders can accomplish. Although leaders are capable of learning, adapting, and shaping their political environment, Bob Michel could not control the larger forces at work: a political party increasingly dominated by movement conservatism and led by Newt Gingrich paired with a decline in comity among members of both parties. As Frank Mackaman (chapter 14) relates in the concluding chapter, Michel found himself out of step and unable "to do what he did best: To get opposing sides to the table. To work out differences. To forge compromises. To give a little here and get a little there and move policy-making forward." This approach—the approach of a statesman—was no longer viable in the increasingly toxic environment on Capitol Hill.

A Note on Structure and Method

Each of the chapters in this book stands on its own as a contribution to understanding Bob Michel and Congress. Taken as a collection of essays they document the extraordinary career of an important American public servant. Unlike a traditional biography, it does not provide a linear narrative of its subject and his life and times. Rather, the editors and authors dismiss that simple narrative device to explore and demonstrate the impact that Bob Michel had in the House of Representatives and on national politics. In this way our approach to biography rewards readers with a distinctive depth of understanding compared to the traditional historical narrative.

The chapters in this book draw heavily on the congressional papers of Bob Michel located at The Dirksen Congressional Center in Pekin, Illinois. Frank Mackaman, an historian, archivist, and director of The Dirksen Center, sought an opportunity to illustrate the tremendous promise of using archival collections to deepen our understanding of Congress and congressional leadership. Beyond the paper record, The Center holds several interviews with Michel that allowed him to explain the contours of his career.

In Sean Kelly, Mackaman found an eager partner. A political scientist, Kelly advocates for using archival collections to better understand congressional politics—to peek behind the curtain and gain admission to rooms otherwise impossible to access. Using archives, we can throw open the "black box."[15] Or as Harris puts it: "To observe politics in real-time."[16] Along with his coconspirators Scott Frisch, Doug Harris, and Dave Parker, Kelly believes that archives hold tremendous promise for researchers.[17] Like archaeologists, archival researchers sift through these enormous collections, finding items left behind—and forgotten decades before—that allow scholars to reconstruct political events, battles, strategies, and ideas that would otherwise go undiscovered. Despite their limitations, archival collections provide insights that are almost impossible to capture any other way.

Invitations to the chapter authors contained only two directives: Keep the focus on Bob Michel, and use The Dirksen Center's archival resources. Mackaman and Kelly hope that this book will help convince scholars, particularly political scientists, that there is value in these collections. Located throughout the country, congressional collections—and other political papers collections, including the papers of presidents, interest groups, judges, and so forth—contain valuable data for political scientists and others who are willing to look.

Acknowledgments

Ray LaHood deserves a large measure of credit for this book. It was he who prompted Frank Mackaman to tell Bob Michel's story. Michel hired LaHood in 1983 as his district administrative assistant before promoting him to chief of staff in 1990. LaHood succeeded Michel in the House in 1995, serving there until 2009. Ray's reflection in this book testifies to his admiration and respect for his longtime friend and mentor. The feeling was mutual. Billy Pitts and Mike Johnson both worked for Bob Michel and were generous with their time, agreeing to multiple interviews with many of the authors in this collection. Both also offer reflections on their years with the Republican Leader.

This Robert H. Michel retrospective is supported by a grant from the Association of Centers for the Study of Congress made possible by the Democracy Fund. Additional support was provided by the Everett McKinley Dirksen Endowment Fund, the Ray and Kathy LaHood Endowment, Busey Wealth Management, and the Institute for Principled Leadership in Public Service at Bradley University.

The editors acknowledge the outstanding work of the contributors to this volume and applaud their skill in placing Robert Henry Michel in the broad sweep of congressional history. We thank Burdett Loomis for advocating for the inclusion of this book in his new series at the University Press of Kansas. Our gratitude extends as well to the hardworking staff at UPK for improving this work with corrections and suggestions. In particular, we thank David Congdon, Jon Howard, Kelly Chrisman Jacques, Karl Janssen, Michael R. Kehoe, and Colin Tripp for their enthusiasm for the project.

The Dirksen Congressional Center owes much of its success to Bob Michel, who represented the central Illinois congressional district in which The Center is located. Through Bob's good efforts, for example, President Gerald R. Ford traveled to Pekin, Illinois, to dedicate the Everett M. Dirksen Congressional Leadership Research Center on August 19, 1975. Three years later, Michel and Senator Howard H. Baker, Jr., secured a $2.5 million congressional appropriation for The Center's endowment. At the time, Michel told his colleagues that The Center "will be a place where students of government, [of] political science and of history, from here and abroad, will come to inquire, to learn, to understand, and, hopefully, to be inspired."[18] One final example: On September 1, 1989, Michel signed a deed of gift conveying his nearly 1,000 linear feet of papers, audiovisual items, and artifacts to The Center's historical collections. Over the course of five decades, Bob Michel championed The Center's work enthusiastically in word and deed.

Frank Mackaman thanks the board of directors of The Dirksen Congressional Center who accepted their congressman's challenge by providing unwavering support for the study of Congress and congressional leadership. He dedicates this book to his partner and wife, Kathleen—forty-six years and counting.

Sean Kelly thanks the two great loves of his life, his wife, Sheen, and their daughter, Shriya, for making his life bearable and for bearing with his frequent absences as he roots through the dusty bowels of libraries near and far . . . but mostly far.

Notes

1. The name "Chowder & Marching Club" has uncertain origins. According to the US House historian, Jackson coined it "whimsically," placing it on the notice for the group's second meeting. A scene from a 1933 Cary Grant movie—in which another founding member of C&M, John Lodge of Connecticut, played a part—may have inspired the name. But no one really knows for sure. The name may have origins in pre-Revolutionary America. Reportedly, concerned citizens met over chowder to discuss the affairs of the day and then marched into town in an airing of grievances. Richard Nixon, Gerald Ford, and the other founders of the group may have discovered and borrowed the title from the 1940s comic strip *Barnaby*. Mr. O'Malley, the fairy godfather character, frequently attended the "Elves, Leprechauns, Gnomes, and Little Men's Chowder and Marching Society." In one story line, O'Malley ran a successful campaign for Congress. Adding to the confusion, "Society," is often substituted erroneously for "Club."

2. Irwin N. Gertzog, *Congressional Women: Their Recruitment, Integration, and Behavior* (Westport, CT: Greenwood Publishing Group, 1995); US House historian, "What's in a Name? Origins of the Chowder and Marching Club," 2014, history.house.gov/Blog /Detail/15032400030.

3. House historian, "What's in a Name?"

4. A contemporary account of SOS describes its fifteen members as "fledgling Republican congressmen who meet weekly to share information and quiz higher-ups about the nation's business." See "Inside Washington," n.d., www.cia.gov/library/reading room/docs/CIA-RDP58-00597R000200060003-9.pdf.

5. J. Brian Smith, *John Rhodes: Man of the House* (Phoenix: American Traveler Press, 2005).

6. William F. Connelly, Jr., *James Madison Rules America: The Constitutional Origins of Partisanship* (Lanham, MD: Rowman & Littlefield, 2010), 300, fn 120.

7. Robert H. Michel interview with Scott Frisch and Sean Kelly, Washington, DC, August 2000.

8. From a transcript of "Frontline: The Long March of Newt Gingrich," www.pbs.org /video/frontline-the-long-march-of-newt-gingrich.

9. David Mayhew's classic formulation of members of Congress as "single-minded seekers of reelection" is one example. Fenno expands the universe of motivations to include constituency, policy, and influence, but the emphasis is firmly focused on individual motivations, not how individual behaviors influence the institutional environment. See David R. Mayhew, *Congress: The Electoral Connection* (New Haven, CT: Yale University Press, 1974); Richard F. Fenno, Jr., *Learning to Legislate: The Senate Education of Arlen Specter* (Washington, DC: Congressional Quarterly Press, 1991); and Fenno, *Learning to Govern: An Institutional View of the 104th Congress* (Washington, DC: Brookings Institution Press, 1997).

10. For instance, Kenneth A. Shepsle, "Institutional Arrangements and Equilibrium in Multidimensional Voting Models," *American Journal of Political Science* 23, no. 1 (February 1979): 27–59.

11. For a comprehensive review of the literature on congressional leadership, see Randall Strahan, "Party Leadership," in *The Oxford Handbook of the American Congress*,

ed. Frances E. Lee and Eric Schickler (New York: Oxford University Press, 2011), chap. 17. Confronting principle-agent models, Strahan argues that "if principal-agent theory . . . captures the most important features of the politics of party leadership, students of Congress would be ill-advised to focus much energy on close study of party leaders, because knowing more about leaders will explain little of importance about what happens in Congress." Strahan, "Party Leadership," 377.

12. We do not contend that this is a unique view. In political science, Lawrence C. Dodd incorporates social learning theory into his theory of congressional change. See Lawrence C. Dodd, "Re-Envisioning Congress: Theoretical Perspectives on Congressional Change—2004," in *Congress Reconsidered*, 8th ed., ed. Lawrence C. Dodd and Bruce I. Oppenheimer (Washington, DC: Congressional Quarterly Press, 2005). See also Fenno, *Learning to Legislate*; and Fenno, *Learning to Govern*.

13. Albert Bandura, *Social Learning Theory* (New York: General Learning Corporation, 1971), 40.

14. RHM to Dear Republican Colleague, RHM Papers, Leadership Series, f. 101st Congress. Dear Colleague, December 19, 1988 (1).

15. See Scott A. Frisch and Sean Q Kelly, "Political Science and Archival Research," in *Doing Archival Research in Political Science*, ed. Scott A. Frisch, Douglas B. Harris, Sean Q Kelly, and David C. W. Parker (Amherst, NY: Cambria Press, 2012), 35–58. See also Scott A. Frisch and Sean Q Kelly, "Dataheads: What Archivists Need to Know about Political Scientists," in *An American Political Archives Reader*, ed. Karen Dawley Paul, Glenn R. Gray, and L. Rebecca Johnson Melvin (Lanham, MD: Scarecrow Press, 2009), 401–418.

16. Douglas B., Harris, "Behavioral Reality and Institutional Change," in *Doing Archival Research in Political Science*, ed. Scott A. Frisch, Douglas B. Harris, Sean Q Kelly, and David C. W. Parker (Amherst, NY: Cambria Press, 2012), 59.

17. Harris, "Behavioral Reality and Institutional Change."

18. *Congressional Record*, April 18, 1978, H 2953.

CHAPTER 1

ROBERT H. MICHEL

A Life Preparing for Public Service

Frank H. Mackaman

R obert Henry Michel was born in Peoria, Illinois, on March 2, 1923, to Anna Baer and Charles Jean Michel. The young family resided in a modest, story-and-a-half clapboard house on the East Bluff, a close-knit neighborhood of middle-class families. The fact that Bob Michel grew up in Peoria rather than in Chicago, in a small town, or on a central Illinois farm proved providential. For most of the twentieth century, Peoria closely reflected the heart of the nation in its diversity of race, income, age, rural and business interests, and educational attainment. In fact, "Will it play in Peoria?" became synonymous with the city's reputation as a test market for new products and as an ideal place to take the pulse of the nation on political campaigns and proposed legislation.[1] Hailing from Peoria gave Michel an intuitive understanding of Main Street, of mainstream values, attitudes, expectations, and aspirations.

Peoria in the 1920s boomed along with most of the rest of the country. Boasting a population of nearly 80,000, among the one hundred most populous cities in the nation and the second largest in Illinois behind Chicago, the town comprised nine square miles with one hundred miles of paved roads, 16,743 dwelling units, 30 public grade schools, 3 public high schools, 147 churches, and 13 parochial grade or high schools. Located midway between Chicago and St. Louis, it became a transportation and distribution center of major importance. Farm-related businesses such as Keystone Steel and Wire undergirded the local economy. In 1925, Holt Caterpillar Company, builder of track-type tractors, and C. L. Best, a competitor, merged to create Caterpillar Tractor Company, today ranking 65 on the Fortune 500 list.[2]

Community prosperity took the form of 684 retail businesses and 254 manufacturing concerns. Peoria was home to the largest traffic signal company in America and among the three leading cities worldwide in washing machine production.[3] The average income for all industries excluding farming amounted to $1,489 per year—the equivalent of about $20,100 in 2018. A carpenter could expect to make $1.08 per hour; a public school teacher, $970 per year.[4] Republican in its politics, central Illinois elected only one Democrat out of the ten men who represented the congressional district in the US House of Representatives during the twentieth century.

A Life Lived Simply

Little is known about Michel's early years beyond his later recollections documented in brief interviews. Bob's father, Charles, was born in 1889 in Alsace-Lorraine, France. He was reared and educated in Nancy, France, a region that Germany occupied by force from time to time. Following an older brother, Charles emigrated in 1910 to the United States, first settling in Oklahoma before moving to central Illinois. A machinist and toolmaker, he retired from Keystone Steel and Wire Company in 1961 after forty-eight years.[5]

Bob's mother was born in the United States, but her parents, Henry and Caroline Baer of Tremont, Illinois, emigrated from Germany and became tenant farmers. Anna was the third of twelve children and, in the custom of the times, took care of her siblings and did not graduate from high school. She worked as a house domestic for some of Peoria's wealthiest families before her marriage to Charles on June 5, 1921. Twin sisters, Mary Ann and Betty Lou, joined the Michel household in 1927.

When asked to describe his upbringing, Michel used such words as "conservative," "frugal," and "penny-pinching." He was grateful, he later said, that his parents were strict, insisting on discipline and respect for one another. If the children came down the stairs in the morning and failed to greet their parents cheerfully, they were marched right back upstairs to try harder. That was the way the day was supposed to begin, Michel recalled, with a bright, optimistic outlook.[6] Charles, an introvert by nature, kept a careful, watchful eye on his brood. Work came first in the Michel household, and the father never hesitated to stroll down to the playground at White Elementary School to call Bob in for chores, putting an end to his son's free time.

Anna held her own, however. "When she felt Dad was a little too stern," Bob remembered, "Mom would step in and make it right."[7]

Young Bob was hired for his first job at age nine, working at Alex Simon's tailor shop on Madison for a dollar a day. A bit later he added two morning paper routes and one evening route to his budding résumé. He mowed the grass up and down the neighborhood for 35 cents a yard. If that were not enough to fill idle time, young Bob spent a few hours weekly cleaning lettuce and doing odd jobs at a grocery store. Early on, Michel learned thrift: "I bought my own clothes with what I earned and the only condition my father put on my earnings was that I had to put away 10 percent in a savings account for a rainy day."[8] Charles would check the accounts periodically to ensure compliance.[9]

Frugality proved an indispensable attribute for a family about to endure the Great Depression. Although his father's job at Keystone was never threatened and the Michels owned their home, Charles made only about $2,000 per year.[10] When hard times struck, two of Anna's brothers rode the rails back from Utah to work as mechanics at Jarvis Chevrolet in Peoria. Finishing up the week's work, they would join Charles, Anna, and their three children for Friday evening dinners. Charles would buy oxtail for soup, and Anna would dress that up with rutabaga ("terrible stuff," according to Bob), bacon, or Swiss chard. As Michel remembered, "The only meat we could eat the first night was that which fell off the bone during the course of the cooking because the second night, she would take the oxtail with the meat that was still on it and make a hash out of that." On one occasion, Uncle Karl volunteered that his pay for the week amounted to $7.65—Bob earned more from his paper routes.[11] His upbringing during the Depression, he later said, "made me all the more conservative"—conservative in spending and conservative in values.[12] Anna and Charles raised their children in the Apostolic Christian Church, a fundamentalist denomination. The doctrine of the church was, and is, based on a literal interpretation of the Bible, which is recognized as God-inspired, infallible, and inerrant. Michel recalled it as a "very strict environment." Young Bob attended Sunday school every week, sang in the church choirs, and, eventually, directed a choir. His father would require one of the children to read a chapter of the Bible after the evening meal, "notwithstanding our desire to go out and play ball."[13]

Baseball

Baseball proved to be an enduring passion for Bob Michel. When asked what, as a youngster dreaming about his future, he saw himself doing as an adult, Michel thought for a few moments before responding: "Being a baseball player." As a teenager, he explained, he kept his own ledger, updated daily, to record every at-bat of every ballplayer for his beloved Chicago Cubs.[14] Not content simply to observe, Michel played ball. He pitched for the Republican baseball team in its annual duel with congressional Democrats, winning fifteen out of seventeen starting assignments during the 1960s and 1970s, and was named to Roll Call's Baseball Hall of Fame in 1993. As he related to a constituent in 1967:

> We play real baseball, man, big-league style and the game is played out at D.C. Stadium just prior to one of the Washington Senators official games. I never pitched hardball before coming to Congress, having caught in high school and played third base in college, but I seemed to be the only one with sufficient control to get the ball over, or around, the plate. In my declining years, however, it's getting more and more difficult to go the route (usually five or six innings), but I am happy to report our new fledging Congressman to the West of us, Tom Railsback of Moline, exhibited a pretty good arm in workouts this year and will undoubtedly be my replacement whenever that time comes. Until then I'm going to hang in there pitching as long as I can, if for no other reason than an inducement to keep my weight down.[15]

America's pastime served as both a release and a source of frustration. "It just burns me that [following] a lead-off double we can't get our guys [referring to the Cubs] to at least attempt to put the ball on the right side of the diamond to move them on to third," he complained to the Cubs broadcasting team of Harry Caray and Steve Stone in 1991. "Bunting is still a problem for some of our guys in the clutch and I must say that I haven't yet through last year and this year seen a Cub outfielder throw out anybody at home plate. Four or five steps to get rid of the ball??!!" The Cubs had squandered two Andre Dawson home runs in a recent game, too, which brought Michel to a boil. "Why am I telling you all this? I don't know," he said. "I'm just so darned frustrated, I'm fit to be tied and thought my only outlet was to get it off my chest to the two of you. . . . Come on fellas, I'm counting on you getting me in a better frame of mind. It's actually gotten so bad it's affecting my legislative work."[16]

Summers provided some relief from the daily household routine during the 1930s. In an interview fifty years later, Bob reflected fondly on the months working on his great uncle's farm. Up at the crack of dawn, he called in the cows before breakfast, which his great aunt made sure featured "the best, thinnest pancakes." At one time or other, Bob did every job on the farm except plant corn, which required too much precision to relegate to hired help. Michel did, however, run a team of horses to cultivate the fields. He also claimed with pride to have been the Woodford County sweet corn–snapping champion, an arduous chore that involved hiking down rows of the crop in the humid July heat, snapping ears of corn from the sharp-edged stocks, and pitching them into a trailing wagon.[17] Charles Michel, as his son recalled, "believed that if you wanted to go up the ladder, you had to start with hard work."[18]

The Michel children heard little of politics around the dinner table. Charles had fled Europe partly out of fear that the constantly shifting political fortunes there might result in war—he had served in the French army and lived in a German-occupied part of France. On those rare occasions when national politics intruded, Charles was quick to denounce Franklin Roosevelt, whom he suspected would entangle the United States in the chaos of European affairs. The family's characteristic parsimony ran counter to the Democratic administration's expansion of federal spending and government programs on the domestic front, too. Bob would cite these factors as steering him gradually to the Republican Party even as a young boy.

In fact, his first outright political activity occurred by happenstance rather than by design. His seventh-grade high-school chum, Paul Herschel, had partisan connections. His father was president of Herschel's Manufacturing and a prominent Republican. The company had what was called Herschel's Republican Headquarters, and Bob volunteered to help in the plant's campaign office for Alf Landon, who was the Republican presidential nominee in 1936. Michel's chore was to hand out sunflower-seed pins with "Alf Landon for President" printed on them. The seventh-grader's efforts fell short—Landon lost all but two of the forty-eight states to Franklin Roosevelt. "That's quite a blow for a young fellow just getting started in politics," Michel said in 1984. "But you have to also condition yourself to taking some defeats along the way."[19]

As he prepared to enter high school, young Bob had acquired, at least in rudimentary fashion, some of the skills, experiences, and qualities that he would employ decades later with great success: hard work, thrift, modesty, self-discipline, faith in God, and integrity. He personified what has come to be known, with respect, as "midwestern values."

Peoria High School afforded Michel the chance to hone additional talents that would serve him well later in politics, although there is no evidence that he envisioned such a path for himself. Mrs. McGrath, his homeroom teacher, was a stickler on parliamentary procedure. She designated Bob as a class officer in charge of running meetings according to prescribed rules that valued reasoned, respectful, and civil discussion. He practiced these valuable skills in a student group that met weekly, much like a city council, with the school's principal. The group offered suggestions about school procedures, sponsored assemblies (Bob moderated some and sang at some), and raised funds for school events. These were consequential activities for a student at a large city high school—so large that it ran two shifts in order to accommodate all the pupils. Michel handled these roles with aplomb, earning election as president of his high school class and holding leadership positions in the school's Young Republicans organization. He met his future political mentor in high school, too, when then-Congressman Everett M. Dirksen visited his civics class—"I was just in awe," Michel recollected six decades later.[20]

The high-schooler developed another useful proficiency that would serve him well. He joined the Boys' Double Quartet and the school's madrigal, launching his amateur career as an accomplished vocalist. Later he would use this talent to forge relationships with a wide variety of politicians and celebrities. Singing brought Michel great joy. In notes for a memoir never completed, Michel described a "special treat" that fulfilled "a life ambition" on a Saturday morning in January 1989 when he sang a solo, "God Bless America," with the Mormon Tabernacle Choir at rehearsal for their concert in Constitution Hall.[21] Beyond joy, music led some years later to the great love of his life—Corinne Woodruff. That serendipity had to wait, however.

The summer following graduation in 1940 found Michel at loose ends. Undecided about his next move, he continued to live at the family home, joined a labor union, and returned to Herschel Manufacturing Company. He started out in the warehouse and then moved to the office, where he took orders for farm implement repair parts—his summers on the farm had paid off. But the job did not pay much; his take-home pay was $12.87 per week with 13 cents deducted for Social Security, a figure Michel kept in mind his entire life. His memory for these details about money served as a harbinger of his obsessive attention to the budgetary fine print that was later to characterize Michel, the congressional budget hawk. This period of searching after high school lasted about two years.[22]

Precisely when and why Michel decided to enroll at the local university are not clear, but the decision was arguably the single most important one in his life. In attending Bradley University, Bob Michel received the academic and extracurricular experiences that prepared him for life in the public eye, met the woman he would marry, and was recommended—by the president of the university no less—for his first job on Capitol Hill. All of that would come later. After just one uneventful semester at Bradley in the fall of 1942, he signed up for military service.

He's in the Army Now

The impetus to serve was strong. "Shoot, we were 19-year-olds, you know?" Michel remembered. "What the heck, there was a war going on! Most of the guys my age [thought], 'We gotta go.' Nobody thought about 'skiddooing' or anything of that nature."[23] Poor eyesight ruled out his first choice—the Navy Air Corps. Called by the draft, he enlisted in Peoria on February 10, 1943, as a private "for the duration of the War or other emergency, plus six months, subject to the discretion of the President or otherwise according to law." His induction papers listed four years of high school education; under the heading "Civilian Occupation," he listed "general industry clerk." Michel stood 70 inches tall and weighed 176 pounds.[24]

Michel took the occasion of military service to address the pronunciation of his surname—a source of confusion throughout his life. Was it "Mike-l" or "Michelle"? His father preferred the Americanized pronunciation of "Mike-l" but Bob and his mother liked the French pronunciation, "Michelle." When he was about to leave for training, "I told my Dad I was going to use the French pronunciation and would not answer to my name unless it was pronounced that way." Although he later converted to the Americanized pronunciation, "there wasn't anyone with whom I served in the army who didn't know Bob 'Michelle,' the French Huguenot."[25]

The prospect of military service presented Michel with a fraught choice. In reaching a decision, he displayed the pragmatic quality that would mark his approach to leadership decades later. During basic training, Michel learned that he could avoid front-line duty by applying for conscientious objector status on religious grounds. When he realized that some of his cousins were already fighting in North Africa, however, Bob could not reconcile refusing to serve with the knowledge that his kin were already out there on the front lines. When recruits were asked to volunteer for combat infantry duty, Michel stepped forward.[26] He nevertheless searched for a way to resolve the tension between the pacifist teachings of the Apostolic Church and the personal obligation he felt to join in combat by seeking a compromise. Military service "made me a man," he recalled in 1999. "I know I've killed people. I never lusted to repeat it as some guys did. If someone was just standing there, I could not pull the trigger. I could not be a sharpshooter."[27] He made another concession to his church's teachings: he refused to leave enlisted ranks for promotion because it always "gnawed" at him, that tension between his religious beliefs and war. Do your duty, but don't be a leader, he explained.[28]

Michel's unit, the "old Fox Company," 39th Infantry, Ninth Division, landed on Utah Beach, part of the Allied invasion of German-occupied France, on D-Day plus 4, June 10, 1944. In a December 18, 1944, letter to "Dear Gang," Private Michel described moving through Germany and foraging for food and supplies from the countryside. Not until the fifth paragraph did he relate "an interesting experience a few days ago" during which he personally captured "eight Jerries by persuading them in German [having taken German in high school] to give up." One of the eight then led Michel to twenty more German soldiers ranging in age from eighteen to forty-five. "They were sure I was going to shoot them and were as scared as can be. When they saw I was going to treat them as human their faces lit up like a Christmas tree."[29]

Michel's fortunes were about to change.

"I lasted until the Battle of the Bulge was just about over, and we were going on the offensive again . . . early in the morning," as Michel recounted the action. His unit had just crossed the Rohr River near the town of Duren early in 1945. "I was out in front of the platoon, and instead of doing what I was always taught to do—hug the tree line, so you've got some protection—our G2 intelligence said, 'they're on the run, all you do is go up and occupy the ground.'" That left Michel wide open, and that's when he was hit in the right hand and then the right leg by German fire. "It was close enough that I could tell . . . his breech had jammed, and he was working back the bolt on his [machine gun]. I could hear it—'clunk, clunk'—so when that happened, boy, of course I lay still after I was down." While the German struggled with his weapon, Michel, unable to use his wounded hand, strained to shed his combat pack. He laid his Browning Automatic Rifle on the pack to support it and "let all 20 rounds go" in the direction of the German. If the German's gun hadn't jammed, Michel said, "He was in a position to saw me right in half."[30] Michel's rounds included tracer bullets, which allowed the platoon behind him to lay down a base of fire. Under that cover, a corpsman treated the soldier's injured hand with a sulfa pack and bandaged it before advising Michel to head back to the town they had just left. As he retraced his steps, Michel lost so much blood that he passed out on a manure pile. First aid personnel who found him there asked if Michel wanted a shot of brandy. "I really don't drink, but I'll take whatever you have," Michel replied.[31]

He was evacuated to Liège, France, and then flown to England for repair and recovery. He spent four months in a hospital near Hereford. After mending, Michel landed back on the Continent precisely on VE-Day, May 8, 1945, at the port city of LeHavre. He spent time at a redeployment camp awaiting orders to ship to the Pacific. Good fortune intervened, however—he was declared disabled and returned to the States just before the semester began at Bradley.

Bob Michel had served in the US Army for nearly three years: February 10, 1943, to January 26, 1946. He was awarded two Bronze Stars, the Purple Heart, and four battle stars for his military service. Those three years proved as formative to his career as any other single factor. Nearly fifty years later, Michel called upon his wartime experience to cast what he termed the most important vote he made as a member of Congress—the January 1991 vote to authorize President George H. W. Bush to use military action to drive Saddam Hussein out of Kuwait. "I guess younger Members are tired of hearing us World War II types always using the prelude to that war as a model for foreign policy," Michel said on the House floor. "But allow me one last reference to the period with a Churchillian quote. He said 'Those who procrastinated in the face of Nazi aggression, were decided only to be undecided, resolved to be irresolute, adamant for drift, solid for fluidity, and all powerful, to be impotent.'" Michel continued: "I, like so many other members of my generation, am haunted by the ghosts of Munich—and the ghosts that Munich produced."[32]

The Bradley University Years

Safely returned to Peoria, Michel readied himself for a new semester at Bradley. The university boasted unusually large curricular offerings for a small college—enrollment in the mid-1940s reached almost 3,000 students. Besides regular liberal arts courses, there were departments in business administration, home economics, industrial education, music, art, and nursing. With the aid of the GI Bill, Michel pursued the four-year course leading to a BS degree. At first uncertain about a major, he dabbled in engineering, noting his fondness for drafting and working with machinery, talents he learned from his father. Michel finally settled on insurance because, as he said, he "liked people, talking with them, protecting them."[33] His class load included accounting, marketing, advertising, salesmanship, business law, finance, insurance, and secretarial training. He also took speech and voice classes, never anticipating how they might aid his political career.

Despite working thirty-five hours a week at Herschel Manufacturing Company, Bob loaded up on extracurricular activities. He played football and baseball.[34] He was elected treasurer of his sophomore class and president of his junior class. Michel joined Pi Kappa Delta Forensic Honor Society and Alpha Pi, the oldest fraternal organization on campus. He volunteered for at least two political campaigns while a student. He served on the university's Board of Control of Student Publications.[35]

It was an impressive résumé for a returning student working nearly full-time. But Bob's campus activities paled in comparison to those of one Corinne Woodruff. The returning veteran met Corinne in the A Cappella Choir at Bradley. Blessed with perfect pitch, she majored in piano and musical education. Their first date was to a Bradley basketball game in the old Peoria Armory, setting on course their mutual love of Bradley basketball. Corinne was three years younger, but Bob had lost about three and half years to the service, so that equalized the age difference. Bob might have been accused of dating above his station. Whereas Bob's entry in the 1947 Bradley yearbook consisted of a single entry and no photograph, Corinne's entry read like this:

> Corinne Woodruff is a senior. Lambda Chi, Political Chairman 4, Inter-Sorority Delegate 4; Music Club 1, 2, 3, 4, Vice President 3; English Club 3, 4; Mask and Gavel 1, 2, 3, 4; Student Federalist 4; chairman of Student Poll committee 4; A Cappella Choir 3, 4; Tech 1; Polyscope 1; Director Lambda Chi Chorus 4; Stunt Show 4; "Midsummer Night's Dream" 3.

Lambda Chi was the oldest social sorority on campus. The purpose of the Student Federalists was "the stimulation of thinking upon the urgency of a federal world government and the support of any steps which might help to attain that form of government." Corinne and her fellow members of Mask and Gavel promoted the "interests of drama and public speaking" and were described as "students with great hopes in the field of speech and acting."[36] Bob and Corinne were a perfectly matched pair—soul mates in today's vernacular—each enjoying the benefits of a well-rounded liberal arts education.

Once the Michels started a family in 1951, Corinne resided in Peoria with their four children. She accompanied local musicians during performances of the Peoria Symphony and theater productions. She helped opera and ballet companies begin in Peoria. She also accompanied Bob when he sang at political receptions and holiday parties. Although Bob made a point of returning to the district on most weekends, it was up to Corinne to raise the children. "The four of us are the way we are because of her," son Scott remarked at her memorial service. "She was always giving me such unique insights and perspectives on people and events. She was very open and understanding of other people and their opinions."[37] Throughout their nearly fifty-five-year marriage, she was recognized as her husband's closest adviser and confidante, possessing keen political insights and an informed understanding of his work. Bob often called upon her to represent him at events in the home district. Corinne Michel died on October 22, 2003, of complications from a stroke she had suffered in January following surgery. It was a devastating loss for Bob.

In early 1948, three or four months before graduation, the president of the university, David Owen, called Bob into his office. Michel described the exchange years later. Owen asked, "Bob, what are you going to do after graduation?" Michel, not at all clear about his plans, replied, "I don't know. I've taken all of the insurance courses I can. I like dealing with people. Or maybe law school." Owen said, "I want you to go and have an interview with a neighboring circuit court judge, Judge Velde. Everett Dirksen is retiring from Congress and he's running for his seat, and he needs a man Friday. He's a good friend of mine." Michel said, "Gee whiz, I didn't take political science. I didn't have journalism." Owen said, "Just go down and have the interview." Michel and Harold H. Velde hit it off, and Bob began immediately to work on the judge's election campaign to replace Dirksen in Congress.[38] He took a pay cut to do so; where Michel made $450–500 per month doing odd jobs at Bradley, his pay with Velde was $30 per week.

Bob still lived at home and had to break the news to his parents. "They were just crestfallen when I said I was thinking about getting involved in politics," Bob often remembered in interviews. "They said, 'This dirty rotten game of politics? You're thinking of getting into it?' I said, 'Dad, I'd like to give it a try. I think you've given us the rearing here at home to be able to tell what's right and what's wrong, and the difference between the two,'" Bob pleaded. "I'd just like to have a shot at it, and if I find out that it's like you say it is, I'll be man enough to come back and tell you, 'You were right Dad, and I was wrong. And I'll get out of this thing.'"[39] Charles and Anna would visit their only son just once after Bob was elected to the House.

Robert H. Michel graduated from Bradley University with a Bachelor of Science degree in business administration in June 1948. Bob and Corinne married on December 26, 1948, just before he moved to Washington, DC, as Velde's aide. She had to fulfill her teaching contract for the balance of that semester and could not join him as he embarked on his new adventure.

To the Nation's Capital

Republicans fared poorly in 1948—losing seventy-five seats and the majority in the House in the bargain—but Velde won his House seat by 5,000 votes. Bob rented a room at the old Dodge Hotel where the rates were "economical." After Corinne joined him, the Michels roomed with Velde and his wife in a two-bedroom, third-story walk-up apartment on 29th Street Southeast, a situation forced by Michel's fiscal conservatism. Although he earned a salary of $12,500 by the early 1950s, "There were $2,500 in expenses or some such thing," he complained. "It was ridiculous with two children and then two homes—or at least, you had the home back home that you were paying the mortgage on. Then you had to have someplace here. And so, Corinne and I and Olive and Harold all lived together in the summertime."[40]

Michel's boss deserves at least a footnote in congressional history. Named to the House Un-American Activities Committee (HUAC) in his first term largely because of his previous stint during World War II as a special agent of the Federal Bureau of Investigation specializing in sabotage and counterespionage, Velde became committee chairman when the Republicans captured control of the House following the 1952 elections. During his chairmanship, the committee launched a series of investigations into reported communist infiltration of the federal government, the military, labor unions, educational institutions, and the clergy. His national profile as a "Red-hunter" would prove to be double-edged, however.

The first three decades of Bob Michel's life featured a series of serendipitous circumstances. Raised neither in privilege nor poverty, he was born into a stable family who survived the Depression without serious hardship; Michel returned from serving in World War II wounded but without debilitating effects; he received a fine education from Bradley University and, most important, met Corinne; and a chance conversation with the university's president sent him to Washington.

The next step required more of Michel.

Taking His Place in the House

As Velde neared the end of his third term in 1954, he seemed ready to retire. An introvert by nature, politics and campaigning ill suited him. His first wife, Olive, had died, and the demands of the office weighed heavily on Velde. His service on the Education and Labor Committee put him squarely in the middle of labor issues, and his conservative stances earned him the enmity of the United Auto Workers, which sponsored an opponent in each of Velde's campaigns. Moreover, as chairman of HUAC, Velde, in Michel's words, "just made an enemy of all the Left and Hollywood."[41] The congressman sat down with his assistant and urged Michel to consider the race.

Michel went so far as to have petitions printed up at a Georgetown printing office so no one back home would know about it. But then Velde remarried, this time to Delores Anderson, his secretary, and she convinced him to run again. Bob naturally deferred to his mentor. But the ambition to win a seat in Congress in his own right had awakened. When Velde decided late in 1955 to retire, he assured Bob that he would not let Delores talk him out of it.[42] Against the advice of his friends, Michel dropped out of Georgetown Law School to seek election.[43]

On January 17, 1956, only six days before the primary election filing deadline, Harold Velde announced he would not seek reelection. The next day, Michel said he would file petitions: "I have harbored aspirations of some day being accorded this opportunity to put into active play in my own behalf the wealth of knowledge and experience I have acquired in the last eight years as Congressman Velde's Administrative Assistant."[44] Although four other Republicans filed for the race, James M. Unland of Pekin emerged as Michel's most formidable opponent. A decorated veteran like Michel, Unland owned a self-named insurance agency in Pekin, served on many nonprofit boards of directors, and headed the Republican Party's finance committee in Tazewell County, the second-most populous county in the district.[45] Unland campaigned against the influence of lobbyists in Washington and the handpicked manner of Michel's selection. In Unland's accounting, political bosses had forced Velde aside as a flawed candidate and had slated Michel in his place at the last possible moment.

Velde's political stances and flagging popularity did not hurt Michel in the district, however. Because Velde was so engrossed in the anticommunist crusade, he had sent Michel back to tend to district chores. "And, that's really what helped me in my primary because I think I could just about name every precinct committeeman in the district in the six counties when I ran."[46] Michel won the Republican nomination over Unland, 19,884 votes to 16,465; two other candidates lagged. Michel did not win a majority, however—opponents captured 21,562 votes all together. But all promised to endorse Michel, and Unland became a lifelong friend and active supporter.

Michel dispatched his opponent, Fred Allen, a self-described "middle of the road" Democrat, in November by taking 58.8 percent of the vote—87,187 central Illinois voters marked Bob's name on their ballots. In true Michel style, he had refused to castigate Allen during the general election campaign. In remarks to the Junior League in October, for example, Michel said: "Now the lines are more clearly drawn and my good opponent and I find ourselves squared off against one another not in personal animosity toward one another but as advocates of the contrasting views and philosophy of our respective political parties."[47] The candidate preferred civility to combat even on the campaign trail.

Michel took his seat in the House of Representatives (which had swung back to the Democrats in 1955) on January 3, 1957. That day's session lasted only one hour and fifty-two minutes, but it was long enough to make Bob Michel the congressman from Illinois's 18th District. Two days later he introduced his first bill, HR 784, to provide for "effecting the disposition of the Illinois and Mississippi Canal" to the Committee on Public Works. Sam Rayburn (D-TX) presided as Speaker, John McCormack (D-MA) as majority leader, and Joe Martin (R-MA) as minority leader. The first session of the 85th Congress counted 234 Democrats and 201 Republicans. Only two years separated Michel and his Republican colleagues from their party's most recent majority in the House. The freshman congressman could not know then that he would never again have as many Republican colleagues as he had in 1957—or that his party would wait almost four decades for another turn at the helm.

One of the ten youngest members of the House when first elected, Michel took the long view of his career. First, he knew that future success depended on satisfying his constituents in central Illinois—he took the lesson from Velde to avoid situations that might compromise his popularity there. "One of the first things I did," Michel said, "was make sure that I didn't have a primary opponent the next time around. I made sure I was in close contact with my party and the 'leaders' on the local scene."[48] He had his marching orders, too. When first elected to Congress, he recalled:

> The charge that the people sent me here with was, "Bob, go down and cut the cost of government and get it off our back. That's all." They didn't say, "Give me more of this. Give me some of this. Give me this. Give me that." Or "What other programs can I qualify for?" That just wasn't the mood at the time. It was, "Cut the cost of government and get it off our back. And we'll be all right."[49]

Such sentiments dovetailed with Michel's personal values and conservative political philosophy. Michel's brand of conservatism differed from the conservatism practiced by the likes of the Tea Party or the Freedom Caucus in the House beginning in 2010. When asked about his definition of the term "conservatism" years later, Michel explained:

> The Founders were conservative, and the Constitution they gave us created a government that is rooted in conservative beliefs about human nature and the absolute necessity to have government that is at once limited and strong. . . . Conservatives and Republicans of all stripes must understand government is not the enemy—wasteful government, intrusive government, irresponsible government, corrupt government is the enemy. The people of the United States are not happy with government when it does not work well. But make no mistake about it: Americans from the beginning have realized that the government system left to us by the Founders is the best in the world.[50]

Close attention to the district and his natural conservatism meant that the new congressman did not see himself as a legislative innovator or a publicity-seeker. His advice to new members included this warning: "The folks back home sent you to the House to be a good legislator not a TV star or a political philosopher."[51] He preferred a behind-the-scenes style more in keeping with his personal modesty—work hard to pass good bills, to defeat bad bills, and to amend bills that needed improvement. Michel offered only fourteen bills and resolutions in the first session of the 85th Congress, all dealing with routine matters. A low-key affair, his maiden speech on the House floor reflected pressure from his farm constituency who sought changes in the corn-acreage allotment. His later remarks during that entire session took up a mere three pages in the *Congressional Record* and dealt with Lake Michigan water diversion and Bradley University's basketball team, which had won the 1957 National Invitation Tournament. He was silent on the dominant issues in 1957, such as the civil rights protests in Little Rock and the Soviet Union's launching of the first man-made satellite, Sputnik 1, into orbit around the earth.

In its first report on their new congressman, the *Peoria Journal Star* highlighted the fit between the district and its representative. The editorial board saluted Michel for "endeavoring to promote economy in governmental operations." As the newspaper noted, he was among the House members who voted to disapprove the appropriation of an additional $2 million to be spent in the administration of state and local public aid commissions throughout the United States. "In taking such an attitude, Rep. Michel is reflecting the attitude of a great many of his constituents." The editorial quoted from Michel's floor speech on the bill: "Even though being a new member of Congress, I have spent enough time here in Washington to be of the frame of mind that if you do not give the bureaucrats the money, they cannot spend it." "We wish more members of Congress had the same idea," the paper opined. "If Mr. Michel continues along the line he laid down in that speech, he'll be giving the people of this district the best kind of representation they could have in Washington."[52]

An Eye to the Future

It is difficult to pin down the precise point at which Michel began to covet a leadership position in the House of Representatives. "When I first got elected," Michel said, "I had no idea how long I was going to be there or to be so ambitious to want a leadership position before my time, or anything like that. That was the furthest from my thoughts."[53] But even early in his career, he took three steps that would propel him—in hindsight if not in foresight—through the party's leadership ranks: (1) He cultivated friendships with his new colleagues; (2) he thought strategically in seeking his first committee assignment; and (3) he took nothing for granted in running his first reelection campaign.

As the only Republican elected in 1956 with previous Hill experience as a staffer, Michel offered to help his freshman colleagues adjust to life on Capitol Hill by suggesting the best office locations, offering ideas about committee assignments, and orienting them to the Hill's folkways. Such generosity with his time and knowledge seems less a political calculation on Michel's part than a natural outgrowth of his personality. As he told an interviewer, "I knew my way around. I knew how the place worked. I was confident that I could do the job because I liked people."[54] His colleagues returned the favor by electing Michel president of the 85th Congress Club, the organization formed by the twenty-two Republican freshman members of the 85th Congress.[55] He also was the only freshman to be appointed to the Republican Policy Committee, which met weekly to chart the course of the party in legislative matters, and he was selected for the Young Republican National Federation Hall of Fame.[56] Thus began Michel's ascent through the GOP's leadership. He kept in mind his father's advice: "If you wanted to go up the ladder, you had to start with hard work. And he believed that if you wanted to be a leader, you couldn't be one by talking all the time—you have to be listening 90 percent of the time."[57]

The conventional view of Bob Michel, congressional leader, is one of modesty and self-effacement—the "aw, shucks" Michel who rarely swore, even in private. That view seriously underestimates Michel's competitiveness and ambition. His sisters noted his drive to win early on the playground of White Elementary School, where young Bob took no prisoners when shooting marbles with his chums and captured the school's championship—Bob recalling that the winner got to keep all the marbles.[58] That competitive streak showed up, too, in the annual congressional baseball game and in his favorite pastime, golf. His close friend, golfing buddy, and colleague Tom Railsback (R-IL) observed: "I don't think I've ever seen anybody as competitive. When you meet him, you don't see that because he is very mild-mannered. But when he wants to compete, he's a real tiger."[59]

Michel may have kept his ambition under wraps in 1957, but he thought strategically in seeking his first committee assignment. Early in the term, he met with Minority Leader (and former Speaker) Joe Martin (R-MA), who assumed the freshman would campaign for a coveted spot on Appropriations or Ways and Means. But Michel surprised him: "Just keep me off of the Education and Labor Committee, and I'll be satisfied." Michel wanted no part of the committee's work on labor legislation, a jurisdiction that had guaranteed an opponent in each of his predecessor's four reelection campaigns. Michel ended up on the Government Operations Committee—his only assignment—and on two subcommittees: Executive and Legislative Reorganization and Intergovernmental Relations. "I was mighty happy simply to just bide my time," he reminisced. "I knew I was young enough, at age thirty-two or thirty-three, that I didn't need to step on people's toes to get up the ladder."[60] In Bob Michel, ambition did not turn him into a hard-charging, ruthless character, unlike some of the generations that followed him in Congress.

Even more consequential in terms of his future as his party's leader in the House, Michel was admitted by secret ballot to the Chowder and Marching Club (C&M)[61] in his first term, one of only two freshmen so honored. A small group numbering fifteen Republican House members, the club based its selections "on factors of intellect, personality, leadership potential and even diversity of background, geography, and current committee responsibility," a club history explained. C&M was formed in 1949 by young Republican House members, all of them, like Michel, veterans of the US armed services during World War II. Their objective: to oppose a pension benefit for themselves. Michel expressed his affinity for the club's charter, and for its endorsement of economy in government, when he described its founding: "We're robbing Peter to pay Paul—what [is] this business about paying pensions to those of us who served our country? That's what we thought we were supposed to do, and now we get ourselves elected to Congress. It's ridiculous."[62] Membership in the club proved crucial later in his career as Michel tapped its membership for support in his leadership races.

Before he could realistically aspire to leadership, however, Michel had to win his first reelection campaign. He announced his bid on December 10, 1957, at the noon luncheon meeting of the Peoria Suburban Kiwanis. In addition to his comparative prominence in the House Republican ranks, and tapping into his audience's aversion to Washington's interference, Michel explained how his subcommittee assignments had given him a perch to oppose "big government" and to find ways by which the federal government "might divest itself of authority, control, regulation, and taxing power." Legislatively, Michel touted his support of the corn, soybean, and livestock producers; his opposition to federal aid to education; his endorsement of the extension of unemployment compensation (under certain conditions); his support of the reciprocal trade program, although he opposed foreign aid (he subscribed to the theory of "trade—not aid"); and his bill protecting the interests of downstate Illinois if there should be an increase in the diversion of Lake Michigan water.[63] Campaigning on the phrase "One Good Term Deserves Another," he prided himself as standing up against "the free-wheeling spenders" in Washington.

Michel could not afford to take the election for granted. Republicans in 1958 campaigned amid the so-called Eisenhower Recession. After thirteen years of postwar growth, the US economy stumbled into its first economic downturn since the Great Depression, a recession that forced over five million people—over 7 percent of the labor force—out of work. Recognizing the headwinds his colleagues faced, Minority Leader Martin advised Michel that their party faced "an unusually hard campaign" as Democrats "will make a heavily-financed and aggressive campaign to completely dominate the Congress as a stepping stone to 1960."[64] As if to confirm the uncertainty of reelection, Michel turned down a request from the Republican National Committee to deliver speeches outside his own district, claiming "that I have my hands pretty full with the United Auto Workers and those growing numbers of unemployed out in Peoria."[65]

Even though Michel had avoided serving on the Education and Labor Committee, labor put up his opponent in 1958. James W. McGee, a forty-year-old Peoria Democrat, longtime party activist, and business agent for the International Association of Machinists local, won his party's nomination. McGee attempted to capitalize on the district's economic hardship: "Not since the days of the dark depression of the 30's has our nation faced a more serious economic problem than it faces today. . . . Our district and our nation cannot be healthy and strong when many of our people are out of work."[66] Responding to McGee's charges that Michel opposed labor on virtually all labor reform proposals in the 85th Congress, Michel said: "In simple defense of my record I will say that I didn't go to Congress as the apple polisher for any special interest. I was quite well aware that I could never please all the people on any one individual piece of legislation."[67] In the same breath, the incumbent cited more than a dozen votes that he characterized as prolabor.

The district's voters returned Michel to the House on November 4 with 59.5 percent of the vote, a modest improvement over his winning margin in 1956 of 58.8 percent. Republicans lost forty-eight House seats in 1958, however, including three Republican incumbents from the Illinois delegation. Robert H. Michel would triumph in seventeen more campaigns, dispatching his opponents with relative ease and averaging over 66 percent of the vote. On only three occasions did his reelection margin seriously falter—in 1964, a result of Republican presidential candidate Barry Goldwater's landslide loss; in 1974, a result of the fallout from the Watergate scandal; and in 1982, when he was forced to defend President Ronald Reagan's economic plan during a recession. The last was his closet call—Republican Leader Michel won a bare majority with 51.5 percent of the vote; thereafter his winning average was 66.9 percent.

In 1958, Bob Michel proved his ability to keep his seat in Congress over the long haul by bucking national trends unfavorable to congressional Republicans.

He chalked up his success to several factors—familiarity with the district beginning with his days on Harold Velde's staff; the fact of his heavily Republican congressional district; the emphasis he placed on constituent service; and a philosophy of conservatism paired with a disdain for federal government overreach that suited the voters back home. His hometown newspaper welcomed Michel's reelection: "It means that his ability, experience and service to the people of the district are recognized by the people and have their hearty approval," adding, "His political future looks bright and we wish him continued success."[68]

The *Peoria Journal Star*'s editors could not know it then, of course, but the congressional elections of 1958 foreshadowed something more ominous for Bob Michel's career: Republicans would remain the minority party in the House for nearly forty more years.

Notes

1. As John Ehrlichman, presidential adviser to Richard Nixon, once explained: "In some conversation or another in the White House . . . I said, 'How is this going to play in Peoria?' meaning how is the average American going to react to this?" See Amy Groh, "The Phrase That Put Peoria on the Map," InterBusiness Issues (2009) at www.peoriamagazines.com/ibi/2009/jun/phrase-put-peoria-map.
2. Jerry Klein, "Peoria!" (Peoria, IL: Peoria Historical Society, 1985), Peoria Public Library Special Collections.
3. "Peoria . . . Impressions of 150 Years" (Peoria, IL: *Peoria Journal Star*, 1995), 83, Peoria Public Library Special Collections.
4. "Peoria . . . Impressions of 150 Years," 84.
5. Other sources have him emigrating in 1913. See RHM Papers, Press Series, f. Subjects: Michel, Robert (2); "Michel Memories," 2002, RHM Papers, Post-Congressional Series, f. Subjects: "Michel Memories."
6. "Bob Michel: Looking Back," WTVP, February 28, 1994, The Dirksen Congressional Center Audiovisual Collection.
7. "Tribute to Our Mom," July 6, 1980, RHM Papers, Personal, f. 1980, M.
8. RHM to Whitfield, January 30, 1992, Personal, f. 1992, W.
9. RHM to Whitfield, January 30, 1992, Personal, f. 1992, W. Charles Michel relied on that 10 percent figure for other advice, too. Bob chalked up one of his leadership traits to his father's admonition: "It's better to listen 90 percent of the time for that leaves only ten percent for talking."
10. 1940 Census, ancestry.com.
11. "First book proposal meeting," August 19, 2003, RHM Papers, Post-Congressional Series, f. Subjects: Memoir.
12. Brien R. Williams interview with RHM, May 24, 2007, RHM Papers, Interfile: Personal, f. 2007, Interviews.
13. RHM to Rev. John J. Steigenga [Christian Reformed Church], August 19, 1993, RHM Papers, Personal, f. 1993, R–S.

14. Shelley Epstein interview with RHM, February 1999, RHM Papers, Audiovisual Series, VHS Tapes.
15. RHM to Stanton Carle, November 28, 1967, RHM Papers, General Series, f. 90th Congress: RHM Personal, A-H.
16. RHM to Harry Caray and Steve Stone, Chicago Cubs, April 24, 1991, RHM Papers, Personal, f. 1991, C–L.
17. Epstein interview with RHM, February 1999.
18. "Robert H. Michel . . . a Biography," ca. 1984 in RHM, Information File, f. Biographical. The RHM Information File was created by the staff of The Dirksen Congressional Center.
19. Epstein interview with RHM, February 1999; Transcript of Michel Speech, "Leadership," February 15, 1984, RHM Papers, Staff Series: Bill Gavin, f. 1984.
20. Epstein interview with RHM, February 1999.
21. RHM Papers, Personal, f. Memoir Notes, 10.
22. Epstein interview with RHM, February 1999.
23. RHM Interview, InterBusiness Issues, July 2013, RHM, Information File, f. Biographical.
24. National Archives and Records Administration, *U.S. World War II Army Enlistment Records, 1938–1946* (Provo, UT: Ancestry.com Operations 2005, search.ancestry.com /cgi-bin/sse.dll?indiv=1&db=WWIIenlist&h=7655708&tid=&pid=&usePUB=true&r hSource=244).
25. RHM to Jeron Michel, March 22, 1989, RHM Papers, Personal, f. 1989. M.
26. Epstein interview with RHM, February 1999.
27. Epstein interview with RHM, February 1999.
28. Epstein interview with RHM, February 1999.
29. Undated news clipping, "Pfc. Bob Michel Persuades 28 Germans 'It's No Use!'" RHM Papers, Scrapbooks, f. Clippings, 1944.
30. RHM Interview, InterBusiness Issues; Epstein interview with RHM, February 1999.
31. Epstein interview with RHM, February 1999. During his recovery, Michel was assigned to interrogate German prisoners because of his fluency in German. One he questioned was the man who had wounded him and who had, in turn, been wounded by Michel. Each was grateful for the other's imperfect marksmanship.
32. RHM, Annotated Draft, January 12, 1991, RHM Papers, Press Series, f. Remarks and Releases; *Congressional Record*, January 12, 1991, H476.
33. Epstein interview with RHM, February 1999.
34. Michel claimed to play both sports, but he is listed on neither team in the university yearbooks of the period.
35. Polyscope [Bradley University Yearbook], 1942–1946, Bradley University Special Collections; Polyscope, 1947–1948, RHM Papers, Scrapbooks, f. Polyscope.
36. Polyscope, 1947, RHM Papers, Scrapbooks, f. Polyscope, 1947.
37. Corinne W. Michel obituary, *Chicago Tribune*, October 24, 2003, www.chicagotribune.com.
38. Epstein interview with RHM, February 1999.
39. RHM Interview, InterBusiness Issues.
40. Fred W. Beuttler interview with RHM, September 5, 2007, RHM Papers, Post-Congressional Series, f. Subjects: Interviews (2).
41. Book proposal meeting, 2003.
42. Epstein interview with RHM, February 1999.

43. RHM to William Avery, January 3, 2009, RHM Papers, Post-Congressional Series, f. Correspondence: 2003, A–C.
44. RHM Press Release, January 18, 1956, RHM Papers, Personal, f. Velde.
45. Clippings, RHM Papers, Campaigns and Politics, 1956, f. Candidates: Unland, James.
46. Book proposal meeting, 2003.
47. Handwritten draft of remarks to the Junior League, October 9, 1956, RHM Papers, Campaigns and Politics, 1956, f. Speeches and Positions.
48. Beuttler interview with RHM, September 5, 2007.
49. Beuttler interview with RHM, September 5, 2007.
50. *Washington Times,* October 19, 1993.
51. RHM Papers, Speech and Trip File, f. National Press Club [not given], 1994.
52. Editorial, "Good Start," *Peoria Journal Star,* February 15, 1957, RHM Papers, Scrapbooks, f. Editorials (1).
53. Beuttler interview with RHM, September 5, 2007.
54. Epstein interview with RHM, February 1999.
55. Book proposal meeting, 2003.
56. Press release, December 10, 1957, RHM Papers, Campaigns and Politics, 1958, f. Public Relations: Press Releases.
57. "Robert H. Michel . . . a Biography," ca. 1984, RHM, Information File, f. Biographical. Interviewed in 1994, even Newt Gingrich claimed to have learned the importance of listening from Bob; he paraphrased Charles Michel's advice as: "You learn less when your mouth is open." See "Bob Michel: Looking Back," WTVP, recorded December 28, 1994, The Dirksen Congressional Center Audiovisual Series.
58. "Bob Michel: Looking Back," WTVP.
59. "Bob Michel: Looking Back," WTVP.
60. Beuttler interview with RHM, September 5, 2007.
61. Early editions of the organization's history begin with this disclaimer: "The Chowder and Marching Club was never formally organized and it was never formally named. In these respects, its origins are probably as unusual as its subsequent activities." See "A History of the Chowder and Marching Club," February 1987, RHM Papers, Post-Congressional Series, f. C&M Club (1).
62. Book proposal meeting 2003; "The Chowder and Marching Club, 1949–1965," RHM Papers, General Series, f. C & M, 89th Congress; "Chowder and Marching Club 1949–1999," RHM Papers, Post-Congressional Series, f. Subjects: C&M (2).
63. Untitled campaign document, RHM Papers, Campaigns and Politics, 1958, f. Speeches/Positions.
64. Martin to RHM, April 9, 1958, RHM Papers, Campaigns and Politics, 1958, f. Congratulations Received.
65. RHM to Meade Alcorn, May 23, 1958, RHM Papers, Campaigns and Politics, 1958, f. Miscellaneous.
66. "James W. McGee," RHM Papers, Campaigns and Politics, 1958, f. Candidates: McGee.
67. Untitled, RHM Papers, Campaigns and Politics, 1958, f. Speeches/Positions.
68. Editorial, "Voter Approval," *Peoria Journal Star,* November 6, 1958.

CHAPTER 2

BOB MICHEL AND THE POLITICS OF APPROPRIATIONS

Scott A. Frisch and Sean Q Kelly

Like his predecessors in the minority leadership, Gerald R. Ford of Michigan and John J. Rhodes of Arizona, he is part of the generation of World War II veterans who remade politics in their hometowns. Blessed with common sense and agreeable personalities, they were spotted early in their House careers as people who were likely to stick around and make their marks.

All three were picked for seats on the Appropriations Committee, the quintessential place of power in the House, a panel that values hard workers with a willingness to compromise and abhors publicity-seekers and bomb-throwers. It was on the Appropriations Committee that Ford, Rhodes, and Michel all learned to function and influence policy in a Democratic-run House, even as they sought to overturn the opposition's majority.[1]

—David Broder, 1993

We believe Broder was right. There is an old saying: "Where you stand depends on where you sit." Individuals are shaped by the perspective from which they observe the world. For half of his congressional career, Bob Michel sat on the House Appropriations Committee, one of the most powerful committees in the chamber. The Appropriations Committee is responsible for determining discretionary funding levels for government programs. A seat on the committee requires hard work and in return confers influence in the House. David Broder, the late legendary political writer, argued that Bob Michel's work on Appropriations presaged his rise to leadership in the Republican Party as it had for John Rhodes and Gerald Ford before him.

In this chapter, we focus on Bob Michel's work on the Appropriations Committee. We begin with a discussion of the Appropriations Committee as it was in the middle of the twentieth century and how Bob Michel found his way onto the committee. We then turn to several of his efforts to use the committee to achieve his fiscally conservative policy goals and to unite his fractured party. In conclusion, we argue that his work on the committee allowed him to learn about the legislative process and to develop the creative skills necessary to be a successful legislator and ultimately the longest-serving House Republican leader in history.

Textbook Appropriations

Richard Fenno's account of the Appropriations Committee, *The Power of the Purse: Appropriations Politics in Congress*, remains the definitive work on the operation of the Appropriations Committees. He stresses the mission-driven organization of the committee toward what he calls their "single, paramount task—to guard the Federal Treasury."[2] Members of the Appropriations Committee conceive of their legislative mission as making decisions about money rather than making policy-oriented decisions: "They deal immediately with dollars and cents. . . . *Theirs is a 'business' rather than a 'policy' committee*" (emphasis added).[3] Members of Congress, in Fenno's textbook committee, gravitate toward the Appropriations Committee because of its power—the "power of the purse." Party leaders choose committee members for their skills and abilities as legislators, that is to say, their ability to adhere to the norms of the institution acting as "responsible legislators."

Fenno highlights the ability of the committee to maintain internal norms that promote unity within the subcommittees and across the "Full Committee." The bulk of the legislative work in the committee occurs at the subcommittee level. A hallmark of the Appropriations Committee is the autonomy of the subcommittees: the degree to which subcommittees defer to one another's decisions, as well as subcommittee "unity"—the obligation of subcommittee members to support internal decisions. Bob Michel characterized committee leaders in 1959: "These fellows want to report a bill that they can all agree on. They don't want any minority report—about all you can do is say, 'I reserve on that question, Mr. Chairman.'"[4] The unity norm is supported by selecting members who are responsible legislators. Unity at the subcommittee level extends to the "Full Committee." According to an appropriator, "I tell them [the Full Committee] we should have a united front. If there are any objections or changes, we ought to hear it now, and not wash our dirty laundry out on the floor."[5]

The power and prestige of the Appropriations Committee, Fenno argues, depends upon the indispensability of its work and its ability to gain passage of its bills on the floor; the unity norm is critical to the legislative mission and to supporting the power and prestige of the committee: "The committee's own conviction is that its floor success depends on its ability to present a united front in its confrontations with the House. And floor success . . . is important to the Committee members because it enhances Committee influence and individual prestige. Unity is the one key variable over which Committee members can exercise some control, and they bend every effort to do so."[6]

Fenno depicts the Appropriations Committee as largely resistant to external influence—it is a closed club. The exclusive club is off-limits even to party leaders: "Party leaders do not normally exercise much influence during Committee decision-making. . . . Committee-based norms far more than party-based norms govern the behavior of members inside the committee."[7] In short, the success of the Appropriations Committee relied on limiting the scope of conflict. Focusing the committee, and the House floor, on spending—how much should we spend rather than whether we should spend and on what—improves the chances of success in committee and on the floor. This reality is reflected in the rules of the House and the Senate. In 1837, for instance, the House adopted a rule stating: "No appropriation shall be reported in such general appropriation bills, or be in order as an amendment thereto, for any expenditure not previously authorized by law." Subsequent changes and additions to the rules have perfected this fundamental principle. Language in the bill or floor amendments that seek to legislate (make policy) in an appropriations bill are subject to a point of order and can be excised from the bill by majority vote or by a ruling of the chair.

Michel and the Appropriations Committee[8]

As a first-term Republican, Michel's committee assignment prospects were limited—something he understood as a Hill staffer.[9] The 1958 midterm elections were not kind to the Republicans. Despite Michel's win, the GOP lost forty-eight seats. Because the ratio of Democrats to Republicans on each committee is a function of the number of seats held by each party, plum committee assignments were in short supply. Michel's willingness to take what he was given without complaint—a slot on the Government Administration Committee—allowed him to demonstrate to party leaders that he was a team player, a workhorse willing to engage in the obscure and undistinguished work of government oversight of the executive branch.

Reflecting on his choice to leave Government Administration, Michel told Richard Fenno that, had he stayed on the committee, "I'd be fifth in seniority, with twenty years in age between me and the next man above me. So I probably could have been chairman of that committee someday. I'll never get to be chairman of Appropriations." But, he continued, "you have to ask yourself whether you want to wait around to be a chairman someday, or whether you want to get in on things and wield a little influence around here before that time."[10]

When Charlie Vursell, a Republican House member from Marion County, Illinois, lost his reelection bid in 1958, his seat on the House Appropriations Committee—a position traditionally filled by a member from Illinois—opened up. Michel wrote to the ranking Republican on Appropriations, John Tabor (R-NY), to make his case: "I said, 'Mr. Taber [sic], I know you are acquainted with my conservative views, and I'd like to get on the [Appropriations] committee.' I know how John works, and I knew that would score points with him. . . . Well, he wrote Joe Martin and . . . said that as far as he was concerned I ought to be on the committee."[11]

One of the most powerful committees in the House, the Appropriations Committee controls discretionary federal spending levels. Using the appropriations process, Michel could seek to influence government spending consistent with his natural fiscal conservatism, to shape government spending priorities, and to help colleagues with federally funded projects in their home districts and states. Assignment to the committee would allow Michel to pursue his policy goals and eventually allow him to become influential within the House GOP. As Michel explained to Fenno: "If you want to get to know some particular area of government, Appropriations is the place to do it." However, "it's no fun to sit in [committee hearings]. . . . You have to pry the information out of these people who are all there to justify their programs. You get no publicity, and for all you know people back home think you're sitting on your prat."

Michel and Harold Collier (from the state's 6th District), both of whom won their first elections in 1956 and who roomed together, appealed to Leo Allen, the dean of the Illinois delegation, for the Illinois appointment. Minority Whip Les Arends, from Michel's neighboring district, told Michel, "Well, we lost a seat on appropriations. Bob, let's see if we can get a spot for you."[12] Arends approached Allen, but Allen remanded the issue, instructing Michel and Collier to settle the matter themselves. The two selected a time-honored method—the flip of a coin. According to Michel, they flipped a nickel in a hall in the Longworth Office Building. The coin rolled on the linoleum floor, rolled up to the sideboard, hung for a split second, and stood upright on its edge. No winner. Michel prevailed on the next attempt.[13] With the endorsement of the Illinois delegation secured, Michel wrote a short letter to the Republican Conference leader Charles Halleck (a close friend of Minority Whip Arends[14]) requesting the open seat on Appropriations:[15]

> Dear Charlie,
>   As Chairman of the Committee on Committees, I should like you to know that I am bidding for one of the vacant seats on the Appropriations committee.
>   Illinois lost its important seat on this committee with the defeat of our good friend Charlie Vursell. It would seem only fair that Illinois should retain a seat on the committee, and I would appreciate very much your support for me in this regard.
>   With expressions of highest esteem.
>   Robert H. Michel, M.C.

The appointment to Appropriations proved fortuitous, providing fertile ground for Michel's characteristic approach to legislating, which emphasized frugality, attention to detail, and willingness to work both sides of the partisan divide. Indeed, according to Fenno's formulation, he was the model of the type of legislator that party leaders sought for the committee. In particular, the Appropriations Committee that Michel joined minimized partisanship. "We had a single staff, not a majority staff and a minority staff," Michel recalled. "If I wanted to propose an amendment to reduce the cost of a popular program, the chief of the staff might say the chairman won't like it, but he honored my request to draw up the amendment. That's how I made my name on Appropriations, by offering amendments to reduce the cost of programs."[16] Michel spent two decades laboring largely behind the scenes on Appropriations. He parlayed appointments on the

Labor, Health, Education, and Welfare (Labor-HEW) and the Agriculture, Environmental, and Consumer Protection subcommittees into a mastery of the far-flung federal bureaucracy. Fated to the minority throughout his service (Democratic Chairman Clarence Cannon could not recall Michel's name until 1960), Michel said, "I wasn't out to make any great big waves. I knew I'm young enough, and if I do my work politically at home well enough, why, I'll bide my time, build up my seniority and then, eventually. . . ."[17] He did not finish the thought.

Bob Michel: Fiscal Conservative, Reluctant Social Warrior

Congress in the 1960s reflected the values developed during the post–New Deal Democratic dominance of the institution. Seniority and apprenticeship norms encouraged young legislators to keep their heads down and learn to legislate. The Texas Democrat and longtime Speaker of the House, Sam Rayburn, reflected the tenor of the House early in Bob Michel's career: "Don't try to go too fast. Learn your job. Don't ever talk until you know what you're talking about. If you want to get along, go along."[18] Mr. Sam's wisdom is reflected in Michel's career on Appropriations. Bob Michel served on the Appropriations Committee starting in 1961, through his service as the minority whip, until 1980, when he was elected minority leader (a title he changed to "Republican Leader" upon taking the office). Service on the committee honed his skills as a legislator, demonstrated his leadership skills to fellow Republicans, and positioned him to rise within the Republican hierarchy. "I always tried to help the president save money," Michel recalled. "As a matter of fact, I think I got my reputation, particularly on the Health, Education, [and] Welfare Appropriations Committee where we offered amendments" aimed at reducing appropriations.[19] Michel's natural fiscal conservatism and service on the committee matched the committee's overall ethos of guardians of the treasury.

Bob Michel's service on the Appropriations Committee allows us to explore two often ignored elements of members' careers: learning and creativity.[20] Congress is a complex political and social institution. It is a combination of formal rules, institutional structures, and intricate social relationships. Successful legislators—that is, legislators who end up influencing policy—must learn to navigate this formal and informal labyrinth. It takes time and effort to learn the necessary skills to be successful. Again, the words of Speaker Rayburn underscore this: "In my many years as a

Representative in Congress it is my observation that the district that is best represented is the district that is wise enough to select a man of energy, intelligence, and integrity and reelects him year after year. A man of this type and character serves more efficiently and effectively the longer he is returned by his people."[21] Close examination of Michel's work on Appropriations provides leverage on the learning process that he experienced serving on the committee.

One characteristic we notice in successful legislators is the capacity for creativity. To outsiders, the institutional machinery of Congress appears to be rigid. In reality, creative members of Congress discover inventive ways to use the rules or innovative legislative language to their advantage. Successful legislators often fail many times, sometimes spectacularly, before they succeed. Success is not simply a product of repetition but of dissecting failures—consulting with staff, interest groups, and other members; adjusting legislative language and floor tactics; and finally developing another approach that might succeed. Focusing on several of Michel's efforts during his career on Appropriations provides an opportunity to explore learning and creativity to illustrate how Michel ultimately developed into a legislatively savvy member of the House Appropriations Committee.

Fiscal Conservative

Labor-HEW Appropriations, 1969. With newly elected President Richard Nixon in the White House, Bob Michel was optimistic that fiscal conservatism would stem, or even turn back, the tide of federal spending that escalated during the Lyndon Johnson administration. When the Labor, Health, Education, and Welfare Subcommittee's appropriations bill hit the floor on June 28, 1969, Michel—the ranking Republican on the subcommittee—was managing the bill for House Republicans for the first time in his career. Managing the bill for the Democrats was the flamboyant former actor and chairman of the subcommittee, Dan Flood (D-PA). In his opening remarks, Michel warned against amendments increasing spending for many of the programs included in the bill. In particular, Michel had readied an amendment to cut spending under the Elementary and Secondary Education Act (ESEA), which provided federal funds to improve education in the states.

"The amending process is the heart of decision making on the floor," Walter Oleszek reminds us.[22] When a bill is considered on the floor it is subject to amendments that change the text of the bill. Amendments are limited to two "degrees": an amendment, and an amendment to the amendment (see Figure 2.1).

When the Labor-HEW Subcommittee bill hit the floor, Bob Michel was prepared with a substitute amendment to replace language in the bill. His intention was to undermine support for larger reductions that he knew would be offered on the floor. His first attempt was struck on a point of order raised by Michigan Democrat James O'Hara. Michel offered the amendment without specifying that other language in the bill would be struck as a result of the amendment. With this ruling, Charles Joelson (D-NJ) responded with his amendment increasing spending by $900 million above the subcommittee proposal, which was $1.3 billion above the previous year's appropriation. Joelson's amendment was in the first degree and thus the last vote that would be taken, improving the likelihood of passage. The most important feature of Joelson's proposal was that 385 House members—Democrats and Republicans—had schools in their districts that would benefit from some of the funding increases that Joelson proposed. Michel then offered his amendment as a substitute for the Joelson amendment. One of Michel's Republican colleagues, Howard Robison (R-NY), moved to amend Michel's substitute by increasing the funding levels suggested by the Michel amendment by $110 million. This amendment provided a sweetener for members attracted to the higher spending levels in the Joelson amendment. A subsequent amendment by Neal Smith (D-IA) increased the Joelson amendment by an additional $73 million. What proponents accomplished through these amendments was to ensure that an amendment increasing the funding levels in the bill achieved a preferential spot in the parliamentary order by "filling the amendment tree," which is to say that no further amendments were in order. In a series of votes, each of the alternatives to the Joelson amendment was defeated and it was adopted by a bipartisan majority. After two days of debate, Michel tasted a bitter defeat to his first amendment as a bill manager.

Perturbed by the outcome, Michel was especially aggravated that a large number of his Republican colleagues abandoned him when the vote was taken on his amendment. In a letter sent to all Republicans, Michel wrote: "As the ranking member of the Subcommittee I personally feel responsible for our having been rolled to a greater extent money-wise than I've ever experienced in my 13 years of the Committee." He continued, "With our Administration in power we've got to have a better reading among our own membership as to why we failed so miserably yesterday." Michel asked

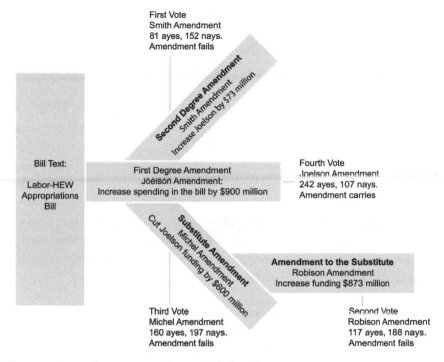

Figure 2.1 Amendment Tree, Labor-HEW bill, 1969

his colleagues to answer three questions: "Why could you not support the [Michel] substitute? Why [was] it necessary for you to support the Joelson Amendment? Why [did] you 'sit out' the teller vote?"

Michel received dozens of responses. Many of them were supportive. Iowa Republican Fred Schwengel, who did not support Michel's amendment, praised Michel, commending him for "the spirit of your letter. Once again you have proven me right in my prediction when I talked to you on several occasions in the past and I commend you as a bright, young forward-looking leader with concern. . . . With this letter [you are] demonstrating a characteristic of good leadership . . . keeping in touch with the troops."[23] And Republican Minority Leader Gerald Ford wrote to Michel: "Before we go on to the next battle, I just want you to know how greatly I appreciated your good teamwork and support in last week's H.E.W. appropriation floor action. Even though we lost, we fought the good fight."[24] Schwengel, like many of Michel's colleagues, expressed concern for local interests; they felt that Michel's cuts would be damaging to the interests of their district. Lawrence Williams (R-PA) wanted to vote for cuts but, having previously challenged his district's educators, wrote: "I saw no reason in further antagonizing an influential group in my District over an already lost cause."[25]

Peter Frelinghuysen, however, responded to Michel with a stinging letter. "Your proposal was obviously just 'bait' to hold enough votes to kill a more attractive proposal." Frelinghuysen continued: "Education—even for Republicans—has appeal; your 'bait' did not. Incidentally, I did not sit out the teller vote; I opposed your proposal at every opportunity."[26] Reflecting on the loss, Florida Republican William Cramer let Michel know in a handwritten note what he thought the source of the problem was: "Better planning and leadership planning needed—we need [a] minority parliamentary expert."[27] According to Frelinghuysen, "you failed because 'we' were in serious disagreement as to what was advisable. Even worse, the leaders never even check to see if they had a team. But perhaps the uses of adversity will be sweet and we'll learn something from the fiasco."[28] There is little doubt that Bob Michel learned from this defeat.

Food stamp fight, 1971–1972. An "appropriations limitation amendment" restricts the amount or scope of spending by the executive branch. In 1971, and again in 1972, Bob Michel attempted to use this maneuver to prevent striking workers' access to federally funded food stamps. Conservatives tend to be critical of unions and many income transfer programs like food stamps. In the late 1960s and early 1970s, strikes were common and often lasted for months. Michel argued that the food stamp program exacerbated the number and duration of strikes. According to a Michel press release, "In 1960 there were 200 strikes which lasted 90 days, and . . . in 1971, seven years after the food stamp program started, the number of over-90-day strikes had nearly doubled to 375."[29] Michel combined two Republican impulses on a tractable level—he could not eliminate food stamps, but he could save money by denying food stamps to a typically Democratic constituency. The wording of the amendment was straightforward: "Provided, That no part of the funds appropriated by this Act shall be used during the fiscal year ending June 30, 1972 to make food stamps available for the duration of a strike to a household which needs assistance solely because any member of such household is a participant in such strike."[30]

Michigan Democrat James O'Hara responded with a point of order arguing that it constituted legislating in an Appropriations bill and imposed duties on the executive branch. Perhaps unknown to O'Hara,

Michel had taken several versions of his amendment to the Parliamentarian's Office and was prepared to defend the amendment. Michel's former floor staffer, Billy Pitts, recalled that "Bob did everything he could to find [rider language] that was in order."[31] Michel recalled several years later that he "took [House Parliamentarian Lewis Deschler] five different versions of an amendment prohibiting food stamps for strikers and said, 'Okay, Judge, one of these has got to be in order.'"[32] Indeed, Deschler confirmed that his rider conformed to the so-called Holman Rule, which provided that a "retrenchment" (phrased in the negative) that does not impose duties on the executive branch—his amendment did not—was in order. The presiding officer, who rarely departs from the advice of the Parliamentarian, ruled that "no substantial affirmative duties are sought to be imposed upon the Secretary which would constitute legislation in violation of clause 2, rule 21. . . . The Chair overrules the point of order."[33]

Michel had gotten over the first hump, and considerable debate ensued. The amendment was soundly defeated 172 for (48 D, 124 R) to 225 against (181 D, 44 R). However, this experience demonstrates Michel's growing sophistication. He made sure that his amendment would not be struck on a point of order; he offered an amendment that a large majority of Republicans could support; and he was able to tie Democrats to striking workers who were often conflated with unpopular antiwar and civil rights demonstrators.

In 1972, Michel returned to the House floor with the same amendment: "Provided, That no part of the funds appropriated by this Act shall be used during the fiscal year ending June 30, 1973 to make food stamps available for the duration of a strike to a household which needs assistance solely because any member of such household is a participant in such strike."[34] Opponents of Michel's amendment were ready, making the case that the amendment legislated in an appropriations bill such that it effectively amended the authorizing language in the food stamp program. The presiding officer, Jim Wright (D-TX), ruled that the ruling of the chair a year earlier made this amendment also in order. Michel lost the vote but by a narrower margin 180 (50 D, 130 R) to 199 (175 D, 24 R).

Michel's effort on food stamps failed. However, unlike his attempt to influence funding for ESEA, this effort demonstrates that he was learning. He chose a narrower target, and he was better prepared for the floor fight. His growing sophistication allowed him to find an approach that united his Republican colleagues.

The Michel Amendment, 1978. Perhaps Bob Michel's signature achievement on Appropriations came almost two decades after he joined the committee. As part of the minority, victories were difficult to come by, but in 1978 Michel scored a win. In the Appropriations Committee and on the floor, Michel's amendments to cut government spending across the board typically failed. With the Labor-HEW appropriations bill on the floor, Michel prepared an amendment that could help highlight his party's fiscal conservatism and produce a victory. The Michel amendment was inspired by an inspector general's report, which indicated that between $6.3 billion and $7.4 billion in HEW losses per year were due to "waste, fraud, and abuse,"

> Sec. 201. Notwithstanding any other provision in this Act, the total amount of budget authority provided in this Act for the Department of Health, Education, and Welfare is hereby reduced in the amount of $1,000,000,000: Provided, That this reduction shall be achieved by the reduction of fraud, abuse and waste as defined and cited in the annual report, dated March 31, 1978, of the Inspector General of the Department of Health, Education, and Welfare: Provided further, That this section shall not be construed to change any law authorizing appropriations or other budget authority in this Act.

Michel recalled that "H.E.W., that was one of those places [with] all kinds of waste, fraud, and abuse." By offering the amendment, he continued, "[We] just let it be known to those who are administering this department particularly, that it's a real thing. And if they just buckle down and find out where are these points that give rise to a press story that we're frittering away or wasting money, and then eliminate it or reduce it."[35] Citing a letter sent by President Jimmy Carter's HEW Secretary, Joseph Califano, Michel noted on the floor that "Califano himself, in his letter of June 6 to the Members of this body, states that he has called upon the Department to make savings of $1.1 billion in fiscal year 1979. That is more than my amendment calls for. I gave him $100 million leeway."[36]

The Michel amendment painted Democrats into a corner. He had, according to Billy Pitts, "caught them by surprise."[37] It is difficult to vote against the amendment and "for" waste, fraud, and abuse. The secretary of HEW, appointed by a Democratic president, had set a $1 billion goal for his department. What could Democrats do? On a voice vote the amendment failed. However, Michel called for a recorded vote and the amendment was adopted overwhelmingly, 290 ayes to 87 nays, with the nays coming exclusively from Democrats. In the Senate, West Virginia Democrat Robert Byrd offered a similar amendment increasing the cut to $2 billion, giving Senate Democrats an opportunity to claim similar fiscal discipline to Republicans. In conference the Senate accepted the Michel language and the $1 billion target was restored. On adoption of the final bill Michel enthused: "We included language in the conference report making clear that the $1 Billion reduction is in fact a real cut which the Secretary of HEW must adhere to."[38]

Secretary Califano and the HEW Office of General Counsel attempted to argue that the language of the amendment did not represent a real cut but expressed a goal. However, the Department of Justice concluded that through the Michel amendment "Congress sought to put the secretary's 'feet to the fire' to compel a reduction in waste, fraud, and abuse. The Amendment embodies Congress' deliberate choice of method to achieve its goal of eliminating unnecessary expenditures."[39] Despite the seemingly small savings projected in the amendment, Michel scored a victory that united his party and provided an important symbolic victory, once again demonstrating his abilities as a legislative and partisan leader.

Reluctant Social Warrior: The Hyde Amendment

One of the hallmarks of the textbook Appropriations Committee described by Fenno was its efforts to restrict the scope of conflict by resisting pressures to include legislative language in appropriations bills. In the 1970s the committee's resolve was tested by the abortion issue. In the landmark 1973 decision *Roe v. Wade*, the United States Supreme Court held that laws criminalizing abortion except when medically necessary are an unconstitutional invasion of privacy. Abortion opponents were outraged by the decision and immediately mobilized to amend the Constitution to outlaw abortion. It quickly became apparent that a constitutional amendment would be difficult, even impossible. Abortion opponents began searching for alternative means of slowing or stopping legal abortions, and their focus shifted to the congressional appropriations process.[40] The initial— and arguably most important—victory for the prolife movement came in the form of a limitation rider on the Labor-HEW appropriations bill. As a senior Republican on the subcommittee, Michel assumed a central and uneasy role in passing what became known as the Hyde Amendment.

Prolife forces took aim at the Labor-HEW bill because HEW (now the Department of Health and Human Services) funded Medicaid (medical insurance for the poor) and Medicaid services that included abortions.

Abortion foes sought to eliminate government funding of abortions through a limitation rider that prohibited HEW from paying for abortion services. In 1974, the first attempt, sponsored by New York Republican Angelo Roncallo, was struck on a point of order that the amendment was legislating in an appropriations bill. In 1975, an amendment offered to the Labor-HEW bill by Maryland Republican Bob Bauman was defeated by a voice vote. However, in 1976 abortion opponents scored their first win when Henry Hyde, a first-term Republican from Illinois, was convinced by Bauman to offer an amendment of Bauman's creation: "None of the funds appropriated under this Act shall be used to pay for abortions or to promote or encourage abortions."[41] Because the Bauman-Hyde language did not contain exceptions (i.e., for rape, for incest, or to protect the life of the mother), it could not be struck on a point of order for "imposing duties on an Executive Official," which is a violation of the rules of the House. The narrow amendment language protected the provision from a point of order that it amounted to legislating in an appropriations bill. In turn, anyone seeking to build in exceptions would be subject to a point of order (legislating in an appropriations bill), thereby maintaining the original language. This was a level of parliamentary sophistication previously missing from earlier attempts to insert antiabortion language into the bill. The Hyde language passed on a bipartisan vote of 207–167. Ultimately, a House-Senate Conference Committee agreed to language that included an exception to protect the life of the mother.[42]

In 1977, Hyde once again offered his amendment to the fiscal year 1978 Labor-HEW appropriations bill. As in 1976, the language was ruled in order and the amendment passed on a bipartisan vote of 201 to 155. This time, reaching agreement in conference was much more difficult. The more conservative House dug in its heels, insisting on the Hyde language, while the more liberal Senate insisted on multiple exceptions. While all of the other provisions of the bill were agreed upon by the two chambers, a failure to reach agreement on the abortion language pushed past the beginning of the new fiscal year. The impasse was not resolved until early December. Congress avoided a partial government shutdown (in the absence of appropriations, the Departments of Labor and of Health, Education, and Welfare could not operate) by passing multiple continuing resolutions.

Bob Michel brokered the compromise that ultimately defined the scope of the Hyde Amendment:

None of the funds contained in this Act shall be used to perform abortions: Except where the life of the mother would be endangered if the fetus were carried to term: Or except for such medical procedures necessary for the victims of rape or incest, when such rape or incest has been reported to a law enforcement agency or public health service or its equivalent: Or except in those instances where severe and long-lasting physical health damage to the mother would result if the pregnancy were carried to term. Nor are payments prohibited for drugs or devices to prevent implantation of the fertilized ovum, or for medical procedures necessary for the termination of an ectopic pregnancy. The Secretary shall promptly issue regulations and establish procedures to ensure that the provisions of this section are rigorously enforced.

In his appeal to the conferees, Michel noted that it was "evident that neither body is anywhere near caving into the other body's position." Continuously bringing back the amendment in disagreement, he observed, would naturally produce the same stalemate. Michel continued: "The only common sense approach, therefore, is for the conference to develop [a] compromise between the two approaches." Since the House proposed one exception and the Senate three, "the logical compromise, therefore, is to provide two exceptions; in effect splitting the difference." One of the ironies of this compromise is that Henry Hyde voted against the bill because he believed the Michel language was too liberal. The amendment that passed in 1977 could legitimately be called the "Michel Amendment" because it was his language that became law.

Michel's involvement with the amendment presented two problems for him. He was a textbook fiscal conservative who seemed uncomfortable pursuing conservative social policy goals. Michel's ambivalence is illustrated in a thoughtful exchange between Michel and a prominent Peoria lawyer, Donald Vonachen. Returning from a visit to his district, Michel received a letter from Vonachen summarizing their recent conversation:

We interpreted your statements the other day to follow a line of thinking that Bob Michel (a) is against abortion; (b) recognizes the fact that there is a human life during the early stages of pregnancy; (c) is against the spending of taxpayer funds for the snuffing out of a human life; (d) has had trouble in the area of forcible rape and

incest cases; and (e) recognizes any exceptions to the Hyde Amendment are and will be flaunted and abused by H.E.W. . . . What I'd
like to ask is your specific commitment to vote for the old Hyde
Amendment . . . and to hold the line at all costs. . . . Will you back
the Hyde Amendment? Will you hold the line?[43]

Michel's response to Vonachen's five axioms is thoughtful and honest. We
doubt that Vonachen was pleased with Michel's response.

> I will agree that your comments embodied in the third paragraph of
> your letter sub-captioned (c), (d) and (e) are right on target. I have to
> tell you, however, that so far as (a) is concerned, I am NOT unalter-
> ably opposed to abortion, period but rather abortion on demand. So, it
> necessarily follows that I have a serious problem with an all-out com-
> mitment to the statement you make in (b). That's the grey area with
> me and that's what the controversy is all about. . . . I don't see how
> I can oppose [abortion] in cases of rape or incest. Those are indeed
> unwanted pregnancies.[44]

In response to Vonachen's request that Michel "hold the line at all costs,"
Michel's response reflected the realities of legislating:

> I can't predict what will happen other than to guess that basically
> what was once the original Hyde language will survive a House test.
> However, when we're thrown into Conference where the Senate will
> be just as adamant this year as it was last year with their 2 to 1 vote
> against the Hyde language, we'll have a prolonged deadlock and if it
> isn't resolved, the Speaker may choose to appoint new Conferees to
> replace those of us who can't agree because we refuse to compromise.

Michel concluded: "I'm sorry that I can't give you the kind of all-out commitment you want to the five points on page one of your letter, but I just can't,
and I don't want you to be laboring under any misapprehension."

Michel was also conflicted over the issue of using the appropriations
process to achieve legislative goals. A Republican partisan and a party leader,
Michel saw the abortion issue as a means of bolstering party unity. However, as an appropriator, he understood the value of limiting legislative language and focusing on conservative fiscal goals. Why did Michel help Hyde?
According to his longtime floor assistant, William "Billy" Pitts, "Henry was
a Republican from Illinois, and Bob liked him."[45] Rather than focusing on

the morality of abortion, Michel preferred to frame the Hyde Amendment as a fiscal issue: "We are asked to reach a decision concerning the wise and judicious use of taxpayers' dollars. . . . Abortion is not the issue here. The funding of abortion with taxpayer dollars is the issue."[46] In a floor statement Michel somewhat unwittingly betrayed his conflicting feelings about using a limitation rider to influence social policy as the Hyde Amendment did:

> I think a word or two is in order on what appears to be a growing practice of attaching legislative provisions to appropriations bills. I have never particularly encouraged this practice because it diverts attention from the dollar amounts included in these bills, which after all is the essential purpose of an appropriation bill. However, I think we have to recognize why this is occurring. It is taking place because of a lack of action by the responsible authorizing committees. If the authorizing committees are going to continue to ignore problems that are of concern to millions of people, then members are going to use the most effective device available to them. In many cases that device is the appropriations bill.[47]

As the 1970s came to a close and Michel prepared for his move up the leadership ladder, he demonstrated his leadership skills by working with Hyde—and allied Democrats like Dan Flood (D-PA) and Bill Natcher (D-KY)—to promote a measure that could unify his Republican colleagues. Michel was a reluctant social warrior, yet the Hyde Amendment spoke to fiscal conservatism. For the Republican Party, which witnessed historic losses in the 1974 midterm elections, abortion was a beacon of hope that the party could be resurrected. Senator James Buckley (R-NY), the brother of the conservative commentator William F. Buckley, Jr., wrote to Bob Michel in July of 1976: "I believe that . . . the Republican Party has a far better answer to [abortion] than do its rivals. . . . The Hyde Amendment is an opportunity to bring together most congressional members of a badly fractured party in the best of causes: the defense of human life." By the 1980s, abortion policy was a defining feature of the two political parties; the Republican Party became the prolife party, and Michel found himself fighting for conservative social policy from the leader's office.

Conclusion

In the estimation of former Michel staffer Billy Pitts, Bob Michel became "one of the best legislators the House has ever seen." He continued: "He could 'breathe through his pores' . . . he could walk on the floor at any given point in time and know what was going on. . . . He developed a sense of knowing what was going on and moved appropriately." However, Michel did not begin his tenure in the House as a well-rounded legislator. As a young lawmaker, he spent his time engaged in the work of his committee. It took time to learn how Congress functioned and to learn how to navigate the social fabric of the institution. The apprenticeship norm of the committee allowed Michel the opportunity to learn. With each battle, and through multiple failures, Michel sought and often found creative ways to achieve his individual goals while promoting the interests of his party. Michel's work on the Appropriations Committee prepared him to become an effective minority leader and the longest-serving House Republican leader in history.

As a political and social institution, Congress shapes individual members and collective outcomes, but members of Congress also shape the institution. Members of Congress often find creative means for achieving their personal and policy goals. They are not automatons—islands unto themselves. Rather, they learn through observation, imitation, and experimentation. Failure is guaranteed. Success is not. However, the capacity for learning, combined with extraordinary resilience, can develop into extraordinary prowess and success. Successful new ideas and tactics adopted by individual members of Congress are incorporated into the formal and social institutions of Congress. On the Appropriations Committee, Bob Michel honed his legislative and leadership abilities. Bob Michel's service on Appropriations shaped him as a party leader. Post-Michel leaders in the Republican House did not typically issue from the Appropriations Committee. None of the Republican Speakers in the post-Michel era benefited from service on Appropriations. It could be that the heightened partisanship since the late 1980s is partially explained by a new generation of leaders who did not benefit from honing their skills in the appropriations process.

Notes

1. David Broder, "Generational Gap," *Peoria Journal Star*, October 8, 1993, RHM Papers, Personal, f. Retirement Press.
2. Richard F. Fenno, Jr., *The Power of the Purse: Appropriations Politics in Congress* (Boston: Little, Brown & Company, 1966), 311.
3. Fenno, *The Power of the Purse*, 312.
4. Robert H. Michel interview with Richard F. Fenno, June 11, 1959, Richard F. Fenno, Jr., Oral History Collection, National Archives and Records Administration.

5. Richard F. Fenno, Jr., "The Appropriations Committee as a Political System," *American Political Science Review* 56, no. 2 (June 1962): 317.

6. Fenno, *Power of the Purse*, 460

7. Fenno, *Power of the Purse*, 415.

8. This section benefited mightily from the efforts of Frank Mackaman.

9. Frisch and Kelly demonstrate that former staff tend to be more successful with their committee assignments. This is likely a function of their experience and willingness to fill roles that other members may see as a burden. See Scott A. Frisch and Sean Q Kelly, *Committee Assignments in the US House of Representatives* (Norman: University of Oklahoma Press, 2006).

10. RHM interview with Fenno.

11. RHM interview with Fenno.

12. Fred W. Beuttler interview with RHM, September 5, 2007, RHM Papers, Post-Congressional Series, f. Subjects: Interviews (2), 15.

13. Shelley Epstein interview with RHM, February 1999, RHM Papers, Audiovisual Series, VHS Tapes; Robert Remini interview with RHM, January 19, 2005, RHM Papers, Interfile: Personal, f. 2005, Interview.

14. According to Michel, "Les Arends . . . was a good friend of Charlie's and told him, 'Here's a young fellow that ought to maybe go places here in the House.'" Beuttler interview with RHM, September 5, 2007, 15.

15. RHM to Charles Halleck, January 7, 1959. Unprocessed collection, University of Indiana, Manuscripts Department, Lilly Library.

16. Shelley Epstein interview with RHM.

17. "First book proposal meeting," August 19, 2003, RHM Papers, Post-Congressional Series, f. Subjects: Memoir.

18. Neil MacNeil, *The Forge of Democracy: The House of Representatives* (New York: David McKay Company, 1963), 129.

19. Beuttler interview with RHM, September 6, 2007, 16–17.

20. We do not contend that this is a unique view. Social learning theory, developed by Albert Bandura, suggests that individuals learn through observing and imitating others. In political science, Lawrence C. Dodd incorporates social learning theory into his theory of congressional change. See, for instance, "Re-Envisioning Congress: Theoretical Perspectives on Congressional Change—2004," in *Congress Reconsidered*, 8th ed., ed. Lawrence C. Dodd and Bruce I. Oppenheimer (Washington, DC: Congressional Quarterly Press, 2005). Richard Fenno highlights the importance of learning in *Learning to Legislate: The Senate Education of Arlen Specter* (Washington, DC: Congressional Quarterly Press, 1991), and *Learning to Govern: An Institutional View of the 104th Congress* (Washington, DC: Brookings Institution Press, 1997).

21. *Congressional Record*, November 2, 1942, Appendix, p. A3866.

22. Walter J. Oleszek, *Congressional Procedures and the Policy Process*, 5th ed. (Washington, DC: Congressional Quarterly Press, 2001), 158.

23. Fred Schwengel to RHM, August 6, 1969, RHM Papers, Interfile, Box 3, f. Appropriations, HEW.

24. Gerald R. Ford to RHM, August 8, 1969, RHM Papers, Interfile, Box 3, f. Appropriations, HEW.

25. Lawrence G. Williams to RHM, August 7, 1969, RHM Papers, Interfile, Box 3, f. Appropriations, HEW.

26. Peter H. B. Frehlinghuysen to RHM, August 8, 1969, RHM Papers, Interfile, Box 3, f. Appropriations, HEW.

27. William Cramer to RHM, August 1, 1969, RHM Papers, Interfile, Box 3, f. Appropriations, HEW.

28. Peter H. B. Frehlinghuysen to RHM, August 8, 1969, RHM Papers, Interfile, Box 3, f. Appropriations, HEW.

29. Press Release, June 23, 1971, RHM Papers, Press Series, f. June 23, 1971.

30. *Congressional Record*, June 22, 1971, 21671.

31. Interview with the authors, July 2017.

32. Robert Michel, "A Warm Farewell to William H. Brown, Parliamentarian," *Congressional Record*, September 20, 1994, 9894.

33. *Congressional Record*, June 22, 1971, 21672.

34. *Congressional Record*, June 29, 1972, 23364.

35. Beuttler interview with RHM, September 6, 2007, 16–17.

36. *Congressional Record*, June 8, 1978, 16787.

37. Interview with the authors, July 2017.

38. "Pertinent Points of Justice Department Ruling," RHM Series, Remarks and Releases, f. June 27, 1979.

39. Memorandum from John M. Harmon, Assistant Attorney General, Office of General Counsel, to Joseph Califano, "Re: The Michel Amendment to the Department of Health Education and Welfare Appropriation Act of 1979," RHM Papers, Remarks and Releases, f. June 27, 1979.

40. For a lengthy discussion of the politics of the "Hyde Amendment," see Scott A. Frisch and Sean Q Kelly, "The 'Hyde Amendment' and the Modern Congressional Appropriations Process," paper presented at the Congress and History Conference, Washington, DC, June 2017.

41. According to recollections by Hyde and Bauman, Bauman chose not to offer the amendment himself because he believed that an amendment associated with him would be immediately defeated. He convinced the "rhetorically gifted" Hyde to offer the amendment instead. Interview with Bob Bauman with the authors, June 2017. See also, Henry Hyde, "Speech to the Maryland Right to Life Banquet October 29, 1977," Henry Hyde Papers, Box 133, f. 16: 1976. Henry Hyde Papers, University Archives, Loyola University, Chicago. Amendment language is from the *Congressional Record*, June 24, 1976, 20410.

42. This compromise language was initiated by Massachusetts Republican Silvio Conte: "None of the funds contained in this Act shall be used to perform abortions except where the life of the mother would be endangered if the fetus were carried to term." By using the Senate-House Conference Committee to build in the exception, legislators skirted the House rule that restricts legislative language in an appropriations bill.

43. Donald Vonachen to RHM, May 3, 1978, RHM Papers, Staff Series: Kehl, f. Appropriations, Labor-HEW FY 1977 (3).

44. RHM letter to Donald Vonachen, May 11, 1978, RHM Papers, Staff Series: Kehl, f. Appropriations, Labor-HEW FY 1977 (3).

45. Interview with the authors, July 2017.

46. RHM Papers, Remarks and Releases, f. June 14, 1976.

47. In a draft of this floor statement, Michel specifically excised language that directly critiqued the Democratic leadership:

> The use of appropriations bills to achieve legislative purposes is thus an indictment of the leadership of the House for not dealing with the concerns of people and for not allowing those who wish to deal with such concerns an effective opportunity to do so. When the leadership recognizes its obligations in this regard, then we may see a return to the traditional legislative processes, but until then, the appropriations bill is likely to be used more and more as a legislative vehicle, and I won't discourage it.

Excising that language likely reflects Michel's bias toward maintaining good relations with Democratic leaders, a quality that would eventually be less well received as the House became more partisan and its members more ideologically polarized. RHM Papers, Remarks and Releases, f. August 2, 1977, "Floor Statement-Labor-HEW Conference Report," 7–8.

CHAPTER 3

BOB MICHEL IN THE LAND OF GIANTS

Relationship Politics in the 1980s

Burdett A. Loomis

Well, Newt's whole idea was that the opposition were our enemies, you know, and I always said, "Newt, they're our political adversaries, not our enemies."

—Bob Michel, 2007

Over the course of his political career representing Illinois's 18th District, Bob Michel had many political adversaries but nary an enemy. As a long-term leader of a minority legislative party, he could not afford to have them, from a pragmatic perspective. More important, Michel's personality harbored no room for enemies; that was not how he approached the world. Michel was a charmer, a singer, and a golfer, a man at ease in almost any venue, with almost any group of people. At the same time, as a politician and party leader, Bob Michel was tough and principled, and he could give as well as he got.

Beginning with his ascension to the minority leader position after the 1980 elections, Michel found himself working, cheek by jowl, with some of the giants of twentieth-century American politics, including Ronald Reagan,

Tip O'Neill, Bob Dole, Howard Baker, Dan Rostenkowski, and Newt Gingrich. Leading a minority that never numbered more than 192 (of 435) members, Michel needed to hold his troops together—a difficult task in an increasingly partisan era—while serving his president and working both across the aisle and between chambers. This chapter, while touching on various pieces of legislation and other congressional actions, largely focuses on Bob Michel in the context of his relationships with other major leaders, with the members of his GOP Conference, and implicitly with the institutions of the House in particular and the Congress in general.

In his research on informal relationships and their decline in the US House of Representatives, Evan Philipson sets the familiar stage of mostly male socializing in the 1960s and 1970s, as recounted by former Speaker Tip O'Neill (D-MA):

> A great way to meet some of my colleagues and to learn what was going on in their districts around the country. On any given night, there would be two or three dozen congressmen, a handful of senators, and several former members eating together in a private room. After dinner, we told stories and played cards. As many as seventy-five men would play during the course of the year, and over the months I got to know them all, Democrats and Republicans alike. There were no parties and no factions in that room. There was only fellowship.[1]

To be sure, this represents a rose-colored anecdote from O'Neill's memoir, but it brings home the role of social ties within the institution.[2] Philipson, basing his definition on both sociological literature and his interviews with former members of Congress, sees strong relationships as interactions "between members of Congress that go above and beyond normal business duties in the House. This includes socializing outside of work, getting to know the family of another member, and forging genuine friendship, regardless of party affiliation . . . more than a business relationship."[3]

This definition is more than serviceable here, in that it moves beyond votes, committee assignments, formal positions, and other linkages. Its essence is the continuing interaction that becomes genuine friendship, a commodity in short supply within the Congress today, especially between members of different parties. Without question, Bob Michel epitomized the ability to build a host of friendships regardless of party or faction.

The Michel Persona: The Basis for Strong Relationships

"I don't personally crave the spotlight of public opinion," Mr. Michel told his colleagues. "My job is to orchestrate your many talents. I know some of you prefer to speak quietly, like wood-winds, and some very loudly, as brass and percussion. But our measure of success is how well we harmonize."

—Bob Michel, quoted by Bob Levy[4]

Harmonize. No word better describes Bob Michel the man, the legislator, the leader. Michel made this statement in his first address to his GOP colleagues after winning the minority leader position in 1980. With 192 members, the Republican minority in the 97th Congress would be the largest in Michel's tenure as leader. He knew that the Republican Conference would provide the core support for Ronald Reagan's ambitious legislative program. With many new, aggressive members, he also knew that orchestrating their many interests would be no simple task. As a singer himself, Michel understood harmony; at the same time, as a leader he had to provide direction so that his choir could sing as one voice.

Michel's colleagues and staff offer systematic, even overwhelming, evidence that he was a most pleasant and convivial individual. Furthermore, they agree that he was no pushover as he sought to make the best deals possible and to pursue his own conservative policy goals. These traits of conviviality and principle played well outside the Congress, as well, and the presidents with whom he worked offer fond and generous assessments. Democrat Bill Clinton observed: "In the best sense he is a gentleman legislator, who, in spite of the great swings in public opinion from year to year, has remained always true to the Midwestern values he represents so faithfully in the House. [Michel is] . . . generally regarded by Democrats and Republicans alike as one of the most decent and respected leaders with which any president has had the privilege to work."[5] Fellow Republican George H. W. Bush noted: "There were some who thought he was too easygoing with his friends across the aisle," but added that "he was a masterful legislator" who could craft bipartisan majorities.[6]

The "easygoing" characterization was correct, but just to a point. Michel's genial nature was genuine, yet his colleagues understood that the congressman harbored a strong and consistent conservatism that—while open to compromise—was central to his character. As he once explained: "Conservatives and Republicans of all stripes must understand government is not the enemy—wasteful government, intrusive government, irresponsible government, corrupt government is the enemy. The people of the United States are not happy with government when it does not work well." Michel also said this: "But make no mistake about it: Americans from the beginning have realized that the government system left to us by the Founders is the best in the world."[7] Michel entered the Congress as a solidly conservative Republican. His placement within the GOP Conference did move toward the center over the years, but not because Michel changed his views. Rather, his responsibilities as party leader pushed him a bit toward the center, and, more important, successive elections in the 1980s and 1990s ushered in a substantial number of new members whose politics stood to the right of the minority leader. (See Table 3.1.)

During his first eleven terms in the House, Michel consistently stood as one of the most conservative of all House members, always ranking among the forty farthest to the right. Among Republicans, through his first nine Congresses, he ranked at about the thirty-fifth most conservative Republican—consistently on the right side of the party, but not the extreme right. After the 1980 election, Michel's position began to change, in part because of his leadership role with its need to relate to all party factions. More important, however, was the influx of a new wave of conservative Republicans who moved the party farther to the right in concert with President Reagan.[8] When he became minority leader in 1981, Michel ranked as more conservative than two-thirds (68 percent) of the GOP Conference. That number steadily declined over the years, as he became—without changing his issue positions—much more of a centrist among his colleagues.

In addition, Michel increasingly came to represent the old guard among Republican members, in a chamber that remained largely bound by seniority. Indeed, Newt Gingrich's speakership, beginning in 1995, demonstrated the power of his attack on the seniority system as part of his overall claim of congressional corruption.

As he assumed his role as minority leader, in the midst of changing ideological and generational forces, Michel led, as he always had, by building strong relationships. Winning election as leader for seven Congresses stands as prima facie evidence that, even as the House Republican Conference evolved, Michel's personal ties prevailed. Equally important, his personal

Table 3.1 Bob Michel ideological placement, 1957–1994

Congress (Years)	% of All Members	% of All Rs	# of Rs in House
	More Conservative	*More Conservative*	
85th (1957–1958)	9%	20%	201
86th (1959–1960)	7%	20%	153
87th (1961–1962)	7%	20%	175
88th (1963–1964)	7%	18%	176
89th (1965–1966)	5%	18%	140
90th (1967–1968)	6%	16%	187
91st (1969–1970)	8%	19%	192
92nd (1971–1972)	7%	17%	180
93rd (1973–1974)	8%	20%	192
94th (1975–1976)	7%	22%	144
95th (1977–1978)	8%	23%	143
96th (1979–1980)	9%	26%	158
97th (1981–1982)	14%	32%	192
98th (1983–1984)	14%	36%	166
99th (1985–1986)	17%	40%	182
100th (1987–1988)	17%	41%	177
101st (1989–1990)	17%	42%	175
102nd (1991–1992)	17%	44%	167
103rd (1993–1994)	20%	50%	176

Source: Voteview.com.

relationships with other major congressional leaders and with Presidents Reagan, Bush, and Clinton allowed him to play an important role in major policy decisions, despite the Republicans' continuing minority status. This chapter emphasizes the 1981–1986 period, when Bob Michel had to work with legendary, powerful figures who either commanded majority legislative parties or, per Reagan, served as the chief executive. The power of his personal relationships would be tested repeatedly over these years.

Bob Michel and His Political Contemporaries

Despite the fact that Republicans did not gain control of the House in 1981, as Michel began his service as minority leader he enjoyed various advantages that the other leaders could not match. To a greater or lesser extent, Michel could count on strong, individual personal relationships with Reagan, Senate Finance Chair (and later Majority Leader) Bob Dole, Senate Majority Leader Howard Baker, Speaker Tip O'Neill, and House Ways and Means Chair Dan Rostenkowski. This leadership group was part of a political generation that had endured the Great Depression and had fought in World War II. All save O'Neill served in uniform, in or directly after the war. Three were from Illinois; three (Dole, Reagan, and Michel) grew up in small-town America, where farming was the major occupation. O'Neill, Rostenkowski, and Michel were avid golfers who often played together in this leisurely pursuit. Finally, all were at or near the acme of their careers between 1981 and 1986. Despite their partisan and ideological differences, they wanted to get things done and make deals that mattered. To be sure, their differences were sometimes great and their rhetoric hot, but they shared a history and a basic worldview that prompted them to work together effectively. (See Table 3.2.)

Bob Michel and Ronald Reagan

At first glance, the political careers of Michel and Reagan look nothing alike: a Hollywood actor turned pitchman (General Electric Company) turned conservative spokesman turned California governor who became president as opposed to a career congressional politician from the solidly Republican American heartland. But both grew up in similar circumstances within a hundred miles of each other in downstate Illinois. After moving several times, the Reagans landed in Dixon, Illinois, where his father was part owner of a store; he was also an alcoholic, which had persistent economic repercussions for the family.[9] Reagan spurned entering the family business to enroll

Table 3.2 Bob Michel and his political contemporaries

	Bob Michel	Ronald Reagan	Tip O'Neill	Bob Dole	Howard Baker	Dan Rostenkowski
Born	1923	1911	1912	1923	1925	1928
Military service	1943–1946	1937–1945; active, 1942–1945	none	1942–1945	1943–1946	1946–1948
Entered nat'l pol	1956	1964; 1976	1952	1960	1964	1958
Became nat'l party leader	1977; 1980	1980	1971; 1977	1971; 1981	1977	1980
Left nat'l politics	1995	1989	1987	1996	1988	1993

Sources: Various editions, *CQ Almanacs, Politics in America*.

in 1928 at Eureka College, close to Peoria, where he received scholarship assistance for both football and academics. At that time, Bob Michel was a five-year-old whose family lived in Peoria, where he had been born. Although Peoria was larger than Dixon or Eureka and was more industrial, the downstate Illinois culture was much the same, with its solid small-government Republicanism. Although Reagan would leave the Midwest in 1937 after working as an announcer at a couple of Iowa radio stations, he spent his first twenty-six years in the heart of the country. His autobiography maintains that his core values—often emphasizing self-reliance—emerged from this environment. Given his background, Bob Michel implicitly understood Reagan's childhood experiences and the related values, thus providing the base of a common worldview when their paths crossed in national politics.

Beyond their childhoods, Michel and Reagan both served in World War II; at first glance, their experiences again seem dissimilar, given Reagan's film-related service. Nevertheless, Reagan's military ties as a reserve officer began long before the war broke out, demonstrating a level of commitment unusual for most Americans, to say nothing of his Hollywood associates. Michel's involvement was more typical and far more fraught, in that he was seriously wounded. Still, in their active-duty roles, given Reagan's early witness to German death camps through film and Michel's battle experience, they shared a firsthand understanding of the necessity and the horrors of war.[10]

After the war, Michel returned to Peoria to attend Bradley University, which was larger than Eureka but similar in many ways—a private institution, typical of many that dot the landscape of downstate Illinois. While Reagan's road toward politics twisted through Screen Actors Guild labor politics and a longtime association with GE as pitchman and public speaker, Michel's path was remarkably direct, as he graduated from Bradley in June 1948 and headed to Washington, DC, as Representative Harold Velde's administrative assistant in December of that year. For both Velde and Michel, the Washington learning curve would be steep. In Congressman Velde's second term, remarkably, he became chair of the House Un-American Activities Committee, a body both noteworthy and notorious. As Velde's administrative assistant, Michel was privy to some of the most contentious proceedings, public and private, in the House; this was a powerful education for a young staff member but great preparation for becoming a representative. In 1956, upon Velde's retirement, Michel would run successfully for his seat, entering the chamber in 1957 for the beginning of a thirty-eight-year run, all in the minority party. In short, despite being younger than Reagan, Michel entered the national political scene almost a decade before Reagan emerged through his historic GOP national convention speech in 1964.

Michel played prominent roles in a host of Republican National Conventions. He served in 1976 as President Gerald Ford's deputy floor manager, as one might expect, given his long-term association with the former House GOP leader. This meant that he had to fight off Reagan's powerful challenge to the incumbent president. Tellingly, in 1980 Michel became Reagan's floor manager as he succeeded in winning the nomination. This informs us a lot about both Michel and Reagan; as one close observer put it: "Of course Michel was a Ford guy, but Reagan never held that against him. He didn't hold grudges."[11] On the surface, Michel's service to Ford, then Reagan, might seem incongruous, but his work in these two conventions attests to his character, his loyalty to the Republican Party, and his ability to work with its distinct factions. Most important, as the Reagan administration began with an ambitious policy agenda, Bob Michel had already established a strong, productive working relationship with the new president.

Bob Michel and Bob Dole

> Bob [Dole] was from Russell, Kansas. We all know that, you know. And I was from Peoria, or am from Peoria. I still regard it as my hometown. I know Bob always has a warm affection for Russell, Kansas. Gosh, all through the years he would make reference to it. I think we all feel, at least he did and I did, felt real strongly about the people who initially sent us into the big arena of politics, and we're always appreciative of that start we got. I share Bob's view that, boy, we never want to forget those roots back there in Kansas or Peoria, Illinois.
>
> —Bob Michel, 2007[12]

Examining the political paths of Bob Michel and Bob Dole, one can easily imagine that each could have had the other's career. Had Michel been successful in seeking the Senate seat of Everett Dirksen upon the senator's death in 1969, he might well have become the floor leader in the Senate, given his insider political skills. Likewise, if Dole had not run for the Senate in 1968, one could envision him using his talents to climb the House leadership ladder. In short, these individuals—both born in 1923, both seriously wounded in World War II, both elected to the House by 1960, both from rural areas, and both traditional conservatives—could and did instinctively understand the other's point of view. Add to that the good humor of each, although expressed differently, and one can easily see how they would build upon their history and friendship to form a close working relationship in 1981, as both ascended to leadership positions in the 97th Congress.

Although Dole's near-death war wounds and his remarkable rehabilitation constitute a well-known narrative,[13] Bob Michel's story is likewise powerful. Although Michel did not have to overcome—and continue to deal with—Dole's range and seriousness of physical obstacles, they shared a sense of good fortune that they had survived the war. For both, a career in public service seemed a natural response to their wartime experience.

Indeed, as the political columnist David Broder observed, they were among several Republican House leaders who emerged from the ranks of war veterans: "Like his predecessors in the minority leadership, Gerald R. Ford of Michigan and John J. Rhodes of Arizona, [Michel] is part of the generation of World War II veterans who remade politics in their hometowns. Blessed with common sense and agreeable personalities, they were spotted early in their House careers as people who were likely to stick around and make their marks."[14] Without question, had Broder considered the Congress as a whole, Bob Dole would have been part of this list.

In many ways, the Michel and Dole political careers developed along similar lines. Dole became Republican National Committee chair in 1971, while Michel served as National Republican Congressional Committee chair in 1973–1974. Both survived and subsequently prospered after extremely rocky tenures, caused largely by the actions of President Richard Nixon. Early in their House and Senate tenures, respectively, both won appointment to a prestigious money committee, Appropriations for Michel and Finance for Dole; these positions allowed them to become, given their talents, effective insiders early in their careers. In the years before the historic 1980 election, Michel rose to become minority whip, while Dole took on the position of ranking minority member on Finance. They were thus well versed in top-level congressional politics before they took key positions in the wake of the 1980 election. Beyond that, Michel knew that Dole could relate to his position within the House. Michel recounted:

> We were in perfect sync with one another. I think the fact that Bob once served in the House always made us more comfortable in the sense that we knew he had an appreciation that there was a different kind of nuance going on in the Senate versus the House. He could quickly understand what it was for those of us in the House to deal with what we were dealing with, because he was once there.[15]

Bob Michel and Howard Baker

Although the Michel-Baker political relationship did not have the deep roots of Michel's ties to Dole, O'Neill, or Rostenkowski, in personal terms they had a long and close relationship in that Baker married Everett Dirksen's daughter, Joy, in 1951. Dirksen had held the House seat that Michel's boss, Harold Velde, first won in 1948. Baker won his Tennessee Senate seat in 1966 and quickly moved into prominent leadership positions, in part due to his highly public role in the Watergate hearings. When Baker became Senate majority leader in 1981, Michel had a close friend to work with, and they conferred regularly, often informally,[16] between 1981 and 1984. Without question, these two seasoned professionals would have had a strong working relationship, but their personal ties made their cooperation all the more seamless.

Bob Michel and Tip O'Neill

Tip O'Neill's rapport with Ronald Reagan is legendary, but his relationship with Bob Michel was, if anything, longer and deeper. Although O'Neill was a decade older than Michel, they shared a status as career politicos, entering the arena as they did, almost immediately after graduating from college. As Michel became GOP whip in 1977, O'Neill rose to the speakership, replacing Carl Albert. Although O'Neill was, at that time, a twenty-five-year veteran of the House, by the late 1960s he had increasingly cast his lot with the reformers and liberals who entered the chamber in 1958 and after. With his decision, after lengthy consideration, to oppose the Vietnam War, the Boston congressman gained a broader constituency within the Democratic Caucus; this led to his rise up the leadership ladder. O'Neill was far more in touch than Speakers John McCormack and Carl Albert with the mainstream of his members, including two large classes in 1974 and 1976; in O'Neill the Democrats had selected a Speaker who both represented the growing liberalism of the Caucus and could negotiate effectively with those on the other side of the aisle. That talent lay largely dormant during Jimmy Carter's administration but became central to the politics of the Reagan era.

Beyond their political relationship, Michel and O'Neill were both first-rate storytellers and avid golfers. They socialized together with their wives and played in numerous charity golf tournaments.[17] Michel's friendship with O'Neill may well have frustrated some in the GOP Conference, but the central fact was that these individuals could be personal friends and political adversaries—but not enemies.

Bob Michel and Dan Rostenkowski

Although both Michel and Rostenkowski hailed from Illinois, their constituencies and backgrounds could scarcely have been much different, with the former representing rock-ribbed Republican Peoria, whereas the latter rose through the ranks of Mayor Richard J. Daley's Chicago machine politics. Still, they both won election to the House in the late 1950s, with Rostenkowski riding the huge 1958 Democratic wave, which swept in a large number of liberals who would do much to change American politics over the succeeding decades. Rostenkowski himself was a loyalist, not a liberal, but he could count votes and understood how to make deals. By 1964, he had won a seat on the Ways and Means Committee, and between 1966 and 1970 he chaired the House Democratic Caucus. Michel's personal ties with Rostenkowski started early, for highly pragmatic reasons. Michel recounted:

> My goodness, we were just "bosom buddies," I should say. In the early days when I was there, you only got reimbursed for one trip back and forth to your district. And, man, with the salary you had, it was hard to get by. So we used to drive, . . . and double up in the car. There would be Rostenkowski, Harold Collier (R-IL), and myself in a station wagon. We'd leave on a Thursday night and drive all night. Then the following Monday, you're coming back again. It was tough to do, but you had to do it.[18]

Beyond their travels, Michel found, as with O'Neill, a welcome golf partner in Rostenkowski, in an era when trips back to the district over a weekend were the exception rather than the rule. Beyond golf and those fifteen-hour, back-and-forth trips, Michel and Rostenkowski, with their seats on Appropriations and Ways and Means, respectively, could work together to help their state on fiscal matters large and small. To be sure, as elected members of their respective party caucuses (Democratic chair, Republican campaign committee head), Rostenkowski and Michel could be formidable political opponents, but the personal bonds never seriously frayed.

Corinne Michel

One additional, major part of Bob Michel's strong set of personal relationships requires acknowledgment. Beyond Michel's great capacity to forge strong ties, his wife created her own relationships with many politicians and their wives. As the former Representative Ray LaHood notes: "Corinne Michel became very good friends with Tip O'Neill's wife Millie. They socialized together a lot, same with Rostenkowski, although his wife never moved to DC. Still, they were friends. So, you had strong relationships beyond politics."[19] In addition, and highly important, Corinne Michel had another close friend: Nancy Reagan. "My good fortune," Bob Michel reflected, "was that my wife was a good friend of Nancy's. They got along famously with one another."[20] In the Reagan White House, there could be no more important social relationship, nor a more important backdoor communication link with the president.

In sum, by happenstance (Baker's marriage), the force of his congenial personality, shared experiences, and the grace of his wife, Corinne, Bob Michel had built, over his thirty-plus years in Washington, a powerful network of political and social relationships that he could use, and even strengthen, during leadership years. These did not give him the power of a House majority leader or the blocking ability of a Senate minority leader, but they did enable him to benefit as much as possible from his Reagan-era spot at the table on issues large and small.

Building on Relationships: Bob Michel, 1981–1986

That [the early 1980s] was a different era. Relationships were so important. In 1981, you had elected leaders who had been around, who had governed. Rostenkowski and Tip O'Neill, and Michel, all had been in the Congress since the 1950s. Reagan had been governor of CA for eight years. They knew how to legislate, they'd done it.

—Ray LaHood, former representative
and Michel chief of staff[21]

This group, along with Senators Dole and Baker, "had done it," to be sure. But the politics of 1981 introduced any number of uncertainties, starting with a new president and a Senate under Republican control for the first time in twenty-six years. Moreover, while relationships are important, they do not broadly determine results, which are shaped by specific agendas and the ability to forge majorities. There would be nothing automatic about lawmaking in an increasingly partisan climate, albeit nothing like the post-1994 levels of partisanship. Other chapters address the initial salvos of the budget and tax battles that raged in 1981, but the pressure remained on congressional Republicans over the first six years of the Reagan presidency; after all, they held the White House and the Senate. In short, legislating meant finding cross-party majorities in the House.[22]

Although House Republicans did have both legislative and political agendas, if not always unified ones, Bob Michel had the difficult, simultaneous tasks of serving both his president and his Conference of GOP members.

Nowhere is this more clear than in the budget/tax politics of 1981, where Michel succeeded in delivering 190 (of 192) votes for the Reagan tax cut package (the Conable-Hance bill), which won on a 238–195 tally. In the end, acting as an agent for the president, Michel managed to hold his members together while generally supporting the Reagan positions. Indeed, Michel's formal and informal relationships with Reagan may well have allowed him to face down Budget Director (and former representative) David Stockman, with whom he had no close ties (and even those disintegrated during the process). At the same time, on major items like the budget/tax cuts of 1981, Social Security reform, and the 1986 tax reform, Michel's leadership consisted largely of serving the president, who could move policies through the system. Reagan "was a wonderful individual to work with. I will always say that I don't think he ever got the kind of credit he is due for helping the legislative process," as Michel put it. "Almost anything I wanted or requested that I thought was going to enhance what he ultimately wanted; he was willing to do everything possible to help me. I can't think of any time when I was at odds with President Reagan on any of the issues where I felt, 'Oh boy, I know what you want Mr. President, but don't count on me.'"[23] In addition, Michel found that President Reagan became a formidable force in enticing some Democrats to vote with the Republican minority, especially in the 1981–1982 period when the GOP membership stood at 192:

> When we were in the minority, he'd just have to have the majority there [at the White House] too; otherwise, you're just rubbing people the wrong way. I think sometimes Tip would get just a little bit ticked off that Reagan was as good as he was in convincing members on his side to split away. [laughs] Because they were the two Irishmen and you used to get that sense of feeling, you know. Tip would say, "Doggone it, you tend to your men and I'll tend to mine," because obviously he lost some votes because of the President's popularity and his deftness in helping win the issue for Republicans, even though being in the minority. But that was fun. That was exhilarating to put it together.[24]

For the most part, Michel's relations with the Senate leaders Bob Dole and Howard Baker generally followed similar patterns to those with Reagan. Even though Senate and House leaders from the same party sometimes disagree, for the most part Michel worked extremely well with both Dole and Baker as they sought to pass the president's agenda, as well as to pass major

Social Security and tax reform, albeit with numerous twists and turns. As Michel stated, addressing his working relationship with Dole:

> On the big issues we were always working together, and in our conferences down at the White House we were both given the opportunity to speak up, and that was required, or express the views of our membership, and we did so as best we could always. It was a good relationship that I had with Bob, no question about it. I guess sometimes you read about leaders at odds with one another, not in sync, and I just can't think of a situation like that where we were at odds.[25]

Michel's relationship with Baker was similar in that Baker, like Dole, continually had to keep tabs on his individualistic senators, who were far more likely to waver than the bulk of House Republicans; indeed, Michel reported only six or so fairly liberal Republicans who posed problems on major tax and Social Security votes.[26] Michel and Baker would often meet after their respective houses had adjourned, in "lots of late-night meetings, down the back hallway, in Baker's office."[27]

Overall, with his links to the Senate majority leaders and to President Reagan, Minority Leader Michel could provide constant, well-informed support to Republican policy initiatives, even through budget difficulties in the wake of the 1981 tax cuts. The mix of strong personal relationships and professional political performance produced, in the 1981–1986 era, the capacity to act effectively on day-to-day matters and to provide the realistic potential for the brokerage of historic, large-scale deals.

Although Michel's GOP linkages with the president and Senate leaders were central to Republican policymaking, his long-term relationship with Speaker Tip O'Neill was at least as important. Michel served on the GOP House leadership team, as either whip or leader, for all of O'Neill's ten years as Speaker. Their continuing, strong personal ties should not obscure the fact that they often clashed swords in partisan battles, which could be fierce and confrontational. O'Neill and Michel might well have played eighteen holes on a Sunday, only to go after each other, tooth and nail, on Monday. Still, their adversarial roles remained political, not personal.

The strength of personal relationships contributed not only to civility within the House but also to legislative productivity. In his farewell address, remarkable for a member of "the other body," Senator John Breaux (D-LA) specifically addressed the relationship between the two House leaders:

> Tip O'Neill and Bob Michel probably differed as much as any two people you could possibly know in terms of philosophy in how Government should work. Tip O'Neill was an FDR liberal Democrat from Massachusetts, and Bob Michel was from Peoria, IL, a middle America Republican. They did not agree on how Government should work necessarily from a philosophical standpoint, but they knew how to make Government work. *They spoke more in one day back then than some of the leaders later on spoke in a year.* . . . I would suggest that government was not any worse off when you had a Tip O'Neill and a Bob Michel traveling together, playing golf together, drinking in the evening and having a cocktail together, betting on sporting events together, which I know they did because they had a relationship that allowed them to find out, "What do we have to do to accomplish what we both realize is best for this country?"[28] (emphasis added)

For all this rhetoric, as well deserved as it might be, the overlapping personal and political relationships of Michel and O'Neill were complex; both needed to be responsive to their respective party caucuses, which meant that, in an increasingly partisan House, they fought for every inch of policy space. At the same time, either in face-to-face negotiations or through their designees, they could come to agreements based on trust. Sometimes, Michel had to parse his friendship with the Speaker and his obligations to his members. Thus, "In 1984, when Gingrich launched a tirade against 10 Democrats advocating negotiation with Nicaragua's leftist government, and O'Neill responded with an intemperate outburst that brought a rebuke from the presiding officer, many House Republicans gave Gingrich a standing ovation. *Michel kept his seat.*"[29] (emphasis added) Likewise, when O'Neill had the House television cameras pan away from Republicans giving postsession speeches, thus showing an empty chamber, Michel could profess outrage. On other occasions the outrage was real, deeply felt, and dramatically presented.

For all his strong relationships with those outside the House GOP Conference, Bob Michel's most important relationships consisted of those within it; if he did not maintain his members' support, as the former leader Charles Halleck (R-IN) had failed to do, he could easily be ousted. Other chapters address Michel's often fraught (but never fatal) relationship with his Conference, but Michel did demonstrate, time and again, the capacity to hold his members together, even in the face of gathering opposition by insurgents from the right. That story played out in the later years of his leadership, but in the 1981–1986 period, as he worked with a Republican Senate and President Reagan, the challenges did not rise to the level of a serious threat. In large part, Michel's security came from his ideological position within the GOP Conference. During these years, he stood as more liberal than just 36 percent of his members (see Table 3.1), although his rating moved from 32 percent in the 97th Congress to 40 percent in the 99th. More conservative members, although not Newt Gingrich, were outflanking him on the right, but Michel remained a conservative, both on his own terms and within the Conference.

Moreover, when the chance came to unify the members of his Conference, he took full advantage. This occurred on many votes, both procedural and substantive, but never more powerfully than on the 1984–1985 controversy over a contested Indiana House seat.[30] In the November 1984 election, on election night Republican Rick McIntyre trailed the Democratic incumbent Frank McCloskey in the Indiana 8th District by 72 votes. Given the narrow result, a recount/canvas was conducted, with McIntyre certified as the winner by a Republican secretary of state by 34 votes. The Democratic-controlled House failed to seat McIntyre, setting off a four-month struggle that resulted in a three-member commission (two Democrats, one Republican) voting to seat McCloskey with a four-vote margin, based on the counting of questionable absentee ballots. Although there was some disagreement within GOP ranks as to the level of aggressiveness in responding to this decision, Michel did lead a walkout of 109 Republicans in protest over the decision. When McCloskey was seated, Michel stated: "If the majority persists in this folly, they will have poisoned the wells of civility in the House. Things will never be the same."[31] Nevertheless, once McCloskey was sworn in, Michel walked over and shook the new congressman's hand, a gesture highly criticized by those farther to the right and newer to the Congress among his fellow Republicans. By fighting aggressively, yet shaking McCloskey's hand, Michel demonstrated the twin pulls of partisanship and institutional loyalty. Those bonds would ultimately be broken in Gingrich's 1993–1994 bid to become leader and his attack on the Congress as he sought, successfully, to build a Republican majority.

Leadership and Personal Relationships

In the post-1994 era of intense and growing partisanship, to the point of trib-
alism, it is easy to romanticize the relative collegiality of the politics between
1981 and 1986. To be sure, there were intense partisan conflicts, but they
pale in comparison to the conflicts of the George W. Bush, Barack Obama,
and Donald Trump presidencies. Likewise, even veteran dealmakers like
Michel and Dole became more hard-edged as their chambers became more
polarized. The leadership politics of the early 1980s still reflected the Capitol
Hill collegiality of the midcentury era, but it took extraordinary efforts to
resist growing partisanship. The extensive personal ties of the World War II
generation exerted moderating forces for both the process of lawmaking and
its results. As House minority leader, Bob Michel enjoyed less formal leverage than his congressional and executive peers, but his store of strong personal ties allowed him to maximize his influence, both for his members and
in his role as President Reagan's agent.

Notes

1. Evan Philipson, "Bringing Down the House: The Causes and Effects of the Decline
   of Personal Relationships in the U.S. House of Representatives," *CUREJ: College
   Undergraduate Research Electronic Journal* (April 8, 2011), University of Pennsylvania,
   repository.upenn.edu/curej/141.
2. This might be the fodder for contemporary network analysis, if social groups could
   be definitively identified, but the strength of these ties, formed over years, have a
   surface validity.
3. Philipson, "Bringing Down the House," 14.
4. Bob Levy, "Robert Michel, Longest Serving Minority Leader in U.S. House, Dies at
   93," *Washington Post*, February 17, 2017.
5. Remarks on Presenting the Presidential Medals of Freedom, August 8, 1994, *Public
   Papers of the Presidents*, The American Presidency Project, at www.presidency.ucsb
   .edu/ws/index.php?pid=48956&st=&st1=.
6. Quoted in Adam Clymer, "Robert Michel Dies at 93. House GOP Leader Prized Conciliation," *New York Times*, February 17, 2017.
7. Quoted in the *Washington Times*, October 19, 1993.
8. See voteview.com/congress/house.
9. Ronald Reagan, *Ronald Reagan: An American Life* (New York: Simon & Schuster,
   1990), 31–33.
10. Reagan, *Ronald Reagan*, 99–100.
11. Ray LaHood interview with author, November 17, 2017.
12. Brien R. Williams interview with RHM, May 24, 2007, RHM Papers, Interfile: Per-
    sonal, f. 2007, Interview, 2.
13. Bob Dole, *One Soldier's Story* (New York: HarperCollins, 2006).

14. David Broder, "Generational Gap," *Peoria Journal Star*, October 8, 1993.

15. Brien R. Williams interview with RHM, May 24, 2007, RHM Papers, Interfile: Personal, f. 2007, Interview, 28.

16. William (Billy) Pitts interview with author, October 27, 2017.

17. Michel's devotion to golf can be seen in one corner of The Dirksen Center's archives, where a host of memorabilia, clothes, clubs, and bags are assembled.

18. Fred W. Beuttler interview with RHM, October 17, 2007, RHM Papers, Post-Congressional Series, f. Subjects: Interviews (2).

19. LaHood interview with author.

20. Fred W. Beuttler interview with RHM, October 17, 2007, RHM Papers, Post-Congressional Series, f. Subjects: Interviews (2).

21. Ray LaHood to Frank Mackaman, email, October 10, 2018.

22. See Matthew N. Green, *Underdog Politics: The Minority Party in the U.S. House of Representatives* (New Haven, CT: Yale University Press, 2015).

23. Beuttler interview with RHM, October 17, 2007.

24. Williams interview with RHM, 32, emphasis added.

25. Williams interview with RHM, 29.

26. His more serious problems with new waves of young, conservative members came more in disagreements over tactics than over supporting major legislation.

27. Pitts interview with author.

28. Chris Wallace interview with John Breaux, "Transcript: Sen. John Breaux Talks about Lessons Learned," December 12, 2004, at www.foxnews.com/story/2004/12/12 /transcript-sen-john-breaux-talks-about-lessons-learned.html.

29. Frank H. Mackaman, "Robert H. Michel Retrospective Collection Notes," 2017, internal Dirksen Congressional Center reference document.

30. This account based on Green, *Underdog Politics*; Mickey Edwards to Ora Mae Bassett, April 4, 1985, RHM Papers, Press Series, f. Subject: McIntyre, Richard; and RHM Papers, Staff Series: David Kehl, f. McIntyre (multiple).

31. "Robert H. Michel," n.d. [1985], RHM Information File, f. Michel. This document is a partial reproduction of an entry published, perhaps, in an unidentified edition of *Politics in America*.

CHAPTER 4

RISING TO LEADERSHIP IN AN ERA OF POLITICAL CHANGE

Bob Michel and the 1970s House Minority Party

Scott R. Meinke

S tudents of the US Congress recognize the 1970s as a time of reform and change in the House of Representatives. Within the majority Democratic Party, younger and more liberal members sought to limit the dominance of conservative committee chairs, bringing about more decentralized committee control. At the same time, Democrats gradually began to strengthen the central party leadership, creating new mechanisms for the Speaker to lead from the center as well as new opportunities for Democrats to participate in the stronger Caucus's activity.[1] Some consequences of these majority party reforms arrived gradually,[2] but other House changes in the 1970s had more immediate impact. The advent of recorded votes in the Committee of the Whole and electronic roll call voting brought about a sharp increase in roll call votes, particularly on controversial amendments.[3] Other changes followed, including closed-circuit monitoring of roll calls and, late in the decade, C-SPAN.[4]

Of course, these changes inside the House were accompanied by—and partly driven by—major upheavals in the broader political system. Watergate roiled presidential and congressional politics and generated an energized House Democratic Caucus while enervating the congressional GOP. Energy crises and broader economic woes changed the issue landscape and the legislative agenda. And a new, more activist, and more ideological brand of politics began to take hold in both parties, with strong reverberations in the House: the liberal Democratic Study Group was at the peak of its influence in the mid-1970s, and a more confrontational breed of conservatives began to make its voices heard in the Republican Conference around the same time.[5]

This is the political environment in which Robert H. Michel (R-IL) began his rise to leadership of the House Republicans. After building a record of party work as a rank-and-file member in the 1960s and early 1970s, Michel won his first elected leadership post in 1973 as chair of the National Republican Congressional Committee (NRCC). At the end of 1974, the Republican Conference elected Michel as minority whip, a post he held until his election as minority leader for the 97th Congress (1981). Michel's quick ascent up the elected-leadership ladder was defined by the particular challenges of this era, and this chapter has a twofold focus as a result. The first subject is Bob Michel, and I trace his leadership elections and his work as a rising House leader. But the second subject is the House minority party of the 1970s: I use Michel's experiences as NRCC chair and as whip to examine the changing strategies, tactics, and institutions of the House GOP.

In each of his two first leadership roles, Michel took over from a predecessor who had held the position for an unusually long time. Taking the reins of the NRCC and the whip organization in quick succession, Michel oversaw changes that responded to the needs of a minority party at an inflection point. With the political changes of the 1970s, the conditions for minority party legislative influence[6] were declining, and the party's electoral and policy goals demanded changes in some tactics, particularly in electioneering and legislating.[7] As I will show, some of these changes, particularly for the NRCC, involved renewed autonomy for the House with less reliance on the White House and the Republican National Committee (RNC). In other instances, House Republicans developed new abilities to respond more rapidly to the floor majority through legislative tactics.

The chapter proceeds in several steps. I very briefly introduce some key conceptual ideas about the roles of the House minority party generally and about House party organizations in particular. Next I consider Bob Michel's first elected leadership role at the NRCC in the 1974 election cycle, discussing how the unfolding Watergate scandal affected Michel and the congressional campaign and providing a picture of the NRCC's role in this period. I then assess Michel's election to the minority whip post, the changes he brought to the Republican whip organization over three Congresses, and examples of the whip system's activity in the Michel era. I conclude with observations about context, constraints, and Michel's leadership of House party organizations.

The House Minority Party: Tactics, Organization, and Influence

Although legislative minority parties have usually received little attention,[8] several recent accounts provide a framework for thinking about the House minority. Matthew Green, for example, focuses on the collective goals of the party, which he identifies as winning the majority and influencing policy as well as advancing both the procedural rights of the minority and the party's presidential prospects.[9] The balance of these objectives can change over time—and can create serious intraparty conflict for the minority.[10] In service of these objectives, minority party actors seek broadly to build party unity, and they employ a set of tactics that includes electioneering, legislating, obstructing, and messaging.[11] The last tactic illustrates the minority's shifting approaches as political circumstances change. Frances Lee[12] has carefully documented the effect of rising congressional party competition on party tactics since about 1980. She shows that the parties have heavily prioritized the collective goal of gaining (or maintaining) the majority and that they have pursued that goal primarily through messaging, broadly defined to include public relations activity as well as legislative actions directed at messages rather than shaping policy.

Jennifer Clark's research provides further insight on this shift away from legislative influence and toward electoral/message politics. In her thorough study of minority parties in Congress and the fifty US state legislatures, Clark demonstrates that "the minority party's capacity to influence legislative decision-making may be enhanced or diminished depending on key features of the legislative and political context."[13] Specifically, she finds that minority influence is diminished with higher levels of polarization and with the reduced uncertainty that comes from greater legislative resources and centralization of "institutional prerogatives."[14]

Together, these perspectives point toward the 1970s as the start of a major change for the Republican House minority. The weaker majority leadership and depolarization that characterized the House around 1970 afforded a meaningful measure of GOP influence in the legislative process[15] that was threatened by the major changes in and outside of the House, as described above. These changes would become more pronounced in the heightened electoral competition and greater polarization of the 1980s, with a more organized effort to push the GOP toward confrontation (e.g., Newt Gingrich's Conservative Opportunity Society of the early 1980s).[16] But we can see in the 1970s an inflection point at which the House GOP began to engage the trade-off between backroom legislative cooperation and a more electorally oriented set of tactics combining legislating, messaging, and obstruction.[17]

The House Minority's Leadership Organizations

In this 1970s context, Bob Michel led two important elements of the House GOP, two among several participatory organizations that are crucial for the minority party's efforts. In my work on Republican and Democratic organizations,[18] I show that structures like the House whip systems prioritize member participation in order to advance collective party goals as well as the goals of individual members. The party leadership gains tools for coordination, persuasion, and external communication, while individual members benefit in their own policy, electoral, and power goals. These organizations have served a distinct role for parties in the minority, providing an outlet for member involvement when other opportunities are limited.[19] The House Republican Conference, during its long stint in the minority, was ahead of the House Democratic Caucus in developing specialized party organizations that substituted for the capacity and resources available to the majority.[20]

"A Very Untenable Position": Leading the NRCC

The National Republican Congressional Committee, the home of Michel's first elected leadership position, stands out as a unique organization in the House Republican system. As Robin Kolodny argues, the congressional campaign committees are distinct in that they "exist to pursue majority status" and to "create an institutional interest" in the collective pursuit of that goal. With their outward focus on fundraising and recruitment, they are a hybrid of "external" and "internal" party organizations.[21] This line-straddling mission reflects the origins and purpose of the congressional campaign committees. The NRCC (the oldest of the House leadership organizations, dating to 1866) and other campaign committees were formed to advance the electoral interests of the congressional party caucus *independent of* the White House and national party organization.[22]

If the history of the NRCC has been shaped by House Republican efforts to distinguish their own campaigns from the national party, Bob Michel's election and brief tenure as NRCC chair is a kind of microcosm of that history.[23] The chair vacancy and Michel's campaign involved controversy about the White House's role in the 1972 cycle and its pressure on the congressional party. As chair, Michel would lead the NRCC in defending its own congressional campaign turf in an increasingly perilous political climate. The 1974 campaign began with the NRCC planning to "pursue majorities"[24] aggressively after the GOP's big 1972 presidential win, focusing on recruitment and considering how to build a majority by flipping southern districts.[25] But the NRCC turned toward defending incumbents as White House scandals dominated the election cycle.

At the start of the 93rd Congress (1973), Bob Wilson (R-CA), who had chaired the NRCC for a decade, found himself in conflict with the White House, which apparently wanted to "force Wilson out."[26] Michel viewed the White House's public campaign to oust Wilson as "shabby treatment" that belied the administration's own responsibility for the mediocre House election results in 1972. According to Michel's recollection, the White House had "shielded" about sixty-six Democratic seats "because the President was indebted . . . for [members'] support of his policy in prosecuting the [Vietnam] war."[27] Under this pressure, Wilson ran again to lead the NRCC, but after winning the post he stepped aside after a few months.[28] Having decided on a run for chair, Michel was prepared for Wilson's announcement, working quietly to cultivate support in early 1973—he had also extracted a promise from RNC Chair George Bush to keep the White House out of the contest.[29]

Michel's race would be against Clarence "Bud" Brown (R-OH). Unlike Michel, who had actively served as a congressional surrogate in GOP presidential campaigns[30] but not on the NRCC, Brown had experience serving on the campaign committee. He had taken charge of candidate recruitment at the start of 1973, and his NRCC chair campaign focused on a detailed recruitment plan.[31] Brown pledged distance from the administration, although a *Washington Post* account indicated that he "had been labeled the choice of the White House."[32] Michel's campaign took more of a person-to-person approach, building support behind the scenes.[33] The NRCC in the 1970s was made up of one GOP member from each state, and members selected their chair in a weighted vote, with each NRCC member casting votes equivalent to the number of House Republicans from his or her state. The weighted vote process introduced some uncertainty, as members could choose to divide the votes they cast, but it also made it easier "to get a pretty good count without covering too many bases and thus arousing a lot of talk and possible discussion in the press," in Michel's words.[34] In the balloting on March 21, Michel won overwhelmingly, at least based on his whip counts (final vote totals were not announced), which estimated his solid support at 132 out of the 192 votes.[35] Analysis of the whip count shows that Michel's votes came from a broad segment of the GOP Conference—his support was not defined by region, and his NRCC supporters were not outliers in ideological position or party voting unity. NRCC members supporting Michel were, however, somewhat more senior than his opponents on average.[36]

Watergate and the 1974 Congressional Campaign

What a time for me to come into the leadership!

—Bob Michel, April 1973[37]

Taking the reins of the NRCC in March 1973, Michel was faced immediately with the growing Watergate scandal. The day after his election as chair, Michel met with Richard Nixon to discuss the 1974 campaign, and he warned Nixon that Watergate "was beginning to have its reverberations out in the hustings, and principally among our own people" on fundraising. Notably, Michel also cautioned Nixon that the House GOP wanted to guard its ability to operate independently of the national committee and the administration in the campaign.[38] Top GOP leaders met in late March and early April for "free-wheeling" discussions about the scandal, coming to a "general consensus that the President would surely have to be told very clearly . . . that somebody better come clean pretty quickly and take the fall, if that's what's necessary. . . . We in the Congress were being placed in a very untenable position."[39] At one gathering, the leadership met with Vice President Spiro Agnew and discussed the difficulty the congressional GOP had in communicating with the president. They heard from Agnew—who spoke frankly about his own frustration—that the problem was in the president's isolating staff arrangement. The congressional leaders agreed on a plan to get a wide-ranging, unfiltered meeting with Nixon and to use it to push the president on Watergate in the course of "confrontation" about other matters. Before that meeting happened, Nixon fired Bob Haldeman and John Ehrlichman. Michel was relieved about the decision, which he believed followed from Nixon learning that "he wasn't being told the truth," but Michel knew it was "not over yet." Michel again pressed Nixon on his concerns about Watergate and fundraising, as well as the administration's accessibility to Congress, in a May meeting in Nixon's Executive Office Building office. At that time, Michel felt that Nixon was "still learning of things that he couldn't conceive of happening in his own Administration."[40]

On the ground, "Watergate [had] taken its toll" on GOP congressional campaigns even before the scandal took its most dramatic turns in late 1973 and 1974. In April 1973, Michel observed that "the average individual really didn't care too much about Watergate itself" but that activists were alarmed, and big donors were cutting off funds until the scandal was resolved.[41] Documents from the NRCC's work in the 1974 cycle reveal the scale of the problem. In fall 1973, fundraising for challengers was running at about two-thirds of its normal pace. A major fundraising event for House Republican challengers in Washington State was canceled in November 1973 because "national uncertainties . . . created an undesirable atmosphere to insure responsible attendance," and at least four other regional events suffered the same fate.[42] RNC and congressional leaders debated whether to hold their major fall fundraising dinner in 1973 given the political climate, eventually choosing to cancel it.[43] Along with the head of the RNC and the National Republican Senatorial Committee (NRSC), Michel issued an unusual public letter noting that these party units had not "been accused of any wrongdoing in their political activities or handling of campaign funds last year."[44] Ultimately, the consequences for the NRCC's work were quite serious. By June 1974, Michel was writing to an Illinois challenger's campaign manager to explain that the committee's fundraising goals "will not be achieved and that means a decided scaling down from what we would hope to be distributing as a maximum to those targeted districts where we feel we have a chance of picking up a seat."[45] Interviewing potential quality challenger Jim Leach (R-IA) in December, NRCC Executive Director Jack Calkins had to explain the same problem.[46]

Despite the optimism about majority-seeking goals after 1972, realism set in early about the party's prospects. The NRCC's executive director warned in summer 1973 that the GOP's high number of marginals combined with a weakening economy created a difficult playing field in the House, even as he downplayed the likely impact of Watergate.[47] The oil crisis, rising inflation and unemployment, and declining economic growth portended a weak year for the White House party in 1974, and Watergate's effect on fundraising, recruitment, and voters' views of the party turned a weak year into a histori- cally terrible loss. A relatively high number of House Republicans (twenty- one) retired, thirteen of these open GOP seats switched hands, and thirty-six Republican incumbents were defeated, with a net seat loss of forty-eight—a quarter of the Republican Conference. Michel himself won reelection with just 54.8 percent of the vote against an inexperienced Democratic challenger.

The NRCC under Bob Michel

Setting aside the disastrous political climate of Watergate, Bob Michel's brief tenure as NRCC chair highlights the role of the NRCC and the changes to party organizations in the 1970s. Taking over as chair, Michel believed that his predecessor had "left so much up to the staff" and took a "limited . . . personal hand" in the operation. He also felt that "the members themselves [had] every right and responsibility to be personally involved" in the core operation of the campaign committee.[48] At the same time, the NRCC by the early 1970s was a century-old organization with a substantial permanent staff and an established set of professional services,[49] so the changes during Michel's single term are mostly evolutionary, and his well-documented ten- ure provides a window into how the committee operated in this era through recruitment, member services, and fundraising.

Recruitment. Early in the 1974 cycle, Republican leaders in and out of the House recognized the importance of candidate recruitment to potential GOP gains. At their first meeting in 1973, Richard Nixon counseled that recruitment should be the NRCC's priority—"It's candidate selection, not the dough. The dough will come."—and urged Michel to find a "mean bastard" to put in charge of candidate selection.[50] In more mild-mannered terms, Michel's dictated diary from May 1973 observes that "we have got to place more emphasis on this business of candidate recruitment." Avoid- ing Nixon's specific advice about staffing, Michel chose to build a regional, member-centered recruitment effort that involved more than twenty Repub- lican members.[51] In assembling this recruitment system, Michel moved the

NRCC in the participatory direction that other party organizations, particularly in the House Democratic Caucus, were taking in the 1970s.[52] And he prioritized regional expertise over central control as a way to recruit winning candidates in a still-diverse party. Michel appears to have chosen a middle ground between members who preferred a more heavy-handed approach to recruitment and those who remained squeamish about active national party involvement in candidate selection.[53]

During the 1974 cycle, this decentralized, participatory recruitment system allowed the NRCC to receive input and develop intelligence on districts and candidates from members with local knowledge.[54] NRCC staff remained heavily involved in screening candidates, however, and despite the new system recruitment remained a challenge, particularly in the Watergate context. NRCC staff and participating members had difficulty recruiting, especially in those southern districts that they viewed as top prospects for pickups.[55] As the general election approached, Michel had put "strong emphasis on the protection of Republican incumbents and the protection of those seats . . . held by retiring Republican colleagues," according to Jack Kemp (R-NY).[56]

Member services and incumbent protection. This shift toward incumbent protection in 1973 reflects the NRCC's ongoing balancing act between supporting races for new GOP members and advancing Republican incumbents' reelection bids.[57] As NRCC chair, Michel inherited a well-developed set of services for incumbent members including, among other things, a news bureau, a photo service, and electronic media assistance. These services were in addition to a modest public relations budget provided to each member by the committee.[58] Under Michel, these traditions were continued, but the NRCC's executive director, Jack Calkins, urged a more aggressive approach to incumbent protection; Calkins observed that the "usual policy" had been to provide incumbents with services "but by and large not to meddle in their political or office operations."[59] Members varied in the extent to which they used these advantages of incumbency, and during the 1974 cycle the NRCC undertook a fairly elaborate effort to single out GOP incumbents who needed to do more to reap the benefits of holding office. The committee, with Michel's strong support,[60] initiated a detailed survey of marginal incumbents, drilling them on their work to build on incumbency. The survey's questions provide a thorough review of the type of activity that David Mayhew and Richard Fenno observed in their contemporaneous writings,[61] for instance: "Do you send [a] newsletter? . . . Do you send

[the] Infant Care book to new parents? . . . Do you have a district luncheon periodically with financial leaders? . . . Do you have weekly public service time [on] TV and radio? . . . How often do you return to [the] District?"[62] The in-person survey revealed "many marginal incumbents who are deficient in maximizing the many advantages of incumbency," requiring follow-up consultation from the NRCC.[63] Although the plan to shore up incumbents was obviously a failure from an election outcome standpoint, there is a bit of evidence that the committee was successful under Michel in expanding use of in-house services for strengthening the electoral connection. In particular, the committee's Radio Actualities Service, which used wide-area telephone service (WATS) to push members' recorded quotes and commentary to local media, grew rapidly in the 1974 cycle.[64]

Fundraising. In the area of campaign funding, Michel's tenure as NRCC chair coincided with the waning of the prereform era in the campaign committees. As Robin Kolodny has explained, the importance of the committees in distributing funds increased as the effects of the 1971 Federal Election Campaign Act (FECA) and subsequent amendments kicked in. But in the 1974 cycle, the new laws had minimal effect on the committees.[65] The NRCC was keeping campaigns informed about compliance with the changing FECA rules,[66] but its fundraising and distribution continued earlier practices. The NRCC executive committee provided funds to incumbents for reelection campaigns, exercising some discretion in allocating its resources to target key races and "cases of special need." Challengers and open-seat candidates were funded separately from incumbents: together with the NRSC, the NRCC operated a "Boosters" program to raise and allocate funds targeted at competitive new candidates. This program, which channeled two-thirds of its resources to House candidates, is a good example of the congressional committees operating independently in the interest of the legislative party.[67] As noted above, this new-candidate funding was especially hard hit by the GOP's fundraising problems during Watergate.

NRCC records from Michel's tenure provide a glimpse of party connection to a key trend in the 1970s: the rising importance of political action committees (PACs) after FECA. While PACs had yet to emerge as a central factor in GOP candidacies,[68] the NRCC appears to have been attentive to PAC activity on behalf of its candidates. A memo by the NRCC's executive director in early 1973 took note of a new PAC for the health insurance sector, observing—correctly as it turned out—that "by 1974 this should be a good source of contributions for candidates and incumbents."[69] More significant, a spreadsheet from late in the 1974 cycle tracked not only each GOP incumbent's allocation from NRCC funds but also contributions from four key PACs.[70] Although the role of PACs remained limited in the Michel era, the NRCC had begun monitoring incumbents' access to PAC funds as it compiled the overall fundraising picture.

The NRCC's records allow for some analysis of how the committee allocated its discretionary funds to incumbents under the constraints of the 1974 cycle. Allocations varied considerably across members, apparently more than in the 1972 cycle.[71] Members' 1972 vote share, unsurprisingly, was a very strong predictor of their 1974 allocation ($p < 0.001$, two-tailed), and seniority was negatively related to members' NRCC funding ($p < 0.01$, two-tailed), while party voting unity had no relationship to funding outcomes. This analysis shows that, on average, a vulnerable (50 percent vote share) freshman would receive about $5,000 from the NRCC, whereas a secure (80 percent vote share) ten-term member would receive $1,818.[72] These general patterns are consistent with what Kathryn Pearson[73] has found for party funding in typical recent Congresses, and they reflect the committee's efforts to direct limited funds where they were most needed to protect GOP seat share, without regard for members' party support.

Kolodny observes that campaign committees are "pulled constantly between pursuing majorities and protecting incumbents" and that parties "struggle internally to determine the maximal common strategy."[74] In the 1974 cycle, the GOP began with hopes of a robust effort to pursue both objectives. New House-centered recruitment efforts joined well-established mechanisms of fundraising and services to incumbents. But as recruitment floundered[75] and fundraising fell dramatically short in the midst of Watergate, protecting vulnerable incumbents took priority. In the end, of course, it was not enough.

Bob Michel as Minority Whip

Would you believe after that disastrous record for me as the chairman of the [NRCC], when the House met after the election, they elected me as their whip?

—Bob Michel, 2007[76]

The Republican Conference elected Bob Michel as minority whip in late 1974 as members prepared for the overwhelmingly Democratic 94th Congress; he would continue in this position until his election as minority leader in 1980. During these three Congresses, the GOP whip organization responded to the two broad sets of changes outlined in the introduction: major changes that transformed House politics, especially on the floor, and long-term shifts in intra- and interparty politics that began to realign the role of the minority. With responsibility for coordinating Republican efforts on the floor and building coalitions of support or opposition in the Conference, the Michel whip organization was at the center of Republican efforts to advance party policy and electoral goals with some of the smallest House GOP contingents since the Great Depression.

The Whip Election

Although Michel would marvel at his election as whip in his "aw, shucks" manner three decades later, he acknowledged in more contemporaneous comments that "no one seemed to blame me specifically for the disastrous [1974] results. . . . Everybody recognized it was simply a product of the times."[77] Former member William Springer (R-IL) expressed this sentiment to Michel in a December letter: "You did a good job as [NRCC] Chairman . . . we were lucky not to lose more than we did."[78] With members judging him based on that counterfactual, and with more than a decade of experience as an appointed assistant whip, Michel jumped immediately into the race for the whip post vacated by the retiring Les Arends (R-IL), who had been Republican whip since 1943.[79] Letters announcing Michel's certain or possible interest (he chose different wording for different members) were ready to go the day after Election Day.[80]

Only sparse records exist of the 1974 whip contest, and it received little national reporting. The tight race for GOP Conference chair, in which the moderate incumbent John Anderson (R-IL) defeated the conservative challenger Charles Wiggins (R-CA), attracted more press attention as an ideological struggle within the party.[81] The whip race was not as close, but the result belied the narrative of a liberal victory in the House GOP as Michel—who was slightly more conservative than Wiggins—easily beat party centrist Jerry Pettis (R-CA) and fellow Illinoisan John Erlenborn.[82] In their campaigns, both Pettis and Erlenborn emphasized the need for faster and more frequent communications as well as the importance of ready accessibility for the whip

Table 4.1 1974 House Republican whip candidates

	Michel (IL)	Erlenborn (IL)	Pettis (CA)	Conference average
DW-NOMINATE (first dim.)	0.310	0.240	0.147	0.196
Age	51	47	58	48
House terms	9	5	4	3.9
1972 vote share	65%	72%	75%	66.9%
1974 vote share	55%	67%	66%	59.6%
Party unity	78%	64%	69%	65.9%
Total votes for whip	75	22	38	

on the floor.[83] Pettis emphasized the "eastern tilt" of the leadership and the need for West Coast representation.[84] Michel's message, at least so far as surviving materials demonstrate, focused more on personal experience and connections, following the approach he took in his NRCC chair campaign.[85]

The descriptive data in Table 4.1 show that Michel (75 votes) had much more House experience than Pettis (38 votes) or Erlenborn (22 votes). He was more party-loyal and more conservative than both opponents. (Michel, in fact, was in the most conservative quartile of the Republican Conference in the 93rd Congress.) Although the whip balloting was secret, records of Michel's own count prior to the vote allow for some analysis of his support. Like Matthew Green and Douglas Harris,[86] I use the archived records to construct a variable for members' votes. In contrast to some of Green and Harris's work, the records here are limited, with only one undated count from at least several days before the vote[87] and no outside sources to fill in gaps. In addition, the Michel records are consistent only in recording his committed support; they do not always note which candidate nonsupporters favored. Still, the totals from my data, which exclude the few newly elected GOP freshmen, are roughly in line with the final outcome, slightly overestimating Michel's final support at eighty-one returning members and underestimating his opposition at forty-six returning members. Based on these data, the logit model in Table 4.2 predicts Michel support based on conservatism (first-dimension DW-NOMINATE score), seniority (terms in the House),

Table 4.2 Michel support in 1974 House Republican whip race

	Michel support
DW-NOMINATE (1)	3.749**
	(1.512)
Tenure	−0.008
	(0.096)
Northeast	−0.944*
	(0.502)
Pacific	−1.198**
	(0.580)
1972 vote	0.012
	(0.020)
Age	0.014
	(0.028)
Constant	−1.114
	(1.793)
N	127

Note: Logit coefficients with standard errors in parentheses. Dependent variable equals 1 for members recorded as Michel supporters in Michel whip count and 0 for all other members. Independent variables based on 93rd Congress data; GOP members elected in November 1974 excluded.

** $p < 0.05$, * $p < 0.01$, two-tailed

electoral security (1972 two-party vote share), age, and region (indicators for Northeast and Pacific states).[88] The results tell a fairly clear story. The more conservative Republicans were significantly more likely to support Michel, whereas members from the Northeast and the Pacific states were less supportive compared with members from interior sections of the country. In contrast to the Conference chair race on the same day, which pitted a losing confrontational leader[89] (Wiggins) against a consensus-builder (Anderson), the whip race went easily to the ideologically conservative but stylistically centrist Michel on a vote that followed traditional ideological and regional divisions in the Conference.[90]

Role of the Whips

Michel's election as whip had a clear parallel to his election as NRCC chair fewer than two years before: he took charge of a party organization that had experienced an exceptionally long period of stable leadership with little change in structure or function. Les Arends's thirty-two-year tenure as Republican whip was (and remains) unmatched in the history of either party's whips. According to Michel, Arends ran the organization "out of his rear pocket," relying on "personal contact."[91] As Michel prepared to take over, a staffer briefed him on the whip office and organization, concluding that Michel could "just about run things any way you choose."[92] His choice was to maintain a similar structure for the whip organization but to move away from the "pocket" operation and rely more heavily on the network of appointed whips to manage new challenges on the House floor.

In the mid-1970s, the majority Democrats were involving more leadership-appointed members in their increasingly sophisticated whip organization.[93] Taking over as whip, Michel broadened member participation in the Republican organization, which had long involved a small hierarchy of regional whips appointed from three regions.[94] Michel added a deputy whip at the top,[95] and he expanded the existing system somewhat by adding a fourth whip region.[96] More generally, Michel joined the participatory trend by making more use of trusted whip appointees to gather and share information. Electronic roll call voting and recorded votes in the Committee of the Whole changed the dynamics on the floor as recorded votes became much more common and floor processes moved faster. As Steven Smith observed, "The House not only made more discrete amendment decisions, but also reserved less time, on average, for each decision."[97] With members arriving and leaving quickly to cast recorded votes, Michel's team put more whips on the floor and positioned them strategically to align the right whip with the types of members who would likely be passing through different entrances to the floor. With timely information becoming more important for the minority's coordination efforts, the whip also increased the volume of written information going to all GOP offices and began some early use of electronic notification systems. To make this more sophisticated operation run, Michel hired a more specialized whip staff, including a whip floor assistant and a staffer in charge of press, in an early move toward professionalizing party communications.[98] In short, Michel took charge of a whip system that was personal rather than institutionalized and revamped its operation and staffing to meet the new coordination and persuasion needs of the mid-1970s party. These reforms responded to demand in the GOP Conference for better and faster connections (as evidenced by the platforms of Michel's opponents in the 1974 whip race) as well as to the needs of the leadership in a changing floor environment.

Whipping to Support a Minority Party Strategy

Of course, there is only so much that even a modernized whip system can do in the House minority, and the Michel whips faced not only significant floor process changes but also several other major challenges. First, Republican efforts to legislate or obstruct from the minority were constrained by their historically small numbers, compounded by the weak Republican president and, after 1976, the loss of the White House. Second, gradually changing partisan politics began to change expectations about what the minority could and should do. Conditions for minority influence on legislative substance[99] had begun to decline somewhat, particularly as the House Democratic Caucus moved to weaken conservative committee chairs and gradually to empower party leaders. Groups of activist Republicans hoped for a more aggressive strategy, and the leadership used some of the new tools at their disposal—including the easily recorded amendment vote—to pursue strategies of messaging and obstruction. But the majority, in turn, began to use control over the rules to limit these opportunities for the minority by the latter part of Michel's tenure as whip.[100] All of this represented the first waves of the rising House partisanship that would characterize the 1980s and 1990s.

In addition to the aggressive floor strategies described above, the Michel whip organization used its regular counting process to support a minority party strategy with messaging, obstructing, and (sometimes) legislating tactics. The formal process involved conveying a whip poll question to a few regional whips, who in turn posed the question to assistant regional whips under their charge. The assistants gathered responses from their assigned members and reported them back up the chain. This formal process was used, on average, about twenty-five times per year during the 1975–1979 period.[101] Beyond this procedure, the whip leadership engaged in more informal persuasive and intelligence-gathering work. Prior to or instead of carrying out a formal count, Republican whips often informally polled "bellwethers," particularly at the liberal end of the GOP Conference, to determine where there might be problems in sustaining the party's position. According

Table 4.3 House Republican whip counts by type, 1975–1979

	Veto override	Proce- dural	Amend- ment	Pas- sage	Gen- eral	Total*
1975	12	0	1	12	2	27
1976	11	3	2	12	0	28
1977	0	2	11	12	1	26
1978	1	3	7	9	2	22
1979	0	2	8	10	1	21

*Totals exclude a small number of unclassified open-ended or follow-up questions. Whip count data from C. Lawrence Evans, *Congressional Whip Count Database* (Williamsburg, VA: College of William and Mary, 2012).

to Michel's floor assistant, William Pitts, the whips frequently started by testing the positions of liberal Northeastern members and proceeded from there. The minority whip also maintained a "pipeline to the other side" in the form of members who had connections to the still-sizable contingent of conservative Democrats and could help the minority assess its chances of success with some Democratic votes.[102]

The content of Michel's whip polls helps to tell the story of the minority party's challenges and tactics in the late 1970s. For the first two years of Michel's whip tenure (1975–1976), Gerald Ford held the White House and used an aggressive veto strategy to battle an energized Democratic Congress. Ford issued thirty-two regular vetoes in these two years, and Congress attempted an override of twenty-one.[103] At the time of the whip election, Michel voiced concern about the emerging veto strategy and a lack of coordination between the president and Congress.[104] In the subsequent two years, however, the Ford administration and congressional Republicans actively worked together to whip members to sustain the vetoes—a tall task with Republicans holding only about one-third of House seats and with the GOP Conference split on the original passage of many vetoed bills.[105] As Table 4.3 shows, Republicans conducted whip counts on overrides about as often as on final passage votes during these two years, covering all but a few of the override attempts.[106] As Richard Conley[107] has shown, Republicans' success in sustaining more than a third of Ford's vetoes in 1975–1976 relied on holding and flipping Republican members through whip contacts.[108]

Ford's loss in the 1976 election swept away the Republicans' last institutional hold on power, and House Republicans saw no improvement in their tiny share of House seats. With the loss of the White House, the minority shifted its organized whip efforts to shape an alternative message and obstruct when possible. After rules changes earlier in the 1970s, Republicans had seized on floor amendments as a useful minority tool; Smith notes that "amending activity and success rates for Republicans . . . shot upward in the 93rd Congress [1973–1974] as Republicans disproportionately took advantage of the new voting procedures."[109] After 1976, the whip organization increased its attention to floor amendments, with about a third of the 1977–1979 polls dealing with amendments compared with just a handful of polls during 1975–1976 (see Table 4.3). And although formal whip activity on procedural votes was relatively rare, the Michel whip organization tracked and built support for some procedural moves in the gradually increasing floor conflict of the late 1970s.[110]

In one notable 1978 example, Republican whips built support for what became a unanimous Republican vote to defeat a special rule on campaign finance. Congressional Democrats had worked since the early 1970s to include public financing for congressional elections in federal campaign law, and they redoubled their efforts at the start of Jimmy Carter's administration. After struggling for more than a year, House Democrats tried to pass public financing as part of a PAC-regulation measure in March 1978. A contingent of sixty-nine Democrats opposed the move, and all 140 voting Republicans joined them to defeat the rule on the bill, 198–209.[111] Republican whips found little opposition to the maneuver, but their initial count found a high level of nonresponse and some undecided votes. By the final vote, the few initial GOP opponents and undecided members all voted against the rule, and this minority party unity made up the margin of the rule's defeat.[112] Republicans helped thwart a subsequent procedural attempt supported by a majority of Democrats to bring the bill to the floor, and a final effort to revive public financing in 1979 also failed. In this instance, Republican coordination through the whip system facilitated minority party obstruction despite the GOP Conference's shrunken size.

Common-site picketing: A case study of minority party victory. Although common-site picketing seems like an obscure debate four decades later, the issue was a heated one in 1977, and it represented a "big win" for Michel as whip, according to Michel floor assistant William Pitts.[113] According to a contemporary account in the *Washington Post*, "Republicans had made a test case out of the bill, telling members that stopping this one could determine how the minority party fared against the rest of the Congress." Organized labor, for its part, "viewed the bill as a test of labor's clout with the heavily Democratic [95th] Congress it helped elect."[114] The vast majority of Republicans joined eighty-eight mostly southern Democrats to narrowly defeat this key measure just two months into the Carter administration after intensive lobbying from inside and outside of the House.

Common-site (or "common situs") picketing, which was barred under a 1951 Supreme Court statutory ruling, involves workers with a grievance against one contractor striking against an entire job site.[115] Construction unions had advocated for reversal of the ruling in Congress, nearly succeeding in 1975 when the House and Senate agreed on a bill permitting common-site pickets. Like all presidents since the court ruling, President Ford had originally supported the action, but he vetoed the bill in January 1976 after "an intense campaign by opposition groups,"[116] leading his secretary of labor to resign abruptly. Democrats quickly brought a version of the bill to the floor in both chambers at the start of Carter's term, with the promise that the new president would finally sign the legislation.

Opposition lobbying against the measure was just as strong in 1977, with interest groups using both grassroots and traditional tactics to pressure Republican and Democratic members. For House Republicans, the vote involved an all-out whip effort with not only a formal whip count (refined in several stages) but also attention to the positions of conservative Democrats and a particular focus on House freshmen, who did not have recorded prior votes on the issue.[117] With both sides seeing high stakes and a close vote, the bill went to the floor of the House on March 23. In a maneuver that Michel portrayed as a desperate Democratic tactic,[118] Democrats and labor supported an amendment from Ronald Sarasin (R-CT), a Republican from the liberal wing of the party. The Sarasin amendment, which passed easily, moderated the bill and moved it closer to the version that Ford vetoed in 1975. But on final passage, the common-site bill failed on a 205–217 vote, with a total of forty members—including fourteen Republicans—who supported the Sarasin amendment voting to defeat the final package. Only fourteen total Republicans supported passage.

Press coverage treated the outcome as "something of an upset" and a "smashing defeat," although the Michel whip counts pointed to very strong

GOP unity early in the process. The earliest regional count identified 119 of the 129 Republicans who would ultimately vote no, and the fifteen undecideds in the earliest count split eight to seven in the party's direction. By the final version of the count, Michel had identified the final positions of all the Republicans correctly with the exception of two leaners and one undecided member, and two of those three voted with the party. Figure 4.1 illustrates the whip tally sheets used on the count, including updated undecided votes as the count proceeded. Although Republican unity seemed relatively easy to come by in this case, the narrow victory and the need to rely on uncertain Democratic numbers put a premium on a very accurate count of Republican positions in getting to the minority party's goal of defeating majority party legislation.

Messaging and the whip organization. Legislative obstruction was a major focus for the minority and its whip organization, but the whips supported other tactics as well, particularly messaging. For example, a 1977 whip poll checked members' willingness to support a message-oriented discharge petition on an early version of the Kemp-Roth tax cut plan:

> Republicans are contemplating a major campaign to publicize our consistent position for individual tax cuts. The leadership urges all members to support the attempt. Will you sign the Discharge Petition #4 on HR 8333, the Kemp Tax Reduction Bill, in support of this effort?

The poll found 105 members of the GOP Conference prepared to sign the petition—hardly enough to win, even assuming some southern Democratic support. But the polling effort likely helped to coordinate the party around a tax-cut message that the leadership was pushing against the Carter administration.[119] In another example two years later, the whips used a poll to urge cosponsorship of a similar Republican tax cut package, an ongoing part of the GOP message.[120]

Summing Up: The Minority Whip in the 1970s

From one perspective, the minority party in the Ford-Carter era was in a historically weak position. Its numbers were decimated by the post-Watergate elections, and conditions for cooperative influence on legislation were declining. At the same time, the whip's activity during Michel's tenure demonstrates the continued relevance of the minority and the role of party

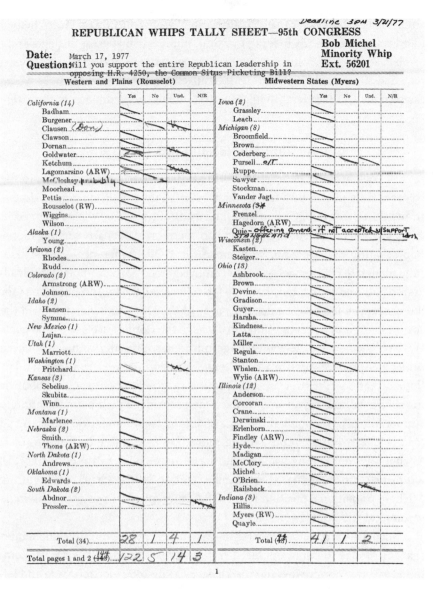

Figure 4.1 Republican whip count on common-situs picketing, March 1977
Source: RHM Papers, Leadership Series, Box 2, f. 95th Congress, Whip Polls, March 7, 1977.

organizations in supporting minority strategies. During 1975–1976, the Republican whips were crucial to the success of Ford's veto strategy. Subsequently, the minority began to make life more difficult for the majority through amendment and procedural activity, reflected in an uptick in whip attention to those issues. And creative use of whip counts sometimes helped to advance Republican messaging. Still, substantive success in legislating or obstructing—as in the campaign finance and common situs examples—required significant help from conservative Democrats, and Michel's whips assisted the GOP leadership in gathering intelligence from across the aisle.

Conclusion: Michel and the 1970s GOP

A close look at Bob Michel's rise through the Republican leadership in the 1970s reveals him to be a transitional figure in the rapidly changing House. In his election as NRCC chair and then as minority whip, Michel stepped in to replace long-tenured leaders who had overseen static party organizations. Representing the conservative wing of the GOP Conference—but stylistically moderate in approach—Michel enjoyed broad party support in his leadership bids and took important steps to rejuvenate the two organizations for the challenges facing the minority party. At the NRCC, Michel defended the committee's independent efforts to advance the Conference's electoral goals and oversaw new House-centered recruitment, addressing points of concern under his predecessor. As whip, Michel professionalized staff and built a floor operation that could respond to the new pressures brought about by the reforms of the 1970s, and he used the participatory whip organization to support the congressional minority's changing tactics under Republican and Democratic administrations. As he moved on from these leadership roles, Michel was replaced by leaders who were more conservative (Trent Lott as whip) or confrontational (Guy Vander Jagt as NRCC chair), highlighting Michel's transitional position in a GOP Conference that was changing in its ideological and strategic outlook.

Michel's transitional leadership was shaped by the multiple challenges that the House Republicans faced in the 1970s. Presidential scandal, combined with economic woes, defined a devastating 1974 election cycle and left Republicans with a weakened president. Michel's NRCC leadership and his first years as minority whip were essentially defensive, with these short-term political struggles taking center stage. But political changes in the House and in the political system of the 1970s put pressure on minority leadership to respond in ways that, in retrospect, are of longer-term significance. New rules and technology were opening up—and speeding up—legislative processes. Majority Democratic Caucus rules were beginning to move power away from old-guard committee chairs. New and more assertive partisans were joining both party caucuses with each election through the mid- and late 1970s. All of this began to restrict opportunities for cooperative legislating and opened new avenues and demand for minority messaging and obstruction in service of the party's electoral and policy goals. As this chapter has illustrated, Michel's 1970s leadership shows the minority party responding in its organization and its regular activity to these new realities. In these responses, the 1970s appear as an inflection point for House Republicans: the GOP Conference was no longer the often-cooperative permanent minority, but it was not yet defined by the highly confrontational approach that would increasingly dominate as the 1980s unfolded.

Notes

I am grateful to Frank Mackaman of The Dirksen Congressional Center for his assistance and insight in the archival portion of this work and to the Association of Centers for the Study of Congress for its support. I thank Lori Curtis of the Loma Linda University Heritage Research Center for assistance in obtaining material from the Jerry Pettis papers, and I thank Larry Evans for making available whip-count data used in the analysis.

1. David W. Rohde, *Parties and Leaders in the Postreform House* (Chicago: University of Chicago Press, 1991).

2. John H. Aldrich and David W. Rohde, "The Consequences of Party Organization in the House: The Role of the Majority and Minority Parties in Conditional Party Government," in *Polarized Politics: Congress and the President in a Partisan Era*, ed. Jon R. Bond and Richard Fleisher (Washington, DC: CQ Press, 2000).

3. Jason M. Roberts and Steven S. Smith, "Procedural Contexts, Party Strategy, and Conditional Party Voting in the U.S. House of Representatives," *American Journal of Political Science* 47 (2003): 308; Steven S. Smith, *Call to Order: Floor Politics in the House and Senate* (Washington, DC: The Brookings Institution, 1989); Jacob R. Straus, "Let's Vote: The Rise and Impact of Roll Call Votes in the Age of Electronic Voting," in *Party and Procedure in the United States Congress*, ed. Jacob R. Straus (Lanham, MD: Rowman & Littlefield, 2012).

4. Jacob R. Straus, "Electronic Voting System in the House of Representatives: History and Evolution," CRS Report for Congress (2008), RL34366.

5. On the 1970s–1980s rise of confrontational conservatives in Congress, see Frances E. Lee, *Insecure Majorities: Congress and the Perpetual Campaign* (Chicago: University of Chicago Press, 2016), chap. 4. On "new breed" House members in the 1970s, see Smith, *Call to Order*, 8, and Rohde, *Parties and Leaders*, 122. On the gradually expanding conservative Republican Study Committee (RSC) in the 1970s, see Ruth Bloch Rubin, *Building the Bloc: Intraparty Organization in the U.S. Congress* (New York: Cambridge University Press, 2017), 261–275, and Edwin J. Feulner, Jr., *Conservatives*

Stalk the House: The Story of the Republican Study Committee (Ottawa, IL: Green Hill Publishers, 1983).

6. Jennifer Hayes Clark, *Minority Parties in U.S. Legislatures* (Ann Arbor: University of Michigan Press, 2015).

7. Matthew N. Green, *Underdog Politics: The Minority Party in the U.S. House of Representatives* (New Haven, CT: Yale University Press, 2015).

8. Earlier exceptions are Charles O. Jones, *The Minority Party in Congress* (Boston: Little, Brown and Company, 1970), and William F. Connelly, Jr., and John J. Pitney, Jr., *Congress' Permanent Minority? Republicans in the U.S. House* (Lanham, MD: Rowman & Littlefield, 1994).

9. Green, *Underdog Politics*, 10–15.

10. Green, *Underdog Politics*, 17.

11. Green, *Underdog Politics*, 19–29.

12. Frances E. Lee, *Insecure Majorities: Congress and the Perpetual Campaign* (Chicago: University of Chicago Press, 2016).

13. Clark, *Minority Parties*, 147.

14. Clark, *Minority Parties*, 8–9.

15. Jones, *Minority Party in Congress*.

16. Matthew N. Green and Jeffrey Crouch, "Newt Gingrich: Strategic Political Entrepreneur," paper presented at the 2017 Meeting of the Congress & History Conference, Washington, DC; Randall Strahan, *Leading Representatives: The Agency of Leaders in the Politics of the U.S. House* (Baltimore: Johns Hopkins University Press, 2017), 138–139.

17. On the challenges of this trade-off, see Lee, *Insecure Majorities*, 53–60, and Green, *Underdog Politics*, 22.

18. Scott R. Meinke, *Leadership Organizations in the House of Representatives: Party Participation and Partisan Politics* (Ann Arbor: University of Michigan Press, 2016).

19. See also Connelly and Pitney, *Congress' Permanent Minority?*

20. Meinke, *Leadership Organizations*, 173–174.

21. Robin Kolodny, *Pursuing Majorities: Congressional Campaign Committees in American Politics* (Norman: University of Oklahoma Press, 1998), 8–9.

22. See also *One Hundred Years: A History of the National Republican Congressional Committee* (1966), RHM Papers, Campaigns and Politics, Box 36, f. NRCC: Chairman's Bulletin; Kolodny, *Pursuing Majorities*, 4–5.

23. For a more detailed account of the NRCC and the 1974 campaign, see Frank H. Mackaman, "In the Shadow of Watergate: Bob Michel Becomes a Congressional Leader," manuscript (Pekin, IL: The Dirksen Congressional Center, 2004).

24. Kolodny, *Pursuing Majorities*.

25. On the southern strategy, see dictated notes by RHM, March 19–20, 1973, RHM Papers, Campaigns and Politics, Box 36, f: NRCC: RHM Notes, 1973. On the southern strategy and the path to a majority, see David Broder, "Watergate: Little '74 Effect but Aftershock for Years," *Washington Post*, May 28, 1973.

26. Kolodny, *Pursuing Majorities*, 120.

27. Dictated notes by RHM, RHM Papers, Campaigns and Politics, Box 36, f. NRCC: RHM Notes, 1973. Elsewhere in these notes, Michel expresses broader concern about the NRCC's independence: "We can't ever again allow our Congressional Campaign Committee to get swallowed up by the National Committee, for when a National

Committee gets all involved in a Presidential election, as they do every four years, there's too much inclination to put all the eggs in the basket of the Presidency and tell the Congress to go to pot."

28. Bob Wilson to Richard Nixon, March 14, 1973, RHM Papers, Campaigns and Politics, Box 36, f. NRCC: Election to Chairman.

29. Dictated notes by RHM, RHM Papers, Campaigns and Politics, Box 36, f. NRCC: RHM Notes, 1973.

30. Michel was a member of Republican "Truth Squads" in 1960, 1964, and 1968, and he was the congressional cochair of the program in 1964. The Truth Squad program, which dated to 1952, involved rotating groups of House members and senators who tailed the Democratic presidential campaign around the country, holding press conferences to refute the candidates' claims. For RHM, participation in this electioneering effort—which some members avoided because of potential costs to their individual goals—showed party commitment and built an early political leadership record. Upon Michel's election as NRCC chair in 1973, a committee press release cited his 1960s experience "carrying the party message to voters." See RHM Papers, Campaigns and Politics, Box 2, f. 1960 Truth Squad, f. 1964 Truth Squad, and f. 1968 Truth Squad, and see RNCC press release, March 21, 1973, RHM Papers, Campaigns and Politics, Box 36, f. NRCC: Election to Chairman.

31. Clarence Brown to Harold Collier, March 15, 1973, RHM Papers, Campaigns and Politics Series, Box 36, f. NRCC. Election to Chairman.

32. Richard L. Lyons, "Michel Heads GOP Campaign Unit," *Washington Post*, March 22, 1973.

33. Dictated notes by RHM, RHM Papers, Campaigns and Politics, Box 36, f. NRCC: RHM Notes, 1973.

34. Dictated notes by RHM, RHM Papers, Campaigns and Politics, Box 36, f. NRCC: RHM Notes, 1973.

35. Annotated NRCC roster, RHM Papers, Campaigns and Politics, Box 36, f. NRCC: Election to Chairman.

36. Ideology is measured here by first-dimension DW-NOMINATE scores, which summarize members' positions based on roll call voting behavior.

37. Handwritten notes on GOP leadership meeting, April 9, 1973, RHM Papers, Campaigns and Politics, Box 36, f. NRCC: RHM Notes, 1973.

38. Dictated notes by RHM, RHM Papers, Campaigns and Politics, Box 36, f. NRCC: RHM Notes, 1973. Also Richard Nixon White House Tapes, March 22, 1973, Tape 887-7.

39. Dictated notes by RHM, RHM Papers, Campaigns and Politics, Box 36, f. NRCC: RHM Notes, 1973. Also Richard Nixon White House Tapes, March 22, 1973, Tape 887-7.

40. Dictated notes by RHM, RHM Papers, Campaigns and Politics, Box 36, f. NRCC: RHM Notes, 1973. Also Richard Nixon White House Tapes, March 22, 1973, Tape 887-7. Also Richard Nixon White House Tapes, May 9, 1973, Tape 432-26.

41. Dictated notes by RHM.

42. John Blume to I. Lee Potter, November 2, 1973, RHM Papers, Campaigns and Politics, Box 36, f. NRCC: Meetings, Fall 1973; Jack Calkins to RHM, September 7, 1973, RHM Papers, Campaigns and Politics, Box 36, f. NRCC: Memos from Executive Director.

CHAPTER 4

43. Jack Calkins to RHM, June 7, 1973, and September 7, 1973, RHM Papers, Campaigns and Politics, Box 36, f. NRCC: Memos from Executive Director.

44. David Broder, "Nixon Dinner Dips under $1 Million," *Washington Post*, May 10, 1973.

45. RHM to Charles Young, June 10, 1974, RHM Papers, Campaigns and Politics, Box 36, f. NRCC: Recruiting Committee. Midwest Region (1).

46. Candidate interview report on James Leach, December 18, 1973, RHM Papers, Campaigns and Politics, Box 36, f. NRCC: Recruiting Committee. Midwest Region (1).

47. Jack Calkins to Bryce Harlow, August 20, 1973, RHM Papers, Campaigns and Politics, Box 36, f. NRCC: Memos from Executive Director.

48. Dictated notes by RHM, 1973, RHM Papers, Campaigns and Politics, Box 36, f. NRCC: RHM Notes, 1973.

49. Kolodny, *Pursuing Majorities*, chapter 4.

50. Richard Nixon White House Tapes, March 22, 1973, Tape 887-7.

51. Jack Calkins to Bryce Harlow, August 20, 1973, RHM Papers, Campaigns and Politics, Box 36, f. NRCC: Memos from Executive Director.

52. RHM to John Conlan, April 13, 1973, RHM Papers, Campaigns and Politics, Box 36, f. NRCC: Candidate Recruitment: "We want everyone who has the time and wants to participate to do so to whatever extent he or she can." See also Barbara Sinclair, *Legislators, Leaders, and Lawmaking: The U.S. House of Representatives in the Postreform Era* (Baltimore: Johns Hopkins University Press, 1995); Meinke, *Leadership Organizations*.

53. "Heavy handed": William Ketchum to RHM (handwritten note on RHM letter dated April 13, 1973), RHM Papers, Campaigns and Politics, Box 36, f. NRCC: Candidate Recruitment. "Squeamish": Charles Wiggins to RHM, April 20, 1973, RHM Papers, Campaigns and Politics, Box 36, f. NRCC: Candidate Recruitment.

54. John Myers to Charles Thone, June 11, 1973, RHM Papers, Campaigns and Politics, Box 36, f. NRCC: Recruiting Committee. Midwest Region (2); Jack Kemp to RHM, April 29, 1974, RHM Papers, Campaigns and Politics, Box 36, f. NRCC: Recruiting Committee. Northeastern Region.

55. Buddy Bishop to Ed Terrill, March 29, 1974, RHM Papers, Campaigns and Politics, Box 36, Folder: NRCC. Recruiting Committee. Southern Region; RHM to Bobby Richardson, February 12, 1974, RHM Papers, Campaigns and Politics, Box 36, f. NRCC: Recruiting Committee. Southern Region; Candidate Interview report on Ward Purrington, December 3, 1973, RHM Papers, Campaigns and Politics, Box 36, f. NRCC: Recruiting Committee. Southern Region.

56. Jack Kemp to RHM, April 29, 1974, RHM Papers, Campaigns and Politics, Box 36, f. NRCC: Recruiting Committee. Northeastern Region.

57. See Kolodny, *Pursuing Majorities*.

58. RHM to Colleagues, April 6, 1973, RHM Papers, Campaigns and Politics, Box 36, f. NRCC: Chairman's Bulletin.

59. Jack Calkins to RHM with attached draft survey, April 19, 1973, RHM Papers, Campaigns and Politics, Box 36, f. NRCC: Memos from Executive Director.

60. RHM to Jack Calkins, April 23, 1973, RHM Papers, Campaigns and Politics, Box 36, f. NRCC: Memos from RHM.

61. Richard F. Fenno, Jr., *Home Style: House Members in Their Districts* (Glenview, IL: Scott, Foresman, 1978); David R. Mayhew, *Congress: The Electoral Connection* (New Haven, CT: Yale University Press, 1974).

62. Jack Calkins to RHM with attached draft survey, April 19, 1973, RHM Papers, Campaigns and Politics, Box 36, f. NRCC: Memos from Executive Director. On the use of infant care books for constituency connections, see Albert D. Cover and Bruce S. Broomberg, "Baby Books and Ballots: The Impact of Congressional Mail on Constituent Opinion," *American Political Science Review* 76 (1982): 347–359.

63. Jack Calkins to RHM, June 22, 1973, RHM Papers, Campaigns and Politics, Box 36, f. NRCC: Memos from Executive Director.

64. Jack Calkins to Bryce Harlow, August 20, 1973, RHM Papers, Campaigns and Politics, Box 36, f. NRCC: Memos from Executive Director. Records of members' RAS use in summer and fall 1973 show that a large number of GOP incumbents used the service, with fifty members using it more than five times during those months. A multivariate model of RAS use shows that more junior Republicans used the service more frequently ($p < 0.01$, two-tailed) and electoral vulnerability had a modest positive effect ($p < 0.10$, two-tailed). Freshmen members were particularly heavy users of the service, with an average of about eight uses in mid-1973 compared with three for other Republicans. Analysis based on data in Jack Calkins to RHM, November 7, 1973, RHM Papers, Campaigns and Politics, Box 36, f. NRCC: Memos from Executive Director.

65. Kolodny, *Pursuing Majorities*, 130–135.

66. Ed Terrill to William Young, October 30, 1973, RHM Papers, Campaigns and Politics, Box 36, f. NRCC: Recruiting Committee. Midwest Region (2); RHM to Jack Calkins, August 8, 1973, RHM Papers, Campaigns and Politics, Box 36, f. NRCC: Memos from RHM; Jack Calkins to Ed Terrill, Paul Theis, and Dave Cole, April 30, 1974, RHM Papers, Campaigns and Politics, Box 36, f. NRCC: Memos from Executive Director. Also see Kolodny, *Pursuing Majorities*, 130.

67. Jack Calkins to Bryce Harlow, August 20, 1973, RHM Papers, Campaigns and Politics, Box 36, f. NRCC: Memos from Executive Director.

68. PAC money made up a slightly larger portion of House race funding in 1974 than in 1972; see Gary C. Jacobson, "Money and Votes Reconsidered: Congressional Elections, 1972–1982," *Public Choice* (1985) 47: 7–62. The explosion of PACs on the campaign-finance scene occurred mostly over the next few cycles; Marian Currinder, *Money in the House: Campaign Funds and Congressional Party Politics* (Boulder: Westview Press, 2009). In total, 608 PACs were registered for the 1974 cycle, but more than five times that number would be registered by the early 1980s. GOP campaigns received only about a third of all PAC contributions in the 1974 congressional races (Jacobson, "Money and Votes").

69. Jack Calkins to RHM, Ed Terrar, and Ed Terrill, April 5, 1973, RHM Papers, Campaigns and Politics, Box 36, f. NRCC: Memos from Executive Director.

70. The spreadsheet is undated, but the set of incumbent Republicans included reflects candidate decisions and primaries from mid-1974. The tracked PACs included LUPAC (life underwriters), ADPAC (dentists), AMPAC (medical), and BIPAC (business/industry). A document from ADPAC dated October 9, 1974, shows that PAC contribution activity was reported directly by the PAC. RHM Papers, Campaigns and Politics, Box 36, f. NRCC: Funding.

71. Jack Calkins's NRCC background memo to Bryce Harlow explains a fairly routine set of allocations that is not reflected in the variable allocations in the 1974 spreadsheet.

Jack Calkins to Bryce Harlow, August 20, 1973, RHM Papers, Campaigns and Politics, Box 36, f. NRCC: Memos from Executive Director.

72. OLS model of combined NRCC allocations from 1974 spreadsheet (see note 70 above). NRCC total = 8255.31(904.30***) Constant—61.10(11.04***) *Vote Share* —149.93(45.83**) *Terms served*—0.75(7.90) *Party unity* (N = 160, R^2 = 0.27, *** p < 0.01, ** p < 0.05).

73. Kathryn Pearson, *Party Discipline in the U.S. House of Representatives* (Ann Arbor: University of Michigan Press, 2015).

74. Kolodny, *Pursuing Majorities*, 11–12.

75. Michel discusses the failings of recruitment in 1974 in his dictated notes from around the time of the 1980 minority leader race: "Prelude to Our Race for Leader (Side B)," RHM Papers, Leadership Series, Box 2, f. 96th Congress, 1979–1980: Leadership contest, 1980 (1).

76. Fred W. Beuttler with RHM, October 17, 2007, RHM Papers, Post-Congressional Series, f. Subjects: Interviews (2).

77. "Prelude to Our Race for Leader (Side B)," RHM Papers, Leadership Series, Box 2, f. 96th Congress, 1979–80: Leadership contest, 1980 (1).

78. William Springer to RHM, December 12, 1974, RHM Papers, Leadership Series, Box 1, f. 93rd Congress, 1973–1974: Whip (1).

79. The exact date of Michel's first appointment as an assistant regional whip is not clear. Archived whip materials indicating his participation date to early 1962, in the second session of the 87th Congress (RHM Papers, Leadership Series, Box 1, f. 88th Congress, 1963–64 Whip), and a mid-1961 *CQ* article lists Michel as the Midwest assistant whip for Illinois and Missouri (*Congressional Quarterly Weekly Report*, "Whips' Effectiveness Tested on Close 1961 House Votes," June 16, 1961). I have not located any Republican whip lists for the 85th or 86th Congresses that would indicate whether Michel was appointed prior to the 87th Congress. Michel's service in Republican leadership organizations also involved several other posts during his first decade in Congress. Michel had been elected as president of his House GOP freshman class in 1957 (Frank H. Mackaman, "Robert H. Michel: Preparing for Public Service," manuscript [Pekin, IL: The Dirksen Congressional Center, 2017], 21), a position that apparently came with an ex officio seat on the Republican Policy Committee in that Congress (*CQ Almanac* [Washington, DC: Congressional Quarterly Press, 1958], 52). In 1965, Michel received another party leadership appointment when he joined Minority Leader Gerald Ford's newly created Committee on Planning and Research (later the Republican Research Committee) (*CQ Almanac* [Washington, DC: Congressional Quarterly Press, 1965]).

80. RHM to various colleagues, November 6, 1974, RHM Papers, Leadership Series, Box 1, f. 93rd Congress, 1973–1974: Whip (2). Some letters signal that Michel is "giving serious consideration to making the race for Whip," while others contain more definitive wording: "I have definitely decided to make a bid for the Whip post."

81. Richard D. Lyons, "House Reform Faces Action Today in Party Caucuses," *New York Times*, December 2, 1974; "GOP, Democrats Pick Liberals as Caucus Heads," *Wall Street Journal*, December 3, 1974; Richard L. Lyons, "GOP Re-elects Anderson," *Washington Post*, December 3, 1974.

82. The *New York Times* reported a "half dozen aspirants" for the whip post on the day of the balloting. In addition to the three with reported final votes, Michel's whip count includes a few notes on support for John Wydler (R-NY), who withdrew in late November. Paul Findley (R-IL) was also an early candidate for the post. See Richard D. Lyons, "House Reform Faces Action Today in Party Caucuses," *New York Times*, December 2, 1974; Whip race whip count, undated, RHM Papers, Leadership Series, Box 1, f. 93rd Congress, 1973–1974: Whip (1); John Wydler to Jerry Pettis, November 27, 1974, Jerry Pettis Congressional Papers, Loma Linda University Heritage Research Center, Correspondence and Miscellaneous Papers '69–'74, Political General/Whip Bid; Paul Findley telegram to Jerry Pettis, November 7, 1974, Pettis Papers, Correspondence and Miscellaneous Papers '69 '74, Political General/Whip Bid.

83. Dear Colleague letters on whip bid, November 18, 1974, Pettis Papers, Correspondence and Miscellaneous Papers '69–'74, Political General/Whip Bid; John Erlenborn to Republican Colleague, November 25, 1974, Pettis Papers, Correspondence and Miscellaneous Papers '69–'74, Political General/Whip Bid.

84. Untitled UPI wire report, November 18, 1974, Pettis Papers, Correspondence and Miscellaneous Papers '69–'74, Political General/Whip Bid.

85. RHM to various colleagues, November 6, 1974, RHM Papers, Leadership Series, Box 1, f. 93rd Congress, 1973–74: Whip (2).

86. Matthew N. Green and Douglas B. Harris, "Explaining Vote Choice in the 1976 Race for House Majority Leader," paper presented at the 2015 Midwest Political Science Association Annual Meeting; Matthew N. Green and Douglas B. Harris, "Choosing the Leader: Explaining Vote Choice in the 1965 Race for House Minority Leader," paper presented at the 2015 American Political Science Association Annual Meeting.

87. The count is undated, but it notes some support for John Wydler, who dropped out of the race officially on November 27.

88. Pacific states include CA, OR, WA, AK, and HI.

89. Wiggins had been "considered one of Nixon's staunchest defenders" until the very end of the Watergate drama. See Eric Pace, "Charles Wiggins, 72, Dies; Led Nixon's Defense in Hearings," *New York Times*, March 8, 2000.

90. Around the time of his election as whip, Michel joined the fledgling conservative group the Republican Study Committee, and he was elected to its executive committee soon after. While RSC membership would become routine for most House Republicans in later decades, Michel's membership in the mid-1970s can be seen as an indicator of his alignment with the GOP Conference's conservatives and his interest in building connections between the RSC and the leadership. See Feulner, *Conservatives Stalk the House*, 131.

91. Beuttler interview with RHM, October 17, 2007.

92. Unsigned staff memo to RHM, November 20, 1974, RHM Papers, Leadership Series, Box 1, f. 93rd Congress, 1973–1974: Whip (1).

93. Meinke, *Leadership Organizations*, 42.

94. "New Congress Organizes; No Role for Mills," *Congressional Quarterly Weekly Report*, December 7, 1974.

95. Funding for a minority deputy whip was added in the 93rd Congress, but the position was not filled under Les Arends. Jerry Pettis was the first Republican deputy whip in the 94th Congress after losing the whip race to Michel, but Pettis died in a

plane accident in early 1975. Republican whip list, undated [94th Congress], Gerald R. Ford Presidential Library, Loen and Leppert Files, Box 28, f. Presidential Meetings with Congressional Leaders, 1974–76 (2); "Pettis to Confer with Ford as Deputy Whip," *San Bernardino Press-Enterprise*, undated, Pettis Papers, Correspondence and Miscellaneous Papers '69–'74, Political General/Whip Bid; Unsigned staff memo to RHM, November 20, 1974, RHM Papers, Leadership Series, Box 1, f. 93rd Congress, 1973–1974: Whip (1).

96. "New Congress Organizes; No Role for Mills," *Congressional Quarterly Weekly Report*, December 7, 1974.

97. Smith, *Call to Order*, 32.

98. William (Billy) Pitts interview with the author, June 19, 2017.

99. Clark, *Minority Parties*.

100. Smith, *Call to Order*.

101. C. Lawrence Evans, *Congressional Whip Count Database* (Williamsburg, VA: College of William and Mary, 2012), wmpeople.wm.edu/site/page/clevan/congressional whipcountdatabase.

102. Pitts interview, June 19, 2017. Pitts suggests that counting of Democratic votes was a fairly common activity, although the minority did not maintain records of these counts as they did for Republican polls.

103. Lyn Ragsdale, *Vital Statistics on the Presidency*, 4th ed. (Washington, DC: Congressional Quarterly Press, 2014).

104. "New Congress Organizes; No Role for Mills," *Congressional Quarterly Weekly Report*, December 7, 1974.

105. Richard S. Conley, "Presidential Influence and Minority Party Liaison on Veto Overrides: New Evidence from the Ford Presidency," *American Politics Research* 30 (2002): 34–65.

106. Twenty-three override-related counts were taken on nineteen unique measures.

107. Conley, "Presidential Influence," 34–65.

108. For examples, see Meinke, *Leadership Organizations*, 148–152.

109. Smith, *Call to Order*, 34.

110. It is important to note that whip activity on amendments and procedural votes was not entirely new to the Michel era, although amendments and procedural votes took on new importance with the changes of the 1970s. The fragmentary existing records of GOP whip counts in the 1960s show that the Arends whip organization conducted some counts on GOP substitutes and on procedural votes. Regional whip count records, RHM Papers, Leadership Series, Box 1, f. 89th Congress, 1965–66: Whip. See also Stanley Bach and Steven S. Smith, *Managing Uncertainty in the House of Representatives: Adaptation and Innovation in Special Rules* (Washington, DC: Brookings Institution Press, 1988); Smith, *Call to Order*, chapter 3.

111. Details on the campaign finance episode are from *Congress and the Nation, 1981* (Washington, DC: Congressional Quarterly Press, 1981), and Steven V. Roberts, "House Blocks Plan on Election Funds," *New York Times*, March 22, 1978.

112. Whip analysis based on data from Evans, *Congressional Whip Count Database*.

113. Pitts interview, June 19, 2017.

114. Mary Russell, "House Defeats Bill on Common Site Pickets, 217–205," *Washington Post*, March 24, 1977.

115. Issue background from *Congress and the Nation, 1981*; Helen Dewar, "Picket Bill Vote Today," *New York Times*, March 23, 1977; Philip Shabecoff, "House Rejects Bill on Picketing Sites by Building Unions," *New York Times*, March 24, 1977; Mary Russell, "House Defeats Bill on Common Site Pickets, 217–205," *Washington Post*, March 24, 1977.

116. *Congress and the Nation, 1981*.

117. Pitts interview, June 19, 2017. Also, Pitts postvote analysis of freshman and Democratic positions on HR 4250 passage and Sarasin amendment, March 24, 1977, RHM Papers, Leadership Series, Box 2, Folder: 3/17/77 Common situs picketing.

118. Handwritten notes for speech on Sarasin amendment, RHM Papers, Leadership Series, Box 2, Folder: 3/17/77 Common situs picketing. See also *Congressional Record*, March 24, 1977.

119. E.g., "Immediate Tax Cut Urged by Republicans," *Wall Street Journal*, October 6, 1977.

120. Whip poll question, July 30, 1979, RHM Papers, Leadership Series, Box 3, f. 96th Congress, 1979–1980: Whip polls, Tax Cut 7/30/79. On the 1979 tax proposal and Democratic reaction, see "GOP Leaders Ask $36 Billion Tax Reduction," *Los Angeles Times*, August 1, 1979, and Don Irwin, "Carter Stands Firm Against GOP Demands for Tax Cut," *Los Angeles Times*, August 7, 1979.

•

CHAPTER 5

MICHEL AS MINORITY LEADER

Minority Party Strategies and Tactics in the Postreform House

Douglas B. Harris and Matthew N. Green

Robert Michel is frequently portrayed as having been pragmatic, conciliatory, and statesmanlike.[1] Critics at the time—particularly those loyal to Michel's chief rival, Newt Gingrich (R-GA)—insisted that these traits were liabilities, not assets. They claimed that Michel lacked the courage to confront majority party Democrats, was disinterested in employing effective communications tactics, and was ultimately an impediment to the Republican majority that Gingrich sought to build.

It is true that Michel did not subscribe to Gingrich's embrace of partisan communications over legislating, his regular attacks on the reputation of Democrats and Congress as a whole, or his laserlike focus on building a conservative movement. But the narrative that Michel was a weak or disinterested leader ignores Michel's substantial efforts to help his party win policy and electoral battles and, more generally, his strategic and tactical responsiveness to a changing congressional environment, which necessarily constrains what minority parties can do.[2] There is substantial evidence that Michel was a skilled practitioner of politics, an occasional innovator of new leadership strategies, and an effective legislator who secured legislative victories even as his party remained mired in the minority.

In this chapter, we evaluate Michel's fourteen-year tenure as Republican Leader in the House of Representatives. Michel's service as Republican Leader—indeed, his entire House career—was exclusively in the minority.

Nonetheless, we find that Michel was not only active and innovative but also relatively successful at helping his party achieve its collective goals. In addition, while Michel frequently differed with Gingrich on tactics and strategy, his relationship with the Georgian was more complicated and complementary than is often portrayed.

Michel's Rise in a Changing House

First elected to the House in 1956, Michel was introduced to Congress during its "textbook era" of independent committees, bipartisan cooperation, norms of comity, and focus on legislative accomplishment over symbolic politics. Michel followed the classic path of a legislative insider, serving on the powerful Appropriations Committee, where policy-oriented bipartisanship was a central ethos.[3] He developed ties to longtime GOP whip and fellow Illinoisan Les Arends and rose stepwise through the party ranks, becoming chairman of the National Republican Campaign Committee (NRCC) in 1973, House Republican minority whip in 1975, and House Republican Leader in 1981.

Just as Michel was moving up the ranks of power, however, the House was undergoing significant internal changes. Party voting was on the rise, and majority party leaders and the House Democratic Caucus were accruing more power through institutional reforms and rules changes.[4] At the same time, the independent influence of committees and their chairs was starting to erode, and new "sunshine" laws and means of communications exposed the legislature to greater outside scrutiny.[5] Institutionally and behaviorally, the House was becoming more partisan and public.

The reasons for these changes have been widely documented and include the rise of more polarized and politically engaged voters; the arrival of party-oriented, media-conscious lawmakers in Congress; the introduction of televised floor proceedings; rules changes that made floor amendments subject to recorded votes; and greater expectations by majority party Democrats that their leaders enforce party discipline.[6] What matters for our purposes is how Michel responded to these developments as minority leader. Since most of his experience and training had prepared him to lead in an earlier era, navigating the distance between his understanding of leadership and how the House chamber was transforming became a central challenge of his tenure.

The first test of Michel's fit with the changing chamber was his race to replace John Rhodes (R-AZ) as minority leader. His opponent in the election, NRCC Chair Guy Vander Jagt (R-MI), was more of an orator and party campaigner than was Michel. Whereas Michel emphasized his experience as whip and the need for legislative wins, Vander Jagt claimed that the GOP should focus principally on building a majority, and his public-oriented politics seemed to fit well with emerging changes within his own Conference and the House as a whole.

Michel bested Vander Jagt, 103–87, thanks in part to his connections with other establishment Republicans and adroit distribution of campaign contributions. But Vander Jagt had won a significant number of votes, especially from more junior lawmakers and those who had narrowly won election in 1980, suggesting that his emphasis on communications and electoral politics resonated with many members of the GOP Conference.[7] Notable among Vander Jagt's supporters was Congressman Newt Gingrich (R-GA), first elected in 1978, who would be a relentless advocate for a more aggressive, partisan, and confrontational minority party stance. Prominent conservative activist Paul Weyrich had also come out against Michel, calling him a "politics-as-usual Republican" who "delivers for the liberals when the chips are down."[8] What remained unclear was whether the new minority leader would pursue the kinds of tactics and strategies that would both satisfy these dissidents and help the House GOP achieve its collective goals.

Michel's Strategies and Tactics as Minority Leader

Minority parties in the House of Representatives have several collective objectives, including winning control of the chamber, enacting policy, protecting the minority's rights, and helping the presidential party (by either defending a same-party president or getting their party elected to the White House). We evaluate Michel's success in achieving these objectives using three major categories of tactics: legislating, messaging (which includes speeches, press outreach, and media events), and electioneering (such as fundraising and candidate recruitment).[9] Though all three are potentially interrelated, considering each independently allows one to identify Michel's particular contributions and evaluate the frequent claim that Michel followed the first category of tactics to the detriment of the other two.

Legislating

The House minority party has relatively few opportunities to legislate. As minority leader, Michel looked for—and often found—ways to shape legislative outcomes. Not only did this jibe with Michel's inclinations as a leader but, it also made sense during his early tenure, when the influence of the Republican Party in national government was greater than it had been in years thanks to a divided majority party, same-party presidents, and an effective whip operation.

Michel made clear from the get-go that a newly elected Republican Senate and White House meant legislating should be the GOP Conference's highest priority. "The bottom line," he told his fellow Republicans, was the "enactment of the Reagan program [and] the battle will be in the House."[10] That meant keeping the 192-member GOP Conference together while conducting what Michel called "commando raids for votes" among the Democratic Caucus.[11] As Michel later recalled, "We weren't going to win anything with 192 votes. We were going to need all of ours, plus twenty-six, twenty-seven or twenty-eight on the other side. And so, for me, that was the challenge."[12]

With Trent Lott (R-MS) as the party's whip, the GOP whipping operation "evolved into an effective machine that rival[ed] the Democrats in its ability to disseminate information, count heads, and build coalitions."[13] The results were impressive. Giving "no quarter in the budget and tax wars of 1981,"[14] Michel and Lott, together with the White House, helped unify Republicans behind major bills while peeling away enough Democrats to pass them on the chamber floor.[15] Most notably, conservative Democrats joined Republicans in late June to pass Reagan's reconciliation cuts to entitlement spending programs, against the wishes of majority party leaders, and passed the president's tax cut bill a month later.

Michel had thus helped his party achieve two key goals: making policy and helping a same-party president. "We helped define a new direction for national government and national politics in this country," as Michel put it, later recalling that his party had been a "force that had to be reckoned with."[16]

The ability of House Republicans to influence legislation declined after the 1982 midterm elections, when they lost more than thirty seats. But Michel remained hopeful that attempts at legislating would bear fruit, especially because the White House and Senate remained in Republican hands. Since intraparty unity was a prerequisite to win floor votes, Lott maintained his formidable whip operation while Michel tried to amend Conference rules to require that floor time available to debate a bill be controlled only by the highest ranking committee member who shared the preferences of party leaders or the full Conference.[17]

Republicans did see some occasional legislative successes in the years that followed, and Michel continued to emphasize the need to win policy battles. For instance, in late 1984, enough Democrats joined Republicans to pass a crime bill proposed by the White House over the objections of the Democratic leadership.[18] In anticipation of Reagan's reelection, Michel and Lott endorsed a proposal by Jerry Lewis (R-CA), chair of the Research Committee, to come up with a postelection legislative agenda for the party.[19] Michel also chided "show horse" members who, he said, "have got to understand that we have a splendid opportunity . . . to build upon the success of the first four years. . . . It's one thing to be out there on the stump, just flapping your gums, and it's another thing trying to put something together. Some of the greatest talkers around here couldn't legislate their way out of a paper bag."[20]

Unfortunately, as time passed, Michel's legislating efforts were increasingly hampered. A shrunken GOP Conference lacked the leverage it once had over votes. House Democrats had begun tightening their procedural control over the chamber, issuing more restrictive rules that prevented Republicans from offering amendments.[21] Ranking minority members were increasingly cut out of the legislative process as well.[22] This environment made it harder for rank-and-file Republicans to see the point of legislating. "Some of the younger members," observed Michel, "don't really know what it's like to be in the position of working on legislation with the thought that it might become law someday."[23]

After the 1982 elections, the most important of those younger members, Newt Gingrich, organized a dozen or so like-minded House Republicans into a new group called the Conservative Opportunity Society (COS). The group sought ways to use publicity—including attention-grabbing floor tactics—as a means of winning elections and, hopefully, a Republican House. Michel soon found himself at odds with the COS's predisposition to think in terms of messaging and public opinion instead of policy influence. For instance, when Democrats seated one of their own in a hotly contested Indiana race in 1985, Michel reiterated the need to keep on good terms with Democratic lawmakers to help Reagan pass his agenda, whereas Gingrich called for "guerrilla warfare" against the majority party.[24]

By the end of the Reagan administration, Michel predicted that the COS would tire of "ringing the bell every day" and follow older House norms.[25] Michel was wrong. COS and Gingrich saw compromise—the key to policy influence, especially for the minority party—as fatal to their party's electoral hopes, and they were even willing to oppose their own party's president to prevent any legislative moves that might tarnish the GOP brand. In 1990, Gingrich, by then minority whip, was among those who came out against President George H. W. Bush (albeit unexpectedly) when Bush struck a budget and tax deal with Democratic leaders in 1990, helping to defeat it against the wishes of Michel.[26] That break may have strengthened the GOP's antitax brand, but it also led the Bush White House to negotiate with Democrats, giving the minority party even less policy influence. As Michel might have predicted, it also weakened Bush's image among voters, hurting his chances of reelection.

Opportunities for legislative influence for the minority Republicans diminished further in November 1992 when President Bush lost reelection and Democrats retained majorities in both chambers of Congress. Michel would be serving for the first time as leader under unified Democratic government, and he adapted quickly to the changed environment. "We're going to be a very militant, forceful force," he told one reporter. "You're going to be hearing from us."[27] Looking back at that period, Michel recalled thinking that "I've got a different role. Instead of being affirmatively for the president's program, I've got to be the official objector, the naysayer."[28]

Sure enough, legislative cooperation between Democrats and Republicans declined in the 103rd Congress. Despite some notable exceptions—such as passage of the North American Free Trade Agreement, for which Michel and his staff helped whip votes[29]—the GOP Conference took a more oppositional role, and any legislating it undertook was designed to defeat bills, not pass them. Not a single House Republican voted for President Bill Clinton's 1993 budget plan, and the party did not lend a helping hand when Democrats tried but failed to pass a major health care bill.[30] Michel may have still preferred cooperation and compromise, and many attributed the change in leadership strategy to pressure from Gingrich and his allies. But Michel also seemed to recognize that positive legislating was neither possible in the changed political context nor a priority for a large faction, if not the majority, of the GOP Conference. With the GOP unable to expect policy victories, messaging took precedence over legislating.

Messaging

In the 1970s and 1980s, messaging became an increasingly important part of congressional politics. Television coverage of the House floor began in 1979, cable TV news grew in popularity, and members began hiring press secretaries and communications directors.[31] The idea of the "permanent campaign"—incumbents continually running for reelection—was also taking hold, creating an incentive to use the legislative process as a backdrop for messaging and improving one's political brand.[32] All of this meant that legislative leaders were expected to play a larger communications role on behalf of their party.

Michel's initial focus was more on legislating than messaging for three reasons. First, he was a consummate legislator and, like others in his generation, skeptical of media politics. Second, the GOP Conference was expected to carry the water of a same-party president (Reagan and then Bush). One Michel aide wistfully recalled that, when Democrat Jimmy Carter had been president, "we had more opportunities to fire on the opposition without having to defend a policy or a program or a position of our own."[33] Third, partisan messaging might drive away moderate House Democrats who would otherwise join the GOP in cross-party coalitions to pass conservative bills.

Michel did not ignore communications altogether, however. Shortly after Michel was elected minority leader, his aide, Billy Pitts, insisted that Michel's staff hone his speechmaking skills and take "every opportunity for legitimate news interviews . . . particularly if there is potential for national coverage."[34] In early 1982, with Reagan and the GOP facing criticism from Democrats for an economic downturn, Michel circulated a series of talking points to colleagues and urged that they repeat them on the floor and in the media to "help keep a lid on the propaganda and drive home some of the facts."[35] He also saw messaging as a means of achieving legislative goals. When a floor vote on Reagan's 1981 budget was scheduled, Michel lobbied newspaper editors to "make your readers aware of this vote so that they may have an opportunity to contact their Member of Congress either way."[36]

Nonetheless, some Republicans—Gingrich first among them—felt Michel was wasting messaging opportunities that would help the party win more House seats. In a 1982 memo to Michel about impending budget legislation, Gingrich insisted that what mattered more was using bills to communicate to voters rather than influence policy:

> The ultimate test of the 1982 budget fight is whether we have a reaffirming or a repudiation election in November. If we win the budget fight on the floor of the House only to lose twenty or thirty seats in November, we have lost everything and gained nothing—because the 1983 Congress will undo everything we have accomplished. However, the budget fight gives us a chance to carry the message to the country that the Democrats are the tax increase/big spending/

high interest rate/job destroying/weak defense party, while we are the tax cut/less spending/low interest rate/job increasing/strong defense party.[37]

Gingrich's view held some sway within the minority leader's office. As Michel staffer Mike Johnson conceded in May 1982, "We tend to give this task [communications] a lower priority than it deserves. . . . You [Michel] get so caught up in the strains of putting together a legislative program on a day-to-day basis, you fail to focus time and energy on the job of making sure the public understands what you're doing."[38]

After the 1982 elections, Johnson advised his boss to turn from legislating to messaging. "With fewer numbers in the House and less chance of shaping legislation," he wrote to Michel, the GOP Conference must "creat[e] the kind of legislative record for ourselves that will enhance the prospect of House candidates." There should be "a far more dominant role by the Republican leadership in the House in defining issues and selling them to the public" and in "develop[ing] positions on issues much earlier so that we have an opportunity to tailor them and promote them politically, instead of having to explain our position after the fact."[39]

More messaging became the order of the day. In September 1983, for example, Michel and Lott organized a special order on the floor to defend Reagan's budget policies.[40] Messaging also became an important tool to help the GOP Conference defend its procedural rights. Michel and other leaders used floor debate and other communications tactics to try to keep Democrats from exploiting chamber rules to seat the Democratic candidate in the contested Indiana election, and they later developed a media strategy to highlight the majority party's use of restrictive rules to limit the minority's legislative options.[41] But Michel admitted that messaging was unlikely to do much to overcome the public's response to procedural matters, which he described as "MEGO—my eyes glaze over."[42]

By the last two years of the Reagan presidency, Michel's office was arranging meetings between lawmakers and reporters,[43] establishing a means of distributing survey data "to Leadership staff and committee counsels,"[44] and pursing political, legislative, and media strategies for policy issues that were expected to help the Republican Party brand.[45] One reporter noted in mid-1987 that Michel was making "a concerted effort . . . to showcase younger members,"[46] and by the 100th Congress (1987–1989) members of the GOP Conference were fully behind efforts by leaders to identify "party issues" that might help them build a legislative agenda, a campaign platform, or both.[47]

One noteworthy move taken by Michel during this period was to form the Project Majority Task Force, a group headed by Lynn Martin (R-IL) and Fred Grandy (R-IA) to find ways to bring Republicans to the promised land of majority status. The task force determined that a bottom-up, localized approach would be best. "National issues only work when they are local issues, too," the group wrote in a November 1987 memo to the minority leader. "We need to develop spots on regionalized issues that will help our candidates with the issues unique to their areas."[48]

Gingrich believed nationalized messaging was better than district-oriented communications, but Michel was not opposed to nationally focused messaging. For example, he and the GOP Conference chair, Jerry Lewis, circulated a letter to colleagues in November 1989 with talking points emphasizing recent economic growth and GOP legislative successes.[49] He also oversaw a gradual expansion of media-oriented congressional leadership activities, and in the early 1990s the GOP leadership considered forming a "Communications Committee" to "develop a wide-ranging plan and strategy to take our message to the media and to the general public" and also "track and exploit committee votes, floor votes and statements from vulnerable Democrats."[50]

After the 1992 elections, with no Republican White House to defend on the airwaves, and with his party completely shut out of power, Michel had fewer GOP voices to compete with.[51] One Republican leadership task force urged that leaders take the party's communications needs more seriously,[52] and the top leadership cited as an "Overall Goal" for Republican leaders the "need to develop and manage issues and resources that will aid us in influencing opinion and in turn . . . gaining control of the House."[53]

In pursuit of these aims, Michel revved up the "Theme Team," a group he had formed in 1991 to coordinate and promote Republican messages, especially during the period of one-minute floor speeches that started each legislative day.[54] The Theme Team became part of a broader messaging operation that included what internal party memos described as "a state of the art communications ability," a "rapid-response team," and regularized "issue briefs and talking points."[55] Michel's office also issued the Blueprint for Leadership that included central messaging aims "to shape the Republican view of America, tell the American people what we believe in, and fully utilize our legislative skills to implement our vision."[56] A new Communications Advisory Group was formed to develop and circulate talking points to party members so they could oppose, for example, President Clinton's tax bill.[57]

In short, though Gingrich sometimes groused that his party's leaders were not willing to use assertive communications tactics, Michel not only supported the use of partisan messaging to help his party but also oversaw several important communications-related developments and new initiatives, such as the Theme Team, to help his party. He also saw messaging as useful for achieving not only electoral goals, as Gingrich did, but also policy, procedural, and presidential objectives, though its effectiveness was not always clear.

Electioneering

Michel had had some experience in election-oriented activity as head of the NRCC in 1973–1974.[58] Once he became minority leader, he remained an ex officio member of the committee but left most of the fundamentals of electioneering, including candidate recruitment and campaign fundraising, to NRCC Chair Vander Jagt.[59] His direct leadership on electioneering was thus relatively limited.

Nonetheless, Michel did oversee some important efforts to improve coordination between the NRCC and the top Republican leadership.[60] He and Vander Jagt hosted several breakfast sessions with GOP lawmakers in late 1982 to encourage coordinated, positive, election-oriented messages from incumbents.[61] Michel wanted to dedicate a portion of the 1984 presidential convention to the theme of creating a Republican majority in the House.[62] In the mid-1980s, Michel's staff recommended regularly distributing NRCC data to leaders and committees and recruiting the NRCC to leverage legislative battles for political purposes. The 1986 budget process, for example, could be used to "politically damage Democrats," while both the NRCC and the Republican Research Committee could organize "watchdog" operations to "create discord" among Democrats on trade legislation.[63]

Michel's electioneering activities continued in the early 1990s. Michel had established a leadership political action committee, the Republican Leader's Fund, which he used to contribute money to Republican candidates, and he gave substantial amounts (more than $200,000 in 1992 alone). He circulated a set of floor speeches by himself and more than a dozen other Republicans laying out the party's plan of action if it won control of the chamber in 1992.[64] Following those elections—in which Republicans gained seats, but not a majority—Michel's Blueprint for Leadership recommended closer coordination between the NRCC and party leaders to help win future elections. The NRCC would continue to help incumbents and challengers, but it would also "implemen[t] political strategy in concert with" leaders, and the NRCC chair would be expected to "participat[e] in the development of House Republican policy."[65] In addition, the votes and public statements of "vulnerable Democrats" would be recorded and used against them in their reelection campaigns.[66]

As the Republican Conference continued to suffer at the polls—losing seats in every election except 1984 and 1992—Michel faced two criticisms related to electioneering. The first was that he followed the wrong electoral strategy. As with messaging, Michel generally endorsed a localized approach to campaigning, focusing on helping individual Republicans win and hold particular seats. But both Vander Jagt and Gingrich advocated nationalizing congressional elections and claimed that Michel's approach contributed to the party's muddled brand and, by extension, its poor electoral success rate.

This criticism appeared to be validated when the GOP took over the House in 1995 following the adoption of the Contract with America, an election-year agenda designed to nationalize the elections in 1994. The House GOP had put forth similar agendas in the past without much electoral success, however, and it is far from clear that voters cast their ballots based on a congressional party's agenda.[67] More generally, Michel was joined by other Republicans who believed the localization approach was better. For instance, the GOP policy chair, Marvin H. "Mickey" Edwards (R-OK), wrote to NRCC Executive Director Ed Rollins in 1989 that the party needed a "greatly increased emphasis on issues polling in local districts" because "without local polling information, in advance of candidate selection, we will not likely find the right candidates or emphasize the right campaign themes."[68]

The second election-related criticism of Michel was that he lacked faith that his party could win control of the House. For instance, Gingrich ally Bob Walker (R-PA) insisted to one reporter that many of his colleagues worried Michel "has been far too satisfied as the minority and hasn't done those things necessary to make ourselves the majority."[69] Even one-time Michel protégé Dennis Hastert (R-IL) reflected, "I don't think Bob Michel believed that we'd ever be in the majority—that was one of his big shortcomings—but the younger leaders sure did."[70]

Though this critique may have made Gingrich more appealing than Michel to majority-starved Republicans, it too is unfair. There is scarce evidence that Michel neither wanted nor tried to make the House GOP the majority party. And if Michel did think control of the chamber was out of his party's immediate grasp, he was far from alone. When Republicans had come close to a majority of seats in the 1980 elections, many found the idea of a Republican-led House exceedingly unlikely.[71] Four years later, one journalist opined that "few GOP leaders or rank-and-file troops expect that the party will soon gain a majority in the House,"[72] and Lott decided to leave the House altogether in 1987, wrote one reporter, partly from the "realization that the Democrats would retain control of the House indefinitely."[73]

The Michel-Gingrich Relationship

Differences of opinion between Michel and Gingrich characterize all three categories of tactics that Michel employed as minority leader. Michel's obvious disdain for confrontation, and Gingrich's frequent criticisms of party leaders, have led many to cast the relationship between the pair as antagonistic.

It is true that Michel was hardly a fan of Gingrich, whom many suspected of harboring ambitions for Michel's job, and the minority leader was disappointed when the Georgian was elected whip in 1989.[74] But their relationship was complex. Though conflicts over strategy and tactics periodically erupted between the pair, Michel also delegated important tasks to Gingrich and was willing to let him pursue aggressive or unorthodox activities that might help advance key strategic aims of the party as a whole.

Delegation is an important task of minority party leaders who wish to apply pressure without sacrificing their personal relationships with the majority.[75] In Michel's case, the minority leader found it useful to assign key messaging and electioneering duties to Gingrich and his allies. In mid-1981, for instance, he and Lott asked Gingrich to lead a task force to defend Reagan's tax legislation,[76] albeit one "limited to generating grass roots support for our legislation."[77] Michel also had Gingrich serve as the conduit of information from the Department of the Treasury to House members on the tax bill.[78] More generally, Michel aide Mike Johnson advised his boss in May 1982 that "where the rhetoric [used by Gingrich] is strictly negative or partisan, there should be no direct link with the leadership other than in an advisory capacity."[79]

The Reagan tax bill was not the only piece of legislation for which Michel delegated important duties to Gingrich. When the White House discussed possible Social Security reform legislation, Johnson encouraged "taking [Democrats] on with every opportunity. It wouldn't hurt to get the Gingrich Guerillas involved with one-minutes and the like."[80] Michel later commended Gingrich for having built "a second [strategic] track" on the politically volatile issue.[81] In 1987, in outlining a case for going "Back to Main Street" to develop a House Republican agenda, Johnson advised Michel to "put Newt Gingrich in charge."[82]

Michel sometimes defended or even supported Gingrich's initiatives to help the GOP Conference. In the fall of 1983, when Gingrich and other COS members suggested an ideas-oriented retreat for lawmakers, Michel "eventually endorsed it and encouraged members to participate."[83] The minority leader permitted Gingrich to hold a seminar for Republican staffers in late 1985 to review arguments their bosses could use against a major tax reform bill.[84] Michel's support extended to Gingrich acolytes as well. When one COS member was subject to a harsh newspaper editorial for aggressive floor tactics, Michel defended him: "It may not be my choice to engage in the tactics of some of our members," he wrote, "but . . . I respect their right and their obligation to do so, and I appreciate their reasons for doing so."[85]

As time passed, Michel demonstrated that he, too, could be confrontational and aggressive against Democrats. When Speaker Tip O'Neill (D-MA) unilaterally decided to show an empty chamber on C-SPAN cameras during the May 1984 speech of COS member Bob Walker, Michel wrote a critical letter to O'Neill and circulated it to other Republicans, declaring that "I just can't let this action go unchallenged."[86] During the 1985 battle over the contested Indiana election, he "ambush[ed] the Democrats" by demanding an unexpected floor vote on seating the Republican candidate, which led Gingrich to call Michel a "leader in transition" toward a more aggressive partisan style.[87] As Gingrich biographer Mel Steely acknowledged, Michel "was willing to communicate with Newt and the COS and to accept some new concepts."[88]

This is not to say that Michel was a full-blown convert to Gingrich's antagonistic mode of leadership. Unlike other Republicans, he did not give Gingrich a standing ovation after he made a point of personal privilege on the House floor in 1985 that led O'Neill to have his words taken down.[89] When the Democrat was seated in the Indiana election case, Michel was the lone Republican who shook hands with the newly seated lawmaker.[90] He also pointedly refused to sign Gingrich's 1988 letter demanding that Speaker Jim Wright (D-TX) be subject to an ethics investigation.[91]

Michel's unhappiness with Gingrich, and resistance to some of his more aggressive techniques, frustrated the Georgian. When Michel was quoted in a December 1987 news article saying he did "from time to time have problems with his [Gingrich's] methodology," Gingrich responded with an angry handwritten note: "I am deeply disappointed. I have taken the risks. I thought you could at least have been positive."[92] Five years later, when Democrats created a professional administrator over Republican objections that it did little to limit the majority's arbitrary authority over the chamber, Gingrich was aggravated that Michel would not agree to stage a walkout from the House floor in protest.[93]

In fact, Gingrich did more than complain. After he was elected whip, he sometimes openly challenged Michel's authority. The minority leader had to give Gingrich a "dressing down" after the whip announced a party strategy on campaign finance and ethics "at odds" with Michel's view,[94] and, most famously, Gingrich led the revolt against Michel and Bush over tax increases.[95] But Gingrich and his allies were also sensitive to the appearance of trying to muscle aside Michel. When Gingrich became whip, for instance, his campaign manager, Bob Walker, quickly rebutted a newspaper article that suggested Walker saw Gingrich's win as a move against Michel.[96] Later that year, after a legislative victory by the GOP, Gingrich wrote to Michel that "we could not have won last week without your patience, flexibility, and leadership."[97]

In sum, there is ample evidence that Gingrich and Michel were hardly the closest of comrades, and they disagreed over what the most effective party strategy would be and whether interparty comity was important enough to dictate Republican tactics. At the same time, Gingrich did try to stay in Michel's good graces, and Michel saw some utility in allowing Gingrich to pursue partisan messaging and aggressive tactics in the name of a shared goal: getting the Republicans into the majority.

Conclusion

Michel was a leader accustomed to operating under a rapidly transforming set of congressional norms and rules. Nonetheless, he found ways to adapt to the changing environment, maintaining a delicate balancing act by keeping one foot in the old order while trying to fulfill the leadership roles suggested by the new order. Michel was also willing to use a plethora of tactics to achieve party goals, including whipping for votes, expanding and professionalizing the leadership's communications operations, and taking on electioneering activities to help Republican incumbents and challengers win office.

Ultimately, Michel did help his party achieve several specific policy goals, and both the Reagan and Bush White Houses saw a number of their legislative priorities become law. However, although Michel did win some small battles to protect his party's procedural rights, he was unable to prevent their gradual erosion over time. Most important, Michel's party never won control of the chamber during his tenure.

The latter two failings rankled many House Republicans and helped fuel the rise of Newt Gingrich, who promised to deliver his colleagues to the promised land of majority status with aggressive, confrontational, media-oriented tactics and strategies. Though Michel and Gingrich found ways to work together, they remained sharp contrasts in both leadership style and strategic outlook. Gradually, Michel's approach lost favor among the rank and file, and as more confrontational party leaders were elected by the GOP Conference, Michel was left "isolated."[98]

The minority leader's reluctance to follow Gingrich's lead was partly due to a fear that it would undermine comity in the chamber. Having good interparty relations mattered to Michel in its own right, but it also gave him some hope of protecting his party's procedural powers. For instance, his negotiations with majority party leaders in 1984 led to the adoption of rules that would protect the GOP's right to deliver floor speeches,[99] and in 1993 Speaker Tom Foley (D-WA) agreed not to show the empty chamber on C-SPAN when Republicans spoke on the floor.[100] In addition, as the minority leader told one reporter, he was "personally uncomfortable being a perpetual antagonist."[101]

Gingrich's confrontational style would eventually win the day—and not just in the House Republican Party. It is telling that behaving as what Michel called "a constant carping critic"[102] has arguably become de facto for minority leaders from both parties. Perhaps declining cooperation and comity between Democratic and Republican leaders was inevitable, given the many outside forces that have pushed our national legislature toward greater politicization and polarization. But it is worth wondering whether another path could have been taken—one that would have helped House Republicans gain politically without sacrificing the chamber's collegiality and quality of deliberation. As Congress remains deeply unpopular and unproductive, perhaps Michel's leadership style and skill should serve as a model for future congressional leaders who care not only about winning the next election but also about making our nation's democratic institutions work.

Notes

1. William F. Connelly, Jr., and John J. Pitney, Jr., *Congress' Permanent Minority? Republicans in the U.S. House* (Lanham, MD: Rowman & Littlefield, 1994); James G. Gimpel, *Legislating the Revolution: The Contract with America in Its First 100 Days* (Boston: Allyn & Bacon, 1996); Douglas L. Koopman, *Hostile Takeover: The House Republican Party, 1981–1995* (Lanham, MD: Rowman & Littlefield, 1996).
2. Charles O. Jones, *The Minority Party in Congress* (Boston: Little, Brown and Company, 1970).
3. Richard F. Fenno, Jr., *Congressmen in Committees* (Boston: Little, Brown and Company, 1973).
4. David W. Rohde, *Parties and Leaders in the Postreform House* (Chicago: University of Chicago Press, 1991); Barbara Sinclair, *Legislators, Leaders, and Lawmaking* (Baltimore: Johns Hopkins University Press, 1995).
5. Leroy Rieselbach, *Congressional Reform: The Changing Modern Congress* (Washington, DC: Congressional Quarterly Press, 1994); Rohde, *Parties and Leaders*.
6. The literature on this subject is vast. See, for example, Alan I. Abramowitz, *The Disappearing Center: Engaged Citizens, Polarization, and American Democracy* (New Haven, CT: Yale University Press, 2011); Timothy E. Cook, *Making Laws and Making News* (Washington, DC: Brookings Institution Press, 1989); James A. Campbell, *Polarized: Making Sense of a Divided America* (Princeton: Princeton University Press, 2016); Douglas B. Harris, "The Rise of the Public Speakership," *Political Science Quarterly* 113 (Summer 1998): 193–212; Matthew Levendusky, *The Partisan Sort: How Liberals Became Democrats and Conservatives Became Republicans* (Chicago: University of Chicago Press, 2009); Burdett Loomis, *The New American Politician: Ambition, Entrepreneurship, and the Changing Face of Political Life* (New York: Basic Books, 1988); Sinclair, *Legislators, Leaders, and Lawmaking*; Barbara Sinclair, *Party Wars: Polarization and the Politics of National Policy Making* (Norman: University of Oklahoma Press, 2006); and Sean M. Theriault, *Party Polarization in Congress* (New York: Cambridge University Press, 2008).
7. Matthew N. Green and Douglas B. Harris, *Choosing the Leader: Leadership Elections in the U.S. House of Representatives* (New Haven, CT: Yale University Press, 2019); Frances Lee, *Beyond Ideology: Politics, Principles, and Partisanship in the U.S. Senate* (Chicago: University of Chicago Press, 2009).
8. "What the Newspapers Don't Tell You," *Weyrich from Washington*, RHM Papers, Leadership Series, Box 2, f. 96th, Leadership Contests, 1980(1). Here and elsewhere we cite materials uncovered in the archives of former Republican congressional leaders. The collections cited herein include: the Robert H. Michel Papers, The Dirksen Congressional Center, Pekin, Illinois (RHM Papers); the Richard K. Armey Collection, Carl Albert Research Center Archives, University of Oklahoma, Norman, Oklahoma (RKA); the Mickey H. Edwards Collection, Carl Albert Research Center Archives, University of Oklahoma, Norman, Oklahoma (MHE); and the Papers of Representative Newt Gingrich, Special Collections, University of West Georgia (NLG).

9. We do not consider a fourth tactic, obstruction, as Michel generally did not practice it, though Gingrich and his allies sometimes did. Matthew N. Green, *Underdog Politics: The Minority Party in the U.S. House of Representatives* (New Haven, CT: Yale University Press, 2015).

10. Congressional Quarterly, "GOP Seeks Fruits of Victory as 97th Convenes," *CQ Almanac 1981*, 37th ed. (Washington, DC: Congressional Quarterly Press, 1982), 3–11.

11. Irwin Arieff, "House Democrats, GOP Elect Leaders, Draw Battle Lines," *Congressional Quarterly Weekly Report*, December 13, 1980, 3549.

12. Fred W. Beuttler interview with RHM, September 6, 2007, RHM Papers, Post-Congressional Series, f. Subjects: Interviews (2), 28.

13. David T. Canon, "The Institutionalization of Leadership in the United States Congress," in *New Perspectives on the House of Representatives*, 4th ed., ed. Robert L. Peabody and Nelson W. Polsby (Baltimore: Johns Hopkins University Press, 1992), 306.

14. John Farrell, *Tip O'Neill and the Democratic Century* (Boston: Little, Brown and Company, 2001), 627.

15. Trent Lott, *Herding Cats: A Life in Politics* (New York: HarperCollins, 2005).

16. Beuttler interview with RHM, September 6, 2007, 12; Congressional Quarterly, "97th Took Bold Steps to Reduce Federal Role," *CQ Almanac 1981*, 37th ed. (Washington, DC: Congressional Quarterly Press, 1982), 14–32.

17. "House Republican Policy Positions," RHM Papers, Staff Series: Billy Pitts Files, f. Republican Conference, 1982–84 (2).

18. Green, *Underdog Politics*, 150–151.

19. RHM and Trent Lott to Rufus Wilson, April 18, 1984, RHM Papers, Leadership Series, Box 6, f. 98th Research Committee.

20. Steven Pressman, "Can Reagan Win with Congress? President's Leadership Style and Split in GOP Ranks are Key to Second-Term Success," *CQ Weekly*, October 27, 1984, 2781–2786.

21. Don Wolfensberger, "Open vs. Restrictive Rules in the House, 94th–113th Congresses," *Bipartisan Policy Center*, bipartisanpolicy.org/wp-content/uploads/2015/10/houserules.pdf.

22. Douglas B. Harris, "Let's Play Hardball: Congressional Partisanship in the Television Era," in *Politics to the Extreme: American Political Institutions in the Twenty-First Century*, ed. Scott A. Frisch and Sean Q Kelly (New York: Palgrave Macmillan, 2013).

23. Alan Ehrenhalt, "Media, Power Shifts Dominate O'Neill's House," *CQ Weekly*, September 13, 1986, 2131–2138.

24. Margaret Shapiro and Dan Balz, "House Seats McCloskey," *Washington Post*, May 2, 1985.

25. Janet Hook, "House's 1980 'Reagan Robots' Face Crossroads," *CQ Weekly*, August 13, 1988, 2262–2265.

26. Ed Gillespie, *Winning Right: Campaign Politics and Conservative Policies* (New York: Threshold Editions, 2006), 42–43.

27. Phil Kuntz, "GOP Moderates Take a Hit in Caucus Elections," *CQ Weekly*, December 12, 1992, 3781.

28. Beuttler interview with RHM, September 6, 2007, 34.

29. See, e.g., RHM Papers, Staff Series: Shelly White, folders NAFTA Correspondence, NAFTA Democratic Whips, and Pitts Working Group.

30. Richard E. Cohen, "Frustrated House Republicans Seek More Aggressive Strategy for 1984 and Beyond," *National Journal*, March 3, 1984; Haynes Johnson and David Broder, *The System: The American Way of Politics at the Breaking Point* (Boston: Little, Brown, 1997).

31. Cook, *Making Laws and Making News.*

32. John B. Gilmour, *Strategic Disagreement: Stalemate in American Politics* (Pittsburgh: University of Pittsburgh Press, 1995); Anthony King, *Running Scared: Why America's Politicians Campaign Too Much and Govern Too Little* (New York: The Free Press, 1997).

33. Johnson to RHM, June 11, 1981, RHM Papers, Press Series, f. Memoranda, 1981–1988 (1).

34. Pitts to Johnson, January 12, 1981, "Subject: Press Relations," RHM Papers, Press Series, f. Memoranda, 1981–1988 (1).

35. Dear Republican Colleague letter, "Budget," February 19, 1982, RHM Papers, Leadership Series, Box 4, f. 97th Congress, Dear Colleague.

36. RHM to "Dear Editor," April 23, 1981, RHM Papers, Leadership Series, Box 4, f. 97th Congress, Dear Colleague.

37. Newt Gingrich to RHM, "RE: Using the budget battle so that we can win the American people in the 1982 election," April 29, 1982, RHM Papers, Press Series, f. Memoranda, 1981–1988 (2).

38. Mike [Johnson] to Bob, "Re: The Gingrich Memorandum," May 5, 1982, RHM Papers, Press Series, f. Memoranda, 1981–1988 (2).

39. Mike Johnson, Memorandum for Bob, January 5, 1983, RHM Papers, Press Series f. Memoranda, 1981–1988 (2).

40. Dear Republican Colleague letter, September 28, 1983, RHM Papers, Leadership Series, Box 6, f. 98th Congress, Dear Colleague.

41. See, e.g., Dear Republican Colleague Letter, April 29, 1985, RHM Papers, Leadership Series, Box 9, f. 99th Congress, Joint Letters; and "A House Corrupted," May 5, 1988, RHM Papers, Staff Series: David Kehl, Box 12, f. Republican Party—House (2).

42. Green, *Underdog Politics*, 73, 106, 208 n. 8.

43. RHM to Trent Lott, May 6, 1986, RHM Papers, Press Series, f. Subjects: News Media—National.

44. Jerry Climer to Mike Johnson, "Re: Leadership Staff Session," March 17, 1986, RHM Papers, Press Series, f. Subjects: Republican Leadership Staff.

45. In the 100th Congress, these issues included agriculture, budget, defense, social policy, and trade. In seeking to build a coalition for Contra aid in the 100th Congress, for example, Michel's office sought to model their plan on the "legislative/political/media strategy" in place in the 99th Congress. See Jerry Climer to Mike Johnson, "Re: Leadership Staff Session," March 17, 1986, RHM Papers, Press Series, f. Subjects: Republican Leadership Staff; Mike Johnson to RHM, "Subject: Legislative/Media Strategy for Contras," March 15, 1987, RHM Papers, Press Series, f. Memoranda 1981–1988 (3).

46. Janet Hook, "House GOP Prepares for Leadership Shuffle," *CQ Weekly*, May 16, 1987, 959–963.

47. Connelly and Pitney, *Congress' Permanent Minority?* 50.

48. Project Majority Task Force, "Report to the Honorable Robert Michel," Re: Television Response, November 10, 1987, MHE, Box 82, f. 17.

49. Dear Colleague letter from Michel and Lewis, November 21, 1989, RHM Papers, Leadership Series, Box 13, f. Dear Republican Colleague Notebook, 1989 (2).

50. "Management Model for Republican Leadership," RHM Papers, Legislative Series, Special Subjects, Other Special Subjects, Box 6, f. 103rd Congress. Reform. Republican Leadership Management Model.

51. "Confidential Draft: Management Model for Republican Leadership," RHM Papers, Legislative Series, Special Subjects, Other Special Subjects, Box 6, f. 103rd Congress. Reform. Republican Leadership Management Model.

52. "What specific functions should be added to the responsibilities of the House Republican Leadership?" RHM Papers, Legislative Series, Special Subjects, Other Special Subjects, Box 6, f. 103rd Congress. Reform. Grandy-Gunderson Task Force on Republican Leadership.

53. "Management Model for Republican Leadership," RHM Papers, Legislative Series, Special Subjects, Other Special Subjects, Box 6, f. 103rd Congress. Reform. Republican Leadership Management Model.

54. Although it is difficult to ascertain the moment of origin for such internal party organizations, the planning documents, rosters, and Michel's own "Dear Republican Colleague" letter encouraging participation in the effort indicates that the Theme Team, originally dubbed the "Theme and Truth (TNT) Team," was created in Michel's office in the fall of 1991; see John Feehery, "TnT Team;" "Leader's Fall Strategy," September 24, 1991; "Theme Team," October 8, 1991; and RHM, Dear Republican Colleague, November 14, 1991, NLG, Box 2684, f. Theme of the Week.

55. "Communications in High Gear," RKA, Box 57, f. 21; "Message and Communications Programs," RKA, Box 57, f. 21.

56. "A Blueprint for Leadership," Office of the Republican Leader, April 16, 1993, RHM Papers, Leadership Files, Box 16, f. Leadership, 103rd Congress, "A Blueprint for Leadership."

57. Dear Republican Colleague, "Clinton Tax Package," May 17, 1993, RHM Papers, Leadership Series, Box 16, f. 103rd Congress. Dear Republican Colleague Notebook, 1993.

58. See chapter 4 in this volume by Scott R. Meinke.

59. "House Leadership and Party Organizations," RHM Papers, Leadership Series, Box 6, f. 98th Congress. National Republican Congressional Committee.

60. Robin Kolodny, *Pursuing Majorities: Congressional Campaign Committees in American Politics* (Norman: University of Oklahoma Press, 1998).

61. Dear Republican Colleague letter, undated [October 1982], RHM Papers, Leadership Series, Box 4, f. 97th Congress. Dear Colleague.

62. RHM to Richard Lugar, May 3, 1984, RHM Papers, Campaigns and Politics Series, Box 39, f. Republican National Convention 1984 (1).

63. See Jerry Climer to Mike Johnson, "Re: Leadership Staff Session," March 17, 1986, RHM Papers, Press Series, f. Subjects: Republican Leadership Staff.

64. "The Republican Congress: A Manifesto for Change in the House of Representatives," RHM Papers, Leadership Series, Box 15, f. 102nd Congress.

65. Office of Republican Leader, "A Blueprint for Leadership," April 16, 1993, RHM Papers, Leadership Series, Box 16, f. 103rd Congress, "A Blueprint for Leadership."

66. Office of Republican Leader, "A Blueprint for Leadership," April 16, 1993, RHM Papers, Leadership Series, Box 16, f. 103rd Congress, "A Blueprint for Leadership."

67. Green, *Underdog Politics*, 67; Donald R. Wolfensberger, *Congress and the People: Deliberative Democracy on Trial* (Washington, DC: Woodrow Wilson Center Press, 2000), 167–168.

68. Mickey Edwards to Ed Rollins, June 5, 1989, MHE, Box 44, f. 1.

69. Robert Walker, Letter to the Editor, March 29, 1989, RHM Papers, Legislative Series, Special Subjects, Legal Cases, Box 2, f. Gingrich, Newt.

70. Dennis Hastert, *Speaker: Lessons from Forty Years in Coaching and Politics* (Washington, DC: Regnery Publishing, 2004), 108.

71. Eleanor Clift and Tom Brazaitis, *War without Bloodshed: The Art of Politics* (New York: Charles Scribner's Sons, 1996), 227; Lee, *Beyond Ideology*, 35–36.

72. Richard E. Cohen, "Frustrated House Republicans Seek More Aggressive Strategy for 1984 and Beyond," *National Journal*, March 3, 1984.

73. Eric Pianin, "House GOP's Frustrations Intensify," *Washington Post*, December 21, 1987.

74. As Michel later put it, "I knew that I'd certainly have to make do with Newt as my Whip." RHM Papers, Personal, Box 2, f. Memoir Notes, 38.

75. Green, *Underdog Politics*.

76. RHM and Trent Lott to Newt Gingrich, March 25, 1981, RHM Papers, Leadership Series, Box 4, f. 97th Congress, Republican Task Forces.

77. Mike Johnson to RHM and Trent Lott, May 18, 1981, RHM Papers, Press Series, f. Memoranda, 1981–1988 (1).

78. Mike to Bob, June 11, 1981, RHM Papers, Press Series, f. Memoranda, 1981–1988 (1).

79. Mike to Bob, May 5, 1982, "Re: The Gingrich Memorandum," RHM Papers, Press Series, f. Memoranda, 1981–1988 (2).

80. Mike to Bob, September 20, 1981, RHM Papers, Press Series, f. Memoranda, 1981–1988 (1).

81. Newt Gingrich to RHM, April 29, 1982, RHM Papers, Press Series, f. Memoranda, 1981–1988 (1).

82. Mike to Bob, March 9, 1987, "Subject: Republican themes for New York and beyond," RHM Papers, Press Series, f. Memoranda, 1981–1988 (3).

83. Diane Grant, "Perspective: Junior House Republicans Seeking 'Zzazip,'" *CQ Weekly*, November 5, 1983.

84. Jane Mayer and Robert W. Merry, "Saving Tax Overhaul Will Require the President to Mollify Republicans, Not Alienate Democrats," *Wall Street Journal*, December 16, 1985.

85. RHM to the Editor of the *New Ulm Journal*, June 1, 1984, RHM, General Series, Box 24, f. 1984 News Media.

86. Dear Republican Colleague, "Camera Coverage of Special Orders," May 11, 1984, RHM Papers, Leadership Series, Box 6, f. 98th Congress. Dear Colleague.

87. Steven V. Roberts, "Forging Alliances to Get Minority's Plans Passed," *New York Times*, December 22, 1985.

88. However, there were rumors that Michel was "intimidated" by Gingrich and fellow hard-liners into being more aggressive against Democrats over the contested election in Indiana ("Gerrymandered Dynasty," *Wall Street Journal*, May 1, 1985). See

also Mel Steely, *The Gentleman from Georgia: The Biography of Newt Gingrich* (Macon, GA: Mercer University Press, 2000), 167.

89. John B. Barry, *The Ambition and the Power* (New York: Penguin, 1989), 158.

90. Roberts, "Forging Alliances to Get Minority's Plans Passed."

91. Letter to Julian Dixon, May 26, 1988, and list of co-signers of the Gingrich letter, NLG, Box 673, f. Ethics Handout.

92. Gingrich note to Michel, December 20, 1987, RHM Papers, Staff Series; David Kehl, Box 12, f. Republican Party–House (3).

93. "The House," *CQ Weekly* 1992; Newt to RHM, April 9, 1992, RHM Papers, Legislative Series, Special Subjects, Other Special Subjects, Box 4, f. 102nd Congress Reform, Michel Proposal.

94. Janet Hook, "Gingrich Finds Rhetoric Must Toe Party Line" *CQ Weekly*, July 22, 1989, 1833.

95. Janet Hook, "Republican Contests Reflect Election Woes, Party Rift," *CQ Weekly*, December 1, 1990, 3997.

96. Robert Walker, Letter to the Editor, March 29, 1989, RHM Papers, Legislative Series, Special Subjects, Legal Cases, Box 2, f. Gingrich, Newt.

97. Note to Bob Michel, May 2, 1989, RHM Papers, Leadership Series, Box 13, f. 101st Congress: Leadership Meeting Notes (1). Gingrich was probably referring to an unexpected defeat of a Democratic spending amendment to the Fiscal Year 1989 supplemental spending bill (David Rapp, "Democrats Stage a Retreat on FY 89 Supplemental," *CQ Weekly Report*, April 29, 1989).

98. Janet Hook and Thomas H. Moore, "Speculation Rampant in House as Michel Weighs Retirement," *CQ Weekly*, September 11, 1993, 2371.

99. RHM and Tom Loeffler to Dear Republican Colleague, August 8, 1984, RHM Papers, Leadership Series, Box 6, f. 98th Congress, Dear Colleague.

100. RHM, Newt Gingrich, Richard Armey, and Henry Hyde to Tom Foley, March 19, 1993, "Special Orders," RHM Papers, Leadership Series, Box 16, f. 103rd Congress, Joint Letters.

101. Eric Pianin, "House GOP's Frustrations Intensify," *Washington Post*, December 21, 1987.

102. Kitty Cunningham, "Goodbye 'Generational Gap'" *CQ Weekly*, October 9, 1993, 2716.

CHAPTER 6

LEADING THE MINORITY

Guiding Policy Change through Legislative Waters

Andrew J. Taylor

For Minority Leader Bob Michel, shepherding the beginnings of the "Reagan Revolution" through the Democratic-controlled House was undeniably a major achievement. But the remaining six terms Bob Michel sat atop the Republican Conference presented him with other, and sometimes equally significant, legislative challenges. He was called upon to move the comprehensive agendas of two Republican presidents—George H. W. Bush as well as Ronald Reagan—and, as we shall see, some of that of a Democrat, Bill Clinton. Particularly during the two years he led House Republicans on Clinton's watch, Michel also worked to revise and obstruct legislation. All of this entailed not just a command of strategy but also an encyclopedic knowledge of policy. Michel oversaw measures that contributed to the end of the Cold War and authorized the prosecution of the Gulf War, unleashed free trade in North America, overhauled Social Security and the federal tax code, reformed criminal justice, expanded opportunities for people with disabilities, ameliorated ballooning budget deficits, and touched upon a multitude of other policy areas. Cumulatively these legislative accomplishments altered American life dramatically. He was responsible, in ways both great and small, for most of the landmark laws of the 1980s and early 1990s.[1]

Michel and Foreign Policy

Foreign affairs were never thought of as central to Michel's policy interests. He is remembered foremost as a master of process—a legislative tactician and coalition-builder. His personal policy interests focused on the economy and government expenditures; prior to becoming Republican Leader he sat on the House Appropriations Committee for twenty-two years, twelve of them as ranking member of the Subcommittee on Labor, Health, Education, and Welfare. The 18th District of Illinois is only 500 miles east of the physical center of the country, and Michel's constituents were overwhelmingly native born, middle class, and Protestant, the type who generally had little interest in international events.[2] Peoria, Michel's hometown, has always been associated with bread-and-butter insular matters. John Ehrlichman, a top aide to President Richard Nixon, famously asked whether an administration policy proposal would be enthusiastically received there, using the city as a bellwether of American public opinion to road-test a plan to bolster the economy. The phrase "Will it play in Peoria?" has been used by politicians in this manner ever since. The district was integrated into the global economy somewhat, largely as home to the construction equipment giant Caterpillar, and Michel was fully aware of the perils of war and the need to confront foreign nemeses—he had participated in the Normandy invasion in 1944 and was later wounded in the Battle of the Bulge. But the minority leader certainly did not have the conventional credentials and experience of a steward of American foreign policy.

Michel's election as GOP minority leader (a title he renamed "Republican Leader" when he took the office) and the events of the 1980s and early 1990s thrust him into such a role, however. Although the administrations of Ronald Reagan, George H. W. Bush, and Bill Clinton clearly forged US policy, Michel's leadership in the House and of his oft-divided GOP Conference was pivotal. Behind the scenes, he produced the Republican votes essential to the country's transition from the Cold War to globalization and to what Bush called a "New World Order." He corralled obstreperous colleagues into coalitions that enabled a huge expansion in American military capability at the end of the Cold War while simultaneously resisting, in the wake of large deficits and deep cuts to domestic programs, administration efforts to go further. More conspicuously, Michel advocated for the traditional liberal international regime against emerging isolationism and worked to check presidential power when he thought it threatened the constitutional system. Four episodes are particularly important to an understanding of Michel's prominence in foreign and national security policymaking during his seven-term tenure at the helm of the House minority.

The first is the Reagan defense buildup and the end of the Cold War. Between 1981 and 1989 nominal federal outlays for defense almost doubled, rising to more than $300 billion when Reagan left office. The huge investment was consistent with the president's philosophy that the Soviet Union was the "Evil Empire," and it underwrote the effort to finally win the Cold War, largely through research and accelerated production of new weapons like the MX missile, B-1 bomber, and, especially, the Strategic Defense Initiative (SDI).[3] It was funded by annual budget resolutions and appropriations and reauthorization bills that had to wend their way through Congress.

Reagan's national security stance had a significant amount of support among House Republican defense hawks who shared his deep animosity toward communism and the Soviets. These included the ranking member of the Armed Services Committee, Bill Dickinson of Alabama, as well as Floyd Spence of South Carolina, Bob Stump of Arizona, and the southern Californians Robert Badham, Bob Dornan, and Duncan Hunter. Melvin Price (D-IL), the committee's chair until after the 1984 elections, did little to provide partisan opposition to the president's agenda, and there were many House Democrats who assisted efforts to pass the administration's proposals, particularly senior members of the Armed Services Committee who were either traditional Cold Warriors or desirous of the lavish pork the panel dished out.[4] Still, generating the votes for Reagan on the appropriations and authorizations bills that were required to support his defense ambitions was not easy. As early as the fall of 1981, fiscal and political pressures began to crimp the endeavor. Michel acted as a go-between, communicating the wishes of his moderate and liberal members to offset Reagan's proposed cuts to domestic programs forced upon him by looming deficits with reductions to the defense budget. Amending his role as "the handmaiden of the president,"[5] Michel, in his trademark understated style, told the White House that "I have to be very practical about what is achievable and what isn't."[6] But he was not unsympathetic. As he explained on the House floor in October 1981: "We cannot allow this budget debate to proceed along the lines of pitting the defense budget against the non-defense budget. We must approach the defense budget with one question in mind: Is this budget adequate to meet our national security needs?" Michel said he would back certain cuts but warned against "balancing the budget not only on the backs, but possibly on the graves of young Americans in our armed forces."[7] The balancing act became considerably more difficult when he faced a minirevolt within his party. During debate on the FY 1983 budget, about a dozen conservative

House Republicans backed a successful amendment to shift defense funds to Medicare in protest of their leadership's opposition to a White House–backed budget plan that protected defense and ostensibly balanced the budget with deep cuts on the domestic side offered by their colleague John H. Rousselot (R-CA).[8]

By the time the House was considering the FY 1985 budget in March 1984, Michel felt so constrained by the nation's ballooning debt, fissures in his Conference, and anxiety about upcoming elections (intensified by bitter memories of the loss of twenty-six seats in 1982) that he told the president proposed defense expenditures must be reduced by $75 billion over the following three years.[9] Not least because of his tireless lobbying, however, the MX missile—a perennial target of Democrats—narrowly survived an effort in the House to block production entirely by just six votes in May 1984.[10] Toward the end of Reagan's presidency, Michel, again the loyal soldier, had pivoted somewhat and embraced the administration's argument that it was the defense buildup that had generated pressure necessary for comprehensive arms control agreements.[11] He now supported administration efforts to continue investments in systems like MX and SDI, even when many Republicans, including Dickinson, the top Republican on Armed Services, pushed to divert resources to traditional military hardware like tanks and helicopters.[12] Michel strongly urged the president to veto a defense authorization bill in the summer of 1988 because the legislation, by greatly reducing support for MX and SDI, dangerously undermined military capacity and the president's strategic position in negotiations with the Soviet Union over the Intermediate-Range Nuclear Forces and START Treaties.[13] Reagan acted on the advice and ultimately signed a version of the measure that inserted greater funding for the weapons systems.

The second episode is Iran-Contra and Reagan's policies toward Central America and the Middle East that preceded it. As an ardent Cold Warrior, the president worked to prevent the spread of communism and opposed insurgent groups and regimes allied with the Soviet Union. Nowhere was this more evident than in the Western Hemisphere. The United States aided right-wing governments facing communist rebels in El Salvador and Guatemala and in 1983 invaded the Caribbean island of Grenada to reinstate its constitution after a Cuba-backed coup. In Nicaragua, the CIA supported Contra rebels that opposed the communist Sandinista government. Following the mining of several Nicaraguan harbors in early 1984, Congress moved to prohibit the CIA and Department of Defense's financial assistance to the group. The so-called Boland Amendment (named after its House sponsor, Edward P. Boland [D-MA]) had originally been passed in 1982 as an effort to prevent arming the Contras, but by the spring of 1984 Democrats were pushing vigorously to prohibit any conceivable kind of military support to the rebels.

Unlike Republican leaders in the Senate, Michel initially stood stridently behind the administration's support of the Contras' military operations. In April, calling the mining episode "a non-binding media event,"[14] he was unable to prevent a lopsided vote on a House resolution condemning the rebels' actions. Just sixteen months later, however, following Reagan's offer to link renewed aid to a peace plan and an antagonistic visit to Moscow by Nicaragua's president, Daniel Ortega, Michel led a charge to reinstate US support so long as it was not deployed for military purposes. After building a coalition including fifty-eight Democrats to defeat an extension of Boland's ban, an amendment Michel sponsored to provide $27 million in humanitarian assistance to the Contras passed by a margin of 248–184. The Republican Leader's passionate enunciation of core Cold War principles won the day. "Where and when do you finally draw the line on our southern border?" he asked. "You tell us we should talk. Well, the communists never listen to talk unless it's backed up by force."[15]

This was not Michel's most famous hour on Contra aid. In March 1986, the House rejected the president's request for $100 million of assistance to the rebels. The measure failed because Democratic leaders promised a future vote on a compromise. In April, the Democratic leadership attempted to usher through its supplemental appropriations bill with what they believed would be a now bipartisan and uncontroversial amendment to greatly reduce the proportion of the $100 million that could be used for military purposes. Simultaneously, Michel directed his fellow Republicans to support a more liberal alternative that effectively stripped the bill of all support for the rebels. The goal was to get a clean, up-or-down vote on Reagan's original request. "I think the president deserves better treatment than what we would propose to be giving him here today by this sham charade," Michel said on the House floor as Republican colleagues rose to their feet in support.[16] After Democratic leaders pulled the supplemental appropriations bill, Michel decided to pursue a discharge petition to force the administration proposal to a vote. The gambit paid off again. Democratic leaders allowed the measure to come up as an amendment when they reintroduced the urgent supplemental in late June. It passed, albeit narrowly. Reagan's lobbying was clearly important in getting fifty-one Democratic votes for the measure, but Michel's leadership was also critical to success. This was quintessential Michel, reveling in the fusion of strategy and policy, working tirelessly and selflessly behind the scenes to secure a victory for his party and his president.[17] "I just think we did the right thing for the long haul," he said.[18]

Unlike Central America, US policy toward the Middle East was, by the time Reagan captured the White House, largely separated from Cold War considerations. Michel's support for the president's course of action, however, was generally undiminished. He was a vocal cheerleader for the retaliatory bombing of Muammar Qaddafi's Libya in 1986, characterizing the action, what he called a response to "unconscionable acts of terrorism," as typical of a "new kind of war" that necessitated "going over the threshold."[19] During the early fall of 1981, in the first real failure of the Reagan agenda in the House, Michel was unable to assuage colleagues' concerns about Israel's security interests and to prevent the passage of a formal resolution of disapproval for the administration's sale of the Airborne Warning and Control System, or AWACS, to Saudi Arabia. One hundred and eight House Republicans deserted the president, although the transaction was rescued when a similar resolution was later rejected by the Senate.

Following the Israeli invasion of Lebanon in 1982, the United States committed to providing Marines for a multinational peacekeeping force there. In October 1983, just six months after seventeen foreign-service and military personnel were killed by a suicide bomb at the embassy in Beirut, 241 marines died in a larger explosion at their barracks on the edge of the city's airport. Michel had found it relatively easy to keep Republicans together and to work with Speaker Tip O'Neill (D-MA) to support a resolution approving a continuation of the Marines' mission under the War Powers Act in late September.[20] But working to block an amendment to a defense appropriations bill that would have withdrawn funding for the operation just nine days after the barracks bombing was much tougher. The minority leader gave an impassioned floor speech in which he said the Marines should be granted their request to "do the job that the commander in chief has asked them to do."[21] By early January 1984, however, Michel began suggesting the administration reassess its decision to keep troops in Lebanon.[22] Under continued political pressure and unable to articulate clearly the purpose of the Marines' continued presence, the commander in chief reversed himself. The troops came home in February.

American policies toward the Middle East and Central America were fused in dramatic fashion by the Iran-Contra scandal. In late 1986, Congress and the country began to learn of a secret deal to sell arms to Iran for the release of Western hostages held in Lebanon that was made by members and staff of the National Security Council. The proceeds were then funneled to the Contra rebels in Nicaragua. The news made it considerably more difficult for Michel to support the president. Both chambers of Congress established committees to investigate the affair. Michel was charged with appointing six of the fifteen members to the House panel and strategically, if somewhat surprisingly, chose a mix of old hands, committee leaders, and junior members. Dick Cheney (R-WY) was made ranking member, a decision that helped propel him into a leadership position on foreign policy within the party. Under him was a combination of Reagan stalwarts like Michigan's William Broomfield and Henry Hyde of Illinois, the ranking members on Foreign Affairs and Intelligence, and younger, more charismatic (charisma was seen as important because the hearings were to be televised) legislators like Jim Courter (R-NJ) and Bill McCollum (R-FL).[23] Michel deferred greatly to Cheney throughout the process. When he did comment publicly about the investigation, he was characteristically measured, tempering his natural support for the president with a dash of political realism. In response to the independent Tower Commission that criticized Reagan for his "hands-off" leadership style and poor management of staff, Michel called on the president to "improve the effectiveness of his administration and ensure sound policy decisions."[24] Wandering public attention and the conclusion of the House hearings in August 1987 permitted Michel to resume a slightly more vigorous defense. He dismissed the House panel's work as "interesting theater" and called for Congress to move beyond it.[25] Together with Cheney, he was able to prevent Democrats from extending the hearings into 1988 and the presidential campaign season. The approach, however, generated criticism from Republicans who felt the administration had heaped unnecessary political pressure on them and sacrificed the conservative domestic agenda to a reckless foreign policy. One of Michel's colleagues anonymously told a reporter after the House panel concluded its work, "I think there is a feeling Bob needs to be reminded he is our leader first before he is the protector and defender of the White House."[26]

Michel persisted in his support of Reagan's fight for Contra aid as well, although now his efforts proved unsuccessful. In March 1987, with the scandal eroding support for the policy, the minority leader could do little to stop seventeen Republicans from voting with the vast majority of Democrats to pass a moratorium on assistance to the Contras until the administration provided a full accounting of previously appropriated funds. "This debate is about responsible United States policy in Central America," he said. "It is about the United States keeping promises. It is about United States reliability. It is about an old-fashioned word called 'honor.'" To support the moratorium, he concluded, was an "inexcusable retreat from a firm, workable United States policy toward Central America."[27] Eleven months later, the House rejected another endeavor to continue military aid and defeated Reagan's biggest foreign policy objective of his final year in office.[28] The following month, Democratic leaders were successful in their attempt to add an amendment replacing a much scaled-down version of the administration's proposal for military assistance with a package of humanitarian aid, only for the House to then reject the altered bill. Many Republicans, in a reprise of the tactic Michel used two years earlier, voted with liberal Democrats to defeat it.[29] This proved to be the end for US financial support of the Contras. The rebels quickly dissolved, many supporting the successful political effort in 1990 to defeat Ortega and the Sandinistas at the ballot box.

With George H. W. Bush's promotion to the Oval Office, Michel continued his work as a loyal foot soldier to the president's foreign policy agenda. The House Republican Leader was steadfast in his support of the administration's diplomatic and military efforts to capture and overthrow Panama's leader, Manuel Noriega, in 1989 and 1990.[30] Bush's most important foreign policy achievement and our third episode was, however, the defeat of Saddam Hussein's Iraq in the Gulf War of 1991. Michel's role in securing House approval for the administration's use of military force was crucial. Throughout the last third of 1990, Bush, Secretary of State James Baker, and Secretary of Defense Dick Cheney worked to shore up a defense of Saudi Arabia and forge a large multinational coalition to oppose Hussein. The activity in the House took place largely within the Committee on Foreign Affairs, but Michel worked back channels to help obtain the body's approval for any military course of action should diplomatic efforts fail. A week into the new year (1991), it seemed unlikely that the Iraqi leader would meet a UN Security Council deadline to withdraw from Kuwait by January 15. On January 10, prompted by a letter from the president requesting congressional assent to proceed with military action, the House began a solemn debate over a resolution, cosponsored by Michel and liberal Stephen J. Solarz (D-NY), that would ultimately authorize Bush to use "all necessary means"—essentially a 400,000 strong force that was in the region—the Security Council had stated would be the consequence for Hussein's recalcitrance. Michel worked his Conference and spoke passionately in favor of war. Invoking the disastrous Munich Conference of 1938, he exclaimed: "Those of our generation know from bloody experience that unchecked aggression against a small nation is a prelude to international disaster."[31] But in reality, Bush's skillful diplomacy and compelling argument won the day. In the lead-up to the vote, a series of prominent Democrats, including a number of committee chairs, said they had lost patience with the existing sanctions regime and would support a military effort.[32] Ultimately, 250 members voted for the Michel-Solarz resolution.

A week later, Michel worked with Speaker Tom Foley (D-WA) to author a resolution praising Bush's decision to initiate Operation Desert Storm and supporting the troops who were executing it. Foley had initially wished to avoid formally commending the president, but the minority leader, following the lead of Senate Republicans, pushed for the inclusion of such language.[33] Michel, who was repeatedly briefed by Secretary of Defense Cheney and the chair of the Joint Chiefs of Staff, Colin Powell, also vocally supported the administration's operational decisions and extended use of an air campaign before invading Kuwait with ground troops.[34]

By the late spring of 1991, however, it was becoming increasingly difficult to mobilize congressional support for President Bush's foreign policy. A supplemental appropriations bill requested by the administration to pay for the Gulf War passed comfortably in March 1991, but there were murmurs from many, including Republicans, that allies needed to pay their share.[35] By May, with a recession nearly a year old, the Democratic majority beat back Michel's efforts to substitute a considerably more generous version of the House leadership's defense authorization bill. Michel's impassioned reference on the floor to the Pentagon's smashing victory just three months earlier fell on deaf ears.[36]

It was a sign of deeper trouble. Michel had spent his congressional career supporting the bipartisan foreign policy consensus. Built on strident anticommunism, the approach advocated a basic internationalism and America's sacrifice for its allies and principles like democracy and human rights. It also succored postwar liberal international institutions like the International Monetary Fund, World Bank, NATO, and the UN. After the Gulf War and with the death of the Soviet Union just ten months later, many American elites, particularly in the Republican Party, began to challenge this consensus. The GOP's foreign policy establishment, of which Bush and Michel were integral members, was rocked on its heels.

The fourth and final episode gave Michel an opportunity to work across the aisle to support the liberal postwar international order. As it has throughout American history, trade made several appearances on the congressional agenda during the Reagan-Bush years. Michel worked to push through the Uruguay Round of the General Agreement on Tariffs and Trade (GATT) in 1986 and the US-Canada Free Trade Agreement in 1988, both important liberalizations of the country's trade policy.[37] When he opposed trade and American investment overseas, Michel's position was the result of other local and unrelated matters, as with the decision to go against Reagan and assist in subjecting the apartheid regime in South Africa to economic sanctions.[38]

But it was on the North American Free Trade Agreement (NAFTA), negotiated by Bush but requiring congressional approval under Clinton, that Michel struck the biggest blow for international liberal economic principles. NAFTA also revealed how high the level of opposition to the postwar global structure had risen within the Republican Party. Throughout the process, Michel struggled with opponents from the right, left, and center— during the floor debate on passage he called the agreement's chief adversaries (Ross Perot, Pat Buchanan, and Ralph Nader) the "Groucho, Chico, and Harpo of NAFTA politics."[39] Perot was more popular in the country— many Americans shared with him the fear that, as it drained American jobs, NAFTA would give off a "giant sucking sound"—but Buchanan's hostility was more problematic because he was a Republican. The former Nixon speechwriter had challenged Bush for the party's 1992 presidential nomination and, after winning at least a quarter of the vote in most states that voted on or before Super Tuesday, he secured himself a sounding board at the convention in Houston. The "America first" concept that was so prominent in Buchanan's message picked up support within the House GOP Conference, bringing with it vocal "no" votes to NAFTA from prominent members like Dan Burton (R-IN), Duncan Hunter (R-CA), Ralph Regula (R-OH), Gerald Solomon (R-NY), and Don Young (R-AK). Some of this Republican opposition to trade liberalization was gone by the time the House got to vote on strengthening GATT in a lame-duck session of the 103rd Congress in late 1994, not least because it included a comprehensive deal on services.[40] But by then, Michel was a lame duck himself. The GATT vote represented the last legislation of any significance he worked on in the House.[41]

It might not be an understatement to say that, without Michel, NAFTA would have been defeated. The principal lobbying operation in the House was run out of his office by top aide Billy Pitts. Pitts's work was critical to coordinating strategy at the staff level. He headed frequent meetings of a large group of seasoned Washington operatives like the Chamber of Commerce's Nick Calio. Members then identified legislators believed to be persuadable and intensely lobbied their staffers. Michel tasked the GOP Conference secretary, Tom DeLay (R-TX), and David Dreier (R-MO) with leading a grassroots and media campaign and the Conference chair, Dick Armey (R-TX), with authoring and disseminating a series of "Dear Colleague" letters to Republican waverers. Newt Gingrich (R-GA) was his lieutenant throughout and took to the task with typical gusto.[42] The targets included many on the other side, and Gingrich began organizing cross-party whip meetings with pro-NAFTA Democrats like Robert Matsui (D-CA) and Bill Richardson (D-NM). Michel also recruited friendly GOP governors to pressure their delegations and orchestrated a letter to colleagues just before the vote that was signed by the four living former Republican presidents. These efforts were particularly important after lawmakers returned from their August recess, many of them pressured by constituents worried about the effects of the accord.[43] Ultimately, NAFTA needed GOP votes to pass, with 132 Republicans among the 234 House members who supported it. Victory constituted an undeniable triumph for Michel's trademark legislative strategy and less acknowledged grasp of policy.

Michel and Domestic Policy

Many of Michel's legislative accomplishments in the domestic realm are discussed elsewhere in this volume. The big Reagan tax cuts in 1981, the reform to Social Security in 1983, and the once-in-a-generation overhaul of the tax code that came with the Tax Reform Act of 1986 were bills of historical importance, and Michel worked adroitly and indefatigably to help them become law. Much of the rest of his time devoted to fiscal matters was spent attending to the broader budget and its health, especially after the disastrous 1982 midterms. Michel's leadership was required for passage of the 1982 Tax Equity and Fiscal Responsibility Act that reversed some of the tax cuts enacted the previous year; the Gramm–Rudman–Hollings deficit reduction process inaugurated in 1985; and the controversial Omnibus and Budget Reconciliation Act (the Bush budget of 1990) believed to have hurt House Republican candidates that fall.[44]

He stood on the outside looking in when House Democrats squeezed through Clinton's 1993 budget reconciliation bill, in this case leading every member of his party in opposition to both original passage and the Senate-House conference report. Unable to launch what he called a "frontal assault" on the president's plan, Michel allowed its energy tax and entitlement reform provisions to galvanize his members and the divisions within the Democratic Caucus in the Senate to draw the attention of the White House and public.[45] The legislation is believed by some to be a principal cause of the Republicans' stunning success in the 1994 elections.[46]

At least partially because federal resources were severely strained during Michel's tenure as Republican Leader, Congress often turned to regulatory and social issues. A large number of these caught his attention and then consumed his time and energy. I will look at his leadership on six of them here. I believe the cases to be both representative and instructive. They all reveal Michel's broadly recognized strategic acumen, as well as his little-understood grasp of complex policy.

The savings-and-loan (S&L) crisis that preoccupied the banking world during the second half of the 1980s and first few years of the 1990s was tremendously complicated and required policy makers to digest numerous technical details. The matter simmered for a while after the Ohio-based Home State Savings Bank became the first S&L to go under in 1985. A few House Republicans, particularly Jack Hiler (R-IN), Stan Parris (R-VA), and the Californians Jerry Lewis and Al McCandless, raised the alarm and set to work on ameliorative legislation and a campaign strategy to use the issue against Democrats—especially after S&Ls were linked to the scandals surrounding Speaker Jim Wright, Majority Whip Tony Coelho, and the "Keating Five" senators, four of whom were Democrats, two years later.[47] These Republicans were acutely aware that the fraud, essentially underwritten by federal deposit insurance, elicited anger, and they worried that the GOP, with its occupancy of the White House and deep roots in the financial sector, would feel its wrath. Many commentators pointed to legislation passed on Reagan's watch, particularly the Garn–St. Germain Depository Institutions Act of 1982, as an accelerant to the problem. Michel, however, was uncharacteristically slow to smell the danger. He was a bystander as the House replaced a $15 billion bailout bill pushed by the Reagan administration with its own $5 billion version that passed almost unanimously in 1987.

It was not until 1989 that the minority leader went to work in earnest, forming a "Savings and Loan Strike Force" led by Hiler and composed of members such as the loyalists and financial experts Hamilton Fish (R-NY), Nancy Johnson (R-CT), and Jim Leach (R-IA). Once focused, he proved a willing and intelligent student. Michel displayed a firm grasp of the issues surrounding the crisis during the passage of the Financial Institutions Reform, Recovery, and Enforcement Act (FIRREA) and continued to devote attention to the matter as its impact became fully understood (according to the Department of Justice, the S&L episode cost $7.7 billion and resulted in 550 criminal convictions between October 1988 and May 1991).[48] Michel's support was critical in assisting the Bush administration and populist Democrats like Henry Gonzalez, chair of the House Committee on Banking, Finance, and Urban Affairs, to pass the contentious FIRREA by a surprisingly comfortable margin.[49] In 1991, Michel played a pivotal role in both House passage and Senate-House conference negotiation of a $30 billion support package for the Resolution Trust Corporation (RTC), the agency supervising the S&L bailout.[50] Two years later, as the episode ground on under a Democratic president, Michel began to dig in his heels and orchestrated successful Republican opposition to another sizeable RTC rescue package.[51]

The S&L crisis assisted the push for campaign finance reform in the early 1990s, another important domestic concern that consumed Michel. The Keating Five and the resignations of both Wright and Coelho in 1989 demonstrated that members received significant financial support from the banking industry and sometimes returned the favor by intervening on its behalf in disputes with federal regulators. Michel frantically counseled his members that "we've got rules and we've got rules," concluding that, although he was unsure of the "doggone fine line," colleagues, if they wanted to "protect" themselves, should keep "well inside the parameters."[52]

Initial campaign finance reform efforts were bipartisan. Two task forces, one on "the congressional code of conduct" and cochaired by Vic Fazio (D-CA) and Lynn Martin (R-IL) and the other focused on "campaign practices" and cochaired by Al Swift (D-WA) and Guy Vander Jagt (R-MI), worked through 1989 and early 1990. Much of their endeavor beyond campaign financing was motivated particularly by the resignation of Speaker Wright in May 1989. (Wright had arranged for bulk sales of his memoir and a sham job for his wife to sidestep House honoraria limits and rules about gifts.)

There were obvious areas of cooperation. Michel, for example, realized that political action committees (PACs) might bolster the Democratic majority, but they gave generously to GOP incumbents as well. Their activities were not overly restricted.[53] During the summer of 1989 the Bush administration proposed, among other items in a broad reform agenda, to eliminate corporate, union, and trade association PACs and to permit parties to coordinate expenditures with candidates. Michel suggested that House Republicans were not "ready to adopt that tight a principle yet,"[54] but the proposal provided considerable momentum to the bipartisan talks.

The effort ultimately broke down in the late spring of 1990, however. Michel felt betrayed by prevaricating Democrats, not least because in 1989 he had left himself vulnerable to criticism from GOP colleagues by publicly stating a willingness to consider spending limits as part of any bipartisan campaign finance overhaul.[55] In June, he responded by introducing ten bills aimed at highlighting Democratic corruption and mismanagement of the House. They contained nascent ideas popular among campaign reformers, such as greater disclosure of donors, limits on union activities, changes to the composition of the Federal Election Commission, and a soft money ban, as well as regulation of members' franking privileges and an effort to change redistricting procedures. In remarks welcoming the League of Women Voters to Capitol Hill, Michel identified three themes running through the reform package: "return power to individuals, instead of special interests; return power to constituents and take it away from big contributors; [and] return competition to House elections."[56] An effort to, in Michel's words, "rid the House of decades of institutional decay and decline and create a new Hill order,"[57] they became part of the Gingrich-led "Project Majority" strategy to gain control of the House in the 1992 elections. Democratic leaders replied with an agenda of their own, one that included reduced limits for PAC donations, government funds to candidates who abide by spending limits, and tax deductions for in-state contributions. Michel upped the ante in a July 7, 1990, *New York Times* op-ed when he wrote that Democrats opposed his party's plans so as to "preserve the system that has given them control of the House for more than thirty years."[58] As he noted, the Democrats liked things as they were. "For them" he explained, "the status quo is good; they're eighty votes out in front."[59]

By the time the Democrats' bill, sponsored by Swift, was ready for the floor in late summer, Michel was in full attack mode. His main goal was to have the bill debated on the floor under an open rule. Aides worked on a detailed media strategy in which Republicans would demonstrate their broad and nonjudgmental approach to reform.[60] "Republicans," Michel claimed, "are for fairness and competition in elections and want an open debate on the connection between the Savings and Loan scandal and the current campaign system's abuses while the Democrats are gagging the House and prohibiting real reform."[61] Democrats ultimately provided him the opportunity to offer a single amendment to restrict PAC donations and activities, but it was inevitably defeated.

With House and Senate Democrats split on the reform effort, however, the issue was ultimately punted into the following 102nd Congress. Concerned by the revelations from the House Bank scandal (in which hundreds of members were caught and several dozen, almost exclusively Democrats, were shown to have particularly abused overdraft privileges), the majority went on the offensive, passing through both chambers legislation that included voluntary spending limits, public financing provisions, and vouchers to purchase television advertising. Michel ended up a spectator, although he was spared the necessity of mobilizing his Republican colleagues by the Senate's widely forecast inability to override Bush's veto of the bill in May 1992.

Michel did not appear especially interested in environmental issues. By the 101st Congress that commenced in 1989, there was intense pressure to amend the Clean Air Act to provide for greater federal regulation over emissions—not least because of the public's increased concerns about acid rain.[62] So as to get out in front of the issue, the Bush administration teamed with John Dingell of Detroit, the Democratic chair of the Committee on Energy and Commerce and longtime supporter of auto manufacturers' interests, to introduce a bill that did much to inject the government into environmental affairs by establishing new and comprehensive permitting and enforcement procedures. The legislation had significant congressional support, and Michel's assistance was not needed by the White House. Instead, the Republican Leader chipped away at it. In early 1989, he worked assiduously to promote complex nationwide cost-sharing among utilities in the bill's acid rain emission reduction plan. Companies like Illinois Power and Central Illinois Public Service had not, unlike power producers in other parts of the country, installed scrubbers in their plants. Without cost-sharing across the entire sector, utilities in central Illinois would each face hundreds of millions of dollars in compliance expenses.[63] Michel ultimately voted for the Clean Air Act Amendments of 1990 (only twenty-two House Republicans did not), but his work with others, especially Phil Sharpe (D-IN), helped generate House support for what became the Byrd-Bond compromise (after Senators Robert Byrd, Democrat of West Virginia, and Christopher Bond, Republican of Missouri). This was an emission trading scheme designed to narrow the interregional economic impacts of acid rain mitigation.

Michel was probably even less stimulated by what we might call social issues. The Americans with Disabilities Act—of which two Democratic versions were introduced in the spring of 1989—presented the Republican Leader with a strategic challenge. The Bush White House supported the effort with reservations, and a number of key GOP allies like the US Chamber of Commerce, perhaps believing there were not the votes to defeat it, tried to get it altered. Steny Hoyer's (D-MD) version rapidly garnered 250 House cosponsors and by September had easily passed the Senate. Michel set to work, securing the opportunity for Republican colleagues to offer amendments and pressuring committees of jurisdiction to move the more liberal House bill closer to its Senate counterpart. He was able to prevail on the Rules Committee to permit the consideration of five Republican amendments during the House floor debate in May 1990. Only two—and they being the most minor—passed. But with the administration silent and unwilling to provide cover, Michel became the reluctant face of opposition. Disabled activists, who had been mobilized throughout the year, publicly targeted him as an obstructionist.[64]

Civil rights put Michel and the Republicans on the back foot as well. In the late 1980s, the United States Supreme Court issued a series of decisions that were interpreted as diluting Title VII of the Civil Rights Act of 1964 by making it more difficult for employees to sue employers for harassment in the workplace, for disparate impact of company policies, and for wrongful dismissal. In 1990, congressional Democrats, led on the issue by Representative Gus Hawkins (D-CA) and Senator Ted Kennedy (D-MA), offered a comprehensive employee rights bill that immediately put the Bush administration and congressional Republicans on the defensive. Working closely with the White House, Michel appointed a House GOP task force on the issue that was chaired by Henry Hyde. It wrote an alternative to demonstrate that the Democrats' bill would have, in the words of a letter written by the president on the day Saddam Hussein invaded Kuwait, "the effect of forcing businesses to adopt quotas" and "foster divisiveness and litigation rather than conciliation."[65] The Republican bill had little chance of progressing, but it helped Michel make his argument that the opposition was unnecessarily antagonistic and would impose unfairly on employers. Twenty-nine House Republicans, mainly from the Northeast and Midwest, voted for the Democratic legislation on original passage the day after Bush's letter, despite the House adopting a Michel motion to instruct its conferees on matters like hiring quotas and limitations on damages. Unsurprisingly, the president ultimately vetoed the bill. In the narrowest of votes, and even with eleven Republicans bucking him, Bush's action was sustained.

Sensing how close they had come, and after picking up seats in the 1990 midterms, Democrats tried again in the 102nd Congress. In fact, HR 1 was reserved for the Civil Rights and Women's Equity in Employment Act of 1991, introduced by Judiciary Chair Jack Brooks (D-TX). Again working with Hyde, and now joined by Senator Jack Danforth (R-MO), who had become a Republican leader on the issue, Michel and the administration offered a substitute that promoted the business community's interests and constituted a kind of marker for the inevitable discussions surrounding a veto that were to follow. As had become customary for the minority leader, he lobbied furiously for a permissive rule on the House floor, noting that "from 1957 to 1981, an open rule was employed almost exclusively for civil rights legislation."[66] He had to be content with a modified closed rule that permitted him to offer a substitute with Hyde. It was defeated in June 1991, with nineteen Republicans defying their leadership.

Any opposition to a civil rights bill melted away in October with the Clarence Thomas Supreme Court confirmation hearings and former Ku Klux Klansman David Duke's victory in the Louisiana Senate Republican primary. Support galvanized around compromise Senate legislation crafted by Kennedy and Danforth. It was passed with huge margins in both bodies. The Bush administration cut its losses and jumped on board, happy just to have secured ambiguity on provisions such as the plausibly discriminatory effects of exams and academic requirements. Michel, probably glad to have the issue off the agenda, was free to focus on other legislative matters.[67]

Law and order consumed a great deal of his attention as well, but it at least permitted Michel an opportunity to craft legislation. Throughout his tenure as Republican Leader, the issue held a prominent place in public debate. Crime, violence, moral decline, and drugs were together regularly cited from the mid-1980s to the mid-1990s by about 25 percent of respondents to Gallup polls as the most important issue facing the United States.[68] Arrests for violent crimes grew significantly from already historically high levels in the period between 1980 and 1994.[69] In 1984, Congress passed a comprehensive anticrime law containing provisions on bail, pretrial detention, the insanity defense, enhanced drug penalties, and sentencing measures. It also established a so-called drug czar. But with crime rates continuing their climb, the American public pressed Washington into further action. Having made law and order and expanded use of the death penalty a component of the House

Republicans' "New Ideas" document that was to shape their agenda in the 99th Congress,[70] Michel worked closely with others on new legislation and, encouraged by President Reagan and the First Lady's intense interest in the issue, played a bit part in the passage of anti–drug use and trafficking legislation in both 1986 and 1988.[71]

The demand for legislative solutions to the country's crime problems only intensified, though. Between 1988 and 1994, Michel emerged as a key figure in the crafting, refining, and obstructing of measures on the issue. In the 100th Congress, collaborating with Republican colleague Michael Oxley (R-OH), he wrote a bill requiring criminal offenders to pay restitution to victims. The measure was approved by voice vote and bundled into the Comprehensive Crime Control Act of 1990, but it was eventually stripped out in Senate-House conference together with provisions related to the death penalty, habeas corpus, the exclusionary rule, and much of the bill's funding for local law enforcement.[72] Calling crime "our number one priority in this country,"[73] Michel returned to the issue at the beginning of the 101st Congress. In March, he introduced the Comprehensive Violent Crime Control Act, responding to President Bush's request for a crime bill within his term's first one hundred days.[74] Preferring to advance a version written by their chair, Jack Brooks, Democrats on the House Judiciary Committee blocked Michel's bill. The minority leader then reluctantly voted for the Brooks measure on original passage but opposed the Senate-House conference report and effectively stood with the administration as the president threatened a veto in October 1991. Explaining his intentions, Bush lauded the Michel legislation and called on Congress to embrace it. The president asserted that Michel's version was superior because it constituted effective application of the federal death penalty, curtailed abuses of habeas corpus, and brought needed reforms to the exclusionary rule.[75] Late in 1992, the Senate ultimately abandoned the conference report, never having voted upon it. Michel was emerging as a leader on criminal justice reform.

This issue did not just divide the parties along the law-and-order plane, with Republicans proposing tougher action on criminals. With the exception of drugs, meaningful bipartisan agreement on anticrime legislation eluded Washington because legislation known as the "Brady Bill" presented a continual sticking point. Named after the Reagan press secretary who was severely injured in the March 1981 effort to assassinate the president, the measure contained mandatory federal background checks and waiting periods for firearms purchases. In August 1993, amid continually escalating crime rates, the new Clinton administration, working closely with the chairs of Congress's two Judiciary committees, Brooks and Senator Joe Biden (D-DE), introduced a bill that was similar to the one left to die by the Senate the previous year. Supported by Michel, Bill McCollum introduced a GOP version that called for more cops on the beat, increased funding for prison construction, mandatory minimum sentencing, restrictions on appeals, an expanded death penalty, and augmented victims' rights. It also, crucially, differed on the Brady provisions by creating a less burdensome "insta-check" for handgun purchases. Michel called the Democrats' bill a "Trojan horse" and McCollum's "truth in labeling."[76] However, he was uncomfortable opposing an anticrime bill that looked likely to pass at a time when the public was baying for action; by 1993 more than 60 percent of Americans believed that prisons were supposed to punish rather than rehabilitate—a significant change from just a decade earlier.[77] In February 1994, Michel did not put his signature to a House Republican letter sent to the White House asserting that Clinton had not gone far enough in efforts to quell the crime epidemic. McCollum, Gingrich, and many other notable members of the extended House GOP leadership appended theirs. Instead, Michel pushed hard for an open rule during floor consideration of the Democrats' bill and experienced a rare victory during the 103rd Congress when the special rule for the conference report was defeated.

Yet, by then, much of the energy for the Republican opposition to the Clinton and congressional Democratic Party agendas emanated from Gingrich. It was he who orchestrated the defeat of the special rule, lambasting the Democratic leadership for waiving the three-day layover standing rule and bringing the report to the floor less than a day after it had come out of conference. Michel was left to make token arguments about substance. During the Sunday debate on final passage, he derided the bill as "Santa Claus wearing a sheriff's badge."[78]

Evaluating Michel's Policy Leadership

By the time the crime bill passed in August 1994, Michel was about to depart the House. He had spent his entire congressional career in the minority, an experience he called "pretty doggone discouraging and debilitating."[79] He was slowly losing his colleagues' allegiance, having suffered not "an electoral cataclysm, just the incremental collapse of high expectations."[80] He was leaving the Republican Conference to a dramatically different, combative, younger, and more conservative leadership, personified by Newt Gingrich—a man who would become Speaker—having secured on his first attempt something that Michel could not do in seven: win the GOP a majority.

Michel's legislative legacy is not one of a decent and gallant loser, however. He is remembered largely as a master strategist and skilled manager. He worked assiduously, using every kind of parliamentary maneuver, to get the agendas of two Republican presidents approved by the House. In his first speech to colleagues upon assuming the leadership of the House GOP in December 1980, he stated "our bottom line has got to be the enactment of the Reagan agenda."[81] He was the "handmaiden" of Reagan and Bush.[82] Depending on the political context, he chose to revise or block Democrats' bills—often, as we have seen in this chapter, pushing the majority to accept floor consideration under an open rule. He also had to keep an increasingly fractious and belligerent GOP Conference together, a task that became particularly difficult after the 1984 elections. Democratic Whip Tony Coelho accused Michel of having "lost control" of his party in 1985, and there was murmuring among GOP colleagues that he was not "tough enough."[83]

There were inevitably personal failures, notably on fiscal issues during the second Reagan term and the Bush term, the Middle East, and social policy. There were also significant victories, however. Other chapters in this volume describe the triumphs of the Reagan Revolution. Here, I detail Michel's successes on legislative matters such as the Reagan-era defense buildup, Contra aid, NAFTA, and the S&L cleanup.

This much is generally appreciated. What is not so frequently recognized is that Michel had a deep and sophisticated understanding of substantive policy on a wide range of foreign and domestic matters, as well as the broader national and global political contexts in which they operated. Michel's position as leader of a minority party in a majoritarian institution with strong and independent committees organized around policy issues did not provide many opportunities for him to reveal his wonkish side. A thorough grasp of technical details and larger political theories was also not compatible with an innate pragmatism that complemented his conservative principles. But, as I have tried to illuminate here, Michel had an encyclopedic knowledge of issues and policy. He demonstrated a strong command of the federal budget, Cold War dynamics, the social and economic effects of trade and environmental policy, the impact of regulation on American businesses, and the federal election processes that shaped his party's fortunes.

Michel also understood that personnel is policy—or that legislative proposals, and therefore outcomes, are likely to be determined by the type of people you pick to craft them. He exploited the expertise of committees' ranking members and, on many of the important bills the House considered, put together a Republican task force made up of a handful of strategically selected knowledgeable and motivated colleagues with divergent viewpoints. The goal was to generate high-quality information through a deliberative process in which the GOP Conference's many views were aired. It had the added virtue of legitimizing final decisions by permitting representation to Republican members' various perspectives.

Michel did not rise through the Republican leadership because he was a bright and conscientious student of American public policy. He did so as a loyal partisan, someone thought to be a skilled manager, electoral strategist, and coalition-builder guided by conservative values. Whether his colleagues in the party judged him fairly or not, it is difficult to tell. What is clear, though, is that he left the minority leader's office in 1994 with an understated yet astute and comprehensive grasp of America and its place in the world.

Notes

1. In an exclusive survey conducted by *U.S. News & World Report* in March 1982, Michel was named more influential in shaping legislation than even Speaker Thomas P. O'Neill. See RHM Papers, Press Series, f. Remarks and Releases: March 9, 1982.

2. Michael Lind, "A Civil War by Other Means," *Foreign Affairs* 78 (September/October 1999): 123–142.

3. Edward Reiss, *The Strategic Defense Initiative* (New York: Cambridge University Press, 1992); Greg Schneider and Renae Merle, "Reagan's Defense Build-Up Bridged Military Eras," *Washington Post*, June 9, 2004, E1.

4. Michael Glennon, "Armed Services Committee Democrats Defend More for Defense," *Congressional Quarterly Weekly*, March 31, 1984, 729–736.

5. Adam Clymer, "Robert Michel, Lawmaker Who Drew Admiration of Both Parties, Dies at 93," *New York Times*, February 18, 2017, D7.

6. Lee Lescaze, "Hill Republicans Tell Reagan Defense Spending Concessions Loom," *Washington Post*, October 1, 1981, A3.

7. RHM Papers, Press Series, f. Remarks and Releases: October 1, 1981.

8. David Broder, "Tactic Reveals GOP Split: Conservative 'Yellow Jackets' Buzz Michel," *Washington Post*, May 28, 1982, A4.

9. Helen Dewar, "Reagan Sways House GOP on Defense Cuts," *Washington Post*, March 30, 1984, A7.

10. Pat Towell, "House Approves MX with Cutback and Strings," *Congressional Quarterly Weekly*, May 19, 1984, 1155–1160.

11. Jonathan Fuerbringer, "Michel Says House Republicans Will Back Cut in Military Budget," *New York Times*, January 17, 1985, A 15.
12. Pat Towell, "Defense Debate Centers Not on Size of Pie, but How to Divide It," *Congressional Quarterly Weekly*, January 10, 1987, 63–68; Pat Towell, "Congress Tightens, Reshapes Defense Budget," *Congressional Quarterly Weekly*, November 28, 1988, 2945–2952.
13. Lou Cannon and Bill McAllister, "Reagan Urged to Veto Defense Bill," *Washington Post*, July 27, 1988, A4.
14. John Felton, "Hill Presses Reagan on Central America Policy," *Congressional Quarterly Weekly*, April 14, 1984, 832.
15. John Felton, "House in Dramatic Shift Backs 'Contra' Aid," *Congressional Quarterly Weekly*, June 15, 1985, 1139.
16. *Congressional Record*, April 16, 1986, H1891; John Felton, "Republicans Go for Broke on Contra Aid," *Congressional Quarterly Weekly*, April 19, 1986, 835–837.
17. John Felton, "For Reagan a Key House Win on 'Contra' Aid," *Congressional Quarterly Weekly*, June 28, 1986, 1443–1447; William F. Connelly, Jr., and John J. Pitney, Jr., *Congress' Permanent Minority? Republicans in the U.S. House* (Lanham, MD: Rowman & Littlefield, 1994), 61; Edward Walsh, "GOP Engineers a Delay in Vote on Contra Aid," *Washington Post*, April 17, 1986, A1.
18. Felton, "For Reagan a Key House Win," 1443.
19. RHM Papers, Press Series, f. Remarks and Releases: April 15, 1986; Bernard Weinraub, "U.S. Calls Libya Raid a Success," *New York Times*, April 16, 1986, A1.
20. John Felton, "Congress: U.S. Marines May Stay in Lebanon," *Congressional Quarterly Weekly*, October 1, 1983, 2015–2020.
21. RHM Papers, Press Series, f. Remarks and Releases: November 2, 1983.
22. Margaret Shapiro and John M. Goshko, "Reagan Moves to Bolster Hill Support on Lebanon," *Washington Post*, January 5, 1984, A1.
23. Steven Pressman, "Reagan Inquiry: A Hot Spot for Republicans," *Congressional Quarterly Weekly*, February 7, 1987, 231–235; Edward Walsh and Helen Dewar, "Rep. Hamilton Named to Head House Iran-Contra Inquiry," *Washington Post*, December 18, 1986, A 29.
24. RHM Papers, Press Series, f. Remarks and Releases: February 26, 1987; Helen Dewar and Edward Walsh, "Lawmakers Say President Must Take Blame and Reassert Control," *Washington Post*, February 27, 1987, A17.
25. Steven V. Roberts, "White House Acting to Control Iran-Contra Damage," *New York Times*, August 5, 1987, A10.
26. Eric Pianin, "House GOP's Frustrations Intensify," *Washington Post*, December 21, 1987, A1.
27. RHM Papers, Press Series, f. Remarks and Releases: March 11, 1987.
28. John Felton, "Contra Aid Denial Shifts Burden to Democrats," *Congressional Quarterly Weekly*, February 6, 1988, 235–238.
29. Connelly and Pitney, *Congress' Permanent Minority?* 84; John Felton and Janet Hook, "House Defeat Clouds Outlook for Contra Aid," *Congressional Quarterly Weekly*, March 5, 1988, 555–558.
30. Ann Devroy and Molly Moore, "Bush Orders More Troops to Panama," *Washington Post*, May 12, 1989, A1.

31. RHM, *Congressional Record* 137, January 10, 1991, H528.

32. Carroll J. Doherty, "Bush Is Given Authorization to Use Force against Iraq," *Congressional Quarterly Weekly*, January 12, 1991, 65–70.

33. Carroll J. Doherty, "Congress Applauds President from Sidelines of War," *Congressional Quarterly Weekly*, January 19, 1991, 176–180.

34. Rick Atkinson, "Gulf Ground War Seen Not Imminent," *Washington Post*, February 7, 1991, A1.

35. Adam Clymer, "House Voting $15 Billion for War, Warns Allies to Pay Their Part," *New York Times*, March 8, 1991, A11.

36. Tom Kenworthy, "House Easily Defeats Bush Defense Budget," *Washington Post*, May 22, 1991, A6.

37. Steven Pressman, "In Capitol Marketplace: Trade Expansion Bills," *Congressional Quarterly Weekly*, March 8, 1986, 554–558.

38. John Felton, "'Less Than Brilliant' Administration Role Led to Momentum for Sanctions," *Congressional Quarterly Weekly*, October 4, 1986, 2340–2341.

39. Stephen W. Stathis, *Landmark Debates in Congress* (Washington, DC: Congressional Quarterly Press, 2007), 455.

40. Deborah McGregor, "Where NAFTA Divided, GATT Finds Unity," *Congressional Quarterly Weekly*, October 29, 1994, 3118.

41. See Michel, Foley, Gephardt, and Gingrich to Clinton, November 16, 1994, reiterating "strong support" for the GATT implementing legislation and explaining their bipartisan efforts "to craft a procedure . . . that would maximize the likelihood that it [will] pass with a large vote of support." RHM Papers, Press Series, f. Remarks and Releases: November 16, 1994.

42. David S. Cloud, "Decisive Vote Brings Down Trade Walls with Mexico," *Congressional Quarterly Weekly*, November 20, 1993, 3174–3178; Gwen Ifill, "The Free Trade Accord: Clinton Extends Unusual Offer to Republicans on the Pact," *New York Times*, November 12, 1993, 1:10.

43. Ann Devroy and Kenneth J. Cooper, "House Republicans Warn Clinton of Eroding Trade-Pact Support," *Washington Post*, September 10, 1993, A11.

44. Gary C. Jacobson, "Deficit-Cutting Politics and Congressional Elections," *Political Science Quarterly* 108 (1993): 375–402.

45. George Hager and David Cloud, "Leaders Scramble to Win Votes for Deficit Reduction Bill," *Congressional Quarterly Weekly*, May 22, 1993, 1277–1279.

46. Gary C. Jacobson, "The 1994 House Elections in Perspective," in *Midterm: The Elections of 1994 in Context*, ed. Philip A. Klinkner (Boulder: Westview Press, 1996), 1–20.

47. William K. Black, *The Best Way to Rob a Bank Is to Own One: How Corporate Executives and Politicians Looted the S&L Industry* (Austin: University of Texas Press, 2005).

48. Ira H. Raphaelson, "Memo to Robert H. Michel," June 6, 1991, RHM Papers, Staff Series: Ted Van Der Meid, f. Banking. Savings and Loan. Justice Department Cases.

49. Kathleen Day, "Surprise Recovery of S&L Measure Was the Result of Unlikely Alliance," *Washington Post*, June 17, 1989, A13.

50. John R. Cranford, "Thrift Industry: $30 Billion RTC Salvage Bill Awaits President's OK," *Congressional Quarterly Weekly*, March 23, 1991, 734.

51. Andrew Taylor, "Thrift Bailout: Democrats Vow to Return to RTC in September," *Congressional Quarterly Weekly*, August 7, 1993, 2147.

52. Taylor, "Thrift Bailout."

53. Guy Vander Jagt, "Memo to Michel: Re: PAC Reform," December 6, 1988, RHM Papers, Staff Series: Ted Van Der Meid, Box 5, f. House Republican Task Force, Working Document.

54. Chuck Alston and Glen Craney, "Bush Campaign Reform Plan Takes Aim at Incumbents," *Congressional Quarterly Weekly*, July 1, 1989, 1648.

55. Richard E. Cohen, "Showdown on Campaign Funds?" *National Journal*, December 16, 1989, 3055.

56. RHM Papers, Press Series, f. Remarks and Releases: June 11, 1990.

57. RHM, Dick Armey, and William F. Goodling, "House Republicans: What We'll Do When We Reach Majority," *Policy Review*, 59 (Winter 1992): 62.

58. RHM, "A Democratic Protection Racket," *New York Times*, July 7, 1990, 1:23.

59. David Broder, "Bob Michel on the Warpath," *Washington Post*, June 24, 1990, C7.

60. Tony Blankley, "Memo to Robert H. Michel, 'Campaign Finance Open Rule Media Plan,'" May 7, 1990, RHM Papers, Staff Series: Ted Van Der Meid, f. Whip Strategy.

61. RHM, "Campaign Reform, Floor Materials," 1990, RHM Papers, Staff Series: Ted Van Der Meid, f. HR 5400, Floor Materials (1).

62. Philip Shabecoff, "Bush to Ask Sharp Cutback in Key Source of Acid Rain," *New York Times*, June 10, 1989, A1.

63. Kennedy Maize, "Has Midwest Benefitted by Ducking Scrubbers?" *The Energy Daily*, November 27, 1989, 1.

64. Julie Rovner, "House Is Nearing Passage of Disability Rights Bill," *Congressional Quarterly Weekly*, May 19, 1990, 1559–1560.

65. George H. W. Bush to RHM, August 2, 1990, RHM Papers, Staff Series: Ted Van Der Meid, f. Civil Rights Bill of 1990, Administration Position.

66. RHM to Joe Moakley, May 20, 1991, RHM Papers: Ted Van Der Meid, f. Civil Rights Bill of 1991, Rule.

67. Joan Biskupic, "Senate Passes Sweeping Measure to Overturn Court Rulings," *Congressional Quarterly Weekly*, November 2, 1991, 3200–3204.

68. Gregor Aisch and Alicia Parlapiano, "What Do You Think Is the Most Important Problem Facing This Country Today?" *New York Times*, February 27, 2017, A3.

69. Howard N. Snyder, "Arrests in the United States, 1980–2009," US Department of Justice, "Patterns and Trends" Report, September 2011, NCJ 234319.

70. Margaret Shapiro, "House GOP Issues List of 'New Ideas,'" *Washington Post*, January 15, 1985, A5.

71. RHM Papers, Press Series, f. Remarks and Releases: August 5, 1986; Julie Rovner, "Parties Compete for Lead, All-Points Bulletin Issued: Act Now on Drugs," *Congressional Quarterly*, August 9, 1986, 1847–1849.

72. Joan Biskupic, "Death Penalty, Other Hot Issues Dumped from Crime Bill," *Congressional Quarterly Weekly*, October 27, 1990, 3615.

73. RHM, *Congressional Record* 137, June 6, 1991, H4130.

74. RHM, "The Comprehensive Violent Crime Control Act of 1991," RHM Papers, Press Series, f. Remarks and Releases: March 13, 1991.

75. George H. W. Bush, "Statement of Administration Policy HR 3371—Omnibus Crime Control Act of 1991," October 11, 1991. Online by Gerhard Peters and John T. Woolley, *The American Presidency Project*, www.presidency.ucsb.edu/ws/?pid=127705.

76. House Republican Conference, "Comparison of the Democrat and Republican Crime Bills," October 26, 1993, RHM Papers, Staff Series: Ted Van Der Meid, f. Crime Bill Comparisons.

77. George Pettinico, "Crime and Punishment: America Changes Its Mind," *Public Perspective* 5 (September/October 1994): 29–32.

78. RHM, *Congressional Record* 140, August 21, 1994, H7951.

79. Janet Hook, "House GOP: Plight of a Permanent Minority," *Congressional Quarterly Weekly*, June 21, 1986, 1394.

80. Janet Hook, "House GOP Hones a Sharper Edge as Michel Turns in His Sword," *Congressional Quarterly Weekly*, October 9, 1993, 2714.

81. RHM Papers, Press Series, f. Remarks and Releases. December 8, 1980.

82. Clymer, "Robert Michel, Lawmaker."

83. Diane Granat, "Splits in Style, Substance: Deep Divisions Loom behind GOP's Apparent Unity," *Congressional Quarterly Weekly*, March 23, 1985, 538.

CHAPTER 7

LEADING GENTLY ON TAXES

Matthew S. Mendez

onald Reagan became president in 1981 after winning a resounding victory over incumbent Jimmy Carter. His election also resulted in a Republican Senate majority that effectively ended unified Democratic control over the federal government. The Democrats' last remaining bastion of power was their durable House majority. With 243 seats, the Democrats should have been in a commanding position, but the majority was in name only due to the deep internal divisions that plagued the party. The Republicans had gained more than thirty seats in the 1980 election to bring their number up to 192, which would be the highest number of House Republicans during the Reagan years.[1] Despite being in the minority, House Republicans were buoyed in this first term by the electoral mandate of the Reagan White House, the ideological fracturing of the House Democrats, and the deft maneuvering of Minority Leader Robert H. Michel. It was in this context that Michel helped shepherd one of Reagan's signature accomplishments, the Economic Recovery Tax Act of 1981, through the Democratic-controlled House of Representatives.

As noted elsewhere in this volume, Michel's leadership style was pragmatic and amiable and was focused mostly on the task of legislating. Michel eschewed the bombast desired by more ideological members of the GOP Conference, as well as the more divisive social issues favored by the Reagan administration, in order to work with the Democratic leadership to advance President Reagan's economic agenda. Michel might have been a self-described "handmaiden"[2] of President Reagan, but he, like Reagan, shared a core belief in limited government, which carried over into a disdain for excessive government spending supported by a tax code that constrained economic prosperity. They came to their faith in tax reduction honestly—through Reagan's experience as governor of California and Michel's tenure on the House Appropriations Committee. A decade's time in the nation's capital, for example, led Michel to say in 1966: "I do not oppose Government. I oppose *surplus* Government. And that is what we have today—surplus Government." "Our Federal Government has grown fat and flabby on high living. It tosses billions around like a drunken sailor. It invents programs, over-funds them, and then spends millions studying the programs it has invented."[3] Following the election of Jimmy Carter to the presidency in 1976 and as Michel climbed his party's leadership ladder in the House, he remarked to the Illinois Association of Manufacturers: "We already have a Federal Government that is trying to (a) do more than its resources will permit, (b) do many things that it cannot do very well, (c) do some things that it should never do at all, and (d) do all of these things at the same time. As a result, we now have more government than we want, more than we need, and more than we can afford."[4] Once installed in the White House, Reagan moved immediately to present a tax reduction plan. In Michel, he found a willing ally.

The US economy was plagued by both high unemployment rates and inflation when the 97th Congress convened in January 1981. President Reagan had campaigned on the promise of reinvigorating the economy by cutting taxes and reducing government expenditures. During the presidential election campaign, Reagan had promised to "cut marginal tax rates by 10 percent a year for three years."[5] Additionally, he had endorsed a proposal by Representative Jack Kemp (R-NY) and Senator Bill Roth (R-DE) that called for reductions in the marginal tax rates for all households but also, most controversially, for businesses and the highest income earners. On February 18, 1981, following a 9:45 A.M. meeting in the Oval Office with Michel and others on the budget and tax plan, President Reagan unveiled his tax proposal to Congress, which called for "$53.9 billion in tax cuts in 1982, starting with a ten percent tax cut in individual tax rates on July 1, 1981 . . . followed by additional ten percent cuts on July 1st in each succeeding year."[6] The proposal also called for various tax cuts for businesses. As the president explained, his plan "is aimed at reducing the growth in government spending and taxing [and] reforming and eliminating regulations which are unnecessary and unproductive or counterproductive."[7] Michel immediately issued a press release lauding the plan: "It is my hope that, working in constant consultation with the Democratic Leadership in the House, we can establish the timetables and procedures necessary to accomplish the President's goals swiftly and completely."[8] Reagan's tax proposal was not at all assured of passage, as the White House's uncompromising position put it at odds with both some fellow Republicans and the House Democratic leadership. Its success owes in part to Bob Michel's legislative skills and diplomatic efforts on behalf of the bill.

Leading from the Minority

As noted by Randall Strahan,[9] Congress was not built for "great men" who led by "sheer force of personality" but for those who are able to adapt to social, institutional, and constitutional factors that are largely out of the leader's control. In his defense of congressional leaders, Strahan argues for a "conditional agency" approach that presupposes that congressional leaders actually lead and, therefore, are causal agents, not simply agents of their followers.[10] "Conditional agency" posits that "major policy . . . changes in Congress . . . occur as a consequence of actions taken by leaders who take personal risks to advance goals about which they care about deeply."[11] The ability to assume risk and convince ambivalent members to follow through on the leader's plan is a hallmark of conditional agency. Michel's role in the passage of the Economic Recovery Tax Act of 1981 is an example of conditional agency. He leveraged contextual factors, such as having a president of the same party, as well as his own personal characteristics to simultaneously negotiate with the House Democratic leadership and the moderate and more militant factions of his own Conference.

While the conditional agency approach was applied originally to House Speakers,[12] it still holds great utility for understanding the role of minority leaders. True, the incentives are different, and the risks are somewhat lower given the disempowered status the minority party holds in the House, but conditional agency nonetheless calls attention to how important individual leaders can be in establishing policy. Michel's personal characteristics deeply informed his leadership style and negotiating tactics. Most notably, he has been described as conciliatory and gentlemanly, focused more on ensuring that Republicans had a voice in the legislative process than on winning the majority. His focus on policy and legislative tactics led him to downplay efforts to win the House majority and to avoid strident, divisive partisan tactics meant to demonize, and alienate, the Democratic House leadership, much to the chagrin of frustrated junior members.

Michel's major goal in 1981 was to enact President Reagan's ambitious economic agenda. Scholars have noted 1981 as Reagan's best year as he went on to see major items of his economic agenda enacted into law. President Reagan won in an electoral landslide with 494 electoral votes but won a bare majority of the popular vote (50.7 percent) and yet acted as if the American people had handed him an electoral mandate. It was not unreasonable for Reagan and his fellow conservatives to assume that at least a majority of the American people wanted a legitimate change. After all, the incumbent Jimmy Carter won only 41 percent of the popular vote and 49 electoral votes. The country's middle class had demonstrated its frustration with Democratic taxation policies and their attendant social welfare programs, as well as with the ailing economy, in what became known as the "middle class tax revolt" of 1978, which saw plebiscitary budgeting approved by the voters of California.[13] The Reagan campaign, and congressional Republican candidates, seized on this issue and pledged to both cut taxes for the middle class and reduce bureaucratic waste.

The stage was set for Michel to lead on tax reform. He had a kindred spirit in the White House who explicitly campaigned for tax relief targeted to the middle class at the expense of federal social programs, and President Reagan had the support of a majority of the American people on this issue.[14] On the institutional front, Republicans controlled the Senate, and Michel had made it a priority to open a direct line of communication with Republican Senate Majority Leader Howard H. Baker, Jr. (R-TN). Michel also sought to strengthen communication between the legislative and campaign arms of the GOP House Conference.[15] This greater coordination among the congressional GOP infrastructure only served to help Michel as he sought to build coalitions for the Reagan tax proposal.

From an institutional perspective, the primary contextual factor that remained involved the House Democratic majority, which controlled the agenda in the House. Yet, there is ample evidence to suggest that the majority was not as powerful as it appeared. First, the Democratic House majority stood alone in the face of a Republican Senate and president in favor of smaller government. Second, the House majority was ideologically fractured, with forty-seven conservative Democrats, many of them southerners, forming the Conservative Democratic Forum (CDF).[16] CDF would serve as an alternative negotiating partner for President Reagan and Michel and often worked to restrain the liberal tendencies of the broader Democratic majority. Third, the Democratic agenda appeared to have been emphatically rejected by a majority of American voters; to make matters worse, it was an agenda that had been endorsed by Speaker Tip O'Neill (D-MA). Finally, Speaker O'Neill had to contend not only with a popular president but also with one who knew how to effectively use the messaging powers of the office.[17]

The Debate Begins

Ronald Reagan threw down the gauntlet in his first State of the Union address to a joint session of Congress. The president's address followed a "pep talk" to the nation on the country's economic ills.[18] At the State of the Union, Reagan laid out an ambitious economic vision that would not only institute supply-side economic theories as government policy but also "re-define the role of government in American society."[19]

While Speaker O'Neill was ready to fight the administration's agenda, Michel used his personal skills to ensure that Reagan's program would find its way to the House floor and to a vote. Michel began the 97th Congress with an appeal to bipartisanship and comity on the House floor. He pledged to work with the Democrats "in the best interest of the American people." But he also hinted at the strategy he would employ to advance the new president's economic programs in addressing Speaker O'Neill: "But I should tell you that during this Congress there will be times when we will be making appeals across the aisle," Michel explained. "And you should know that the inherent logic of our arguments, the persuasiveness of our appeal, and the all-around good nature of Republicans will often find success in rallying Democrats to our cause."[20]

At least partly due to Reagan's popularity and Michel's conciliatory tone, O'Neill and the Democratic leadership agreed to abide by a firm legislative timetable for consideration of all the major components of the Reagan economic package. In response to this development, Michel said: "This is the first time in my memory that there has been bi-partisan agreement on the consideration of a program of this magnitude."[21]

The legislative agreement called for the consideration of budget resolutions for FY 1981 and FY 1982, as well as a final reconciliation bill, by June 1981; it also called for final consideration of a tax bill immediately upon the adoption of the budget resolutions and reconciliation bill.[22] This meant that all of the major spending and tax decisions would happen concurrently.[23]

Elated by these events, Michel's pragmatic instincts revealed themselves when he remarked to Reagan at a breakfast on March 17, 1981, that the "timetable is a good sign of bipartisan cooperation, but I should caution against complacency."[24]

It is here that Michel's personal characteristics influenced the Democratic House leadership's decision to agree to this timetable, thereby effectively removing the majority's ability to stall Reagan's agenda through delay. Michel's commitment to civility allowed him to build trust with Democratic leaders, including House Majority Leader Jim Wright (D-TX). Wright described Michel as "decent, honorable, and straightforward."[25] Michel's unwillingness to engage in destructive character attacks or unseemly partisan maneuvering also won praise from Wright: "When he gives you his word, you know he will keep it."[26] Michel's reputation for civility was as much of a factor as Reagan's efficient use of the bully pulpit in securing a timetable for Reagan's economic agenda.

The administration's plan was to enact deep spending cuts to federal social welfare programs, along with a reform of the tax code that would cut taxes across the board for individuals and businesses. Reagan's tax proposal included the aforementioned 10 percent cuts for three successive years, in addition to "a speed-up rate at which businesses could deduct the cost of purchasing new plants and equipment."[27] The business cuts were initially referred to as the "10–5–3" proposal, as they officially classified which properties could be written off (i.e., depreciated) in ten, five, or three years. The 10–5–3 proposal had great bipartisan support when it was introduced in the House in 1980.[28] The White House also wanted "a second tax parcel, including proposals to index income tax brackets; do away with the marriage penalty, which discriminated against working married couples; provide tuition tax credits; and revise inheritance taxation."[29] Initially, President Reagan refused to compromise or negotiate with House Democrats.

Democrats attempted to head off Reagan's tax proposal when Dan Rostenkowski (D-IL), the new chairman of the House Ways and Means Committee, released his own tax bill. While it was probably more conservative than liberal Democrats wanted, it differed significantly from the president's proposal. Rostenkowski's bill was written to attract the support of Republicans as it "included two proposals that had widespread GOP support: reducing the top marginal rate on unearned income from 70 percent to 50 percent, which would benefit those at the upper end of the income scale, and easing the marriage penalty, which would benefit two-earner families."[30]

The chairman's proposal also differed from the administration's proposal in that it only cut taxes for one year instead of the proposed three and did not include the 10–5–3 tax schedule for businesses. Rostenkowski's proposal received a cool reception from Republicans who were careful to support principles of the proposal, which were modeled closely after President Reagan's goals, while rejecting the chairman's specific changes. Michel's remarks on the Rostenkowski proposal encapsulated the Republicans' general feeling toward the bill and the majority party: "They are still the party of a strong, expansive central government. . . . How else can you propose lower taxes, lower deficits, lower spending . . . all without reducing services?"[31] Barber Conable (R-NY), the GOP's ranking member on the Ways and Means Committee, also came out publicly against the proposal.[32]

Discord among House Republicans

As Democrats held faithful to their end of the legislative bargain, Michel began to confront discontent within his own Conference. As a general proposition in those early months of the Reagan presidency, Michel had to work with the White House to sweeten legislation for conservative Democrats without alienating moderate Republicans, most of whom hailed from the urban Northeast. He adopted different approaches for each Republican faction. He made it clear to the moderate "Gypsy Moths" from the Northeast and Midwest that their overall budget support would count later on when they wanted specific financial help for their districts. And he persuaded militant Reaganites not to pick fights with the moderates while the key legislation was still pending.[33] As a concession to the conservatives, for example, Michel appointed Newt Gingrich (R-GA) ally Bob Walker (R-PA) as one of the party's "official objectors" to the consent calendar on the House floor. In a letter to Walker, Michel complimented his parliamentary acumen and told him the "the job of objector is crucially important to safeguarding the rights of the Minority."[34] Despite such gestures, Michel continued to hear criticism from his more conservative and confrontational colleagues.

Junior Republican lawmakers first challenged Michel's carefully laid legislative strategy when Gingrich inserted into the *Congressional Record* on May 6, 1981, a letter to Wright signed by two Republican freshmen, Thomas J. Bliley, Jr. (R-VA), and Ed Weber (R-OH).[35] Gingrich was seen as the leader of conservative members who were elected in 1978 and 1980, and he sought to use overtly hostile, partisan tactics in order to embarrass the Democratic majority. The Bliley-Weber letter demanded that the Democratic leadership schedule a vote on the tax rate reductions in May 1981, well before the agreed-upon June deadline.[36] The communication quickly won support from other House Republicans, eventually gaining the endorsement of 150 members. Michel was furious upon learning about the letter and demanded that the authors make several changes. But the letter was presented to Wright without the changes sought by Michel—and in front of the press no less, much to the Republican Leader's chagrin.

According to press accounts, the incident reflected a basic disagreement over tactics. "It makes no sense to embarrass the majority leader," said Michel, "because he is certainly capable of embarrassing us."[37] Michel understood the political ramifications of angering Majority Leader Wright and the Democratic leadership, who still controlled the agenda-setting powers of the House. Michel's commitment to seeing the tax legislation through the House of Representatives was not enough for these junior members who wanted to create bad press for the Democratic House leadership.[38] Yet, this did not assuage the discontent among his ranks. "The trouble is that Michel is still a minority leader, and hasn't yet become a real Republican leader," commented one junior congressman.[39] Such a comment by a low-ranking colleague both mocked and accurately described Michel's behavior. The Republican Leader was perfectly fine observing institutional norms while advocating strongly for his legislative agenda. He refused to engage in antagonistic, excessively partisan leadership.

The resulting fallout from this episode led to negative press from reporters who charged that Michel could not control members of the GOP Conference. Michel staffer Mike Johnson wrote that the episode demonstrated a "failure of basic professional courtesy" because Bliley and Weber did not inform Wright that they intended to deliver the letter with the national press in attendance.[40] He added: "Attempting to embarrass the Majority Leader in that manner could have very easily cost us future Democratic votes."[41]

Much like his boss, Johnson was concerned that a lack of civility could damage the legislative process. In response to reports in the press that Michel was feuding with his own members, Johnson wrote the following:

> If such a perception persists, it may ultimately injure your efforts
> to convince Conservative Democrats that we are united and capable
> of delivering votes on our side. Furthermore, it will suggest that at
> any given time, we may turn on them. I don't think you can afford,

under any circumstances, a split of the appearance or a split in the Republican ranks. This is exactly what the Democrats have been looking for.[42]

Johnson's letter emphasized the strategic imperative of maintaining not only a cordial relationship with the Democratic House leadership but also GOP unity in order to keep hope alive for a cross-partisan bill.[43] Johnson, like Michel, knew that the only hope for a tax bill that adhered closely to President Reagan's specifications would require the votes of at least twenty-six conservative Democrats. It called for a gentle touch, one that constrained but did not exclude junior members' participation. For example, Johnson advised his boss to let Gingrich and his ilk generate grassroots support for the tax legislation but prohibit them from participating in any activities on the House floor.[44]

Committee and Legislative Breakthroughs

Reagan had initially refused to compromise with the Democrats on taxes. His popularity with the public and Congress, along with the steadfast support of Michel, kept reluctant Republicans in line. Even Barber Conable, Michel's close friend, was not overly enthusiastic about the administration's proposal, but Conable decided to toe the line on Reagan's budget. By refusing to budge, Conable and the Republicans left Rostenkowski without any potential avenue more amenable to the Democrats. Not helping matters were divisions among the Democrats as Speaker Tip O'Neill, Majority Leader Wright, Chairman Rostenkowski, and the conservative southern Democrat Kent Hance (D-TX) all staked out different positions.[45]

In late May 1981, Michel sent a "Dear Colleague" letter to Republican members laying out his argument for why they should continue to stay unified behind the president's plan. "Make no mistake about it," he wrote, "there is a reason behind the hard-line approach taken by the Speaker. The House that Tip built will topple without an ever escalating flow of tax revenues into the Treasury." He concluded the letter by stating that House Republicans must continue to strive for "multi-year, across the board tax reductions this year," adding that he "hopes all Republicans will continue to press hard for these goals."[46]

After a meeting with the House Democratic leadership on June 1 ended in further stalemate, President Reagan finally yielded and offered concessions to House Democrats. His alternative bill proposed $37.4 billion in tax cuts for 1982, reduced the first rate reduction to 5 percent, delayed it until October 1, 1981, and put in some sweeteners, including savings incentives and marriage penalty relief. It continued proposed rate cuts of 10 percent on July 1, 1982, and 1983. It also dropped the top rate on investment income to 50 percent, cut almost 30 percent of the business tax relief in the original plan, and added a host of tax bonuses for individuals that were selected to lure support from conservative Democrats.[47] For example, the bill included tax breaks on oil royalties meant to entice support from Democrats from oil-producing states.[48] The new bill was to be introduced in the House by Hance and Conable.[49]

In a press release after the Oval Office meeting, Michel hoped that Democrats would cooperate on the tax proposal. "Our economy thirsts for tax relief," the minority leader said. "It is as dry and parched and barren as the Mojave Desert. The drought must end."[50] The president thanked Michel for his leadership in drafting the tax program a few days later in a personal letter.[51]

Not to be outdone, Chairman Rostenkowski and the majority of Democrats on the Ways and Means Committee came up with a plan that called for a two-year tax break, which would provide a 5 percent tax cut the first year and 10 percent the second.[52] The tax measure also included targeted relief to the middle class and had support from the majority of House Democrats. The conservative Democrats, however, were initially divided. Charles W. Stenholm (D-TX) reported that the forty-seven-member group of conservative Democrats, which he led, was split between those who supported the president and those who would opt for Rostenkowski's two-year measure. Another CDF member, Phil Gramm (D-TX), claimed the president had twenty solid votes among these same conservative Democrats.[53] The conservative Democrats were now split between groups supporting Hance-Conable and a majority of House Democrats.

During this time, the Michel papers reveal the deep appreciation that President Reagan had for Michel's efforts on behalf of his economic program. After the successful passage of his budget through the House in late May 1981, Reagan gave Michel a jar of jelly beans to thank him, telling him that he "could bring the jar back for a refill—if he has equal success with the President's tax cuts."[54] Michel referred to his president as a "jewel to work with." To an interviewer years later, Michel explained the process he had so carefully coordinated with the White House:

There were times, on a critical issue, when I would take members down to see the president personally in the Cabinet room for his kind of soft treatment. On a real critical issue, we'd set aside a day. I'd take two groups in the morning and two groups in the afternoon. It was never more than ten or twelve, and it was mixed—those for or against an issue, and those who were swing votes in the middle. I'd give the President a card to let the president know where they were from because he couldn't remember every member's name, etc. But the White House and those in the group were very good in helping us develop that thing like a violin. I mean, he was so good at it.[55]

Michel defended the president in the strongest possible terms after Speaker O'Neill said on national television that Ronald Reagan "doesn't understand the working class of middle America . . . because of the fact he doesn't associate himself with those types of people." Michel responded: "I understand the Speaker's position. He is a spokesman for a failed philosophy of government. . . . It must be frustrating for him to know that the vast majority of the American people trust and believe in President Reagan. But this does not excuse the personal attack."[56]

The Hance-Conable bill and the Rostenkowski proposal set off a bidding war in the House of Representatives. As Barber Conable's biographer later explained it, the outcome of tax legislation depended on conservative Democrats. The president and Michel not only had to hold on to all 190 Republicans but also attract at least twenty-seven of the forty-seven members of the Conservative Democratic Forum. That combination would give Michel a 217-vote majority in the House, which at the time, with three vacancies, had a total membership of 432. If, however, Rostenkowski and the House Democratic leadership could persuade their Democratic colleagues to stay with the party, they had a chance to defeat the Reagan tax bill and replace it with one of their own and, equally important to them, reestablish their partisan control over the House.[57] As Michel himself admitted in remarks to the Insurance Information Institute titled, "Republican Strategy in the 97th Congress": "The Republican leadership has to first keep its own people on the reservation and convince a number of Democrats to join us."[58]

The messaging strategy adopted by Michel was to trumpet support for President Reagan's plan, as well as to signal Democrats that Republicans were working in good faith. While Michel praised Reagan's leadership and considered it "a vital part of the strategy of the Republicans in the House," he acknowledged that "it is only part. The battle has to be won here [in the

House]. The tactics to make the strategy work have to be developed here."[59] The Republican strategy sought to emphasize common values that some Democrats might share instead of a nakedly partisan strategy that might alienate conservative Democrats.

In June, Michel, who had been working more behind the scenes, was urged to take a more active role by Mike Johnson, his press secretary, who worried about what Johnson called "the politics of confusion" surrounding the tax and budget issues. One of Michel's innovations intended to appease conservative Republicans was to create a series of working groups or task forces in order to give colleagues a voice in developing the party's positions. But, according to Johnson, they had become a problem when they went off track. Michel had not given these groups enough guidance, and they had developed party messages and positions that contradicted the leadership.[60] Regrettably, the Michel papers do not reveal if Michel took the advice.

Competing Proposals

The cross-partisan House coalition and the Democratic majority continued to add sweeteners to their bills in order to attract support from conservative Democrats and keep moderate Republicans in the fold. Conable added provisions designed to appeal to the moderates, such as "tax credits for rehabilitating old buildings and for wood burning stoves."[61] House Democrats, meanwhile, offered a "tax credit of $4,300 for oil royalty owners."[62] This all supplemented the giveaways and concessions negotiated by the Senate to attract support. Conable later said, "If I were writing the bill, I would write it differently."[63]

With a vote on tax proposals coming up in the House at the end of July 1981, both parties ramped up their efforts to lobby potential swing votes in the House and influence public opinion. The Democratic Party sought to encourage their supporters among the general public, especially those in labor unions, to pressure moderate Republicans from the Northeast and Midwest to oppose the administration's tax measure. This included an advertising blitz in newspapers that accused Republican lawmakers of putting the president's agenda before their constituents' interests.[64]

The votes of these moderate Republicans were seen as critical to the survival of the bill, but Michel had always been able to keep them in the fold due to his goodwill efforts. These included facilitating meetings between the president and party moderates who were not pleased with the Reagan budget.

Michel also appointed an official liaison to the Gypsy Moths,[65] Edward Madigan (R-IL), to show his appreciation for their efforts. The Gypsy Moths were comforted by the fact that Michel was immediately "sympathetic and supportive" of their concerns regarding the Reagan budget and communicated said concerns to the White House on their behalf.[66] These efforts by Michel soothed early tensions between the White House and the moderate Republicans, making it virtually impossible for the House Democratic leadership to peel off a significant number of Gypsy Moths for their rival tax proposal.

The Republicans had their own media and lobbying blitz in order to get Hance-Conable across the finish line in the House. President Reagan was heavily involved in the final round of lobbying. He first reached out to House Republicans, "personally urging them to stick together in 'these last crucial days,'" calling the tax cut "the most crucial item left on our agenda for prosperity."[67] For example, he invited fourteen wavering members to a barbeque at Camp David on Sunday, July 26, 1981. Eleven eventually supported the president's tax cut.[68] Republicans also paid for a series of radio ads in swing districts to sway public opinion and protect potentially vulnerable members of Congress.[69] President Reagan's most consequential contribution to the lobbying effort culminated in his television address to the nation on Monday, July 27.

The president originally wanted to discuss both his proposed Social Security reform package and his tax bill in his remarks that night. However, Republican legislative leaders, including Senate Majority Leader Baker and Bob Michel, strongly opposed combining the two and convinced Reagan to focus on the tax measure.[70]

Reagan made a masterful and powerful plea that elated Republicans and infuriated Democrats. He told the nation it was a choice between his bill, which promised a tax cut, and a Democratic bill, which promised a tax increase. This was despite the fact that the Democratic alternative also cut taxes.[71] The president went on to ask the American people to call their member of Congress to register their support for the bill. The Democrats could not overcome the overwhelming response from voters, who inundated their offices with calls and telegrams mostly in favor of Reagan's tax proposal. Michel issued a press release on July 28, 1981, stating that the president's speech was "a vital step" toward the passage of the cross-partisan tax package.[72]

In July 1981, Michel seemed to have disappeared, at least publicly, from the legislative battle over the tax bill. Nothing could be further from the truth, however, as he did what he always did—worked effectively behind the scenes planning and collaborating with his allies. He held a series of meetings on

July 9, 22, 23, and 28 with President Reagan, Speaker O'Neill, Senate Majority Leader Baker, Treasury Secretary Donald Regan, and House colleagues Conable, Hance, and Gingrich. Michel listened to his members' concerns, keeping them together, and worked closely with the White House. His investment paid off. As he said: "The remarkable aspect of this whole debate is that the question is not whether to cut taxes, but when and by how much. I never thought I would see the day Democrats and Republicans were both advancing billions of dollars' worth of tax relief toward final deliberation in the House."[73]

Passage and Republican Victory

On July 29, 1981, the House convened at 9:00 A.M. and formally adopted the modified closed rule from the Rules Committee, which called for no amendments and up-or-down votes on three tax bills.[74] The first bill would be the version drafted by liberal Democrats and sponsored by Morris Udall (D-AZ), which called for a scaled-down version of the committee bill and balanced the budget in 1982. The second option was the bipartisan Conable-Hance substitute favored by Reagan.[75] If both of those bills failed to achieve a majority, the committee bill sponsored by Chairman Rostenkowski and the other Democratic members of the Ways and Means Committee would follow.

Voting commenced after the House resolved itself into the Committee of the Whole with all members present. The Udall measure was soundly defeated by a vote of 144–288 with one member voting present. The Hance-Conable substitute was up next, and Michel made the final argument on behalf of the Reagan tax bill. "This is another one of those issues where our philosophical kinship rather than our political division will be the decisive factor in determining whether the bipartisan substitute will prevail over the Committee bill," the minority leader began in a final appeal to those across the aisle. "Unfortunately," he continued, "the Committee bill before us embraces a philosophy that has dominated this Congress for generations. . . . It is classically traditional. I dare say it is the only kind of tax bill the Speaker of the House could support. On the other hand," Michel said, "the philosophy underlying the Conable-Hance bill is the antithesis of the Committee bill. Its direction, its dynamics, its dimensions have no equal." He ended: "The Conable-Hance substitute gives back to the people what is theirs to begin with. Conable-Hance means that those who govern must get their license to govern—to spend and tax—from those who are governed."[76] Michel's comments channeled the aspirations of the Reagan Revolution, as well as the conservative principles that he had always held dear.

The Committee of the Whole then voted to pass the Conable-Hance substitute by a vote of 238–195, with all but one House Republican, Jim Jeffords (R-VT), in support. The Democrats fractured as forty-eight deserted their leadership to vote for the Reagan tax measure, including thirty conservative Democrats. A motion to recommit the bill was defeated when the Committee of the Whole reported the bill back to the House, and it was then passed by a bipartisan majority of 328–107. Michel had delivered on his promise to President Reagan, handing him his third major legislative victory of the year. "Your vote yesterday for the Conable-Hance tax bill fulfilled a vital commitment to the American people," Reagan wrote to Michel, "and I thank you for it." Admitting that the task "of rebuilding our country's economy, and thereby restoring prosperity" was far from finished, the president concluded: "Please accept my appreciation for your help, along with my personal pledge to complete the job we have together undertaken."[77]

Bob Michel had helped shepherd the biggest tax cut in American history through the House of Representatives. The Senate had passed a similar, but not identical, version by a vote of 89–11. Conferees for both chambers assembled on July 31 and worked furiously to hammer out a compromise over the minor provisions that separated the House and Senate bills. On August 3, the final version of the bill, the Economic Recovery Tax Act (HR 4242, PL 97-34) passed the Senate, 76–8, and on August 4, it passed the House, 282–95. Ronald Reagan signed the bill on August 13, 1981, at his California ranch, Rancho del Cielo.

Conclusion

Bob Michel later told an interviewer that his "most exhilarating days were those during the first Reagan administration."[78] It was during 1981–1982 that he had the most influence over the GOP Conference as his party basked in the afterglow of the Reagan victory, and his members responded well to his leading by "gentle persuasion."[79] Michel saw himself as an "institutionalist" and "servant of the president."[80] He expertly melded both as he sought to implement President Reagan's economic agenda. He did so by honoring the traditions and formal rules of the House.

This chapter began with a discussion of the conditional agency approach and used the story of the legislative process related to the Economic Recovery

Tax Act of 1981, with the aid of archival documents from the Robert H. Michel Papers, to reveal how Michel deftly maneuvered through the political contexts of the time to deliver this pathbreaking bill. In keeping with the conditional agency approach, Michel had a clear goal: to pass President Reagan's tax cuts. He did so by convincing ambivalent party members to stay in the fold and resist negotiating with the Democrats on a compromise bill.

Michel's choices reflected his leadership style and his own personal characteristics. They are as much a part of the explanation for the successful passage of this bill as Ronald Reagan's political skills or other contextual factors, such as the ideologically divided House Democrats. Michel best described his agency, so to speak, when he explained his interaction with his members:

> Each member is a separate entity. You can't treat two alike. I know what I can get and what I can't, when to back off and when to push harder. It's not a matter of twisting arms. It's bringing them along by gentle persuasion. Sometimes they don't realize they're being brought into the orbit. You get down to the end of the walkway and you say, "Hey, we aren't 2 cents apart, are we?" and he says, "Well, I guess we aren't."[81]

Michel chose to treat his members with respect, listen to their concerns, and find ways to incorporate them into the political process, whether it was creating working groups to channel the energy of restless conservatives like Newt Gingrich or setting up meetings with the Gypsy Moths to ensure their policy priorities were heard by President Reagan.

Reagan's talents were formidable, and his use of the powers of the presidency still remains among the most storied to this day, but the successful passage of the tax bill belongs as much to Michel as it does to him. Michel made a choice to eschew strategies designed to win the House majority in order to win legislative and messaging battles. As Matthew Green notes, winning the majority is among the primary goals of the minority leader,[82] but Michel wisely and controversially deemphasized this goal and the confrontational tactics that came with it. He led gently by leveraging the good relationships he had with the House Democratic leadership to ensure a fair and timely hearing for Ronald Reagan's agenda.

The end of 1981 saw looming threats to the fiscal health of the country, and Michel did not always enjoy the same level of success in the legislative battles to follow. As criticism of Reagan's tax plan mounted, Michel said: "The Congress has set more records in the past nine months than any Congress in my memory. A good many Members took these historic and unprecedented actions at considerable political risk, based on their strong conviction in what we are attempting to do."[83] House Republicans and the 97th Congress achieved these goals because of Michel. It is very plausible that another minority leader with a different temperament and leadership style would have produced a different outcome. Bob Michel's leadership on what became the Economic Recovery Tax Act demonstrates the importance of understanding *who* political leaders are and *how* they make strategic decisions in the legislative process.

Notes

1. Fred W. Beuttler interview with RHM, September 6, 2007, RHM Papers, Post-Congressional Series, f. Subjects: Interviews (2).
2. Adam Clymer, "Robert Michel Dies at 93; House GOP Leader Prized Conciliation," *New York Times*, February 17, 2017.
3. RHM Papers, Speech and Trip File, f. August 29, 1966.
4. RHM Papers, Speech and Trip File, f. November 11, 1976.
5. "Congress Enacts President Reagan's Tax Plan," *Congressional Quarterly Almanac 1981* (Washington, DC: Congressional Quarterly Inc., 1982), 91–104, at library.cqpress.com/cqalmanac/cqa181-1171841.
6. "Congress Enacts President Reagan's Tax Plan."
7. "Address Before a Joint Session of the Congress on the Program for Economic Recovery," February 18, 1981, *Public Papers of the Presidents of the United States, Ronald Reagan, 1981* (Washington: US Government Printing Office, 1982), 108.
8. RHM Papers, Press Series, f. Remarks and Releases: February 18, 1981.
9. See Randall Strahan, *Leading Representatives: The Agency of Leaders in the Politics of the U.S. House* (Baltimore: John Hopkins University Press, 2007), 4–5.
10. Strahan argues against the principal-agent model of congressional leadership popularized in the 1990s in favor of evaluating individual characteristics. See Barbara Sinclair, *Legislators, Leaders, and Lawmakers: The U.S. House of Representatives in the Post Reform Era* (Baltimore: John Hopkins University Press, 1995).
11. Strahan, *Leading Representatives*, 4.
12. Strahan, *Leading Representatives*, 4.
13. Art Pine, "Revolt Against Taxes . . . and Performance," *Washington Post*, June 11, 1978.
14. Ronald Reagan entered his first term with public support, which yielded a high approval rating of 60 percent in mid-March 1981. See Frank Newport, Jeffrey M. Jones, and Lydia Saad, "Ronald Reagan from the People's Perspective: A Gallup Poll Review," at news.gallup.com/poll/11887/ronald-reagan-from-peoples-perspective-gallup-poll-review.aspx.
15. *Congressional Insight*, May 15, 1981, RHM, Press, f. Subject. Michel, Robert (1).
16. David W. Rohde, *Parties and Leaders in the Postreform House* (Chicago: University of Chicago Press, 1991), 47.
17. Martin Tolchin, "The Troubles of Tip O'Neill," *New York Times*, August 16, 1981.
18. "Address Before a Joint Session of the Congress on the Program for Economic Recovery," at www.history.house.gov.
19. RHM Papers, Speech and Trip File, f. March 24, 1981.

20. RHM Papers, Speech and Trip File, f. Introduction of the Speaker, January 5, 1981; RHM Papers, Press Series, f. Remarks and Releases: January 5, 1981.
21. RHM, Press Series, f. Remarks and Releases: March 11, 1981.
22. RHM, Press Series, f. Remarks and Releases: March 11, 1981.
23. See chapter 8 by Daniel Palazzolo in this volume for a detailed analysis of the legislative process concerning the 1981 budget reconciliation bill.
24. RHM, Press Series, f. Remarks and Releases: March 17, 1981.
25. *Congressional Insight*, May 15, 1981, RHM Papers, Press Series, f. Subject: Michel, Robert (1).
26. *Congressional Insight*, May 15, 1981, RHM Papers, Press Series, f. Subject: Michel, Robert (1).
27. "Congress Enacts President Reagan's Tax Plan."
28. "Congress Enacts President Reagan's Tax Plan."
29. "Congress Enacts President Reagan's Tax Plan."
30. *Congressional Quarterly Almanac*, 97th Congress, First Session, 1981, vol. 36 (Washington, DC: Congressional Quarterly Inc., 1982), 91–104.
31. RHM Papers, Press Series, f. Remarks and Releases: April 9, 1981.
32. "Congress Enacts President Reagan's Tax Plan."
33. "Robert H. Michel," ca. 1985, RHM Papers, Information File, f. Michel. The original source of this document is not noted but may have come from *Politics in America*.
34. RHM to Bob Walker, April 27, 1981, RHM Papers, General Series, f. 97th Congress: News Media.
35. Rowland Evans and Robert Novak, "Reagan's Men Turn Up the Heat," *New York Post*, May 16, 1981, RHM Papers, Press Series, f. Memoranda 1981–1988 (1).
36. Evans and Novak, "Reagan's Men Turn Up the Heat."
37. Evans and Novak, "Reagan's Men Turn Up the Heat."
38. Evans and Novak, "Reagan's Men Turn Up the Heat."
39. Margot Hornblower, "The Master of Gentle Persuasion," *Washington Post*, August 10, 1981.
40. Mike Johnson to Michel and Lott, May 18, 1981, RHM Papers, Press Series, f. Memoranda 1981–1988 (1).
41. Mike Johnson to Michel and Lott, May 18, 1981, RHM Papers, Press Series, f. Memoranda 1981–1988 (1).
42. Mike Johnson to Michel and Lott, May 18, 1981, RHM Papers, Press Series, f. Memoranda 1981–1988 (1).
43. Like Palazzolo in this volume, I also use the term "cross-partisan" instead of "bipartisan" because the former refers to a situation where a minority of one party joins the majority of another in passing a bill. See also Charles O. Jones, *The Presidency in a Separated System* (Washington, DC: Brookings Institution Press, 2005).
44. Mike Johnson to Michel and Lott, May 18, 1981, RHM Papers, Press Series, f. Memoranda 1981–1988 (1).
45. Joseph White and Aaron Wildavsky, *The Deficit and Public Interest: The Search for Responsible Budgeting in the 1980s* (Berkeley: University of California Press, 1991), 161.
46. RHM Papers, Leadership Series, f. 97th Congress: Dear Colleague, May 29, 1981.
47. *CQ Almanac*, 97th Congress, First Session, 1981, 91–104.
48. Steven R. Weissman, "President Accedes to Major Revisions in Tax-Cut Package," *New York Times*, June 5, 1981.

49. James S. Fleming, *Window on Congress: A Congressional Biography of Barber B. Conable Jr.* (Rochester, NY: University of Rochester Press, 2004), 290

50. RHM Papers, Press Series, f. Remarks and Releases: June 1, 1981.

51. RHM Papers, Presidential Scrapbooks, f. 50.

52. Weissman, "President Accedes to Major Revisions," 1981.

53. *CQ Almanac*, 97th Congress, First Session, 1981, 91–104.

54. *U.S. News & World Report*, May 25, 1981, RHM Papers, Scrapbooks, f. Clippings, 1981.

55. Beuttler interview with RHM, September 6, 2007.

56. RHM Papers, Press Series, f. Remarks and Releases, June 8, 1981.

57. Fleming, *Window on Congress*, 291–292.

58. RHM Papers, Speech and Trip Series, f. June 23, 1981.

59. RHM Papers, Speech and Trip Series, f. June 23, 1981.

60. Johnson to Michel, ca. June 11, 1981, RHM Papers, Press Series, f. Memoranda 1981–1988 (1).

61. White and Wildavsky, *The Deficit and Public Interest*, 174.

62. White and Wildavsky, *The Deficit and Public Interest*, 172.

63. White and Wildavsky, *The Deficit and Public Interest*, 29.

64. Thomas B. Edsall, "Rostenkowski Aside, House Likes Indexing," *Washington Post*, July 18, 1981.

65. "Gypsy Moths" was a pejorative term used by some conservative Republicans to describe moderate members of their party who mostly represented the northeastern or midwestern urban parts of the country—an area that is also the habitat for the invasive Gypsy moth, which damages trees.

66. David S. Broder, "The Gypsy Moths," *Washington Post*, July 27, 1981.

67. Fleming, *Window on Congress*, 297–299.

68. Fleming, *Window on Congress*, 297–298.

69. White and Wildavsky, *The Deficit and Public Interest*, 176.

70. White and Wildavsky, *The Deficit and Public Interest*, 177.

71. Fleming, *Window on Congress*, 297–298.

72. RHM Papers, Press Series, f. Remarks and Releases, July 28, 1981.

73. RHM Papers, Press Series, f. Remarks and Releases: The Michel Report: "Tax Cut Alternative Nearing Final Consideration," July 27, 1981.

74. Fleming, *Window on Congress*, 299.

75. Fleming, *Window on Congress*, 299–300.

76. RHM Papers, Press Series, f. Remarks and Releases: July 29, 1981.

77. Ronald Reagan to RHM, July 30, 1981, RHM Papers, Scrapbooks, Presidential Scrapbooks, f. 50.

78. Beuttler interview with RHM, September 6, 2007.

79. "Robert H. Michel," ca. 1985 [perhaps *Politics in America*], RHM Information File.

80. Hornblower, "The Master of Gentle Persuasion."

81. Hornblower, "The Master of Gentle Persuasion."

82. Matthew N. Green, *Underdog Politics: The Minority Party in the U.S. House of Representatives* (New Haven, CT: Yale University Press, 2015), 10.

83. RHM to Dallas Williams, October 15, 1981, RHM Papers, Legislative Series, f. 97th, Budget.

CHAPTER 8

FROM "EXHILARATING DAYS" TO PRAGMATIC POLITICS

Bob Michel's Leadership in the Budget Process, 1981–1994

Daniel J. Palazzolo

B ob Michel's leadership in the budget process during his time as minority leader was influenced by both the political and institutional context from 1981 to 1994 and his personal qualities. Divided party control, large deficits, and divisions within the House Republican Party positioned Michel to serve as an agent for Republican presidents and to pursue a "middleman" style of leadership, reconciling varying views within the party.[1] Those conditions also afforded Michel some leeway, and his approach to leadership reflected his personal choices and individual qualities. A fiscally conservative, probusiness, midwestern Republican and a pragmatic legislator who was oriented to House politics in the 1950s, Michel preferred to serve Republican presidents and favored the middleman style. Indeed, Michel maintained this posture in spite of institutional and political changes that encouraged a more partisan and confrontational approach to leadership.

Michel was most influential in the budget process when Republican presidents—Ronald Reagan and George H. W. Bush—sought agreements with Democrats. Michel played a vital and perhaps underappreciated role in the passage of the 1981 budget reconciliation bill. Thereafter, during the 1980s, Michel found himself in the middle of debates within the party over whether tax increases should be a part of deficit reduction plans. Although

Table 8.1 Major ways in which House Republicans
divided in the 1980s–1990s

West and South	vs.	Northeast and Midwest
Younger Party Activists	vs.	Older "District Guys" and "Committee Guys"
"Bomb Throwers"	vs.	"Responsible Partners in Governing"
Conservatives	vs.	Moderates
Congressional GOP Loyalists	vs.	Presidential GOP Loyalists
Supporters of a "National Strategy"	vs.	Supporters of a "Local Strategy"

Source: William F. Connelly, Jr., and John J. Pitney, Jr., *Congress' Permanent Minority? Republicans in the U.S. House* (Lanham, MD: Rowman & Littlefield, 1994), 20.

he personally opposed raising taxes, Michel sided with Reagan and Bush and some House Republicans and against majorities of House Republicans to support deficit reduction plans that included spending cuts *and* tax increases. During the first year of Bill Clinton's presidency and unified Democratic Party control of government, Michel adopted some aspects of opposition party leadership, but he did not abandon a commitment to constructive engagement and resisted the more aggressive and confrontational tactics of his successor, Newt Gingrich (R-GA).

Bob Michel's Leadership Style

Congressional leadership style, tactics, and influence are affected by institutional and political contexts and the personal qualities of leaders.[2] Several studies on Speakers of the House find that their leadership style and ability to advance legislative goals depend on the degree of party unity; leaders exercise more influence and leverage when the members are highly unified or are in agreement on public policy goals.[3] Other studies show that institutional and political conditions provide leaders with leeway to pursue their own goals, and individual qualities can have independent and consequential effects on congressional leadership.[4]

The degree of party unity affects minority party leadership, though the minority leader faces different challenges than the Speaker. In varying degrees, minority parties seek four goals: gain majority standing, advance policy favorable to the party's interests, protect procedural rights, and support the president if he is of the same party.[5] Divisions within the minority party, together with a president of the minority leader's party, can create conflicting goals for the minority leader. Thus, while Speakers of the House must be responsive to the policy preferences of the majority of members who elect them to office,[6] minority party leaders have more leeway when the president is setting the party's priorities.

Several conditions affected Michel's role in the budget process: the degree of party unity, the size of the minority party, the party of the president, and budget deficits. As William Connelly and John Pitney point out, the House Republican Party was divided along several dimensions during Michel's tenure as minority leader (see Table 8.1).

In addition, electoral changes during this period accelerated a shift in geographical representation. From the 97th Congress (1981–1982) through the 103rd Congress (1993–1994), the number of Republicans from the Midwest and Northeast declined from 108 to 81, while the number from the South and West increased from 84 to 95.[7] The party grew more ideologically conservative and more focused on winning the majority during Michel's tenure as minority leader. Meanwhile, the House Democratic Party became more unified and more liberal over time (Figure 8.1). In addition, the largest minority Michel worked with during his time as minority leader was in the 97th Congress (Figure 8.2), a time when he had the most influence in the budget process. Finally, large and persistent budget deficits dominated the policy agenda throughout Michel's tenure as minority leader,[8] forcing Republicans to confront tradeoffs between two competing policy priorities: lower taxes or lower deficits. (See also Figure 8.3.)

Yet these conditions also provided Michel with some leeway to choose from among the four primary goals of a minority leader—electioneering, messaging, legislating, and obstructing.[9] Although Michel devoted some time to electioneering and messaging, he clearly favored legislating above

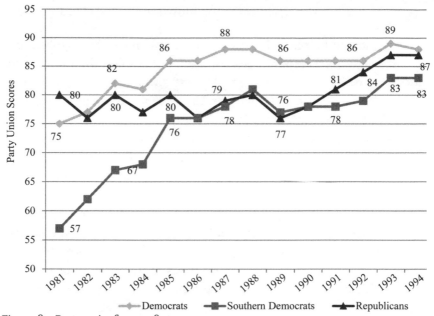

Figure 8.1 Party unity from 1981 to 1994

Source: Party unity scores are extracted from Harold W. Stanley and Richard G. Niemi, eds., "Table 5-10 Party Unity in Congressional Voting (1954–2014)," in *Vital Statistics in American Politics* (Washington, DC: Congressional Quarterly Press, 2015), 211–212.

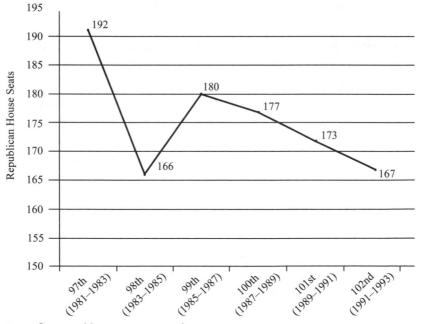

Figure 8.2 Republican House seats by Congress

Source: "Party Divisions in the House of Representatives: 1789–Present," history. house.gov/Institution/Party-Divisions/Party-Divisions.

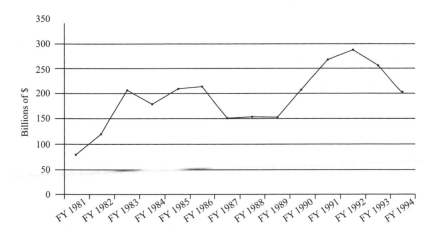

Figure 8.3 Annual deficits, FY 1981–1984 (in billions)
Source: Congressional Budget Office, Historical Budget Data, www.cbo.gov/about
/products/budget-economic-data#2.

the rest, and his leadership in the budget process reflected a pragmatic, prob-
lem-solving approach. He was aligned more with the members who shared
the qualities on the right-hand side of Table 8.1, supporting the priorities of
Republican presidents (even when those priorities conflicted with the majority of House Republicans) and compromising with Democratic leaders, but
he also sought to reconcile differences among Republicans.

Michel's reflections on leadership reveal his personal preference for the
middleman style, acting as agent of the president and bipartisan pragmatist.
When talking about the factions within the party, Michel said: "You can't treat
two alike. I know what I can get and what I can't, when to back off and when
to push harder. It's not a matter of twisting arms. It's bringing them along by
gentle persuasion."[10] And: "The great task of political leadership is not to get
caught up in factions and divisions but to transcend them and move forward."[11]

A minority leader's commitment to serving the president of his or her
party is also partly a matter of choice and conviction,[12] and Michel's support for
Reagan and Bush corresponded with his goal of legislating. He noted: "I was
elected leader in a Republican administration to help a Republican administration."[13] And: "I'm the servant of the president. I like being a good soldier."[14]
Although Michel did not always agree with the policy details advocated by Reagan and Bush, he was committed to advancing their budget priorities.

Finally, at a time of growing party polarization, when insurgent, younger
Republicans in the House sought confrontation with the Democrats, Michel's

pragmatic, bipartisan approach to governing was a throwback to a bygone era. Michel noted: "I recalled the days of Joe Martin and Sam Rayburn. I said, 'When they switched back and forth, depending on who was in the majority, they always had a great respect for one another.'"[15] He believed that "there is a lot of responsibility to being the leader. . . . In that role you have to deport yourself in a manner in which you can submerge the partisanship and the confrontation for the good of the country. That's what's expected of you."[16] And: "I think it's more acceptable to the American public, to see that the leaders of the opposite parties with widely divergent views can still get together, talk about it, and resolve the differences."[17]

The following analysis of budget politics from 1981 to 1993 shows that Michel's actions reflected a combination of the political and institutional context and his personal view of leadership.

1981: Realizing the Reagan Revolution

Reflecting on his career, Michel remarked, "My most exhilarating days were those during the first Reagan Administration. We only had 192 members, but we enacted his program. . . . Now that was satisfying. You'd go home at night and say, 'Well, I did the Lord's work today (laughs).'"[18] Although President Reagan was clearly the driving force behind major shifts in spending and tax policy in 1981, Michel contributed to the enactment of budget policy in the House. He complemented the White House communications strategy with outside constituents, managed the budget process through the House, and mitigated the losses of House Republicans on key roll call votes, especially on the most difficult piece of the budget: a reconciliation bill that cut domestic spending.

In his campaign for president, Reagan promised to cut taxes, lower government spending, restore the national defense, and balance the federal budget. He defeated the incumbent president, Jimmy Carter, by nearly 10 percent of the popular vote and carried forty-four states with a total of 489 Electoral College votes. Meanwhile, the Republicans gained twelve Senate seats and majority control of the Senate (marking the first time in twenty-eight years the Republicans had won a majority in either chamber), as well as thirty-three House seats. The surge in GOP House seats together with a faction of forty, mostly southern Democrats—the Conservative Democratic Forum—created a conservative majority in the House. The elections essentially delivered a conservative policy mandate.[19]

Table 8.2 Votes on major budget actions in the House (1981)

Date	Subject of roll call vote	Yeas–Nays
May 7	Gramm-Latta I: FY 1982 First Budget Resolution	253–176 R 190–0 D 63–176 SD 46–32
June 24	Previous Question on Budget Reconciliation Bill	210–217 R 1–188 D 209–29 SD 54–24
June 25	Resolution for Considering Gramm-Latta II	214–208 R 188–0 D 26–208 SD 22–55
June 26	Gramm-Latta II: Budget Reconciliation Substitute	217–211 R 188–2 D 29–209 SD 26–52
July 29	Conable-Hance: Substitute Tax Cuts	238–195 R 190–1 D 48–194 SD 36–43

Source: Compiled by author from *Congressional Quarterly Almanac*, various editions.
Note: R = Republicans, D = Democrats, SD = Southern Democrats

Bob Michel welcomed the opportunity to build a governing coalition in the House. As he explained to his colleagues following the election of Democrat Thomas P. "Tip" O'Neill as Speaker on January 5: "I should like to feel . . . that when the really big issues of great importance are considered in this House, there will be many occasions when partisanship will be laid aside and a significant number of you [meaning Democrats] will be so persuaded by our logic, good sense and compelling arguments that you will actually vote with us." Michel continued: "You do have it within your power, in this House, to give life and breath to the new President-Elect's proposals, modify them slightly or drastically, or to kill any one of them outright. I simply want to pledge to you Members of the Majority my desire as the Republican Leader to work with you in the best interests of the American people."[20]

Yet, because the majority party almost always dictates the rules for considering legislative acts in the House, Speaker O'Neill had the leverage to disrupt the process and potentially undermine President Reagan's budget. Michel's first move in the budget process was to make sure that O'Neill followed through on a promise (made during a January meeting with Michel and President Reagan) to give Reagan's budget a fair hearing in the House.[21] To ensure that O'Neill followed through on that promise, Michel quietly warned O'Neill after the meeting that he would not hesitate to deploy an arcane and seldom used procedure dealing with presidential rescissions of appropriations. Reagan included a slew of spending rescissions in this budget that were referred to the House Appropriations Committee. Under Title X of the Budget and Impoundment Control Act of 1974, those rescissions could be discharged from the committee at the request of an individual member with the support of just one-fifth of the House.[22] The motion to discharge a rescission is highly privileged and not debatable in the House. The discharge rule enabled the minority leader to force the majority to vote on spending legislation, tie up the floor, and put members on record as either supporting or opposing spending items. The Speaker, Michel believed, would not want to incur the inconvenience and disorder, to say nothing of the political damage, a repeated use of the discharge rule could bring to the House.

In order to translate Reagan's campaign goals into law, Congress needed to pass three major initiatives: (1) a budget resolution with spending, revenue, and deficit targets and instructions to congressional committees to cut taxes, increase defense spending, and cut spending in domestic programs (the Gramm-Latta I substitute); (2) a tax bill that codified proposed instructions on tax cuts into law (the Conable-Hance substitute); and (3) a reconciliation bill that codified proposed instructions on spending cuts into law (the Gramm-Latta II substitute). In addition, before approving the reconciliation bill, the House had to pass two procedural votes: one on the previous question to end debate, and the other on the rule for debating and amending the bill. As Table 8.2 shows, the House approved all of those votes, with cross-partisan majorities in each case (i.e., overwhelming majorities of Republicans and a decisive minority of Democrats).[23]

The political conditions—a sweeping electoral victory, the conservative coalition, and Reagan's popularity—contributed to the success of Reagan's budget priorities. President Reagan also benefited from the budget reconciliation process, used for the first time the previous year, which allowed Congress to package individual spending cuts into a single omnibus bill.[24] White House tactics to lobby conservative Democrats also made a difference. David Stockman, the director of the Office of Management and Budget (OMB), revised Reagan's original budget by lowering the deficit and increasing defense spending; Reagan invited members to the White House and promised not to campaign against them if they voted for the budget;[25] and White House political director Lyn Nofzinger coordinated a grassroots campaign with direct mail and phone calls in fifty-one targeted congressional districts (forty-five in the South) that strongly supported Reagan in the 1980 election.[26] In a speech to a joint session of Congress on April 28, just two days prior to the House vote on the budget resolution, Reagan urged members to support the "bipartisan" Gramm-Latta substitute.[27]

Michel applauded Reagan's leadership on the budget resolution and the tax and reconciliation bills: "When you've got the right president, like Reagan, to really help you at the top and to be the kind of leader that he was, then, even though we were in the minority, it was possible, through the president's influence over conservative Democrats, to wean them away from their party line and have some wonderful winning ways."[28] And: "I have to give a lot of credit to the president himself, who I had never thought got near the credit he should have been given for helping the legislative process as much as he did."[29]

After the House passed the budget resolution, Michel announced: "Let history show that we provided the margin of difference that changed the course of American government."[30] On April 23, about a week prior to the vote on the budget resolution, Michel sent to editors of newspapers across the country a fact sheet comparing the Gramm-Latta I substitute with the budget resolution developed by the House Budget Committee and sponsored by its chairman, Jim Jones (D-OK). He noted that the Gramm-Latta substitute contained lower spending, more tax cuts, and larger increases in national defense than Jones's budget resolution. The "fundamental difference," though, was the "economic benefit" from "reordering government priorities."[31] Michel said that tax cuts will spur economic growth, spending cuts will lower inflation, and block grants will give states flexibility to provide government services. Michel noted that Gramm-Latta "has the full support of the Republican Leadership in the House as well as the support of Congressman Charles Stenholm, the Chairman of the Conservative Democratic Forum." He urged the editors to write opinion pieces "to make your readers aware of this vote so that they may have an opportunity to contact their Member of Congress either way."[32]

Michel's pragmatic and bipartisan approach to legislating was evident at a potentially divisive moment in the budget process. When Delbert Latta (R-OH), the ranking Republican on the House Budget Committee, and several colleagues protested naming the budget resolution "Gramm-Latta" (with the Democrat Gramm's name coming first) rather than "Latta-Gramm," Michel explained: "I can only have so many things my way because I'm pleading for support from the other side of the aisle. The way to get it was to not stick it back to the opposition in a partisan sort of way but show conciliation from the very beginning. And of course, that was the way we were successful."[33]

The White House also depended on Michel's legislative skills and ability to maintain Republican support throughout the budget process. "Through the months of bargaining and lobbying over President Reagan's budget and tax bills, Bob Michel was the man the White House depended on for a sense of strategy and timing in the House." The trick was to work "with the White House to sweeten the legislation for conservative Democrats without alienating moderate Republicans from the urban Northeast."[34]

Shortly after the budget resolution passed, Reagan proposed cuts in Social Security spending, and Michel's response is a good example of how he sought to manage differences between the president and House Republicans. In a letter to colleagues on May 21, 1981, Michel urged the need to "communicate with our constituents on this subject," which "will require an extensive educational process." Seeking to address the concerns of the members without undermining the president, Michel stated: "Frankly, I do not agree with all of the changes proposed by President Reagan and I am sure many of you have some of the same reservations I have. However, there is no question in my mind that the President acted with courage in facing this problem head-on and not pulling any punches with phony solutions that won't get us beyond next year." He framed the Reagan proposals as a "first volley in a debate that promises to be drawn out and lively." Still, "we ought to reaffirm our commitment to those currently on Social Security and reassure those who are near retirement that we will not abandon those who have legitimate needs." Michel supported the president's efforts even as he disagreed with some of the details. Reagan, Michel said, "faced controversial issues forthrightly and did not shy away from the political consequences of a spirited public debate. . . . That is the meaning of political leadership." The letter listed numerous possible reforms and took a positive tone: "It can be done if we all work together, deliberate openly and honestly, and exercise courage any difficult decision demands." Michel stated that Congress should not "pull the rug out from under those individuals and families who are economically locked into retirement years that depend on benefits derived from the Social Security system."[35]

The 1981 Reconciliation: House Democrats versus Gramm-Latta II

Analysis of documents in the Michel collection on the budget process suggests that Michel's most significant contribution came when Reagan needed the most help. The reconciliation bill (Gramm-Latta II), which cut spending by $35.2 billion, passed the House by only six votes. Because only twenty-nine Democrats voted for this bill, compared with the sixty-three who voted for the initial budget resolution, Michel's task leading up to the vote was to limit defections of House Republicans, which became very real just two weeks prior to the vote when Stockman released the details of a proposed reconciliation bill favored by the White House. Michel worked behind the scenes to gather critical intelligence on the preferences of House Republicans who dissented from Stockman's proposal. He then worked with the White House to make policy changes before the final draft of the bill, ultimately introduced by Gramm and Latta, reached the House floor. Without those efforts, a key element of the Reagan Revolution may have failed. Michel's leadership during this part of the budget process deserves attention; it must be among his most consequential efforts as Republican Leader.

Before analyzing Michel's role, we should clarify the reconciliation process and the highly unusual sequence that culminated in the passage of Gramm-Latta II, a substitute to the House Budget Committee's reconciliation bill. How unusual? It has not happened before or since. To begin, the House used reconciliation for the first time in 1980, thus setting a precedent the following year, and Michel was strongly in favor of the process: "I think it is absolutely essential to the viability of the budget process that we establish the principle of reconciliation."[36] The process typically begins after a budget resolution is approved by the House Budget Committee and voted on by the

House, both institutions controlled by the majority party. The budget resolution includes reconciliation instructions to committees to reduce spending or change tax policy in programs under their jurisdictions. The resolution sets a deadline for committees to report legislative changes to the House Budget Committee, which compiles the myriad changes into a large package, an omnibus reconciliation bill. The House Rules Committee then crafts a resolution defining the terms for debating and amending the committee's reconciliation bill, and the House acts on it as it would any other bill.

There is a crucial difference between a budget resolution and a reconciliation bill: the resolution is a nonbinding agreement that *recommends* legislative changes, whereas the reconciliation bill *prescribes* specific changes in existing law. The vote on a reconciliation bill comes with greater political risks than a budget resolution, particularly if the bill contains tax increases or spending cuts. Yet the great advantage of an omnibus reconciliation bill is that it allows party leaders and members to frame potentially politically difficult choices (cuts in programs supported by interest groups or constituents, for instance) in favorable terms.[37] By voting for a total package of spending cuts rather than cuts in a particular program, members can say they voted to "reduce government spending" or to "lower deficits" rather than to take a way benefits or to cut spending for a particular program. Nonetheless, in order for the House to approve a reconciliation bill, members must value the aggregate benefit of deficit reduction over the particular spending cuts contained within the bill; otherwise, they may vote against the total package.

In 1981 the reconciliation process was dramatically altered by the fact that the House approved a budget resolution (Gramm-Latta I) that was opposed by the majority party, including the majority party leadership, the majority of the Budget Committee, almost all of the chairs of authorizing committees who received reconciliation instructions, and the Rules Committee.[38] The question was: Would the institutions controlled by the majority party and designed to carry out the reconciliation process follow through on the will of the House (i.e., the cross-partisan coalition of Republicans and conservative Democrats that approved Gramm-Latta I)? As the process unfolded in late May, it became clear to the president's staff and congressional Republican leaders that the answer was "no."

Since the committees controlled by the majority party would not abide by wishes of the majority of the House, Stockman and congressional Republican leaders would need to craft an alternative reconciliation bill outside of the committee system. This process required extraordinary coordination, communication, and organizational leadership, and Michel would play a critical role in steering the process. Initially, Michel instructed Republican members to work through the normal process by advocating policy changes through the authorizing committees that complied with the reconciliation instructions contained in Gramm-Latta I. On May 28, Michel notified members that committees would mark up reconciliation instructions the following week: "It is important that you make your feelings known and seek change within the budget totals so that when the bill comes to the floor we can have a unified Republican position." He invited members to make changes, but adding spending required them to come up with "alternative cost reductions."[39]

By June 4, after realizing that the authorizing committees would fall short of carrying out the reconciliation instructions, Michel notified Republican colleagues that the administration would propose an alternative consistent with the terms of Gramm-Latta I. The coordinating mechanism would be an "information center," consisting of staff from OMB and White House government relations, to handle inquiries from committees and government agencies. The center would handle "reports of problems in achieving reconciliation targets or securing adoption of the President's proposals." It called for "requests for comparative analyses of reconciliation packages" and "requests for Administration positions on proposals that differ from the President's program." The OMB program associate directors were responsible for coordinating evaluations and working with Congress, agencies, the White House, and OMB. Any "major policy issues" would be "taken up with agency heads, Senior White House staff, and where necessary the President." Michel's letter listed the desk officers assigned to each of the nine committee pairs in the House and Senate that had jurisdiction over reconciliation instructions.[40]

By June 12, Stockman presented a draft of the Republican alternative reconciliation bill, including substantial spending cuts and policy changes in a broad range of programs. Michel sent a "Dear Colleague" letter to House Republicans "requesting comments and major concerns" on the "proposed bi-partisan reconciliation substitute" that was prepared by OMB. He noted that the final version of the bill would be drafted by minority leadership staff working with committee staff, and "the primary concern will be to develop a package that will appeal to a majority in the House and minimize differences that would have to be worked out in conference with the Senate. As this potential substitute is drafted, please be assured that the proposals developed by our Members in the several committees will receive priority consideration."[41] Members were given three days to reply.

Michel's mailbox was flooded with responses from forty-four House Republicans concerned about various parts of Stockman's proposal.[42] A few members expressed concerns about public policy effects, but most dealt with issues related to constituent interests, including concerns about getting reelected. Fifteen of the members were from competitive districts and twelve represented districts in which Reagan won 50 percent or less of the popular vote.[43] Twenty-six of the members were from the Northeast or Midwest, and eighteen were from the South and West.

The letters focused on a range of policy issues: block grants for education, regulation of the Guaranteed Student Loan program, pricing of natural gas, impact aid for communities with military bases, termination of the Clinch River Breeder Reactor, Conrail subsidies, dairy subsidies, cost-of-living-adjustments (COLAs) for civil servant retirees, and on and on.[44] Numerous members stated that their support for the reconciliation bill would depend on changes to Stockman's proposal, and the bill was in jeopardy of failing to pass the House if certain provisions were not removed or enhanced. Here are a few notable examples of objections made by GOP members:

James Broyhill (R-NC), ranking member on Energy and Commerce, wrote that OMB recommendations would "mean the loss of several Republican votes on the Energy and Commerce Committee."[45]

Clair Burgener (R-CA), writing for himself and Bill Lowery (R-CA), listed two items that were "absent": the High Temperature Gas Cooled Reactor program and the Geothermal Binary Cycle Demonstration Plant. "The inclusion of these items in any bipartisan substitute would greatly enhance our chances of adopting the substitute."[46]

Bobbie Fielder (R-CA) expressed concerns about losing votes over the elimination of the twice-per-year COLA for civil service retirees. "This is an inequitable cut. By the way, President Reagan is a double dipper. He gets his government paycheck and Social Security."[47]

Steve Gunderson (R-WI) expressed major reservations about cuts in student loans and dairy price supports: "The facts are, Bob, I have tried everything I know of to get this Administration to give me something to take to my dairy farmers. At this point, it is very difficult not to agree with those who charge this is an anti-dairy administration." And: "My election is due in large part to the fact that I carried each of the campuses in my district by almost 2–1 margins, with a pledge to work for and with students." Thus, "I might consider voting against the Administration, if necessary to properly represent my district. . . . My district is the largest dairy district in the country. And I have 46,000 college students as well."[48]

Stewart McKinney (R-CT) opposed the OMB proposal of eliminating the lending and borrowing power of the National Consumer Cooperative Bank: "I could not support such a substitute."[49] McKinney also signed, along with eleven other Republicans, a separate letter from Chalmers Wylie (R-OH) that stated: "We could not support a proposal so long as it would, for all practical purposes, kill the National Consumer Cooperative."[50]

Michel took the intelligence from those and many other letters back to Stockman, who made numerous adjustments to the substitute bill, which would become Gramm-Latta II. Stockman spent the next two weeks making deals with wavering Republicans and southern Democrats who had complained about specific provisions in the bill.[51]

When the House convened to take up the Budget Committee's reconciliation bill, Michel noted that almost half the authorizing committees had failed to comply with reconciliation instructions. The Republican leadership requested to offer Gramm-Latta II as a single omnibus substitute to the Budget Committee's bill. But the Democratic-controlled Rules Committee approved a resolution that required the Republicans to offer a series of amendments rather than a single bill. Under this scheme, the House would vote on proposed spending cuts in individual programs rather than the whole package. This approach made the votes much more politically difficult for Republicans wary about voting to cut programs and harder for Republican members to stay together behind Gramm-Latta II. Michel criticized the Democratic leadership's tactic: "You have denied what I believe is a majority of this House a clean vote up or down on our package. You are denying the President a clean cut expression of what he prefers."[52]

Thus, Republicans and a minority of Democrats would need to defeat the Rules Committee's resolution and replace it with a rule that allowed the House to vote on Gramm-Latta II as a single substitute bill. Ultimately all but one Republican voted to defeat the previous question, which would have ended debate and allowed the House to move forward with the rule. With the support of twenty-nine Democrats, the previous question was defeated by seven votes, and the Republican leadership effectively took control of the floor. The House proceeded to pass Gramm-Latta II. Only two Republicans—Claudine Schneider (R-RI) and Charles Dougherty (R-PA)—voted against the bill, and it passed the House by six votes.

Given the number of objections to Stockman's original draft, without Michel's leadership the bill may very well have failed. As the *Washington Post* reported: "It was almost anti-climactic when the reconciliation bill passed 232 to 193. As the vanquished general, Speaker Thomas P. (Tip) O'Neill, Jr. (D-Mass.) supplied the battle's final commentary. Recognizing Minority Leader Robert H. Michel (R-Ill.) as a matter of routine at the session's end, he referred, intentionally or otherwise, to him as the 'majority leader.' Republicans cheered, Democrats winced."[53] The president privately acknowledged Michel's pivotal role in a letter the next day: "You have once again proved your political courage and commitment to restoring the vitality and strength of the American economy."[54]

1981–1992: Deficit Politics and the Problem of Taxes

The enactment of President Reagan's economic and budget plan unified the Republican Party around the promise that tax cuts would stimulate economic growth and raise federal government revenues. Theoretically, spending cuts in domestic programs plus the economic growth from the tax cuts would result in lower deficits. But by the fall of 1981, it became clear that the numbers were not adding up. With revenues falling short, a growing deficit would put upward pressure on interest rates, which in turn could undermine or erase positive growth effects from the tax cuts.

Concerned about the market effects of larger deficits, Stockman called for an additional $15 billion in spending cuts.[55] Michel urged Republicans to keep faith with the president: "The President has put before us a challenge to reduce the cost of government more than we have already, and I am prepared to meet that challenge. I am hopeful there will be a concerted effort by Members of both parties in the coming months to enact legislation necessary to accomplish the President's goal of a balanced budget and reduced interest rates."[56] Yet a group of Northeast and Midwest Republicans—the so-called Gypsy Moths—opposed cutting more than $5 billion.[57] Placing his concerns about the adverse effects of budget deficits above all else, Stockman negotiated a deal with Senate Republican leaders that included a mix of tax increases ($80 billion) and spending cuts ($70 billion).

House Republicans opposed the plan, but a deficit reduction proposal by a Republican administration that contained a mixture of tax increases and spending cuts foreshadowed a debate within the party that would last for a decade. Republicans divided generally into two camps: the supply-siders (or the "growth" wing of the party), who opposed tax increases to reduce deficits; and fiscal conservatives (or the "budget balance" wing of the party), who preferred not to raise taxes but would support "revenue enhancements" together with spending cuts to lower deficits.

The decision-making calculations of individual Republicans over deficits and taxes—what Connelly and Pitney refer to as the Rubik's Cube of institutions, interests, ideas, and individuals[58]—defined the challenge to leadership on budget matters for most of Michel's tenure as minority leader. His institutional commitment was to support the Republican president; his policy preferences aligned with fiscal conservatives; and his political approach was to act as a middleman, seeking to bridge differences among House Republicans. As the years progressed, and the tax-cut wing of the party strengthened, Michel struggled increasingly to bring those three goals together. On several occasions, in order to carry out the role of agent for the president's priorities, he would vote with a minority of House Republicans for deficit reduction plans that included revenue increases.

1984: Deficit Reduction Act

On April 11, 1984, majorities of both parties in the House passed a bill that would raise revenue by $50 billion, mainly by closing loopholes and increasing taxes on alcohol and cigarettes. The vote was 318–97 in favor (Democrats 223–31 and Republicans 95–66). Michel explained his support: "I do not like raising taxes, it runs against my grain. . . . However, I am going to vote for . . . the bill. One reason is that we do have a commitment to reduce expenditures that comes from down the avenue." He then read a letter from President Reagan, in which Reagan emphasized that this bill would be part of a larger compromise of spending cuts and tax loophole closings. "I will vote for this tax bill because the president is committed, if no one else is." And: "This legislation is the product of the good faith of Members of both sides of the aisle. . . . This legislation is realistic as a component of deficit reduction."[59]

But Republican support for the bill eroded after the conference with the Senate produced a bill with limited spending cuts. The final bill included $50 billion in new taxes and just $13 billion in spending cuts. Michel noted again that he did not like the taxes, but it was "part of a three-legged stool . . . on deficit reduction." The main policy rationale for the bill was that, even though the economy was growing, financial markets, the press, and the

Federal Reserve ("those who influence interest rates") wanted to see deficit reduction. "What I have to be today is a realist. . . . If we don't take steps to make a down payment on the deficit we will be contributing to that negative psychology. . . . We will be defeating our own purpose." Thus, "Today we must do what the political and economic facts of life dictate."[60] The bill passed on June 27 by a vote of 268–155. Michel voted for the bill, along with seventy-six House Republicans; but the majority of the party, eighty-six House Republicans, voted against it.

1987: The Omnibus Reconciliation Bill

Three years later, the House GOP's support for a package of spending cuts and tax increases had eroded further. The Omnibus Reconciliation Bill of 1987, which reduced deficits by $76 billion over two years, contained nearly a two-to-one balance of spending cuts to revenue increases. It cut spending by $49.6 billion ($30 billion in mandatory spending cuts, $19.6 billion in discretionary spending cuts) and raised revenues by $26.6 billion. The Democrats needed Republican support to pass the bill, but the vast majority of Republicans voted against it. On December 12, the bill passed 237–181, with 193 Democrats in favor (51 against) and just 44 Republicans in favor (130 against). Michel voted with the minority of his party again, saying that he preferred a GOP proposal to freeze spending: "But we do not always get our way in this body, especially when having to deal with the majority here, the other body and our own President when he has to be part of the negotiations."[61]

1990: Budget Enforcement Act and Omnibus Reconciliation Bill

The tension between the supply-siders and the fiscal conservatives resurfaced in the epic battle over a budget summit agreement in 1990, which was forged by a group of Democratic and Republican leaders, including Michel. Facing the possibility of automatic spending cuts to meet the deficit reduction targets set by the Gramm–Rudman–Hollings law, President Bush reneged on his campaign promise not to raise taxes. Five months of high-level negotiations produced a plan with $289 billion in spending cuts and $177 billion in tax increases and user fees. Anticipating opposition within his party led by Minority Whip Newt Gingrich, Michel stated on the House floor:

"I wish there were a better way of doing it. Suffice it to say that the strong point of our agreement can be found only in its totality. We have to accept it as a whole, as it provides the only bipartisan basis for attacking the deficit problem." He also stressed the importance of making "savings in entitlement programs."[62]

But in a rebuke of both Democratic and Republican leaders, on October 4 the House (including majorities of both parties) rejected a budget resolution containing the terms of the budget summit.[63] Democratic leaders and the Bush White House rallied to develop an alternative package that reduced the deficit by $496.2 billion, including $146.3 billion in revenues. The bill contained higher taxes on upper income earners, more cuts in defense, and smaller cuts in Medicare spending, as well as caps on spending and pay-as-you-go provisions for subsequent proposals to increase spending or cut taxes. Like the 1987 Omnibus Reconciliation Bill, the 1990 Budget Enforcement Act (BEA) and Omnibus Reconciliation Act depended on a cross-partisan coalition. The bill passed on October 27 by a vote of 228–200; forty-seven Republicans, including Michel, voted for the bill, and 126 voted against it.

The 1990 BEA and Omnibus Reconciliation Act capped a twelve-year stretch in which Michel loyally supported Republican presidents and constructive compromises with Democratic leaders. Commenting on his support of the controversial budget, Michel noted: "George Bush is still our president for another two years. As the leader, I have an obligation to support him, try to do everything I possibly can do to the best, not only for him but for the country."[64] Reflecting later on a conversation Michel had with Bill Frenzel about his governing philosophy, Michel put it this way:

I said, "Bill, we've got to have a substitute on the budget resolution." The guys just said, "Let's vote against it. We don't want anything." And I said, "But Bill that isn't being very constructive. . . . You maybe feel that you'd like to be for something. Why, let me give you all of the encouragement that I possibly can to come up with an alternative." Then, of course, over time it developed that we had what we called the Constructive Republican Alternative to pieces of legislation. That's because we just couldn't be constant naysayers over that period of time. We just thought it was good politics to be for something, even though the prospects for winning might be very dim.[65]

The Clinton Presidency: Confrontation
or Constructive Leadership?

The 1992 elections presented a new challenge for Bob Michel. For twelve years, if either of the two Republican presidents sought compromises including tax increases, Michel could choose constructive engagement with Democratic leaders. He could defer to presidential priorities, even if it meant siding with a minority of Republicans on taxes. The political and institutional context corresponded with his personal view of leadership. But the election of President Bill Clinton and unified Democratic majorities in the House and Senate marginalized Michel and House Republicans. Unlike Reagan and Bush, Clinton did not need Republican votes to enact budget policy in 1993.

Moreover, years of confrontational tactics by the Conservative Opportunity Society and vigorous efforts by Gingrich to recruit conservative candidates designed to build a Republican majority worked against constructive engagement with the Democrats. The 1992 congressional elections delivered fresh troops to assist Gingrich's effort to take over the House. Michel referred to the 1993 Republican Conference as "the most conservative and antagonistic to the other side." Of the forty-seven freshmen elected in 1992, "seven are thoughtful moderates, and the other forty are pretty darn hardliners, some of them real hard line."[66]

How did Michel respond to those conditions? If only the context mattered, the minority leader would act as the loyal opposition—confront the president, oppose the Democratic budget, and perhaps even offer no alternative to the opposition's budget. In terms of tactics, legislating would be replaced by messaging, electioneering, and possibly obstructing.[67] While Michel pivoted somewhat by publicly opposing Democratic plans to raise taxes and endorsing the party's messaging strategy, he remained open to a constructive approach to minority party leadership. Matthew Green observes: "By 1993, every Republican leader except Robert Michel 'believed in partisan confrontation.'"[68]

Michel's posture as opposition party leader was showcased on February 17, 1993, when he gave the Republican response to President Clinton's State of the Union address. Michel identified differences between the parties, but he wanted to engage the president in the early stages of the process, and he preferred constructive partisanship when the Democrats presented their budget resolution. Clinton highlighted the need for a short-term economic stimulus and a longer-term deficit reduction plan of $493 billion over four years, half of which would come from tax increases. Michel's strategy was to deliver a response in which "the tone is deliberately civil, if candid, in raising questions about the Clinton administration. At this point it would be wrong—and politically stupid—to launch an all out attack on a new President."[69]

Michel's tone was nonconfrontational.[70] He explained: "Rather than give the so-called traditional response to the President's speech, I would like to talk with you as though we were having a cup of coffee in Joe's Restaurant in my hometown of Peoria, IL." Instead of rebuking or criticizing the president: "It is a chance to ask some questions about where our nation is heading." And so it went: "All of us—Democrats, Republicans and Independents—want our new president to succeed." He listed points of agreement with Clinton—welfare reform, cutting the deficit, investment tax credits, and the importance of family and community. Michel, however, opposed tax increases: "Higher taxes and more federal mandates don't create jobs—they destroy jobs,"[71] and he stated that President Clinton's economic plan thus far was "fragmented and ad hoc." But Michel mainly asked questions, almost as a way of seeking clarification of the stimulus plan, the prospect of inflation, and the overall strategy. "Where is it all leading?" "Is it really unfair to ask to see the general blueprint, the grand strategy, the vision . . . ?" "How can we tell if the new Clinton program is good unless we see it in the context of the budget at large?"

While Michel stood by Republican principles, compared with other Republicans he pulled his punches. John Kasich, ranking Republican on the House Budget Committee, said: "I want to make spending reductions now and worry about taxes later." Pete Domenici, ranking Republican on the Senate Budget Committee, complained about Clinton's speech: "I'm really disappointed. . . . This is a program to dramatically increase taxes."[72] Gingrich stated: "It was a good speech and a very destructive program."[73]

On March 18, the House acted on the administration's budget resolution. The night prior to the debate, the GOP Conference voted for a resolution to oppose tax increases. In addition to the budget resolution drafted by the House Budget Committee and a Congressional Black Caucus substitute, the House considered a budget endorsed by Kasich and one by Gerald Solomon (R-NY), the ranking Republican on the Rules Committee. Kasich's budget, which cut spending by $500 billion over five years and contained no tax increases, was supported by 132 Republicans; 41 voted against it. Solomon's budget, which cut spending $555 billion and added $172 billion in revenue, received just 19 Republican votes; 153 Republicans voted against it.[74]

Michel voted with the majority of his party in favor of Kasich's budget, and his speech on the House floor struck a balance between constructive engagement in the process and opposition to the president: "I charged each and every one of those [Republican] members with the role and responsibility to act as though we were a majority party, to put together the kind of budget, on our own, that we thought would sell with most of our members. Obviously, we had no President to lead us; so it was up to us . . . to produce an alternative budget." He was critical of the Clinton budget, a "Madison Avenue product," which was "sold to the public in a slick, expensive telemarketing campaign." He criticized the Budget Committee markup as a "blatant partisan act" and criticized the Democratic plan for increasing taxes and cutting defense spending. "Our plan does not raise taxes on the American people" and "makes a real down payment on the deficit."[75]

Yet, in spite of his differences with the Democrats over taxes,[76] Michel continued to call for constructive bipartisanship. Reflecting on President Clinton's first one hundred days in office at a news conference on April 16, Michel noted the spending cuts in the Republican budget and pointed to a proposal by Solomon and Mike Castle (R-DE) for a line-item veto. He asked the president "to examine these proposals from House Republicans and begin a true bipartisan approach to legislation in the coming months."[77]

On May 17, a few weeks before the House would vote on the reconciliation bill, including an energy tax, Michel told his colleagues the "House Republican leadership is engaging in several efforts to 'turn up the heat' on the Democrats' bill." The letter included talking points on the Ways and Means bill, titled "Clinton's Energy Tax: What Every Taxpayer Should Know." The essential message: "The Clinton energy tax will hurt the consumer, generate unemployment, fuel new spending, and drive the Federal deficit up, not down."[78] Michel highlighted the leadership's new Leader's Communications Advisory Group, which had developed a messaging strategy that assigned responsibility to members with media markets shared by Democrats to explain opposition to the tax bill.

Yet, in early August, after the House completed its work on the budget for 1993, Michel reflected ambivalence about the Republican position on taxes and deficit reduction. He expressed reservations about the unanimous GOP opposition to Clinton's deficit reduction plan: "I'm more comfortable and feel much better about what I can be doing constructively to make things move." The GOP Conference, Michel stated, "wanted a resolution stating flat-out opposition to any tax increases. I had to tell my guys don't talk about a half-trillion-dollar deficit reduction plan if you're absolutely opposed to raising taxes because you can't get there and I'll take you through it anytime."[79] In spite of overwhelming Republican opposition to the Democratic budget, Michel continued to support bipartisan legislating. Two months later, he would announce his decision not to run for reelection.

Conclusion

For twelve of fourteen years during his time as minority leader, Bob Michel played a key legislative role in the budget process—leading efforts to support the budget priorities of Republican presidents. His ability to gather and accommodate the interests of wavering Republican members was crucial to the passage of spending cuts in the 1981 budget reconciliation bill. After 1981, caught between Republican presidents and the majority of House Republicans on taxes, Michel consistently chose to serve the president, a reflection of his pragmatism and preference for legislating. The cross-partisan coalitions around spending and tax packages that Michel helped to forge were critical to the progress Congress and the president made toward reducing the deficit. Of course, as Michel was leaving the House, the party had essentially abandoned its struggle over taxes: given a choice between a compromise containing tax increases and spending cuts and no package at all, Republicans were even more likely to choose the latter. Bipartisan and cross-partisan politics are much less likely today, as polarization has limited the choices of Republican leaders seeking legislative solutions to budget deficits.

Notes

1. David B. Truman, *The Congressional Party: A Case Study* (New York: Wiley and Sons, 1959).
2. For a good review of the literature on the effects of context and personal qualities, see Randall Strahan, *Leading Representatives: The Agency of Leaders in the Politics of the U.S. House* (Baltimore: Johns Hopkins University Press, 2007), chap. 2.
3. See, for example, Joseph Cooper and David W. Brady, "Institutional Context and Leadership Style: The House from Cannon to Rayburn," *American Political Science Review* 75 (1981), 411–426; David W. Rohde, *Parties and Leaders in the Postreform House* (Chicago: University of Chicago Press, 1991); Barbara Sinclair, "The Emergence of Strong Leadership in the 1980s House of Representatives," *Journal of Politics* 54 (1992): 658–684; and Barbara Sinclair, *Legislators, Leaders, and Lawmaking: The House of Representatives in the Postreform Era* (Baltimore: Johns Hopkins University Press, 1995).
4. See, for example, Ronald M. Peters, Jr., *The American Speakership: The Office in Historical Perspective* (Baltimore: Johns Hopkins University Press, 1990); Strahan, *Leading*

Representatives; Matthew N. Green, *The Speaker of the House: A Study of Leadership* (New Haven: Yale University Press, 2010).

5. Matthew N. Green, *Underdog Politics: The Minority Party in the U.S. House of Representatives* (New Haven, CT: Yale University Press, 2015), 10–18.

6. Charles O. Jones, "Joseph G. Cannon and Howard W. Smith: An Essay on the Limits of Leadership in the House of Representatives," *Journal of Politics* 30 (1968): 617–646; David W. Rohde and Kenneth A. Shepsle, "Leaders and Followers in the House of Representatives: Reflections on Woodrow Wilson's Congressional Government," *Congress & the Presidency*, 14 (1987): 111–133; and Sinclair, *Legislators, Leaders, and Lawmaking*.

7. William F. Connelly, Jr., and John J. Pitney, Jr., *Congress' Permanent Minority? Republicans in the U.S. House* (Lanham, MD: Rowman & Littlefield, 1994), 20.

8. Joseph White and Aaron Wildavsky, *The Deficit and the Public Interest* (Berkeley: University of California Press, 1989).

9. Green, *Underdog Politics*, 10.

10. Alan Ehrenhalt, ed., *Politics in America, 1984* (Washington, DC: Congressional Quarterly Inc., 1983), 467.

11. RHM Papers, Speech and Trip File, f. RNC Gala Leadership Breakfast, February 3, 1994.

12. Green, *Underdog Politics*, 15–16.

13. Quoted in Green, *Underdog Politics*, 13.

14. Margot Hornblower, "The Master of Gentle Persuasion," *Washington Post*, August 10, 1981, RHM Papers, Press Series, f. Subject: Michel, Robert.

15. Brien R. Williams interview with RHM, May 24, 2007, RHM Papers, Interfile: Personal Series, f. 2007.

16. Tom Strong, "'Nice Guy' Finishes Last Session in Congress," *Peoria Journal Star*, October 9, 1994, RHM Series, Scrapbooks, f. Clippings 1994 (1).

17. Fred W. Beuttler interview with RHM, September 6, 2007, RHM Papers, Post-Congressional Series, f. Subjects: Interviews (2).

18. Beuttler interview with RHM, September 6, 2007.

19. Charles O. Jones, "Ronald Reagan and the U.S. Congress: Visible Hand Politics," in *The Reagan Legacy: Promise and Performance*, ed. Charles O. Jones (Chatham, NJ: Chatham House Publishers, 1988), 32.

20. RHM Papers, Speech and Trip File, f. Introduction of the Speaker, January 5, 1981.

21. The following account is based on an interview with Billy Pitts, legislative assistant for RHM, November 9, 2017.

22. Discharge of rescissions can occur after the committee has not reported them at the end of twenty-five calendar days. See Congressional Budget and Impoundment Control Act of 1974, Sec. 1017 [2 U.S.C. 688].

23. Politicians often use the term "bipartisan" to describe support for a bill that attracts members of both parties. But I take "bipartisan" to mean majorities of both parties supporting legislation formed by leaders of both parties. "Cross-partisan" is more appropriate for when the majority of one party wins by joining with a minority of the other party, as witnessed on the budget items passed in the House in 1981. See Charles O. Jones, *The Presidency in a Separated System*, 2nd ed. (Washington, DC: Brookings Institution Press, 2005).

24. David Stockman, director of the Office of Management and Budget and chief architect of Reagan's budget, believed reconciliation was the critical vehicle for translating Reagan's goals into legislation. David A. Stockman, *The Triumph of Politics* (New York: Harper & Row, 1986), 159.
25. Hedrick Smith, "Taking Charge of Congress," *New York Times Magazine*, August 9, 1981, 18.
26. Barbara Sinclair, *Majority Leadership in the U.S. House* (Baltimore: Johns Hopkins University Press, 1983), 194–195.
27. Ronald Reagan, *Public Papers of the United States President: Ronald Reagan, 1981* (Washington, DC: US Government Printing Office, 1982), 394.
28. Beuttler interview with RHM, October 15, 2007, 20–21.
29. Beuttler interview with RHM, October 15, 2007.
30. "First Budget Resolution Follows Reagan Plan," *CQ Almanac* 1981, 37th ed., 247–254 (Washington, DC: Congressional Quarterly, 1982), library.cqpress.com/cqalmanac /cqa181–1172387.
31. "Fact Sheet: The Latta-Gramm and Jones Budget Resolutions: An Analysis," from the Office of the Republican Leader, House of Representatives, April 23, 1981, RHM Papers, Leadership Series, 97th Congress, Box 4, f. Dear Colleague Letters 1981–1994.
32. "Dear Editor," April 23, 1981, RHM Papers, Leadership Series, 97th Congress, Box 4, f. Dear Colleague Letters 1981–1994.
33. Beuttler interview with RHM, October 15, 2007.
34. Ehrenhalt, *Politics in America, 1984*, 467.
35. "Important Notice for Members," May 21, 1981, RHM Papers, Leadership Series, 97th Congress, Box 4, f. Dear Colleague Letters 1981–1994.
36. "General Debate—Budget Reconciliation," RHM Papers, Staff Series: Kehl Box, f. Budget FY 81.
37. John B. Gilmour, *Reconcilable Differences? Congress, the Budget Process, and the Deficit* (Berkeley: University of California Press, 1990), 7.
38. Daniel J. Palazzolo, *The Speaker and the Budget: Leadership in the Post-Reform House of Representatives* (Pittsburgh: University of Pittsburgh Press, 1992), 104–110.
39. Dear Colleague, May 28, 1982, RHM Papers, Leadership Series, 97th Congress, Box 4, f. Dear Colleague Letters 1981–1994.
40. The information in this paragraph is from Dear Colleague, June 4, 1981, RHM Papers, Leadership Series, 97th Congress, Box 4, f. Dear Colleague Letters 1981–1994.
41. Dear Colleague, June 12, 1981, RHM Papers, Staff Series: Kehl, Box 9, f. Budget FY 82 Reconciliation.
42. There were thirty-seven letters, but several were signed by more than one member. RHM Papers, Staff Series: Kehl, Box 9, f. Budget FY 82 Reconciliation.
43. I use a threshold of 55 percent or less for a competitive district. To be more exact, eight won by 51 percent or less; twelve 53 percent or less; and fifteen 55 percent or less. In addition to the twelve where Reagan carried 50 percent or less in another four districts, he carried 51 percent.
44. For a complete list of objections and concerns with the bill, see "Response on the 'Dear Colleague' on Reconciliation," RHM Papers, Staff Series: Kehl, Box 9, f. Budget FY 82 Reconciliation.

45. James Broyhill, Ranking Member on Energy and Commerce, to RHM, June 15, 1981, RHM Papers, Staff Series: Kehl, Box 9, f. Budget FY 82 Reconciliation.

46. Clair W. Burgner and Bill Lowery to RHM, June 15, 1981, RHM Papers, Staff Series: Kehl, Box 9, f. Budget FY 82 Reconciliation.

47. Bobbie Fielder to RHM, June 15, 1981, RHM Papers, Staff Series: Kehl, Box 9, f. Budget FY 82 Reconciliation.

48. Steve Gunderson to RHM, June 15, 1981, RHM Papers, Staff Series: Kehl, Box 9, f. Budget FY 82 Reconciliation.

49. Stewart McKinney to RHM, June 15, 1981, RHM Papers, Staff Series: Kehl, Box 9, f. Budget FY 82 Reconciliation.

50. Chalmers Wylie to RHM, June 15, 1981, RHM Papers, Staff Series: Kehl, Box 9, f. Budget FY 82 Reconciliation.

51. Stockman, *The Triumph of Politics*, 205–223.

52. House Republican Policy Committee Statement No. 5, June 23, 1981, RHM Papers, Staff Series: Kehl, f. Legislative, Budget FY 82 Reconciliation (Gramm-Latta) (2).

53. Helen Dewar and Richard L. Lyons, "Reagan Triumphs in House Budget Vote," *Washington Post*, June 27, 1981.

54. Ronald Reagan to RHM, June 27, 1981, RHM Papers, Presidential Scrapbooks, f. 50.

55. David to Bob, September 18, 1982, "Results of meeting with Stockman on Budget changes," RHM Papers, Press Series, f. Memoranda 1981–1988 (1).

56. Robo Letter, October 5, 1981, RHM Papers, Legislative Series, f. 97th, Pro/Latest Budget Cuts.

57. RHM Papers, Staff Series: Pitts, f. Budget 1981 (16).

58. Connelly and Pitney, *Congress' Permanent Minority?* 114–123.

59. *Congressional Record*, 98th Congress, April 11, 1984, H 2591–92.

60. *Congressional Record*, 98th Congress, June 27, 1984, H 7119.

61. *Congressional Record*, 100th Congress, December 21, 1987, H 37080.

62. *Congressional Record*, 101st Congress, October 4, 1990, H 27642.

63. The vote was 179–254; 71 Republicans voted for it and 105 voted against.

64. Christopher Madison, "Pint-Sized Elephant," *National Journal*, January 19, 1991.

65. Beuttler interview with RHM, October 15, 2007.

66. Timothy J. Burger, "Bob Michel Defends Statement Labeling Frosh as 'Hard-Line,'" *Roll Call*, August 16, 1993.

67. Green, *Underdog Politics*, 10.

68. Green, *Underdog Politics*, 28.

69. "A Rationale: Why We Are Making This Speech," February 11, 1993, RHM Papers, Speech and Trip File, f. February 17, 1993, Part 1.

70. Unless otherwise noted, the following quotations are from remarks by RHM, *Clinton State of the Union Speech*, February 17, 1993, RHM Papers, Speech and Trip File, f. February 17, 1993.

71. Dear Colleague, February 17, 1993, RHM Papers, Leadership Series, Box 16, f. 103rd Congress, Dear Republican Colleague Notebook, 1993(1).

72. Both Kasich and Domenici quoted in George Hager, "President Throws Down Gauntlet," *CQ Weekly Report*, February 20, 1993, 355.

73. "The Spin Cycle: 24 Hours of Very Intense," *Washington Post*, February 19, 1993, C1. From Lexis/Nexis Academic.

74. George Hager, "House Democrats Easily Back Clinton Budget Blueprint," *CQ Weekly Report*, March 20, 1993, 653.
75. *Congressional Record*, 103rd Congress, March 17, 1993, H 5348.
76. Michel echoed his preference for cutting spending and opposing Clinton's tax increases in his constituent correspondence. See RHM Papers, Legislative Series, Box 69, f. 103rd Congress 1993 Budget Deficit.
77. Statement of the Republican Leader Bob Michel, RNC Clinton First 100 Days Press Conference, April 16, 1993, RHM Papers, Speech and Trip File, f. April 26, 1993.
78. Dear Colleague, May 17, 1993, RHM Papers, Leadership Series, Box 16, f. Dear Republican Colleague Notebook, 1993 (2).
79. Editorial, "Message from a Statesman," *Peoria Journal Star*, August 15, 1993, RHM Papers, Scrapbooks, f. Clippings 1993 (2).

1. Michel as a youth, undated. RHM Papers, Audiovisual Series, Still Photographs.

2. Bob Michel joins the US Army, 1942. RHM Papers, Audiovisual Series, Still Photographs.

3. (*Above*) Vice President Richard M. Nixon endorses Michel in 1956 by misspelling the candidate's name: "To Bob Mitchell with every good wish for victory in '56." RHM Papers, Audiovisual Series, Still Photographs.

4. Early days in the US House of Representatives. RHM Papers, Audiovisual Series, Still Photographs.

5. Michel's staff celebrates his first election as minority leader, December 8, 1980. RHM Papers, Audiovisual Series, Still Photographs.

6. Newt Gingrich and Michel celebrate House passage of President Reagan's tax cut, the Economic Recovery Tax Act of 1981, July 29, 1981. RHM Papers, Audiovisual Series, Still Photographs.

7. Meeting with President Ronald Reagan following passage of federal budget reconciliation and tax reduction legislation, August 5, 1981. *Left to right*: Jack Kemp, Michel, Pete Domenici, Reagan. RHM Papers, Audiovisual Series, Still Photographs.

8. Meeting with President Ronald Reagan following passage of federal budget reconciliation and tax reduction legislation. *Left to right:* Reagan, Robert Dole, Michel, Howard Baker. RHM Papers, Audiovisual Series, Still Photographs.

9. Michel campaigns for reelection,
September 2, 1982. RHM Papers,
Audiovisual Series, Still Photographs.

10. President Ronald
Reagan campaigns for
Michel's reelection in
Peoria, Illinois, October
20, 1982. RHM Papers,
Audiovisual Series, Still
Photographs.

11. At the Republican National Convention, August 17, 1988. RHM Papers, Audiovisual Series, Still Photographs.

12. (*Above, left to right*): Corinne Michel, President George H. W. Bush, Michel, Barbara Bush, January 20, 1993. RHM Papers, Audiovisual Series, Still Photographs.

13. President Clinton awards Michel the Presidential Medal of Freedom, August 8, 1994. RHM Papers, Audiovisual Series, Still Photographs.

14. Four Speakers of the House and one minority leader, Cannon Centenary Conference, November 12, 2003. *Left to right:* Tom Foley, Dennis Hastert, Jim Wright, Michel, Newt Gingrich. RHM Papers, Audiovisual Series, Still Photographs.

15. Michel and Henry Gonzalez warm up for the annual congressional baseball game, undated. RHM Papers, Audiovisual Series, Still Photographs.

16. Speaker of the House Tom Foley with Michel, undated. RHM Papers, Audiovisual Series, Still Photographs.

17. Speaker Thomas P. "Tip" O'Neill with Michel, undated. RHM Papers, Audiovisual Series, Still Photographs.

18. Michel in his leadership office, undated. RHM Papers, Audiovisual Series, Still Photographs.

CHAPTER 9

ANTICIPATING THE REVOLUTION

Michel and Republican Congressional Reform Efforts

Douglas B. Harris

W hat I Would Do as Speaker of the House" was the title of a brief
essay that Bob Michel penned as part of House Republicans'
1992 Manifesto for Change in the House of Representatives.
The Manifesto was one of several late 1980s/early 1990s GOP critiques
of forty years of Democratic rule of the House and Michel's contribution, accompanying fourteen essays written by other House Republicans,
focused on House organization and processes. Noting that "process is
substance" and promising the "first comprehensive reform of the House
of Representatives in modern times," Michel proclaimed that the "goal"
of a Republican majority and his speakership would be to reform the
internal workings of the House in order "to restore institutional virtues
that have been lost, preserve strengths that have survived, and protect
traditional American values."[1]

Michel's decidedly conservative and traditionalist tone—to "restore,"
to "preserve," and to "protect"—explicitly recalled the House Michel first
entered as "a relatively small and efficient institution," harkening back
to what scholars refer to as the "textbook Congress" of the mid-twentieth century.[2] Dominated by committees and noted for its bipartisanship,
the textbook Congress instilled in its members a pragmatic sense of the
primacy of legislation (valuing actual bills actually passed), comity and
cooperation (including with colleagues from across the aisle), and institutional patriotism. If Michel's early tutelage in the House was steeped

in these textbook-era norms, given the longevity of his career (from the Eisenhower administration to the Clinton administration), Michel was witness to considerable changes in American politics generally but also in terms of 1970s House reforms that posed key challenges to the House norms he valued.

Throughout the postreform era, Michel frequently lamented institutional changes generally, but he particularly decried those changes that threatened the participatory rights and role of the House minority.[3] These twin imperatives—a nostalgic commitment to the old school of legislative politics exemplified by the textbook Congress, plus a fervent advocacy for the minority party's rights—impacted Michel's views of legislative change and reform throughout his career and guided his own reform efforts as Republican Leader in the 1980s and 1990s. Amid a ratcheting up of majority party control of the House in the late 1980s, a consequent marginalization of the minority, and calls for more fierce oppositional politics (from Newt Gingrich and other Republicans) that challenged the legislative norms of the institution, Michel was fighting a war on two fronts—with sometimes heavy-handed majority party Democrats, as well as with growing dissent in his own party, even as he contemplated the potential of his own would-be speakership to restore, preserve, and protect the House he valued so highly.

Michel would, of course, never become Speaker, retiring just as the 1994 midterm elections swept Republicans into power in the House for the first time in forty years, a partisan turnover that made Newt Gingrich the first Republican Speaker since Joe Martin of Massachusetts. But Michel's repeated projections of the House under a Republican majority and his multiple proposals for legislative reform merit attention both as precursors to reforms ushered in by Gingrich during the Republican Revolution and, in some respects, as alternatives to the more polarized and partisan and less collegial House that emerged in Gingrich's wake. This chapter explores Michel's views of the proper functioning of the legislative process as expressed through his various reactions to institutional changes in the 1970s and then considers his calls for reform, as Republican Leader, in the years just before the 1994 Republican takeover of the House. In all, Michel's views of the institution and his reform proposals can be viewed as something of a road not taken in the history of the House and, perhaps, one worthy of reconsideration to address the "brokenness" that some see in the contemporary Congress.[4]

The House in Change: The Postreform Era and Party Polarization

If Bob Michel had the misfortune of serving his forty years in Congress *all in the minority*, his early years had the dubious distinction of being among the best in congressional history to be a minority party member.[5] The mid-twentieth-century's textbook Congress was led by the legendary Speaker of the era, Sam Rayburn (D-TX), who served as Speaker seventeen of the twenty-one years from 1940 to 1961, all the while protecting the House's institutional prerogatives and guarding and passing on its norms. Not simply a backbencher in this era, Michel was plugged in early to House power centers. Formerly a congressional staffer and named president of his freshman class in the House, Michel also represented the district adjacent to the long-serving Republican whip, Les Arends (R-IL), and was selected as a member of the influential Republican group, the Chowder and Marching Club. He rubbed shoulders, too, with the Democratic floor leader, John McCormack (D-MA), who was chair of Michel's first subcommittee and Rayburn's chief lieutenant.[6] To be sure, this era's institutional norms and leaders left their impression on Michel, who claimed to have "looked up to" Rayburn "like he was God Almighty as Speaker."[7]

What were the norms of the era? First, the textbook Congress was focused on legislating. Policy passage was a chief purpose of the legislature, and it was thought that Congress should approach its legislative work with a deliberative spirit.[8] If electoral politics were necessary to return to Congress, they were for the most part compartmentalized to the politics back home; in this era the electoral season was distinguishable from the normal legislative politics under the Capitol dome.[9] In support of this, Speaker Rayburn famously valued workhorse members over showhorse members, and his efforts to shield the House from television and media politics generally can be thought of as an effort to create a deliberative sphere of action for the legislature that was insulated—if only to some degree—from broader politics outside the chamber. Resisting calls for televised committee hearings (decades before C-SPAN), Rayburn once said: "If we allowed the televising of everything that comes along up here we would never get anything done."[10]

The legislative focus also counseled a second key feature of the textbook Congress: deference to committees, which had become the policy centers—the little legislatures—of the era.[11] Committees were controlled by their chairs, who, selected by virtue of seniority, tended to be southern and more conservative than the whole of the majority party Democrats and were prone to work with ranking minority members across the aisle on committees and, not infrequently, build conservative coalitions for policy passage on the floor. Because legislative coalitions were regularly built with bipartisan and cross-partisan alliances, minority party members had some hope that they could strike legislative bargains and enact some of their policy aims even in a chamber dominated for most of the era by Democrats.

Third and related, the textbook Congress was highly collegial as Rayburn preached to colleagues both institutional patriotism as well as the kinds of interpersonal comity and accommodation ("to get along, go along," the Speaker would advise colleagues) necessary for bargaining. Bargains were essential to effective legislating when the majority party was deeply divided, and legislative coalitions were apt to be built across the aisle and with ad hoc coalitions from one bill to the next; thus, "reciprocity and compromise" were "the prime behavioral rules" normed "for all members."[12] Rayburn had "friendly relations with minority party leaders" and "extended advice and favors to rank-and-file minority members."[13] The House that Michel entered in the 1950s was one in which members (from leaders to the rank and file, in the majority and the minority alike), less likely to go home regularly, would not only work together but also socialize together, bonding—across the aisle—over cards, drinks, or games in the House gym. As Michel recalled: "More members had their families here; it was a village."[14]

Fourth and more generally, House rules and processes offered participatory opportunities to all members, including, again, those in the minority party. Rather than operating by whim of the Speaker or with a rigged system of rules tilting processes to majority party outcomes, the textbook Congress was one in which minority party members could call upon rules and precedents, as well as a sense of collegial fairness, at least, to have their views heard and, sometimes, even to influence outcomes. Michel recalled his sense that the minority party was afforded considerable deference in the mid-twentieth-century Congress. Looking back, Michel said of Rayburn that he was "Speaker of the whole House. They [Rayburn along with McCormack] respected the fact that the minority had something to say."[15]

For all of its strengths, the textbook Congress had obvious shortcomings. It was prone to obstruction, particularly by a conservative coalition alliance of minority party Republicans and conservative Democrats, and legislating was dominated by sometimes autocratic committee chairs. Consequently, the majority will could be thwarted by committee chairs or the conservative coalition, or from simply a lack of active coordination to overcome those and other institutional impediments. Beginning in 1958 and with increasing numbers throughout the 1960s and into the 1970s, liberal Democrats, chafing at Congress's conservative biases, began to call for institutional reforms. With an early victory to expand the House Committee on Rules in 1961 (which had promised to stall the Kennedy legislative program), liberal impetus for reform increased as their numbers grew, especially in the landslide elections of 1964 and 1974. With the Legislative Reorganization Act of 1970 and, especially, reforms in the House Democratic Caucus (many of which occurred in early 1975), liberal reformers succeeded in limiting committee power, empowering the top party leadership and party organizations more generally (particularly the majority party), and opening up the Congress to greater press and public scrutiny through "sunshine reforms."[16]

If the sum total of these reforms made the House more efficient and more responsive to the will of the House majority,[17] the minority party had reasons for concern.[18] First, the comity and forms of bipartisan cooperation of the textbook Congress had been weakened. Second, committee government (which allowed for cooperation between chairs and ranking minority members) was being displaced not only by stronger party leadership but also by an increasing number of subcommittees, each of which had its own jurisdiction and increasing legislative authority. Third, the general trend toward greater party leadership power meant, specifically, a growth in *majority* party leadership power and thus a greater ability of the majority to rule and, where it wished to do so, to marginalize the minority.

These tendencies toward efficiency and party leadership power were met with increasing internal agreement within the parties, and, consequently, partisanship in Congress began to take off. If proponents could claim that Congress was better organized under stronger party leaders, and that its legislative program was arguably more ideologically coherent and politically representative of what a majority of the public voted for, it was nevertheless also true that the minority party (not to mention the voters that it represented) was increasingly marginalized. The majority's newfound power to refer bills to multiple committees and to control the Rules Committee, which regulates access to and amending of legislation on the House floor (as but two key examples), allowed the party leadership greater influence in the content of legislation and more opportunity to legislate without consultation of the minority or its leadership. Complaining about Tip O'Neill's (D-MA) partisanship, Minority Leader John Rhodes (R-AZ) quoted the soon-to-be-Speaker: "Republicans are just going to have to get it through their heads that they are not going to write legislation!"[19] With O'Neill as Speaker during President Jimmy Carter's administration, the new opportunities that reform afforded the majority were met with this more aggressive style of partisanship. And, by the time of the Reagan presidency, partisanship was spiraling upward in the House: not only were the percentage of party votes on the floor and average party unity on the rise, but, procedurally, the minority was further marginalized as Speakers O'Neill and, especially, Jim Wright (D-TX) ratcheted up majority party control of the process.

Minority party Republicans, increasingly frustrated by decreasing opportunities to participate, responded with an increased appetite for dramatic ways to disrupt the House majority, to dramatize procedural abuses by the majority, and to offer embarrassing amendments. In turn, the majority party's response to such dramatic acts was to limit further still their prospects for participation by using the Rules Committee, which after reform was dominated by the party leadership, to further restrict debate and amendments on the House floor. In addition to increasingly frequent use of restrictive rules, the leaders would also engage in more aggressive efforts to structure special rules or self-executing rules designed to further advantage the majority party at the expense of the minority, as well as to limit the minority party's right to offer a motion to recommit with instructions—a long-standing procedural safeguard for the House minority. Increasingly aggressive both procedurally and politically, the majority party was looking to govern with minimal minority consultation and, as a result, increased restrictions on minority participatory rights.[20]

The changes of the postreform, partisan era struck at the heart of Michel's view of the proper role of the minority in the legislative process. Not only were Republican voices being muted in the legislative process; the growing tensions across the aisle seemed to eclipse the kinds of floor exchanges that Michel thought essential to deliberation: "Today everybody gets up and gives a blurb in one minute when they're given the time. Nobody yields to anybody else when they're given a question. But in the old days, 'Would the gentleman yield for a question?' 'Yeah, sure.' Then you get a good mix of debate, but you don't get that in the House anymore today, unfortunately."[21] Viewed this way, the decline in minority party participation in the legislative process was not only to limit their voices (as well as, in turn, those of their constituents); it also hampered the give-and-take essential to compromise or the kinds of deliberative practices that might improve the quality of legislation.

These changes toward greater partisanship in the House were accompanied and exacerbated by greater openness of House politics. Sam Rayburn's efforts to insulate the House from television coverage and other external pressures were giving way to a variety of sunshine reforms that began with increased recorded votes and open votes and proceeded in quick fashion to include open committee hearings by rule and, in March 1979, continuous national broadcast coverage of House proceedings on C-SPAN. Like most of his generation, Michel was reluctant to embrace television politics when the issue of gavel-to-gavel coverage emerged in the late 1970s. Explaining his "apprehension," Michel said:

> I'm basically a traditionalist. What I was concerned about was: Who was going to operate these cameras? Who were they going to be covering? Would they be distracting from the one speaking on the floor to someone whose reaction was one of those things that today's television would love to pick up over anything. . . . In other words, how much show boating was going to go on?[22]

Like many of the members of his generation, Michel was concerned that broadcast coverage of House proceedings would bring out the worst in show-horse members whose television-inspired "antics . . . were demeaning to the House of Representatives." He asked: "How many show boaters are we going to have up there hogging the doggone screen instead of legislating?"[23]

Michel worried about the impact on the institution more broadly. He noted instances of members bringing props to the House floor to "dramatize" their points and worried that the House would "becom[e] a show, you know, a theatrical type of thing."[24] In a *Washington Post* op-ed titled "Politics in the Age of Television," Michel expressed concern that media politics posed challenges to the very meaning of Congress and its ability to deliberate:

> Communications in this media age are faster and in more detail. Few words uttered on the floor are left unrecorded or unreported. In this environment there is less chance—and, yes, less desire—to sit down and work our problems out in a bipartisan fashion. There are fewer opportunities to work compromises, to deliberate, to "come together" (which, after all, the definition of Congress is—a "coming together") prior to the members' being locked into positions or forced into partisan exchanges by the swiftness of mass communication.[25]

These changes were also challenging the norms of civility that Michel practiced and cherished. Michel was increasingly troubled by the pattern of personalized attacks that he saw in Gingrich, someone he claimed had raised the "visibility" of the "conduct of members in the institution."[26] Claiming to be actually more conservative than Gingrich, he identified his own value on comity as a key differentiating point between the two: "It's just that I talked to people, and because I talked to people on the other side, therefore, that made me a moderate."[27] Successor to both, Speaker Dennis Hastert (R-IL) contrasted Gingrich's confrontational style with Michel's "'go along to get along' school," echoing, of course, Rayburn's famous dictum.[28] If polarization led to decreased civility, other reforms, too, limited the kinds of incidental contacts that strengthened collegiality and comity. Michel cited electronic voting, as well as the relative lack of downtime in the cloakrooms and on the floor waiting for votes, as yet another cause of the decline of comity.[29] In these and other ways, the House was no longer the "village" that Michel recalled from the Rayburn era.

The prior era's broader sense of collegiality among the House membership was exemplified, and perhaps reinforced, by strong interpersonal relationships with House Democratic leaders. Much like Rayburn's friendship with Republican Leader Joe Martin or Senator (and then President) Lyndon Johnson's (D-TX) good relationship with Senate Republican Leader Everett Dirksen (R-IL), Michel had very strong personal relationships with both Tip O'Neill (the two were golf partners) and Tom Foley (D-WA).[30] Of O'Neill, Michel said: "We could go at it hammer and tongs verbally during the course of the day and after it was all over go back to the office and play a little gin rummy and have a brew or something."[31] In a joint oral history with Michel and Foley, Michel characterized their closeness even as he lamented the decline of such comity; he said to Foley that "things have changed considerably from the time you and I were leaders of our respective parties and even though we'd get involved in very vigorous debates on key issues, we never let it degenerate to a fight between personalities."[32]

Michel's penchant for institutional comity and good relationships across the aisle served practical purposes. Throughout most of his time as leader, Michel was actively trying to build coalitions in support of Ronald Reagan's and George H. W. Bush's programs and was thus always in need of Democrats to get the 218 votes needed to win. Explaining his strategic assessment of this, Michel contrasted his approach to Gingrich and compared it instead to the textbook-era Senate leader Dirksen:

> You don't get some on the other side by condemning them outright
> and calling them your enemies as my friend Newt Gingrich used to

call them. We had several conversations about that. I said, "Newt, they are our political adversaries. They're not our enemies." And I think Dick Armey, when he became the majority leader, also realized that you've got to use a little syrup, sugar, candy, and the things Everett Dirksen used to talk about in winning over the opposition to your side to get a majority of votes.[33]

Recalling Michel's style, Representative Randy Hultgren (R-IL) summed up the practical advantages of Michel's fundamental decency and collegiality: "Treating others with respect and care was essential to making deals and moving forward solutions to American problems."[34]

Whereas it is true that Congress scholars should not be too quick to look back on the textbook era with nostalgia, Bob Michel himself seems to have been nostalgic for that era, and this thinking and sentiment would continue to color his perceptions of the Congress as it changed during the Democratic reform era and as the institutional norms Michel valued were flagging during Gingrich's rise to power. To the extent that 1970s-era reformers could celebrate the House's greater openness and responsiveness, traditionalists such as Michel saw the changes as weakening the norms of the textbook era, overpoliticizing House politics, polarizing it, excluding the minority, and challenging the comity necessary to bargains, compromise, and legislative productivity.

Republican Reform Efforts before the Revolution

Michel did more than lament these changes. Restless for change himself, as Republican Leader Michel was active in reform conversations throughout the 1980s and early 1990s, particularly where the rights of the minority party were at stake.[35] Amid these more general Republican criticisms of Democratic Congresses, he offered a series of alternative rules packages and other proposals for House procedural reform. If Gingrich and others were challenging Democratic rule in the hopes of taking over the House, where Michel was concerned the calls for reform can just as well be read as conservative calls for a restoration and revitalization of more or less older forms of House procedures.[36]

Frustrated by seemingly perennial minority status, Republicans were increasingly willing to criticize Congress in the 1980s and 1990s. During the first six years of the Reagan administration when the Senate was under Republican control, the focus on the procedural rights of the House minority was particularly intense. But when the Democrats took control of the Senate after the 1986 elections, national party Republicans were clear to aim rhetorical fire at Congress as a whole. The 1988 and 1992 national party platforms were replete with anti-Congress rhetoric; the latter platform had a section titled "Cleaning Up the Imperial Congress" and observed that "the Democrats have controlled the House of Representatives for longer than Castro has held Cuba." Republican objections included not only attacks on member perquisites, campaign finance, and incumbent protection but also internal procedures like the use of restrictive rules and perceived abuses of the budget process.[37] These efforts accelerated as the potential for taking the majority grew and as the resignations of Speaker Jim Wright and Majority Whip Tony Coelho and the House Bank and Post Office scandals increased public concern over internal House politics.

Whereas Newt Gingrich stoked these concerns outside Congress by leveling charges of corruption at House Democrats, Bob Michel focused his attention on internal reforms. In successive years from 1991 to 1994, Michel established several reform task forces: the Leader's Congressional Reform Task Force (1991); the Task Force on House Reform (1992); the Deliberative Democracy Task Force (1993); and the Leader's Advisory Task Force on Congressional Reform (1994). This general impetus toward reform was perhaps most pronounced in a series of named reform projects and organized special orders—the Bicentennial House Restoration Project (1987), the Broken Branch of Government (1988), the Republican Manifesto for Change (1992), the Republican Leader's Blueprint for House Reform (1992), and A Mandate for Change in the People's House (1993)—that Michel and the Republican leadership used both to offer Republican alternatives to the Democratic rules of the House and to publicize Republican calls for wholesale institutional reforms.

In tone and approach, each of these named reform efforts and organized special orders combined criticism of Democratic rule with a decidedly conservative, restorative tone consistent with Bob Michel's hope to return to House processes more in line with the textbook Congress in key respects than with the postreform and more partisan Congresses of the 1970s and 1980s.

The Bicentennial House Restoration Project and the Broken Branch of Government, 1987–1988

Pegged to the bicentennial of the US Constitution, the 1987 Republican rules package, offered on the House floor on January 6, 1987, promised "restoration" of congressional productivity, which Republicans argued had waned in recent years. Critical of years of Democratic rule and marginalization of the minority, the House GOP bemoaned "the inability of Congress to forge . . . a consensus in a rational and deliberative fashion" and argued that "the policy-making process of Congress is virtually in shambles."[38] Diagnosing problems in three categories—House Organization & Scheduling, the Committee System, and the Budget & Appropriations Process—the Bicentennial House Restoration Project offered a series of reforms in each of these three areas in an avowed effort to "consider [Congress's] current condition in the context of the Framers' original intent" and to overcome the "parliamentary paralysis" of the contemporary Congress.[39]

Of course, the Republican minority's rules were not adopted, and Republicans continued throughout the 100th Congress—particularly given Jim Wright's aggressive use of speakership prerogatives—to complain about Democratic abuse of power. Later in the 100th Congress, House Republicans revisited these and other reform questions, instantiating "abuses" under Wright in an organized special order on May 24, 1988, dubbed the "Broken Branch of Government." The Broken Branch effort included many of the internal reform topics of the prior year's effort but widened the scope of consideration to include policy matters and separation of powers politics (e.g., applicability of civil rights laws to Congress; congressional "interference in foreign policy," and incumbent protections) to appeal to broader audiences.[40] Indeed, the effort was designed as much for media and public consumption; it would play to C-SPAN cameras and, as leadership staff planned, "be accompanied by a substantial media communications effort to attract greater interest from columnists, editorial commentators, etc., and to develop a package which Republicans [sic] Members can use in their districts to educate their constituents."[41]

A Manifesto for Change in the House of Representatives, 1992[42]

The Republicans began the 102nd Congress with a rules substitute they titled "A Republican Reform Manifesto for a New House Revolution," which elaborated a series of organizational, committee, and budget reforms reminiscent of the Bicentennial House Restoration Project.[43] With an eye on the 1992 national elections, Republicans began the second session of the 102nd Congress by compiling a manifesto that outlined a series of potential changes to the House and to public policy. Originally offered as another organized special order effort, the speeches were compiled in a document titled the Manifesto for Change. This manifesto included Michel's essay "What I Would Do as Speaker of the House" (discussed at the beginning of this chapter) and fourteen other essays (each authored by a prominent House Republican) that ranged from the procedural and organizational (Marvin H. "Mickey" Edwards [R-OK] penned "Reforming the Way We Do Business in the House," and Gerald Solomon [R-NY] wrote "A Working Committee System in the Republican House") to a series of Republican policy comments on the welfare state, national security, the economy and budget, energy, education, crime, and health care.

Michel, in particular, took a very critical tone by comparing the House Democrats to one-party dominance "in eastern Europe" or "in China"; he noted the Democratic majority's "arrogant lack of responsiveness," its "delusion that the entrenched party is irreplaceable and above criticism," and its "compulsion to build bureaucracies." He charged that Democrats could not "deliver free and open debate" or produce "efficiency in legislating," "a lean, mean staff for the micro-chip age," "a sense of purpose to our deliberations," or "an institution worthy of its history, its promise, and its responsibilities."[44] In support of these claims, the Manifesto for Change also included a summary of GOP reform proposals, data comparing the legislative performance of the 101st Congress to that of the 91st and 96th, clippings of news articles on Republican proposals, and supporting policy statements.[45] Publicizing the potential value of Republican rule in conservative circles, a version of Michel's essay was published alongside essays by Dick Armey and William Goodling (R-PA) in the Heritage Foundation's *Policy Review* in January 1992 titled "House Repairs: What We'll Do When We Reach Majority."

The Republican Leader's Blueprint for House Reform, 1992[46]

Internal scandals involving the House Post Office and House Bank provided opportunities for Republicans to renew their complaints about Democratic administration of the House later that year. Resignations of the House sergeant-at-arms and the House postmaster in March 1992 and the subsequent release of the names of House members who had made overdrafts of their House banking accounts raised press and public awareness of internal operations; the House GOP pressed their case for administrative *and procedural reform.*[47] In addition to proposing that the House hire a chief financial officer ("elected by 2/3 vote of the House," thus ensuring minority participation), "eliminate office of Doorkeeper and Postmaster," and "create an Inspector General Office to conduct independent audits and investigations," House Republicans also proposed that control of the House Administration

Committee and the Appropriations Subcommittee on the Legislative Branch be made bipartisan—all the while renewing calls for many of their procedural reforms regarding committees (e.g., ratios, staffing, proxy voting bans, and oversight reform), budget and appropriations processes, and deliberation on the floor. Michel seized on the public attention to the scandals to propose reforms, as he wrote to Speaker Tom Foley, to restore "the functions of the Officers of the House . . . to [their] original functions" and to revitalize committees and the floor as deliberative and participatory spaces.[48]

Seeking to broaden public awareness of this effort, Michel also wrote "An Open Letter to the Citizens of the United States" claiming that true reform required "more than housecleaning" and that "the real scandal is the way the Congress does its legislative business." In a call to "utterly reform the tyranny of the Majority over the legislative process," Michel again struck his conservative tone: "Our reform proposal attempts to restore the House to its place as the premier legislative body in the world. We do this by guaranteeing the existence of open debate, one that both allows any Minority to participate in the legislative process and remains consistent with the founders' intent."[49]

A Mandate for Change in the People's House, 1993[50]

With the election of President Bill Clinton, House Republicans were freed to be more oppositional than they were with Republicans in the White House, all the while continuing their assaults on long-term Democratic dominance of the House. Citing Woodrow Wilson's famous conclusion that "Congress in committee rooms is Congress at work," Mandate for Change observed that, in the 1980s, the congressional "committee system has broken down into a fragmented system of subcommittee government which has proven to be incapable of developing coherent, cohesive, or consensus-producing legislation."[51] Of increased restrictions of the minority on the floor, Republicans complained that "when one considers which amendments are allowed and which are not," it is clearly done by the majority "for purposes of political expediency and legislative outcome management and predictability." Deeming these and similar efforts to use the suspension of the rules procedures to expedite majority-preferred legislation, the minority railed against "the majority leadership's undemocratic tactics."[52]

Citing these and other (mostly deliberative) failures, Mandate for Change argued that there had been "endemic, structural deterioration" in Congress that had made the institution itself "a contradiction in terms: instead of epitomizing 'a coming together,' in recent years it has increasingly evinced a falling apart."[53]

· · · · ·

Although each of these efforts varied in terms of context and presentation, the tone of each was traditional and conservative: they all, in one form or another, called for a restoration of House norms seemingly lost during the eras of reform and partisan polarization. Moreover, there was a notable consistency in terms of the specific legislative reforms espoused: (1) Republicans proposed a professionalized, streamlined, and bipartisan administration of the House of Representatives to provide for greater institutional effectiveness and accountability; (2) looking to restore the role of committees in the legislative process, they advocated a rationalized and revitalized committee system; and (3) to promote participation and deliberation, the GOP proposed a greater openness for debate and amendment on the House floor.[54]

Collectively, these themes provide a statement of how the Michel-led House Republicans of the late 1980s and early 1990s believed the House should be reformed and reorganized.

Republicans proposed a professionalized, streamlined, and bipartisan administration of the House of Representatives to provide for greater institutional effectiveness. Table 9.1 outlines the major proposals in each of the named reform projects related to the institution of the House and its overall performance. Reform proposals for a more professionalized system of operations and accounting were included in the Manifesto, Blueprint, and Mandate documents. Following the House Bank and Post Office scandals, House Republicans called for the hiring of a chief financial officer, for example, who would be selected with minority party input, thereby taking away some of the potential for abuse in the majority party patronage positions that ran the administration of the House. The overall idea reflected a desire to have greater shared responsibility for House organization between the majority and the minority. They advocated, too, equalizing the proportions of majority and minority members on the House Administration Committee and the Legislative Appropriations Subcommittee. In the same vein, after the Republicans no longer controlled the White House, the 1993 Mandate recommended that the Government Operations Committee be controlled by whatever party (regardless of majority/minority status) does not control the White House. This recommendation actually echoed one that Bob Michel made in an essay published in *We Propose: A Modern Congress*, a 1960s Republican reform document;[55] in that piece, Michel sought to empower the Republican minority to

Table 9.1 Administration of the House and institutional performance

	Bicentennial House Restoration Project (1987)	Reform Manifesto/ Manifesto for Change in the House (1992)	Blueprint for House Reform (1992)	Mandate for Change in the House (1993)
House Organization				
Speaker's Schedule Plan	X	X	X	X
Submission of Oversight Plans	X	X	X	X
Prompt Committee Organization	X	X		X
Deadlines for Authorization Bills		X		X
House Administration				
House Chief Financial Officer			X	X
Limitations on Reprogramming of House Funds			X	X
Minority Representation/Role				
Out-Party Control of Government Operations				X
Bipartisan Control of House Administration Committee			X	X
Majority/Minority Equal Representation on Legislative Appropriations			X	X
Congressional Responsiveness				
Application of Laws to House of Representatives			X	X

Author-compiled from RHM Papers, Legislative Series, Special Subjects, Other Special Subjects, Box 4, f. 102nd Congress: Reform; RMH Papers, Leadership Series, Box 18, f. Leadership Series, 100th Congress, 1987–1988: Special Order, Broken Branch; and RHM, Staff Series: Karen Buttaro. f. Opening Day of the 103rd Congress.

check and counter the rise of the imperial presidency. Nearly three decades later, Michel called again for out-party control of government operations in not only Mandate for Change but also in his testimony before the 1993 Joint Committee on the Organization of Congress.[56]

In addition to such broader institutional accountability measures, efficiency was central to Republican efforts. All of the reform documents advocated better planning by the Speaker and clear oversight plans for committees; in addition, three of the four advocated prompt organization of House committees at the beginning of each Congress. Each reform document also proposed reductions in congressional staff, which had increased considerably in the second half of the twentieth century. In his contribution to "House Repairs: What We'll Do When We Reach the Majority" in *Policy Review*, Michel critiqued the "bureaucracy" that the House had become—in terms of staff, offices, and budget—during his time in the House, and he vowed to reduce and streamline the operation, including specifically a promise to "cut committee staffs in half" to the tune of $26 million in savings.[57]

Looking to restore the role of committees in the legislative process, the House GOP advocated a rationalized and revitalized committee system. If the GOP's proposed institutional reforms were efforts to complain about Democratic "misrule" and to chart a path toward greater public confidence in Congress, Michel-led reforms went directly to redressing imbalances in the legislative process, too. For the most part, the demands regarding committee politics were consistent from the Bicentennial House Restoration Project to Mandate for Change, focusing on rationalization of committees, representativeness, and deliberation. All four documents called for the abolition of joint referral processes (whereby a bill would be referred simultaneously to more than one committee) as well as a significant decrease in the number of subcommittees. Deeming the current committee system "chaotic and impotent," the Bicentennial House Restoration Project complained that subcommittee government had produced "a sprawling jungle of semi-autonomous subcommittees . . . and excess staff, overlapping jurisdictions . . . the referral of the same bills to more than one committee, skewed party ratios that produce unrepresentative bills, and phantom voting devices like proxy voting and one-third quorums necessitated by poor attendance."[58] In addition to limiting subcommittee government, two of the documents took the additional step of calling for the study of committee jurisdictional realignment, including the abolition of specified select committees.[59]

Table 9.2 House committee reforms

	Bicentennial House Restoration Project (1987)	Reform Manifesto/Manifesto for Change in the House (1992)	Blueprint for House Reform (1992)	Mandate for Change in the House (1993)
Rationalization Joint Referral Abolition	X	X	X	X
Jurisdiction Realignment (or study thereof)		X		X
Limits on the Number and Power of Subcommittees	X	X	X	X
Abolition of Specified Select Committees			X	X
Representation/ Responsiveness Proportional Committee Ratios	X	X	X	X
Term Limits for Chairs and Ranking Members				X
Committee Staff Cuts	X	X	X	X**
Deliberation Proxy Voting Bans	X	X	X	X

	Bicentennial House Restoration Project (1987)	Reform Manifesto/ Manifesto for Change in the House (1992)	Blueprint for House Reform (1992)	Mandate for Change in the House (1993)
Majority Quorum Requirements	X	X	X	X
Sunshine Recorded Votes on Motions to Report		X	X	
Open Committee Hearings & Disclosure		X	X	

**The percentage of recommended committee staff cuts varied from a 10 percent cut in the Manifesto to a 50 percent cut in the Blueprint and a recommended 30 percent cut in the Mandate.

Source: Author-compiled from RHM Papers, Legislative Series, Special Subjects, Other Special Subjects, Box 4, f. 102nd Congress: Reform and RHM Papers, Leadership Series, Box 18, f. Leadership Series, 100th Congress, 1987–1988: Special Order, Broken Branch.

In terms of committee representation and responsiveness, all four documents called for committee membership ratios proportional to the majority–minority ratio in the House, and by 1993 Mandate for Change called for term limits on committee chairs and ranking minority members.[60] Accompanying these reforms were well-worn minority calls to promote deliberation in committees with majority quorum requirements in committee and bans on proxy voting—these calls, too, were present in all four documents.[61] See also Table 9.2.

In all, the thrust of House Republicans' committee-related reforms of the late 1980s and early 1990s aimed to revitalize the committee system by updating its jurisdictions, streamlining its performance (by eliminating subcommittees in efforts to reempower full committees), and bringing back the actual give-and-take in full committee that might reassert the committees' deliberative processes and roles. Of course, for committees to contribute to such roles they have to not only promote actual discussion of legislative matters; they must do so in ways that fully reflect the minority party's input and viewpoints. If the Rayburn Congresses offered bipartisanship and committee government, under decades of subsequent Democratic rule and reform, Michel said, the committee system had become "cavalier in its treatment of the minority," treating them as "vassals" subject to the will of the majority, a matter he sought to address.[62]

To promote participation and deliberation, House Republicans proposed a greater openness for debate and amendment on the House floor. Of course, for Congress to perform its deliberative functions, it must also have active and participatory floor debate. Beginning with the Bicentennial House Restoration Project, House Republicans complained about Democrats' increased use of suspension of the rules (a process that sets strict time limits for debate and forbids amendments) for substantive, important, and sometimes even controversial legislative matters. Even more prominent were complaints about the restrictiveness of rules and calls for greater openness for debate and amendment on the floor, which were present in the Manifesto, the Blueprint, and the Mandate documents, as were limits on self-executing rules. The Manifesto for Change in the House and the Blueprint for House Reform were probably the House GOP's most elaborate statements on the value of open floor debate, as both called as well for explicit guarantees of the minority's right to a motion to recommit and a variety of sunshine reforms that would promote greater public scrutiny of the actual workings of the floor as a venue for debate and legislative decisions. See also Table 9.3.

Such advocacy for greater openness on the floor served, again, the minority's interest in participation. House Democrats' dominance of the Rules Committee since the 1970s and its increasing use of restrictive rules to limit debate and amendments in the 1980s and 1990s were perceived as choking off minority viewpoints in the legislative process. As Michel observed, Democratic use of "closed or semi-closed rules, effectively disenfranchis[es] millions of Americans, who lose the chance to have their representatives offer amendments."[63] Michel's commitments were not only to representativeness but also to deliberative values as well. As he said: "The phrase 'free and open debate' becomes meaningless when the chance for such debate is effectively eliminated by closed rules." Thus Michel committed himself, should he become Speaker, to greater openness

Table 9.3 Reforms of House floor procedures

	Bicentennial House Restoration Project (1987)	Reform Manifesto/Manifesto for Change in the House (1992)	Blueprint for House Reform (1992)	Mandate for Change in the House (1993)
Floor Participation				
Suspension of the Rules (limited use)	X	X	X	X
Limitations on Use of Restrictive Rules		X	X	X
Limits on Budget Process Waivers	X	X	X	X
Limits on Self-Executing Rules		X	X	X
Motion to Recommit Guarantees		X	X	X
Budget and Appropriations				
Continuing Resolution Limits	X	X	X	X
Enhanced Presidential Rescission Authority		X	X	X
Biennial Budgeting		X		X
Sunshine				
Roll Calls on Tax, Appropriations, and Pay Raise Bills		X	X	
Publication of Alternative Views on Conference Reports		X		
Discharge Petition disclosures		X		

Source: Author-compiled from RHM Papers, Legislative Series, Special Subjects, Other Special Subjects, Box 4, f. 102nd Congress: Reform; RHM Papers, Leadership Series, Box 18, f. Leadership Series, 100th Congress, 1987–1988: Special Order, Broken Branch; and RHM, Staff Series: Karen Buttaro, f. Opening Day of the 103rd Congress.

and a fairer treatment of the minority: "In order to make the House more responsive I would insure that all controversial bills come to the floor with rules guaranteeing free and open debate."[64]

These long-standing Republican complaints about the restrictiveness of rules had broader political appeal, and Michel espoused them publicly and in official settings throughout the rest of his House career. In his 1992 "Open Letter to the Citizens of the United States," Michel argued for greater protections of the minority (and their constituents) in the House: "We seek to reform utterly the tyranny of the Majority over the legislative process. Republicans, and their constituents, have much to offer the political process. Over the last thirty-eight years of Democratic control of the House, our views have been effectively ignored."[65] Testifying before the Joint Committee on the Organization of Congress in 1993, Michel complained that the "trend" of more restrictive rules was "disturbingly clear" in that it "sharply curtail[ed] the rights of members to offer amendments on the floor"; summing up this point, he said that "legislative debate on the Floor has degenerated into a majority monologue."[66]

Conclusions: The Road Not Taken

The legislative process that Bob Michel advocated was not one of majority party dominance but instead one of broad participation, debate, and deliberation. Although we cannot know how he would have actually performed as Speaker, the consistency of his statements on the legislative process and legislative reform over the course of decades gives us good reason to expect that Bob Michel's House and his speakership would have reflected his efforts to restore and revitalize key components of the textbook Congress, including explicit protections for the role that the minority played in contributing to the performance of Congress's functions. Having generally viewed the changes and reforms of the 1960s and 1970s as lamentable and deleterious both to Congress and to the minority party's role therein, most of Michel's reform proposals are best understood as efforts to recover and to restore the textbook norms of the Rayburn era.

Immediately upon Michel's retirement, Republicans were able to reform the House after the historic 1994 elections returned the GOP to a House majority for the first time in forty years and made Newt Gingrich Speaker. The GOP's Contract with America contained promises not only to hold floor votes on ten legislative provisions but also to reform the internal operations of the House itself. In addition to promises to implement zero-based budgeting, to require three-fifths majorities to increase taxes, and to compel Congress to live under the laws it passes for the nation, the Contract promised, too, administrative reforms (hiring an "independent auditing firm to conduct a comprehensive audit of Congress") as well as committee reforms ("cut the number of House committees, and cut committee staff by one-third," term limits for chairs, and to "ban . . . proxy votes in committee").[67]

The 1994 Republican takeover—a key moment in House history—implemented these and other reforms. In addition to the elimination of three committees, Republicans restructured the jurisdictions of several other committees, reduced both the number and the autonomy of subcommittees, imposed term limits on committee chairs, and increased party leader power over committee assignments and even the selection of chairs.[68] Other aspects of the legislative process would change as well: the Gingrich-led Republicans succeeded in eliminating joint referral of bills and abolished proxy voting and rolling quorum procedures.[69] On the floor, the Republican majority would continue to use restrictive rules but with somewhat less frequency and eliminated some of the more extreme limitations on minority rights, at least initially. This led a more open floor than House Democrats had provided, although the Republicans returned to restrictive patterns by the beginning of the twenty-first century.[70]

Read in light of Michel's reform efforts, it becomes clear that key elements of the Republican Revolution's institutional reforms had antecedents in Republican reform proposals dating back at least to the 1980s.[71] The elimination of subcommittees, the abolition of joint referral, and banning proxy voting in committees were all mere extensions of proposals that Michel had been championing for the better part of a decade. Gingrich's staff reductions in addition to his efforts to reform committee jurisdictions were, in fact, more restrained versions of reforms for which Michel had called.[72] By the same token, Gingrich's postelection promises to do a thorough audit of the House and to compel Congress to adhere to the laws it passed for the rest of the country were faint echoes of more robust House Republican reforms proposed since the Bank and Post Office scandals.[73] These seemingly dramatic reforms appear instead to be less personally attributable as Gingrich reforms and more as long-standing House Republican reforms; viewed in this light, they seem considerably more evolutionary than revolutionary.

This is not to say, however, that Gingrich merely adopted Michel's views of the proper functioning of the House—he did not. Most scholarly assessments of the effects of Gingrich's reforms emphasize the enhanced power of the majority party leadership at the expense of both the committee system and the Democratic minority rather than the restoration of committee power and minority participation that Michel had championed. By the end of 1995, Gingrich was criticized by some House Republicans for what was viewed as a preference for task force leadership over traditional committee deliberations, a move that, if implemented, would empower the Speaker at the expense of committees. It is noteworthy that government by task force had been anathema to Republican views just a few years prior. In the Manifesto, the Rules Committee's ranking member, Gerald Solomon, specifically denounced the practice: "Secret task force government is hardly an acceptable alternative to subcommittee government if deliberative democracy is our ideal."[74] Quite apart from Michel's views, the Gingrich reforms were "an unequivocal attack on committee autonomy and power."[75]

Perhaps the key differentiating point between Michel and Gingrich was that Michel's reform aims were institutionally conservative, whereas Gingrich's were radical and revolutionary. Gingrich did not have deliberative aims per se. He was driven more by movement conservatism, personal power, and a devotion to building the Republican majority than he was by concerns over the House as an institution or its place in the constitutional separation of powers.[76] Gingrich's move to limit subcommittees (which at first blush seems just an implementation of a Michel-proposed reform) was meant to empower party leaders rather than full committee chairs, who would be subject to term limits and who had lost a great deal of autonomy to Gingrich, who wielded extraordinary levels of influence in the determination of committee chairs.[77] In all, Gingrich preferred the majority party (if it was his majority) over the minority, party leadership over committees, and sunshine and messaging rather than privacy and compromise. Stronger centralized leadership, weakened committees, and more openness? These seem much more like continuations of the 1970s Democratic reforms than the "corrections" of those reforms that Michel advocated.[78] Whereas scholars have noted that Gingrich was motivated toward reform by partisan and personal power,[79] Michel's reform motivations seem to have been more institutional and partisan, a mix of enhanced deliberation and minority rights.

Consequent to Gingrich's rise, the House became more politicized, its parties more polarized, and its politics more given to personal conflict than to comity, with its public standing hitting abysmally low levels.

While this is true, and these tendencies have been exacerbated since, it is worth remembering that Bob Michel and the House Republicans of the 1980s and early 1990s offered a different path forward. In his testimony to the Joint Committee on the Organization of Congress in 1993, Michel connected the decades of Democratic control and what he deemed the consequent ineffectiveness of the House as perilous to the public standing of the institution. Of Democratic rule and reform, he said: "As the House has become more autocratic, it has become more unpopular. As it has become less democratic, it has become less effective. If it continues to become more unfair, it will continue to be an object of scorn for the American people as a whole."[80] Rather than a restoration of the regular order of the Rayburn era, Gingrich took the House farther down the road of partisanship and exclusion of the minority that Democratic reformers had begun decades before. To the extent that he made the House more partisan-efficient, he made it less prone to deliberation and—if Michel is right—less popular an institution.

It is worth noting another fact: Not only did Gingrich perpetuate partisanship and polarization in the House; he also hastened the decline of the comity and bipartisan friendships that Michel prized. This divergence could be seen as Gingrich and Michel were vying for power in the late 1980s and early 1990s. Not only would Gingrich openly challenge rank-and-file Democrats—he would also provoke Tip O'Neill, champion ethics complaints against Jim Wright, and seemingly encourage an early smear attempt against Tom Foley.[81] Michel, by contrast, sought cooperative relationships with these and other Democrats even when he disagreed with them politically. Looking back, Michel touted the advantages of such cooperation and the dangers of its loss: "You did have the respect of the other side to the degree that, 'Hey, we're in this thing together, but we've also got to be opponents.' One of my problems with Newt during my leadership, I said, 'Newt, they're not our enemies. They're our political adversaries and you've got to treat them with respect.'"[82]

In 2017, almost a quarter-century after Michel's retirement, Steny Hoyer (D-MD), leader of the Democratic minority, said this on the House floor in remembrance of Bob Michel: "Mr. Speaker, I did not want to lose the majority in 1994, but when we lost, I lamented the fact that Bob Michel did not become the Speaker of the House of Representatives. In my opinion, if he had, America would be a more civil place today and this body would be a more collegial body than it is."[83] It's not only that the House would likely have been a more civil and pleasant place to work: this very point goes directly to the ability of Congress to legislate effectively. The civility that Michel championed was essential to a House politics that was less partisan and more deliberative and, as a result, more likely to lead to legislative achievements than is currently the case.[84]

One wonders what the House would have been like had Bob Michel become Speaker after 1994. Whereas Gingrich's revolution was a partisan revolution—a *Republican* revolution—and he steered the House (and seemingly much of American politics) in a more partisan direction, Michel's vision was conservative in the sense that it aimed to restore, preserve, and protect the House as an institution. Michel's vision saw the House of Representatives as a policy problem-solver, a deliberative assembly. Notably, his vision was simultaneously less partisan and more conservative (in a traditional sense) than Gingrich's in that it prized institution and nation over individual, ideology, and party. In today's polarized America and in the post-Gingrich polarized House, the path that Michel offered is worthy of reconsideration as one that might help Congress (and the nation) find a way back to the spirit of deliberation, comity, and compromise that it once embodied.

Notes

1. RHM, "What I Would Do as Speaker," in "The Republican Congress: A Manifesto for Change in the House of Representatives," 3–5, RHM Papers, Leadership Series, Box 15, f. 102nd Congress, 1991–1992: "The Republican Congress: A Manifesto for Change in the House of Reps" (1).
2. RHM, "What I Would Do as Speaker."
3. Indeed, an early reform RHM advocated proposed that the House Government Operations Committee be chaired and controlled by members of the party not controlling the presidency, even if that party was in the minority in the House. See RHM, "Reorganization of the Committee on Government Operations and Minority Control of Investigation," in *We Propose: A Modern Congress*, ed. Mary McInnis (New York: McGraw-Hill, 1966), 163–176.
4. On Congress as the "broken branch" of American government, see Thomas E. Mann and Norman J. Ornstein, *The Broken Branch: How Congress Is Failing America and How to Get It Back on Track* (New York: Oxford University Press, 2008).
5. RHM's career was near-perfectly bookended by Congresses with Republican majorities (the 83rd and 104th) given that his first Congress was the 85th and his last was the 103rd. On the broader point, House minorities in the late nineteenth or late twentieth centuries had far fewer opportunities to participate and to affect legislative outcomes than did minorities in the mid-twentieth century. See David W. Brady, *Congressional Voting in a Partisan Era* (Lawrence: University Press of Kansas, 1993); Joseph Cooper and David W. Brady, "Institutional Context and Leadership Style: The House from

Cannon to Rayburn," *American Political Science Review* 75 (1981): 411–425; and William F. Connelly, Jr., and John J. Pitney, Jr., *Congress' Permanent Minority?* (Lanham, MD: Rowman & Littlefield, 1994).

6. On the importance of these connections in RHM's own words, see Fred W. Beuttler interview with RHM, September 7, 2007, RHM Papers, Post-Congressional Series, f. Subjects: Interviews (2), 8; Richard Norton Smith interview with RHM, Gerald R. Ford Oral History Projects, April 28, 2009, 14–15.

7. Smith interview with RHM, 14–15.

8. Joseph Bessette, *The Mild Voice of Reason: Deliberative Democracy & American National Government* (Chicago: University of Chicago Press, 1997).

9. These norms were slipping in the 1960s and 1970s as incumbent protections became more central to House behaviors and processes. See David Mayhew, *Congress: The Electoral Connection* (New Haven, CT: Yale University Press, 1974).

10. H. G. Dulaney and Edward Hake Phillips, *Speak, Mister Speaker* (Bonham, TX: Sam Rayburn Foundation, 1978), 459. On the broader point, see Douglas B. Harris, "Rayburn as Leader: Strategic Agency and the Textbook Congress," in *Reflections on Rayburn*, ed. James W. Riddlesperger, Jr., and Anthony Champagne (Fort Worth: Texas Christian University Press, 2018).

11. George Goodwin, Jr., *The Little Legislatures: Committees of Congress* (Amherst: University of Massachusetts Press, 1970).

12. Cooper and Brady, "Institutional Context and Leadership Style," 420.

13. Cooper and Brady, "Institutional Context and Leadership Style," 420.

14. Smith interview with RHM, 17.

15. Smith interview with RHM, 14–15.

16. Leroy Rieselbach, *Congressional Reform: The Changing Modern Congress* (Washington, DC: CQ Press, 1994), and Julian E. Zelizer, *On Capitol Hill: The Struggle to Reform Congress and Its Consequences, 1948–2000* (New York: Cambridge University Press, 2004).

17. See, for example, David W. Rohde, *Parties and Leaders in the Postreform House* (Chicago: University of Chicago Press, 1991).

18. There were protections of the minority included in the 1970 LRO as well as in regard to hiring of staff on committees. See Rieselbach, *Congressional Reform*, 62.

19. John J. Rhodes, *The Futile System: How to Unchain Congress and Make the System Work Again* (Garden City, NY: EPM Publications, 1976), 33.

20. Sarah A. Binder, *Minority Rights, Majority Rule: Partisanship and the Development of Congress* (New York: Cambridge University Press, 1997), 154–165.

21. Smith interview with RHM, 14–15.

22. Fred W. Beuttler interview with RHM, September 6, 2007, RHM Papers, Post-Congressional Series, f. Subjects: Interviews (2), 19.

23. Fred W. Beuttler interview with RHM, September 6, 2007; Smith interview with RHM, 20.

24. Smith interview with RHM, 20.

25. RHM, "Politics in the Age of Television," *Washington Post*, May 20, 1984.

26. Beuttler interview with RHM, October 15, 2007, RHM Papers, Post-Congressional Series, f. Subjects: Interviews (3), 37.

27. Beuttler interview with RHM, September 5, 2007, Part I, RHM Papers, Post-Congressional Series, f. Subjects: Interviews (2), 25.

28. Dennis Hastert, *Speaker: Lessons from Forty Years in Coaching and Politics* (Washington, DC: Regnery Publishing, 2014), 94.

29. Ron Sarasin, "Interview with Bob Michel and Tom Foley," June 14, 2006, United States Capitol Historical Society, transcript, 8, at uschs.org/wp-content/uploads/2017/03/USCHS-Oral-History-Thomas-Foley-Robert-Michel.pdf. Broadcast coverage further exacerbated these individualistic tendencies by allowing members of Congress to spend less time on the floor by monitoring House activity from their offices or even from their homes. See Douglas B. Harris, "PanoptiCongress: Policy Deliberations in the Post-C-SPAN Congress," paper presented at the conference on "Public Broadcasting and the Public Interest," University of Maine, Orono, 2000.

30. This was less the case with Speaker Jim Wright perhaps because Wright failed to cultivate this relationship with RHM; see Beuttler interview with RHM, September 6, 2007, 24–25.

31. Sarasin interview with RHM, 7.

32. Sarasin interview with RHM, 7.

33. Beuttler interview with RHM, September 6, 2007, 12.

34. *Congressional Record*, February 27, 2017, H 1343.

35. In fact, House Republicans had been making reform proposals and levying criticisms since the 1960s. High-profile works proposing institutional reforms and taking aim at Democratic control included *The Republican Papers*, edited by Melvin Laird (Garden City, NY: Anchor Books, 1968); Rhodes, *The Futile System; The Case Against the Reckless Congress*, edited by Marjorie Holt (Ottawa, IL: Green Hill Publishers, 1976); and *View from the Capitol Dome*, edited by Richard T. Schulze and John H. Rousselot (Bridgeport, CT: Caroline House Publishers, 1980).

36. Notably, there were some mentions of modernizing the House and improving its organizational operations, but, legislatively, the efforts seemed much more to counsel a return to "textbook" legislating.

37. Amy Fried and Douglas B. Harris, "On Red Capes and Charging Bulls: How and Why Conservative Politicians and Interest Groups Promoted Public Anger," in *What Is It about Government That Americans Dislike?* eds. John R. Hibbing and Elizabeth Theiss-Morse (New York: Cambridge University Press, 2001), 168–169.

38. *Congressional Record*, January 6, 1987, 9.

39. *Congressional Record*, January 6, 1987, 9. See also RHM and Trent Lott, "Dear Colleague," January 2, 1987, RHM Papers, Leadership Series, Box 10, f. 100th Congress, 1987–1988: Dear Colleague, January 2, 1987. RHM and Lott urged colleagues to vote to allow the minority to offer and debate its rules proposals. In addition to the reform proposals discussed in Tables 9.1–9.3, House Republicans also called for budget and appropriations reforms that included limitations on continuing resolutions, restoring the power of authorizing committees and limiting appropriations power, as well as a streamlining and rationalization of timetables for the budget and appropriations processes.

40. "Proposal for House Republican Leaders: Timeline for Special Order/Conference," May 24, 1988, RHM Papers, Leadership Series, Box 18, f. Leadership Series, 100th Congress, 1987–1988: Special Order, Broken Branch.

41. "Proposal for House Republican Leaders," May 10, 1988, RHM Papers, Leadership Series, Box 18, f. 100th Congress, 1987–1988: Special Order, Broken Branch.

42. "A Republican Reform Manifesto for a New House Revolution," RHM Papers, Legislative Series, Special Subjects, Other Special Subjects, Box 4, f. 102nd Congress: Reform. Michel Proposal, Part 1; "The Republican Congress: A Manifesto for Change in the House of Representatives," RHM Papers, Leadership Series, f. Leadership 102nd, "The Republican Congress: A Manifesto for Change in the House of Reps." In addition to reforms listed below, the Reform Manifesto also called for consideration of campaign reform and a process for improved foreign travel reporting by members of Congress.
43. "A Republican Reform Manifesto for a New House Revolution." This is the "Manifesto" document analyzed in the section that follows.
44. "The Republican Congress: A Manifesto for Change in the House of Representatives," 4.
45. "The Republican Congress: A Manifesto for Change in the House of Representatives."
46. "The Republican Leader's Blueprint for House Reform," RHM Papers, Legislative Series, Special Subjects, Other Special Subjects 1987–1994, box 4, f. 102nd Congress: Reform. Michel Proposal.
47. Whereas Democrats were actively searching for administrative reforms in response to the scandals, RHM seized the opportunity to renew calls for procedural reform as well and noted this as the first of several "key differences between Republican and Democratic approaches" to the House Republican Conference; see "Michel Talking Points on House Reform," April 1, 1992, RHM Papers, Legislative Series, Special Subjects, Other Special Subjects 1987–1994, box 4, f. 102nd Congress: Reform. Michel Proposal. Among the administrative reforms proposed (not discussed here) were changes in the elections and duties of officers of the House, the creation of a chief financial officer, an inspector general, and a general counsel, as well as the establishment of a bipartisan task force on measures aimed at "restoring public confidence in the House of Representatives"; see "The Republican Leader's Blueprint for House Reform." In addition to the procedural reforms discussed in greater detail below, they also proposed new processes for treatment of vetoed bills and timelines for presentment of legislation to the president, the establishment of a commemorative calendar, oath requirements for members of the Intelligence Committee, and prohibitions on franked mail outside of members' districts.
48. See RHM to Speaker Thomas S. Foley, March 11, 1992, RHM Papers, Legislative Series, Special Subjects, Other Special Subjects 1987–1994, box 4, f. 102nd Congress: Reform. Michel Proposal.
49. RHM, "An Open Letter to the Citizens of the United States," April 8, 1992, RHM Papers, Legislative Series, Special Subjects, Other Special Subjects 1987–1994, box 4, f. 102nd Congress: Reform. Michel Proposal.
50. "The Republican Congress: A Manifesto for Change in the House of Representatives; A Mandate for Change in the People's House: Republican House Rules Substitute, 103rd Congress," January 5, 1993, RHM, Staff Series: Karen Buttaro, f. Opening Day of the 103rd Congress. In addition to the reforms discussed below, the Mandate for Change document renewed prior calls for prohibitions on franked mail outside of a member's district, the creation of a general counsel and a commemorative calendar, as well as consideration of campaign reform legislation.
51. "Mandate for Change," 2.
52. "Mandate for Change," 3.

53. "Mandate for Change," 1.

54. The following comparison excludes the Broken Branch of Government Special Order for two reasons: (1) It was largely an echo of the Bicentennial House Restoration Project; and (2) it took the form of a Special Order effort that, though organized, was constituted of disparate speeches by different members as opposed to a consolidated and comprehensive leadership reform effort. Readers should note that important budget and appropriations reforms were proposed as well.

55. RHM, "Reorganization of the Committee on Government Operations and Minority Control of Investigation," in *We Propose: A Modern Congress*, ed. Mary McInnis (New York: McGraw-Hill, 1966), 163–176.

56. See RHM's testimony before the Hearing of the Joint Committee on the Organization of Congress, January 26, 1993 (Washington, DC: US Government Printing Office, 1993), 35, 42.

57. RHM, Dick Armey, and William F. Goodling, "House Repairs: What We'll Do When We Reach the Majority," *Policy Review* (Winter 1992): 62–65.

58. *Congressional Record*, January 6, 1987, 10.

59. The "Blueprint" called for the abolition of specified select committees. See RHM Papers, Legislative Series, Special Subjects, Other Special Subjects 1987–1994 box 4, f. 102nd Congress, 1991–1992: Reform. Michel Proposal.

60. Phil Duncan, "Quietly Assertive Freshmen Arrive for Orientation," *CQ Weekly*, December 5, 1992, 3746.

61. The "Manifesto" also specified sunshine reforms to ensure the openness of committee meetings as well as to demand record votes on committee motions to report legislation to the floor. See "The Republican Congress: A Manifesto for Change in the House of Representatives."

62. See RHM's testimony before the Hearing of the Joint Committee on the Organization of Congress, January 26, 1993 (Washington, DC: US Government Printing Office, 1993), 33.

63. RHM, Armey, Goodling, "House Repairs," 63.

64. RHM, Armey, Goodling, "House Repairs," 63.

65. RHM, "An Open Letter to the Citizens of the United States."

66. See RHM's testimony before the Hearing of the Joint Committee on the Organization of Congress, January 26, 1993, 33–34.

67. "Contract with America," in *Contract with America*, ed. Ed Gillespie and Bob Schellhas (New York: Times Books, 1994), 8; and C. Lawrence Evans and Walter J. Oleszek, *Congress under Fire: Reform Politics and the Republican Majority* (Boston: Houghton Mifflin, 1997), 83–84. Republican commitments to the openness of rules were implied by the contract's promise to "giv[e] a clean and fair vote" to each of its ten legislative provisions, "Contract with America," 1994, 9.

68. David C. King, *Turf Wars: How Congressional Committees Claim Jurisdiction* (Chicago: University of Chicago Press, 1997); Douglas L. Koopman, *Hostile Takeover: The House Republican Party, 1980–1995* (Lanham, MD: Rowman & Littlefield, 1996), 152–156; Evans and Oleszek, *Congress under Fire*, 93–101; and Nicol C. Rae, *Conservative Reformers: The Republican Freshmen and the Lessons of the 104th Congress* (Armonk, NY: M. E. Sharpe, 1998), 70.

69. Evans and Oleszek, *Congress under Fire*, 90; John E. Owens, "Taking Power? Institutional Change in the House and Senate," in *The Republican Takeover of Congress*, ed. Dean McSweeney and John E. Owens (New York: St. Martin's Press, 1988), 40.

70. James G. Gimpel, *Legislating the Revolution: The Contract with America in Its First 100 Days* (Boston: Allyn and Bacon, 1996), 116–117. Still, under continued Republican rule in the Gingrich and Hastert years, the leadership continued to gain influence, use more restrictive rules as the years went on, and ratchet up party control as the House polarized further still. See Barbara Sinclair, *Unorthodox Lawmaking: New Legislative Processes in the U.S. Congress*, 4th ed. (Washington, DC: CQ Press, 2012), 28.

71. Indeed, the antecedents to much of this can be found, generally, in James C. Cleveland, ed., *We Propose: A Modern Congress* (New York: McGraw-Hill, 1966), and Laird, ed., *Republican Papers*; and, specifically, in Rhodes, *The Futile System*. Note, for example, the list of proposed reforms in the appendix's inclusion of the report from the House Republican Task Force on Reform; these 1975 reform proposals included calls for open rules and restraints on use of the Suspension of the Rules, open committee meetings and recorded votes, submission of oversight plans at the beginning of a Congress, improved scheduling, and maintenance of strong quorum rules and bans on proxy voting, all of which would emerge again with RHM's efforts in the 1980s and 1990s.

72. Evans and Oleszek, *Congress under Fire*, 100–101.

73. Even though Gingrich approached the transition with a tone of suspicion, insisting, for example, that Democrats not destroy any documents at the end of the 103rd Congress.

74. Gerald Solomon, "A Working Committee System in the Republican House," 15–18, in "The Republican Congress: A Manifesto for Change in the House of Representatives," 17.

75. Owens, "Taking Power?" 39.

76. Indeed, even fellow conservatives worried that Gingrich was willing to "tear down" the institution; see Amy Fried and Douglas B. Harris, "On Red Capes and Charging Bulls: How and Why Conservative Politicians and Interest Groups Promoted Public Anger," in *What Is It about Government That Americans Dislike?* 172–173.

77. Owens, "Taking Power?" 39.

78. A notable exception to this is Gingrich's efforts to reduce the number and influence of subcommittees.

79. Evans and Oleszek, *Congress under Fire*, 43–44.

80. See RHM's testimony before the Hearing of the Joint Committee on the Organization of Congress, January 26, 1993, 35.

81. Douglas B. Harris, "Sack the Quarterback: The Strategies and Implications of Congressional Leadership Scandals," in *Scandal! An Interdisciplinary Approach to the Consequences, Outcomes, and Significance of Political Scandals*, ed. Alison Dagnes and Mark Sachleben (New York: Bloomsbury, 2014), 29–50.

82. Richard Norton Smith interview with RHM, 17.

83. *Congressional Record*, February 27, 2017, H1344.

84. See Frank H. Mackaman, "Growing Apart: 'Civilista' Attempts to Bridge the Partisan Rift," in *Politics to the Extreme: American Political Institutions in the Twenty-First Century*, ed. Scott A. Frisch and Sean Q Kelly (New York: Palgrave Macmillan, 2013).

CHAPTER 10

BOB MICHEL AND THE LEGACY OF COMMITTEE REFORM

Colton C. Campbell[1]

> Traditionally, the committee system has been the heart and soul
> of the House. It is in the committees where legislation begins
> its journey.

—House Republican Leader Robert H. Michel, May 24, 1988[2]

Even before the electoral earthquake of 1994 that shifted party control in the House of Representatives for the first time in forty years, the self-proclaimed revolutionary Newt Gingrich (R-GA) asserted his leadership over the Republican Party by introducing the Contract with America. The Contract was a ten-point party program (e.g., balance the budget and impose term limits on lawmakers, etc.) that Republicans promised to enact within the first one hundred days of the 104th Congress (1995–1997) if they won majority control of the House. As such, it is Gingrich's political entrepreneurship that is often credited with engineering the Republican takeover and for pushing the House to adopt a package of amendments to the rules that put in place a series of institutional changes designed to advance the party's agenda. Yet several of the reforms that Gingrich and the new majority implemented reflected what some observers call a "Republican frame of reference" that was built in the preceding years under the leadership of Robert H. "Bob" Michel (R-IL).[3]

Throughout his tenure as leader of the House Republicans, Bob Michel routinely offered alternative rules changes aimed at making the legislative process more deliberative and representative for his party. As Table 10.1 highlights, several efforts were directed at the committee system,[4] such as overlapping jurisdictions, imbalanced party ratios and staffing levels, proxy voting, and running quorums. Committees have long been central, if not dominant, in shaping the legislative agenda of the House. They help to write legislation that goes before the full chamber, oversee the implementation of legislation, educate members, and manage an expanding workload. As Woodrow Wilson observed nearly a century before Michel, the committee system is the very heart of the legislative process.[5]

The purpose of this chapter is to highlight the less familiar pursuit by Bob Michel to reform various aspects of the House committee system during his tenure as House Republican Leader. The antecedents for change that he advocated were rooted in his party's criticisms of the Democratic majority and the transformation it brought about during the reform decade of the 1970s. Collectively, the reforms of this era were designed to redistribute influence in the House—both downward toward the subcommittee level of the legislative process, as well as upward toward the centralized party leadership—in order to make the committee system more accountable and responsive to the Speaker and to the party caucus as a whole.[6] Many of the recommendations shepherded under Michel's leadership reflected counterproposals developed through intraparty groups such as the Conservative Opportunity Society and the 92 Group, as well as various Republican alternative rules packages and recommendations of the bipartisan Joint Committee on the Organization of Congress, all of which culminated with the Contract with America.[7]

Entering Congress in the Era of Committee Barons

Bob Michel entered the House during a period when weak party cohesion encouraged autonomous and powerful committees in Congress. Each committee generally had the right to proceed at its own pace with relative autonomy over its own agenda in ways that satisfied the parochial interests of committee members. Party leadership—the Speaker, floor leaders, and the whips—held little ability to enforce disciplinary action across a fragmented, decentralized institution.[8] Instead, the House resembled a feudal-like oligarchy largely controlled by

Table 10.1 Summary of proposed reforms to House committee system under Republican Leader Robert H. Michel (1981–1995) and changes to the committee system in the 104th Congress (1995–1997)

REFORM PROPOSAL	PROPOSED REFORM PLANS						
	Amendment in the Nature of a Substitute by Republican Leader 98th Congress (1983–1985)	Republican Blueprint for a House That Works 99th Congress (1985–1987)	The Bicentennial House Restoration Project 100th Congress (1987–1989)	A Bicentennial Mandate to Restore the People's House 101st Congress (1989–1991)	A Republican Reform Manifesto for a New House Revolution 102nd Congress (1991–93)	Republican Manifesto for Change 103rd Congress (1993–1995)	Changes Under Republicans 104th Congress (1995–1997)
Jurisdiction				Realign and rationalize committee jurisdictions along functional lines	Realign and rationalize committee jurisdictions along functional lines	Realign and rationalize committee jurisdictions along functional lines	Eliminate three standing committees and shift some jurisdictions

Multiple Referral of Legislation	Eliminate joint referrals (while retaining sequential and split referrals); Speaker gains authority to designate a committee of principal jurisdiction	Eliminate joint referrals (while retaining sequential and split referrals); Speaker gains authority to designate a committee of principal jurisdiction	Eliminate joint referrals (while retaining sequential and split referrals subject to time limits with a principal committee designated by the Speaker)	Eliminate joint referrals (while retaining sequential and split referrals)	Eliminate joint referrals (while retaining sequential and split referrals)	Eliminate joint referrals	Eliminate joint referrals; Speaker gains enhanced authority over split and sequential referrals, including authority to designate a lead committee with deadline for reporting
Subcommittee Limits	Reduce subcommittees by limiting committees (excluding Appropriations) to no more than six each	Reduce subcommittees by limiting committees (excluding Appropriations) to no more than six each	Reduce subcommittees by limiting committees (excluding Appropriations) to no more than six each	Reduce subcommittees by limiting committees (excluding Appropriations) to no more than six each	Reduce subcommittees by limiting committees (excluding Appropriations) to no more than six each	Reduce subcommittees by limiting committees to no more than six each	Limit most committees (excluding Appropriations, Government Reform and Oversight, and Transportation) to no more than five subcommittees*

Table 10.1 (continued)

	PROPOSED REFORM PLANS					
Assignment Limits	Reduce members' subcommittee assignments to no more than four	Reduce members' subcommittee assignments to no more than four	Reduce members' subcommittee assignments to no more than four	Reduce members' subcommittee assignments to no more than four	Reduce members' subcommittee assignments to no more than four	Reduce members' committee assignments to two full committees and four subcommittees
Proxy Voting Ban	Prohibit proxy voting	Prohibit proxy voting	Prohibit proxy voting	Prohibit proxy voting and one-third quorums	Prohibit proxy voting and one-third quorums	Prohibit proxy voting and rolling quorums in both committees and subcommittees
Committee Documents	Require verbatim transcripts of hearings and meetings (distinguished from extensions or extraneous materials); (subject any substantive alteration (excluding "technical, grammatical or typographical corrections"))		Publish members' committee votes or, in the case of non-recorded votes, the names of those members present	Publish members' committee votes	Publish members' committee votes	Publish members' committee votes and require verbatim transcripts of hearings and meetings

of verbatim accounts to investigation by Ethics; require committee approval of documents and prints or carry a clear disclaimer to the contrary on their cover

Committee Staffing						
House Administration Committee to establish committee staff size; investigative staff allocated according to a committee's past and anticipated legislative and oversight activities; subject increase in staff size to two-thirds approval by the House	Reduce committee staff by 10 percent from previous Congress; House Administration Committee to establish committee staff size; subject committee funding to a point of order if committee staff size exceeds ceiling set by the House	Reduce committee staff by 10 percent from previous Congress; House Administration Committee to establish committee staff size; minority allowed up to one-third of the investigative staff	Reduce committee staff by 10 percent from previous Congress; House Administration Committee to establish committee staff size; minority allowed up to one-third of the investigative staff	Reduce committee staff by 10 percent from previous Congress; House Administration Committee to establish committee staff size	Reduce committee staff by 10 percent per Congress over three Congresses	Reduce committee staff by one-third; House Oversight Committee gains authority to establish committee staff sizes; subcommittee staff hired by full committee chair

Table 10.1 (continued)

	PROPOSED REFORM PLANS						
Oversight Reform	Require committees to adopt oversight plans by March of that Congress	Require committees to adopt oversight plans at the start of each Congress	Require committees to adopt oversight plans by March of that Congress	Require committees to adopt oversight plans at the start of Congress and report on implementation of the agenda at the end of each Congress	Require committees to establish realistic oversight agendas at the start of each Congress	Require committees to adopt oversight plans and submit them to the House Oversight and Government Reform and Oversight Committees by February 15 of the first session	
Committee Ratios	Require party ratios on committees, excluding Standards (bipartisan) and Rules (two-thirds majority), to reflect the party ratios in the House	Require party ratios on committees, excluding Standards (bipartisan), to reflect the party ratios in the House	Require party ratios on committees, excluding Standards (bipartisan), to reflect the party ratios in the House; extend requirement to select and conference committees as well	Require party ratios on committees to reflect the party ratios in the House	Require party ratios on committees to reflect the party ratios in the House		

Sunshine			Require majority quorums for committee business	Require open committee meetings; only allow closed meetings for national security, personal privacy, or personal reasons	
Majority Quorums	Require majority quorums for committee business	Require majority quorums for committee business	Require majority quorums for committee business		
Leader Limits				Six-year term limit or committee chairs and ranking members	Six-year term limit on committee chairs and ranking members

*In conjunction with the abolition of three full committees, the number of House subcommittees is reduced by thirty-one.

*Sources: Information derived from *The Republican Congress: A Manifesto for Change in the House of Representatives*, The Dirksen Congressional Center, www.dirksencongressionalcenter.org; *Congressional Record*, 97th Cong., 1st sess., vol. 127, January 5, 1983, 94–111; *Congressional Record*, 98th Cong., 1st sess., vol. 129, January 5, 1983, 36–41; *Congressional Record*, 99th Cong., 1st sess., vol. 131, January 3, 1989, 394–403; *Congressional Record*, 100th Cong., 1st sess., vol. 133, January 6, 1987, 5–17; *Congressional Record*, 100th Cong., 1st sess., vol. 133, October 29, 1987, 29934; *Congressional Record*, 101st Cong., 1st sess., vol. 135, January 3, 1989, 68–81; *Congressional Record*, 102nd Cong., 1st sess., vol. 137, January 3, 1991, 46–55; *Congressional Record*, 103rd Cong., 1st sess., vol. 139, January 5, 1993, 92–97; and *Congressional Record*, 104th Cong., 1st sess., vol. 141, January 4, 1995, 462–469.

committee barons, where the process of coordinating the activity of the chamber shifted from a basis of centralized command and control to one of bargaining. Representative Carl Vinson (D-GA), chair of the Naval Affairs Committee, exhibited this point. He was fond of calling the Navy "My Navy," ordering its admirals around like cabin boys, and he treated his twenty-six-member panel the same way, scarcely allowing junior members to question witnesses.[9]

Sam Rayburn (D-TX), the first Speaker under which Michel served, and whom he "looked up to like he was God Almighty,"[10] was one leader who challenged committee barons and was able to assert a degree of authority under these conditions. Though substantially unable to reestablish the institutional bases of the power of the speakership, he was able to work within existing arrangements in politically effective ways by adopting an informal leadership style of "quiet persuasion, combined with patience and a willingness to compromise."[11] One way, for example, was by seeing to it that allies were named to Democratic vacancies on the Ways and Means Committee, where they had the power over committee appointments. This arrangement gave him indirect influence on further committee assignments. By this means Rayburn was able, for example, to turn the Education and Labor Committee from a predominantly conservative panel into a liberal one during the 1950s.[12] His success in this respect was also illustrated by his ability, after the 1948 election, to secure the removal from the House Committee on Un-American Activities of three Democrats who had supported then–South Carolina Governor Strom Thurmond's bid for the presidency as candidate of the States' Rights Party, which had splintered from the Democrats in that year.[13]

Rayburn's occasional attempts to control committee activities more directly met with mixed success. For example, four years before Bob Michel arrived on Capitol Hill, Rayburn banned the televising of committee hearings after many House panels began the practice of what Rayburn considered the courting of television crews. His concern originated with hearings of the Senate Special Committee on Organized Crime in Interstate Commerce (referred to as the "Kefauver Committee"), which had prompted controversy over the rights of witnesses and led to portrayals of congressional proceedings as "three-ring circuses."[14] At first Rayburn quietly advised chairmen to refrain from similar activity. When this met with resistance, he solidified his decision to ban the televising of committees, asserting that "the rules of the House are hereby made the rules of its standing committees so far as applicable."[15] Since there was no House rule authorizing televising or broadcasting House sessions, he held that the committees also lacked such authority.

Rayburn's efforts to assert effective control over the operations of the House, and specifically the activities of committees, remained handicapped by his lack of control over the Committee on Rules, whose chairman not only acted as yet another autonomous baron but also often acted in harmony with other powerful and independent chairs to protect and foster their preferences, rather than those of the Caucus as a whole. By the end of the 1950s, the more liberal wing of the House Democratic Caucus had been continually frustrated by obstruction of their program by the chairman of the Committee on Rules, and many of them urged Rayburn to redress the situation by challenging the seniority system. Rayburn instead chose a less defiant course and secured the enlargement of the committee by three members. Afterward, lawmakers privately acknowledged that Rayburn had selected the new Democratic members of the committee partly on the basis of whether they had supported the Speaker on the question of enlargement. The Rules assignment, they said, was "a gentle reminder" to the Speaker's opponents that "the way to get along is to go along."[16]

Although Rayburn did not live to see the Speaker reestablish full control of the Committee on Rules, this success was the first step in that development. It also laid the groundwork for the reform era of the 1970s that collectively redistributed influence in the House by decentralizing the power structure, as well as the eventual counter-recommendations advocated by Michel and the Republican Conference.

Rebelling against the Committee Barons

In the years after Speaker Rayburn, many rank-and-file House Democrats expressed increasing dissatisfaction with the role of the conservative coalition of Republicans and conservative, mostly southern, Democrats in inhibiting enactment of liberal social and economic legislation. These disaffected members, presenting themselves as mainstream or national Democrats, considered that the dominance of the conservative coalition was facilitated by the continued concentration of power in the hands of a few committee chairs, predominantly senior and conservative Democrats from safe districts, who exercised broad control of their panels' decision-making. The reformers accordingly sought to facilitate enactment of a liberal program by democratizing the House, making committee chairs more accountable to the Democratic Caucus, and offering more members a greater chance to influence congressional policymaking and oversight.[17]

Many of these reform-minded members were unwilling to heed Rayburn's frequent advice: "To get along, go along." They rejected norms of apprenticeship that required them to restrain their active participation in congressional deliberations. Instead, they developed an organization to promote both their own policy goals and internal House reforms. On the Democratic side of the aisle the chief organ was the Democratic Study Group (DSG), which served as their strategy and research arm and became the largest informal group in the House at the time.[18] By the early 1970s, the Democratic reformers had become strong enough to bring about a revitalization of the party caucus and used it to institute an array of significant changes in the party practices, as well as in House rules that had supported conservative control of the congressional agenda. Many of these changes, which reallocated political and policy power away from committee chairmen and shifted it to junior members, subcommittee chairs, and the party caucus,[19] reflected proposals originally developed through the DSG.

In the mid-1970s, buoyed by a large freshman class of seventy-five new Democratic members (the so-called Watergate Babies), the Democratic Caucus took a major step toward the reformers' goals by adopting a new party rule prohibiting Democrats from chairing more than one legislative subcommittee. The majority Caucus also adopted a "subcommittee bill of rights," under which subcommittee leaders were to be selected not by the committee chairman but by the Caucus of the Democrats on each committee. These changes had the effect not only of distributing leadership positions among a greater number of members[20] but also of reducing the control of committee chairs over that distribution. In addition, the bill of rights increased the potential power of these more widely distributed leadership positions by requiring that subcommittees have fixed jurisdictions, that legislation within their jurisdictions be referred to them, that each subcommittee have a dedicated staff and its own budget, and that each subcommittee be authorized to meet, hold hearings, and act. Together, these changes were later seen as having given rise to a system of government by subcommittee, where more members of the Democratic Caucus gained an opportunity to influence congressional decision-making at all stages of the legislative process.[21]

A further change adopted by the Democratic Caucus empowered its Committee on Committees to breach the seniority principle, under which the majority member with the longest continuous committee service was automatically entitled to chair each committee. The Caucus relieved the Ways and Means Committee of the job of serving as its Committee on Committees and assigned the task of committee assignments instead to the Democratic Steering and Policy Committee. The reformers then used these new rules in the Caucus to challenge several sitting committee chairs and removed three. To reflect the party's increased strength, the Caucus expanded party ratios on committees.

In several ways, the reforms of the 1970s also placed more resources in the hands of the party's leaders. In the first place, the Speaker and other major party leaders regained a more direct influence on committee assignments, because they were ex officio leading members of the new Steering and Policy Committee. The Speaker also regained a degree of influence over the referral of measures to committees as a result of other reforms of the period, which permitted him to refer measures to more than one committee (such multiple referrals were typically open-ended joint referrals, where Speakers could submit an entire measure to two committees) or to several committees (where legislation went first to a "primary" committee of jurisdiction for action, after which additional panels received the bill on a sequential basis). The Speaker could also divide up legislation and refer parts to different committees, as well as set time limits on committee consideration of bills. In addition, changes to Caucus rules permitted the Speaker personally to nominate the chair and Democratic members of the Committee on Rules, enabling him to place reliable supporters on this panel, and thereby enhanced his influence on the conditions under which the House considered measures.

Alternative Proposals to Democratic Reform

Not all of the congressional reform efforts were seen as evenhanded or "good government" by Michel and his Republican colleagues. The partial restoration of proxy voting (a practice that allowed a chair or panel member to cast votes for an absent member) and rolling quorums in both committees and subcommittees, for instance, encouraged absenteeism in committee meetings. They also allowed members to abdicate their responsibility to follow legislation closely. Members could simply leave their proxy with the committee, often without knowledge of how it would be used. As a result, proxy voting elevated the power of those present in committee markups.[22] Combined with the proliferation of subcommittees and subsequent dispersion of authority from a few committee leaders to a broader range of members, this was, Michel warned, altering the relationship of committees to the larger House environment. "Mark my words," he declared, on the opening day of the 95th Congress (1977–1979), "our major concern should be the fantastic growth and proliferation of committees and subcommittees."[23] With members spread too thin across subcommittees, the "net result," Michel reasoned, would be fewer members on the House floor engaged in meaningful debate, particularly with the "big, key decisions" affecting the country.[24] "Democracy is not neat, it is not even tidy for that matter, and it is not convenient," he noted. "It demands full debate; open, free and candid."[25]

Two years later, Michel argued that the majority Democrats had gone too far with "partisan reforms," causing an "erosion of the effectiveness of the House as a deliberative body."[26] The rules changes before the 96th Congress (1979–1981), he contended, transferred to the Speaker more power over the order of business and took away from the House some of its traditional rights to determine how it proceeded with its consideration of legislation. The result, he stated, was "more and more power being concentrated in the office of the Speaker and away from the true Representatives of the people."[27]

Later, on the heels of President Jimmy Carter's last State of the Union address to Congress in 1980, Michel offered his own "State of the House" speech, where he assessed the aforementioned Democratic reforms and their impact on the committee system: "If I had to choose a single image to describe Congress today, I'd chose a 'maze,'" he declared, "and our committee system has become a 'jungle thicket.'" He further stated:

> At a time of continuing and expanding energy crises, we have no central focal point, single committee dealing with energy. We do, however, have subcommittees, all the overlapping jurisdictions anyone might want, multiple referrals, proliferation, duplication, and rubber-stamping of subcommittee work by full committees.
>
> A Democratic Caucus of subcommittee chairmen looks like a meeting of the Amalgamated Indian Chiefs run amok.
>
> Yet even with all of those subcommittees, the committee work does not get done. We have in recent years been subjected to a new phenomenon: the floor mark-up. We are now doing on the floor the work on amendments and so forth that should have been done way back at the subcommittee level, and we're wasting valuable hours and days of floor time doing it. The Committee of the Whole has turned into a catch-all, do-it-yourself standing committee.
>
> And problems with the committee structure are just the tip of the iceberg. There are serious problems with staffing, duplication, research, liaison with the departments and practically every other function of the Congress.[28]

Speaking on January 5, 1981, to the 97th Congress (1981–1983) as the newly elected Republican Leader (an official title he changed from "Minority Leader" to symbolize a change in style from his predecessor), Michel contended that the proposed rules changes before the chamber "perpetuated the gradual concentration of power in the hands of a few." "Having said that," he continued, "I will tell you it is not my intention to fight these rules. The country does not have the time to spend on these issues, and we do not have the votes. You know it and I know it."[29] An important matter worth drawing attention to, however, was committee ratios and the barriers they presented to successfully implementing Ronald Reagan's economic agenda. Michel stated:

When it comes to the composition of House committees, the majority seems to believe that a little representative government is better than none, and a lot of representative government is worse than a little. The majority has provided for representation on some committees and not on others. On two major committees, Rules and Ways and Means, the majority has substituted autocracy for democracy.

Since the 95th Congress, Republicans have increased their membership in this House by 45. Yet in those 4 years, we have not been allowed one single additional seat on either Rules or Ways and Means. Ways and Means is the tax writing committee of the Congress through which the very cornerstone of President Reagan's economic program must pass. If the majority intends to work with the new administration on tax reform, why then does the majority assume such an arbitrary and obstructionist attitude toward who sits on that committee? There is a message in those numbers and it must not escape the attention of the American people.[30]

Speaker Thomas P. "Tip" O'Neill (D-MA) was using his leverage with the Committee on Rules to secure restrictions on the amendment process on the House floor.[31] In the 94th Congress (1975–1977), for instance, the last before O'Neill became Speaker, 81 percent of special rules were "open," meaning that any member could offer any germane amendment to the measure under consideration on the floor. By the 99th Congress (1985–1987), the last of O'Neill's speakership, only 50 percent of special rules were considered under open rules.[32] Without the votes to modify a rule from the Committee on Rules, the minority was often precluded from offering amendments and thus lacked access to the legislative process. For Michel, this was akin to converting the House into "robots, in a glass-covered dome, who come only when they are called, speak only when they are told, and cast their votes only when it is unavoidable."[33] He added: "It is more than tradition we are discarding. It is the fabric, character, and personality of an institution that for almost 200 years has stood as a symbol of freedom, open deliberation, and true representative democracy worldwide. This was once the House of the body politic. It is becoming a House of political bodies who have no purpose other than the service of the master."[34]

Further frustrating Michel and his Republican colleagues was the Speaker's effective use of referring measures to more than one committee or to several committees in sequence. O'Neill employed multiple referrals to safeguard committees' jurisdictional prerogatives, impose or extend reporting deadlines on panels, or coordinate policymaking.[35] This use of his referral authority tied him more directly into committee decision-making and involved him directly in committees' jurisdictional concerns.[36] Chairmen, for example, consulted with the Speaker about referral decisions or worked with him to clarify jurisdictional disputes.[37] The practice of multiple referred bills, Michel and the Republican Conference argued, consumed "four times as much meeting and hearing time as singly-referred measures, yet had half the chance of being reported from committees, and more than three times less chance of being passed by the House."[38]

At the start of the 99th Congress, Republicans offered an alternative rules package based on recommendations from the Republican Blueprint for a House That Works. The minority plan called for smaller committees, fewer subcommittees and staff, more equitable committee ratios, streamlined committee rules and procedures, evenly distributed workloads, less committee jurisdiction overlap, and greater oversight and accountability. "We waste too much public funds on too many subcommittees, too much staff, and too much paperwork," Michel argued. "We put very little meat on the public platter and a lot of fat and gristle, but the taxpayers pay for it as though it was all 100-percent prime beef."[39] Subcommittee proliferation and inequitable party ratios impaired the minority's ability to advance alternative viewpoints, pass amendments, or implement changes. Republicans calculated that there were 1,642 subcommittee seats and 154 members who had five or more subcommittee assignments in the 93rd Congress. By contrast, in the 98th Congress there were 1,721 subcommittee seats (a 5 percent increase from the 93rd Congress) and 198 members who had five or more subcommittee assignments (a 28 percent increase from the 93rd Congress). The increase in committees reflected a corresponding growth in staff. In the 93rd Congress, House committees had 848 committee staff; in the 98th Congress, committees had 1,732 committee staff, a 104 percent increase. The ratio of committee staff to committee member jumped from 1 to 1 to 2.1 to 1.[40]

The Republican Blueprint for a House That Works reiterated the imbalanced ratios on key committees and subcommittees. While the ratio of Republicans to Democrats in the House in the 98th Congress was 38 percent, Republicans represented just 34 percent of seats on the Ways and Means Committee, 30 percent on the House Administration Committee, and 29 percent on the Education and Labor Committee. This adherence to improperly aligned ratios, contended Michel, "disparages the very spirit of representative government and is equivalent to political disenfranchisement."[41] By his estimate, the minority party was underrepresented on committees by twenty-three seats and on subcommittees by sixty-two seats—"effectively disenfranchising 11.5 million Americans at the committee level and 31 million Americans at the subcommittee level."[42]

Calls for Further Committee Repair

Known for his conciliatory and bipartisan approach with Democratic leaders, Michel had a strained relationship with Democrat Jim Wright of Texas.[43] In Wright's relatively short tenure as Speaker (January 1987 to June 1989), Wright wielded the powers of his office with determination. Perhaps his most important tool as Speaker, however, was his use of the Rules Committee to shape floor consideration of Democratic bills through special rules.[44] He worked more directly, closely, and assertively with panel members than did his predecessor, Speaker O'Neill. According to Representative Claude Pepper (D-FL), chair of the Committee on Rules at the time, O'Neill had normally communicated his wishes to the committee through staff, though he occasionally also summoned its members to his chambers. By contrast, Wright met routinely with Rules Committee Democrats in the committee's own rooms to give them their marching orders.[45] "Wright has acted more upon the assumption that the Rules Committee is a branch of the leadership than Speaker O'Neill did," said Chairman Pepper. "Sometimes Members chafe a little at that."[46] Michel and Republicans portrayed the Committee on Rules as a gag-rule enforcer, barring GOP amendments from reaching the House floor. Wright's tactics prompted one of Michel's lieutenants at the time, the House Minority Whip Trent Lott (R-MS), to accuse the Democratic leadership of "trying to turn the Rules Committee into the stranglehold on this institution that it was 30 years ago."[47]

A notable example of Wright's use of the Committee on Rules to advance his legislative priorities occurred in October 1987, when the House rejected a special rule for consideration of a major tax bill, largely because many members found one of the bill's provisions too controversial. Wright directed the Committee on Rules immediately to report a new rule that would bring to the floor a version of the bill lacking the controversial provision. Then, in a move reminiscent of Speaker Joseph G. Cannon, a Republican from Illinois who presided over the House from 1903 to 1911, he maneuvered around a requirement that a special rule cannot be considered on the same day it is reported from the committee without a two-thirds vote of the House. To circumvent that requirement, Wright adjourned the House, then reconvened it in a new legislative day less than two minutes later. The House then considered and adopted the new rule for consideration of the tax bill. In order to secure passage of the bill itself, however, Wright had to keep the roll call open well beyond the minimum required fifteen minutes, bringing down the gavel only when his fellow Texas Democrat, Representative Jim Chapman, changed his vote, giving the bill a one-vote majority.

Actions of this kind often generated intense personal animosity among House Republicans, especially by young, aggressive conservative members of the Conservative Opportunity Society.[48] Representative William Dannemeyer (R-CA) protested Wright's manipulation of the legislative day by saying: "Genesis tells us our Lord created the world in seven days. We are now witnessing the creation of an eighth day. I just ask the gentleman: Does he have a name for this new creation?"[49] "The House is convinced the sun rises and sets over it," added Representative Hank Brown (R-CO), "but this is the first time I've ever seen us readjust the sun."[50] In a way similar to Speaker Cannon, Wright's aggressive use of the Committee on Rules and his procedural prerogatives as chair to forward his legislative priorities ultimately eroded his political base of support and contributed to his eventual downfall.

By the start of the commemorative 100th Congress (1987–1989), Michel and the Republican Conference criticized Wright and the committee system for being "chaotic" and "impotent" due in large part to the lack of legislative or oversight agendas. They cited the "sprawling jungle" of semiautonomous subcommittees (148 in the 99th Congress) and excess staff, overlapping jurisdictions both within and among committees, the referral of the same bills to more than one committee, skewed party ratios that produced "unrepresentative bills," and "phantom voting devices" like proxy voting and one-third quorums "necessitated by poor attendance." As Representative Trent Lott commented, "The heart of the policy process in the House, our committee system, has clogged arteries as a result of layers of fatty tissue." "For another thing," he added, "our committees—like Gulliver—are hamstrung and tied down by a Lilliputian system of subcommittees and staff, ensuring duplication, conflict, and delays."[51] Michel added during a special order organized by the Republican leadership to draw further attention to issue: "The fact is that the committees are not doing their jobs, and when the committees are not doing their jobs, the Congress has failed in its obligation."[52]

Using red-white-and-blue charts, Republicans proposed the Bicentennial House Restoration Project, a thirty-point reform package that consisted of various changes to the committee system. These included requiring committees to organize earlier, within three legislative days after their election; abolishing joint referral of the same bill to more than one committee while retaining split referrals subject to time limits and with a principal committee designated by the Speaker; requiring all committees (except Ethics) to reflect the party ratio of the House; limiting all committees (except Appropriations) to no more than six subcommittees; limiting members to no more than four subcommittee assignments; banning proxy voting; restoring majority quorums for transacting business; and requiring the House to adopt an overall committee staff limit with conforming sublimits for each committee; entitling the minority to up to one-third of the investigative staff; and reducing the overall staff by 10 percent from the previous Congress.

In a Republican "Dear Colleague" letter, Michel and Marvin H. "Mickey" Edwards (R-OK) highlighted the importance of reform:

> Our 30-point House reform package is aimed at restoring our committee system, floor procedures, and budget process to ensure a more deliberative, representative and accountable House. The House reform revolution of the Seventies, with its proliferation of subcommittees and staff, its tangled jurisdictions, and diffusion of power, over-democratized the House to the point of paralysis.
>
> The counter reform movement of the Eighties has concentrated more powers in the leadership at the expense of our committee system and individual responsibilities. As you, the people's Representative, have been increasingly dealt out of the process, your constituents have been disenfranchised. The time has come to put the people back in the People's House by giving their Representatives more of a voice and a vote in shaping our Nation's laws. That is what our Bicentennial Mandate is all about: Restoring the People's House.[53]

Leader Michel: Change through Gentle Persuasion

As a matter of practice, Bob Michel was the sort of leader who generally let the committee process operate with little interference.[54] He was, however, a master of "gentle persuasion," who succeeded by "downplaying his own role."[55] "If you're not concerned over who gets the credit," he would say, "you might be doggone surprised over how many things you can get accomplished."[56] This was especially on display on the opening day of the 101st Congress (1989–1991). After self-deprecating the fact that he was the first member in history to lose the contest for Speaker five times in a row, Michel quoted Representative Fisher Ames as a way to draw attention to the hazards of prolonged one-party control: "Two hundred years ago when Congress met," he stated, "Fisher Ames, a member from Massachusetts, said the House consisted of sober, solid folks but few geniuses. There are few geniuses."[57] He continued:

> I believe much the same can be said for our House membership today. Perhaps we are not the shining geniuses some others in this town think they are, but our Members in the main continue to be solid and hard-working, and we still bring to this House from our hometowns, the virtues of the heart.
>
> But even a hard-working and most well-meaning body of men and women needs periodically to examine its behavior and analyze its rules and regulations, and it is my belief that in this 101st Congress is one that should deal right up front in a bipartisan and comprehensive way with reforms dealing with campaign reform and our ethical code of conduct.
>
> The key words are "comprehensive" and "bipartisan."[58]

In its effort to make the committee system more responsible and responsive to leadership and members, the Republican Conference offered A Bicentennial Mandate to Reform the People's House. Similar to the reforms proposed in the previous Congress, this round of reforms also encouraged committees to organize earlier, reduce subcommittees and member assignments, abolish proxy voting, and require majority quorums for any committee business—all to allow for more legislating and less duplication of effort. In addition, it proposed that committee meetings only be closed for national security, personal privacy, or personal reasons and that committee reports on bills include the names of those members voting for and against reporting a measure or, in the case of a nonrecorded vote, the names of those lawmakers present.[59]

Repeated calls for repairing the committee system continued into the 102nd Congress (1991–1993). Although retitled, the Republican Reform Manifesto for a New House Revolution echoed the Bicentennial House Restoration Project by representing how a Republican majority would govern if given the opportunity. The rules package, contended Michel, was very similar to a "genetic code." "It does not determine our fate entirely," he declared, "but it is the structure in which much of the fate of this Congress will be determined."[60] The Democratic majority's rules package, Michel pointed out, offered members "an inheritance of misery." "Think of it," he told colleagues: "22 committees, 158 subcommittees, with hopelessly tangled and knotted lines of responsibility."[61]

Among the committee reforms offered in the Manifesto for a New House Revolution were: realigning committee jurisdictions along more rational and functional lines; abolishing joint referrals of legislation (while retaining sequential and split referral); limiting committees (other than Appropriations) to six subcommittees and members to no more than four subcommittee assignments; ending proxy voting and one-third quorums; requiring party ratios to reflect the party ratio in the House; establishing staff ceilings as well as reducing committee staff by 10 percent from previous Congresses; requiring that oversight agendas be adopted at the beginning of a Congress and that their implementation be reported on at the end of each Congress; and requiring roll call votes on reporting measures from committees.[62]

By the 103rd Congress (1993–1995), Michel and the GOP offered a second, slightly narrower rules manifesto, the Republican Manifesto for Change, which included a six-year term limit on committee chairmen and ranking members; committee realignment; a ban on proxy voting and joint referrals; equitable party ratios in committees; a reduction in subcommittees to six per committee and a limit of four committee assignments; a one-third reduction in committee staffs; and publication of committee votes. Michel especially urged members to stop the use of rolling quorums in the House: "Now rolling quorums may sound like one of those bits of esoteric jargon we legislators like to throw around to impress each other," he said, but they defeated "the purpose of collective deliberation and decision making." "The very word Congress," he reminded his colleagues, "has at its roots in the concept of coming together, of being together, of political community, and to institute procedures that fragment the collective sense of decision making and responsibility in the House is to demean the very concept of the Congress."[63]

Republican Takeover—Michel Retires

Michel's decision to retire from Congress came on the cusp of the historic Republican takeover of Congress in 1995. One commentator likened it to Moses: "He [Bob Michel] was given a glimpse of the promised land he could not enter."[64] Michel himself reflected on his missed opportunity in a manner befitting his folksy, plainspoken manner: "There are times when I feel like a small boy who has dutifully eaten his spinach and broccoli but who leaves the dinner table before Mom brings in the strawberry shortcake."[65]

On the first day of the 104th Congress (1995–1997), the newly elected Speaker, Newt Gingrich, and the Republican majority not only presented the Contract with America agenda to the new House, but also adopted a package of amendments to the rules that put in place a series of long-awaited institutional changes that Michel stewarded. House Republicans passed a series of reforms that affected most parts of the House committee system. These changes were part of the overall concession of authority upward to party leaders and were intended to make the committee system more accountable to the Republican Conference.[66] By recasting the committee system through the majority party, consistent with the underlying goals of the 1970s, the Republican Party could impose its agenda on committees accustomed to charting their own course.[67]

One of the rules changes under the new Republican majority imposed term limits on committee and subcommittee chairs of not more than six years of service. Among other things, this restriction had the effect of making committee leaders less formidable as competitors to the Speaker for power in the chamber. A second change abolished proxy (or absentee) voting on committees and subcommittees. This change was important to the Speaker because, by the 103rd Congress (1993–1995), Democratic committee chairs were extensively using proxies to win votes on amendments during markups even when many of their party colleagues were absent. Gingrich argued that prohibiting proxy voting would promote member participation in markups.

The power dynamic between leadership and committees was also affected by changes in rules affecting the referral of measures to multiple committees. The new rule authorized the Speaker to designate a "primary" or lead committee among the several panels receiving legislation and also expanded his authority to require a committee to report legislation within a specified time or be discharged. These changes increased the Speaker's flexibility in deciding whether, when, and for how long other panels might review a bill.[68] At the same time, it increased the accountability of the committees to the Speaker for their handling of legislation.

Gingrich was able to use these rules changes, together with the loyalty he enjoyed within the Republican Conference, to influence the composition of the committees, as well as to assert central direction over many of their activities. He used his control over committee assignments to name loyal and energetic members to key committee positions, often in a way that also reinforced the allegiance to his leadership felt especially by many of the Republican freshmen. He was able to depart in at least three instances from the seniority principle in naming committee chairs, bypassing more senior GOP committee members in favor of ones more assertive and dedicated to his program. Also, in a manner reminiscent of Speaker Cannon decades earlier, he asked that Republican members of the Appropriations Committee sign a statement that they could be removed if they did not adhere to the Republican Conference's agenda.[69] In addition, in an unprecedented move, he placed freshmen members on several "exclusive" committees including Appropriations, Commerce, Rules, and Ways and Means.[70] And he saw that two Republican freshmen received appointments as subcommittee chairs.[71]

Rotation of chairs was assured by a GOP Conference provision that committee chairs could serve no more than six years in leadership. By changing the structure of the Republican Steering Committee, Gingrich acquired far more power to appoint committee chairpersons and a greater say in the selection of committee and subcommittee members. And the House's own staff and budget came under the party leadership's control, which gave the Speaker broad discretionary authority and control over insider resources, the ability to reward or punish members, and a broad network of patronage.

Especially in the 104th Congress (1995–1997), Gingrich made frequent use of ad hoc task forces to write legislation reflecting the views of the majority leadership.[72] Freshmen (class of 1994) and sophomores (elected in 1992)—who constituted more than half of the Republican membership—often predominated on these panels. By this means, Gingrich was able to involve supportive noncommittee members in the decision-making process, generate party consensus, and circumvent jurisdictional and other committee-related obstacles.[73] For instance, Gingrich formed the "design team on Medicare," a group consisting of eight members from the leadership and from the Ways and Means and Commerce Committees, which worked out of the Speaker's conference room over four months to draft Medicare legislation. In the process, subcommittees were relegated to the role of holding hearings without considering specific legislative proposals. As Representative Henry A. Waxman (D-CA) complained: "The subcommittees are practically irrelevant."[74]

Gingrich also persuaded committees to report legislation quickly; hearings on the GOP's Contract with America items—its governing agenda during the first one hundred days of 1995—were perfunctory, and markups often pro forma, largely because committee chairs, at the request of the Speaker, set aside their own priorities to focus on Contract legislation.[75] "There has not been time to implement items of my personal agenda," Henry J. Hyde (R-IL), then chair of the Judiciary Committee, said: "But they are small potatoes. I'm full in accord with the priorities of this leadership. On the whole, it is a salutary way to proceed, because we have focus and direction, not drift."[76]

In the judgment of one commentator, the various changes that augmented the Speaker's power produced an "American version of a prime minister in a system of party government and a legislative process with a lot less of the deliberative and incremental pacing that a committee-centered system can provide."[77]

This manner of structuring power in the House did not, however, prove enduring in all respects. The 1996 elections gave the Republicans a reduced majority in the 105th Congress (1997–1999), which precipitated disputes among frustrated party factions. As divisions over specific policy objectives increasingly disrupted party unity, confidence in Gingrich's leadership declined, and consequently the willingness of Republican lawmakers to defer to centralized party leadership diminished. The disciplined Republican Party organization that characterized the start of the 104th Congress was absent in the 105th. Speaker Gingrich was forced to reverse some of his more ambitious methods of circumventing committees; he left the House at the end of the Congress. Thereafter, the House reverted once again to a heavier reliance on committees for the processing of legislation and the achievement of legislative and political goals.

Conclusion

At a swift glance the landmark committee reforms implemented by Gingrich and the new Republican majority in 1995 seemed to tear up the traditional rule book and offer a revolutionary way of doing business on Capitol Hill. Yet like other attempts at change, several of these reforms were rooted in earlier efforts. In this respect, Gingrich capitalized on the legacy of his colleague and the longtime GOP minority leader, Bob Michel. Yet Gingrich's success did foreshadow the changing face of the House Republican Party, one that was young and impatient, one that favored his more activist and confrontational tactics[78] compared to Michel's self-effacing and harmonious ways.

Michel's entire congressional career (with the exception of the 83rd Congress, 1953–1955)—both as a staffer to Representative Harold H. Velde (R-IL) and as a representative—was spent in the minority of a majoritarian institution that conformed to many Republicans' views toward Congress and their roles as legislators.[79] At a press conference shortly after his retirement announcement, Michel reflected on the expectations of him and other junior members upon arriving in Congress: "It wasn't anything about revolutionizing this or changing this or that, to that degree," he said, "other than on pretty much plain old philosophical ground."[80]

This outlook and approach separated Bob Michel not only from his replacement as the Republicans' leader of the House but also from the regime of "conservative reformers" within his own party who viewed comity and compromise as relics of a bygone era.[81] He, instead, was an affable institutionalist who understood well the central part that committees play in Congress—how they shape policy, advance party agendas, disentangle complexity, and manage workloads—but who rationalized that their proliferation had bureaucratized the legislative process. Senator Richard "Dick" Durbin (D-IL) summarized this well when he noted that Michel was "the face of decency and public service."[82] Moreover, Michel would not blindside a political opponent, or consider "comity" and "compromise" bad words, according to his longtime aide and successor in the House, Representative Ray H. LaHood (R-IL).[83]

Notes

1. The views expressed in this chapter are those of the author and not necessarily those of the National Defense University, the Department of Defense, or any other entity of the US government.
2. RHM, *Congressional Record*, May 24, 1999, 12178.
3. Michael L. Koempel and Judy Schneider, *A Retrospective of House Rules Changes since the 104th Congress*, CRS Report RL 33610 (Washington, DC: Congressional Research Service, 2006), 1 and 14. See also Rafael Gely and Asghar Zardkoohi, "Understanding Congressional Reform: Lessons from the Seventies," *Harvard Journal on Legislation* 35 (1998): 509–535; and Christopher J. Deering and Steven S. Smith, *Committees in Congress*, 3rd ed. (Washington, DC: CQ Press, 1997), 47–50.
4. Roger H. Davidson, "Congressional Committees as Moving Targets," *Legislative Studies Quarterly* 11 (1986): 19–33. Committees have long been agents of change. In 1811, as the system of permanent, or standing, committees began to emerge in the House, Henry Clay (R-KY) used his authority over the appointment process to stack key

panels with the allies who had elected him. House Speakers Thomas B. Reed (R-ME) and Joseph G. Cannon (R-IL) centralized committee power through the majority party and its control of the Rules Committee to achieve their party goals. Much later, Speakers Nicholas Longworth (R-OH) and Sam Rayburn (D-TX) revamped committees to reclaim power in order to advance their party's agenda. And Speakers Thomas P. "Tip" O'Neill (D-MA) and James C. Wright (D-TX) recentralized authority through skillful management of the Rules Committee and by circumventing committees with leadership-appointed task forces to draft legislation.

5. Woodrow Wilson, *Congressional Government* (New Brunswick, NJ: Transaction Publishers, 1885 [2002]), 79.

6. Colton C. Campbell and Roger H. Davidson, "US Congressional Committees: Changing Legislative Workshops," in *The New Role of Parliamentary Committees*, ed. Lawrence D. Longley and Roger H. Davidson (New York: Frank Cass, 1998), 132.

7. Koempel and Schneider, *A Retrospective of House Rules Changes*, 1 and 14

8. See Leroy N. Rieselbach, *Congressional Reform* (Washington, DC: CQ Press, 1986), chap. 2.

9. Robert A. Caro, *Means of Ascent: The Years of Lyndon Johnson* (New York: Alfred A. Knopf, 1990), 76.

10. Richard Norton Smith interview with RHM, April 28, 2009, Gerald R. Ford Presidential Foundation, geraldrfordfoundation.org/centennial/oralhistory/bob-michel.

11. Donald C. Bacon, "Sam Rayburn," in *The Encyclopedia of the United States Congress*, ed. Donald C. Bacon, Roger H. Davidson, and Morton Keller (New York: Simon & Schuster, 1995), 1672.

12. Robert A. Diamond, ed., *Origins and Development of Congress* (Washington, DC: Congressional Quarterly, Inc., 1976), 140.

13. D. B. Hardeman and Donald C. Bacon, *Rayburn: A Biography* (Austin, TX: Monthly Press, 1987), 424. Thurmond joined the Dixiecrats, a group of southern Democrats who bolted from the Democratic Party's national convention in opposition to President Harry S. Truman's civil rights program. The rebellious act ruffled Rayburn, who served as Truman's chief House advocate, often hammering out compromises on the administration's legislative proposals.

14. John D. Morris, "Rayburn Bars TV and Radio from All House Inquiries," *New York Times*, February 26, 1952; and John D. Morris, "House Ban on TV Has Wide Political Impact: Speaker Rayburn's Ruling Is Not Likely to Be Changed in Near Future," *New York Times*, March 2, 1952.

15. *Congressional Record*, February 25, 1952, 1334–1335.

16. Quoted in John D. Morris, "Democrats Admit Rules Reprisals: Concede Voting on Rayburn Plan Influenced Choices for House Committees," *New York Times*, February 3, 1961, 11.

17. Leroy N. Rieselbach, *Congressional Reform in the Seventies* (Morristown, NJ: General Learning, 1977).

18. Arthur G. Stevens, Jr., Arthur H. Miller, and Thomas E. Mann, "Mobilization of Liberal Strength in the House, 1955–1970: The Democratic Study Group," *American Political Science Review* 68 (1974): 667–681.

19. Rieselbach, *Congressional Reform in the Seventies*; and C. Lawrence Evans and Walter J. Oleszek, "The Politics of Congressional Reform: The Joint Committee on the

Organization of Congress," in *Remaking Congress: Change and Stability in the 1990s*, ed. James A. Thurber and Roger H. Davidson (Washington, DC: CQ Press, 1995), 73–98.

20. Roger H. Davidson, "Subcommittee Government: New Channels for Policymaking," in *The New Congress*, ed. Thomas E. Mann and Norman J. Ornstein (Washington, DC: AEI Press, 1981).

21. Donald R. Wolfensberger, "A Brief History of Congressional Reform Efforts," prepared for use by the Bipartisan Policy Center and the Woodrow Wilson Center, Washington, DC, 2013; Roger H. Davidson, "Two Avenues of Change: House and Senate Committee Reorganization," in *Congress Reconsidered*, 2nd ed., ed. Lawrence C. Dodd and Bruce Oppenheimer (Washington, DC: CQ Press), 107–133; and Christopher J. Deering, "Subcommittee Government in the U.S. House: An Analysis of Bill Management," *Legislative Studies Quarterly* 7 (1982): 533–546.

22. Campbell and Davidson, "US Congressional Committees: Changing Legislative Workshops," 137.

23. *Congressional Record*, January 4, 1977, 63.

24. *Congressional Record*, January 4, 1977, 63.

25. *Congressional Record*, January 4, 1977, 63.

26. *Congressional Record*, January 15, 1979, 13.

27. *Congressional Record*, January 15, 1979, 13.

28. RHM, "State of the House," February 4, 1980, RHM Papers, Staff Series: Bill Gavin, f. 1980, "State of the House."

29. *Congressional Record*, January 5, 1981, 99.

30. *Congressional Record*, January 5, 1981, 99.

31. Steven S. Smith, *Call to Order: Floor Politics in the House and Senate* (Washington, DC: Brookings Institution Press, 1989), 68–71.

32. Stanley Bach and Steven S. Smith, *Managing Uncertainty in the House of Representatives: Adaptation and Innovation in Special Rules* (Washington, DC: Brookings Institution Press, 1988), 51.

33. *Congressional Record*, January 3, 1983, 37.

34. *Congressional Record*, January 3, 1983, 37.

35. Roger H. Davidson, Walter J. Oleszek, and Thomas Kephart, "One Bill, Many Committees: Multiple Referrals in the House of Representatives," *Legislative Studies Quarterly* 13 (1988): 3–28.

36. Roger H. Davidson, "The New Centralization on Capitol Hill," *Review of Politics* 50 (1988): 345–364, 357.

37. Davidson, "The New Centralization on Capitol Hill," 359.

38. *Congressional Record*, January 3, 1985, 396.

39. *Congressional Record*, January 3, 1985, 394.

40. *Congressional Record*, January 3, 1985, 394.

41. *Congressional Record*, January 3, 1985, 396.

42. *Congressional Record*, January 3, 1985, 396.

43. Adam Clymer, "Robert Michel Dies at 93; House G.O.P. Leader Prized for Conciliation," *New York Times*, February 27, 2017, www.nytimes.com/2017/02/17/us/robert-michel-dies.html?_r=0; see also Adam Clymer, "Michel, G.O.P. House Leader, to Retire," *New York Times*, October 5, 1993, A24.

44. Janet Hook, "Jim Wright: Taking Big Risks to Amass Power," *CQ Weekly Report*, March 12, 1988, 625.

45. Janet Hook, "GOP Chafes under Restrictive House Rules," *CQ Weekly Report*, October 10, 1987, 2451.

46. Quoted in Hook, "GOP Chafes under Restrictive House Rules."

47. Quoted in Hook, "GOP Chafes under Restrictive House Rules," 2450.

48. Nicol C. Rae, *Conservative Reformers: The Republican Freshmen and the Lessons of the 104th Congress* (New York: Routledge, 1998).

49. *Congressional Record*, October 29, 1987, 29934.

50. Anne Swardson and Tom Kenworthy, "Wright Ekes out Tax Bill's Passage: Speaker Literally Turns Back Clock to Overcome Party Rebellion," *Washington Post*, October 30, 1987, A16.

51. *Congressional Record*, January 6, 1987, 8–10.

52. RHM, *Congressional Record*, May 24, 1999, 12178.

53. RHM and Mickey Edwards to "Dear Republican Colleague," RHM Papers, Leadership Series, f. 101st Congress: Dear Colleague, January 11, 1989.

54. Scott A. Frisch and Sean Q Kelly, *Committee Assignment Politics in the U.S. House of Representatives* (Norman: University of Oklahoma Press, 2006), 187.

55. Margot Hornblower, "The Master of Gentle Persuasion," *Washington Post*, August 10, 1981, A1.

56. Quoted in Hornblower, "The Master of Gentle Persuasion."

57. *Congressional Record*, January 4, 1989, 68.

58. *Congressional Record*, January 4, 1989, 68–69.

59. *Congressional Record*, January 4, 1989, 79–80.

60. *Congressional Record*, January 3, 1991, 53.

61. *Congressional Record*, January 3, 1991, 53.

62. *Congressional Record*, January 3, 1991, 47.

63. *Congressional Record*, January 5, 1993, 94.

64. Ed Kilgore, "R.I.P. Bob Michel, the Last GOP Leader before Anger Took Over," *New York*, nymag.com/daily/intelligencer/2017/02/r-i-p-bob-michel-the-last-house-gop-leader -before-anger-took-over.html.

65. Quoted in Katherine Skiba, "Robert Michel, Illinois Republican Leader Skilled at Compromise, Dies at 93," *Chicago Tribune*, February 17, 2017, www.chicagotribune .com/news/obituaries.

66. C. Lawrence Evans and Walter J. Oleszek, *Congress under Fire: Reform Politics and the Republican Majority* (Boston: Houghton Mifflin, 1997), 129.

67. Walter Pincus, "Centralized Republican Power House: Strategy Apparatus Gives Gingrich and Company Structure to Manage Hill Agenda," *Washington Post*, September 6, 1995, A19.

68. Roger H. Davidson and Walter J. Oleszek, *Congress and Its Members*, 5th ed. (Washington, DC: CQ Press, 1996), 215.

69. Connie Bruck, "The Politics of Perception" *New Yorker*, October 6, 1995, 72.

70. Democrats and Republicans designate "exclusive" committees in the assignment process and generally limit service to one such panel. For Republicans, at the time, these included the Committees on Appropriations, Rules, Ways and Means, and Energy and Commerce.

71. Representatives David M. McIntosh (R-IN) and Thomas M. Davis (R-VA) were appointed chairs, respectively, of the Government Reform and Oversight Committee's Subcommittee on National Economic Growth, Natural Resources, and Regulatory Affairs, and its Subcommittee on the District of Columbia.

72. Richard E. Cohen, "Crackup of the Committees," *National Journal*, July 31, 1999, 2214.

73. Evans and Oleszek, *Congress under Fire*, 132.

74. Quoted in Jackie Koszczuk, "Gingrich Puts More Power into Speaker's Hands," *CQ Weekly Report* (1995), 3052.

75. Barbara Sinclair, *Unorthodox Lawmaking: New Legislative Processes in the U.S. Congress* (Washington, DC: CQ Press, 1997), 26.

76. Quoted in Koszczuk, "Gingrich Puts More Power into Speaker's Hands," 3052.

77. Richard F. Fenno, Jr., *Learning to Govern: An Institutional View of the 104th Congress* (Washington, DC: Brookings Institution Press, 1997), 31.

78. David Hawkings, "Bob Michel, Last Leader of the 'Old School' House GOP, Dies at 93," *Roll Call*, February 17, 2017, www.rollcall.com/news/politics/not-publishbob -michel-last-leader-old-school-house-gop-dies-xx; Douglas L. Koopman, *Hostile Takeover: The House Republican Party, 1980–1995* (Lanham, MD: Rowman & Littlefield, 1996). See also Elizabeth Drew, "Washington: When Decency Prevailed," *NYR Daily*, www.nybooks.com/daily/2013/11/01/foley-memorial-decency.

79. William F. Connelly, Jr., and John J. Pitney, *Congress' Permanent Minority? Republicans in the U.S. House* (Lanham, MD: Rowman & Littlefield Publishers, 1994).

80. Quoted in Connelly and Pitney, *Congress' Permanent Minority?* 60.

81. Rae, *Conservative Reformers*. See also Ed Kilgore, "R.I.P. Bob Michel, the Last House GOP Leader before Anger Took Over," *New York Magazine*, February 17, 2017, nymag .com/daily/intelligencer/2017/02/r-i-p-bob-michel-the-last-house-gop-leader-before -anger-took-over.html.

82. Senator Richard Durbin (D-IL), February 17, 2017, www.c-span.org/video/?424202–2 /senator-durbin-tribute-representative-bob-michel.

83. Quoted in the *Peoria Journal Star*, "Editorial: Remember Bob Michel," February 17, 2017, www.pjstar.com/opinion/20170217/editorial-remembering-bob-michel.

CHAPTER 11

BOB MICHEL, NEWT GINGRICH, AND THE REPUBLICAN LEADERSHIP DILEMMA

C. Lawrence Evans

During the second decade of the twenty-first century, observers of Congress have repeatedly questioned whether the House Republican Conference can be governed. Following the midterm elections of 2010, the most ideologically conservative elements of the Conference were often unwilling to compromise on major legislative issues and were at best reluctant team players when whipped by their leaders on party priorities. This turn toward conservative intransigence, many argued, reflected broader changes within the GOP activist base across the country, especially the rise of the national Tea Party movement, as well as increasing distrust of government, politicians, and elites more generally.[1] An early warning shot was the primary defeat of House Majority Leader Eric Cantor (R-VA) in summer 2014. The next year, conservatives within the GOP Conference signaled that they might support a motion to vacate the chair, which led to the resignation of Speaker John Boehner (R-OH). During 2011–2018, the Republican majority in the House repeatedly confronted potential insurgencies from within its right wing that complicated efforts to pass appropriations bills, debt limit hikes, and other measures that the party mainstream viewed as critical to maintaining the GOP name brand. Not surprisingly, the response was a cacophony of criticism from pundits and scholars. Congressional Republicans had become dysfunctional, said many.[2] The House Republican Conference had become an "ideological freak show," claimed some.[3]

The factionalization that exists within the House GOP Conference is real and reflects enduring conditions within the congressional party dating back at least to the late 1980s and the relationship between two leaders at the time—Minority Leader Robert H. Michel (R-IL) and GOP Minority Whip Newt Gingrich (R-GA). Indeed, the current difficulties that Republican leaders face in building majorities during the Trump era have roots in internal divisions that emerged within the House Republican Conference of Michel's and Gingrich's days.

Building on recent scholarship about the congressional parties, this chapter maintains that there are important differences between the internal politics of the two political parties in the House, and there is something that can be usefully called the "Republican leadership dilemma." While Democrats are best viewed as a coalition of interests primarily concerned about securing benefits and services from government, Republicans long have been a more ideologically oriented party focused on limiting the expanse of federal programs, especially as that relates to domestic policy. As a result of these important substantive distinctions between the policy agendas of the two parties, the process of building coalitions within them are somewhat different. While coalitions among congressional Democrats can be constructed via logrolling and the dispersion of programmatic benefits, forging agreements among Republicans relies more on broader appeals rooted in ideological conservatism. Since Bob Michel's time in the leadership, especially when the Republicans have been the House majority, GOP leaders have routinely confronted the possibility of defections at the ideological extremes within their party on major votes.

In short, the job of Republican leaders in the House—and to some extent the Senate—is different from the set of challenges that routinely confront leaders of congressional Democrats. To understand Bob Michel, it is critical to consider the practical exigencies of his role as a leader of congressional Republicans, rather than as a leader of a past minority or the representative from Peoria, Illinois. And the substantial coalition-building difficulties that Paul Ryan (R-WI), John Boehner, and other recent GOP House leaders have confronted likewise are not completely new and can be traced back to the leadership struggles that occurred between Michel and Gingrich decades before.

Asymmetric Polarization and the Rise of Movement Conservatism

There is a tendency within political science to conceptualize party leadership without drawing qualitative distinctions between the two major political parties. The party cartel model of Gary Cox and Matthew McCubbins, for example, maintains that the majority party in the House has had something approaching monopoly control over the floor agenda since the late 1800s.[4] Regardless of party, according to this view, the leaders of the House majority control which measures are placed on the chamber agenda and will take steps to ensure that issues or bills that would be opposed on final passage by a majority of the majority party never see the light of day. Occasionally referred to popularly as the "Hastert Rule," the implication is that the procedural prerogatives of the House majority can be used to block changes to existing policy and thereby pull outcomes in the direction of the majority program. When Democrats control the chamber, the prediction is that outcomes (or nonoutcomes, if you will) will skew toward the left, and when the GOP is in the majority, the tilt will be toward the right. As another example, according to the "conditional party government" theory of John Aldrich and David Rohde, members of the majority party are expected to empower their leaders when policy preferences within that party are relatively homogeneous and a wide ideological gap exists between the two party programs.[5] Conversely, if viewpoints within the partisan majority are ideologically dispersed and the two party positions are less distinct, then power tends to be more dispersed within the chamber, party leaders are somewhat less consequential, and the locus of decision-making is more centered at the committee level. Just like the party cartel model, then, the conditional party government theory is posited to hold regardless of whether the Democrats or Republicans are organizing the House.

The two congressional parties, however, are not mirror images of each other. For one, the well-known trend toward increased ideological polarization between the parties appears to derive primarily from burgeoning ideological conservatism among Republican members, while aggregate movements in the liberal direction among Democrats have been far less pronounced. Figure 11.1 shows the number of Democrats and Republicans falling along different portions of the liberal-conservative ideological spectrum during four Congresses stretching across the 1970s to the 2010s. The ideological measure is the first-dimension DW-NOMINATE value that is standard in congressional scholarship.[6] As you can see, the two House parties have become increasingly polarized along left-right ideological lines. In 1979–1980, the years during which Michel rose to lead the House Republicans, there was substantial overlap between the parties, with a considerable number of conservative Democrats falling to the ideological right of several dozen Republican moderates. A decade later, in 1989–1990, as Michel began to consider retirement at least partly in response to challenges from more conservative House Republicans

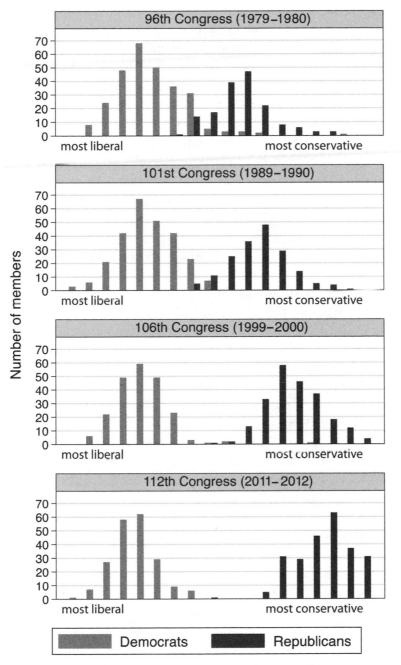

Figure 11.1 Roll call ideology of House members by party, selected Congresses
Source: The DW-NOMINATE values used in this chapter encompass roll call data
from the 1st through the 113th Congresses and were downloaded from Keith Poole,
Voteview: Congressional Roll-Call Votes Database (2017), legacy.voteview.com.

led by Gingrich, this overlap had shrunk to a dozen or so members, and by the end of the 1990s they had all but disappeared. As we move into the contemporary era, the open ideological ground between the two congressional parties has become quite large. The figure also clearly reveals, however, that while there has been some movement over time among Democrats toward the left, the rightward shift among the GOP is much more dramatic.

When we consider the substantive disputes that have divided the parties and the divergent interests of which they are composed, the case for asymmetric polarization grows still stronger. In influential research, Matt Grossmann and David Hopkins argue that the Republican Party is most properly viewed as a coalition of interests tied together by common ideological preferences for limited government and traditional values, while the Democratic coalition is composed more of interest groups seeking programmatic benefits from the federal government.[7] As a result, ideological purity receives greater emphasis on the GOP side of the aisle, while Democrats can rely more on logrolling and compromise when constructing legislative coalitions. These differences in the factional makeups of the two political parties, Grossmann and Hopkins maintain, are reinforced by critical features of public opinion. While Americans are generally supportive of limited government and highly skeptical about concentrations of power and governing institutions more generally, when they are asked about particular programs and benefits they tend to want more government rather than less.

Not surprisingly, Democratic and Republican identifiers use different criteria in evaluating the parties. While GOP partisans focus disproportionately on ideological concerns like free markets and traditional values, Democrats place more emphasis on group benefits like Medicare funding and aid to the disadvantaged.[8] Similarly, the financial donors and organized groups that ally themselves with one or the other party are also distinct. On the GOP side of the aisle, they tend to share a common commitment to broad conservative values, while the groups under the Democratic umbrella are far more ideologically diverse.[9]

The challenges that Republican and Democratic congressional leaders confront are substantially different. Republican leaders, in particular, are more likely to face cross-pressure between the demands of ideological purists on their far right, on the one hand, and the kinds of compromises needed to win elections and pass legislation within a system of separate institutions sharing power on the other. Michel certainly understood the dilemma: "Ideological rigidity in a democracy is the political equivalent of the kiss of death," he told an audience in 1987. "Demands for ideological purity in a democracy—especially among those who call themselves conservatives—is lunacy," and he warned that "ideological thought police of the right or left tell the rest of us that defeat is better than victory so long as no compromise was involved. They love a loss better than a bit of progress. They see a slight deviation from some ideological abstraction as the first step on the road to political perdition. That's nonsense."[10] Relative to Democratic congressional leaders, in other words, the coalition-building challenges that Republicans face are more likely to be U shaped, with significant dissention arising from both party moderates and from the most conservative elements of the party.

Traces of this dilemma date back to the 1950s or earlier, but the importance within the Republican Party of what has come to be called "movement conservatism" has increased substantially since the 1970s.[11] The nomination of Barry Goldwater (R-AZ) as the GOP presidential candidate in 1964 jump-started the movement and gave rise to demands from the grassroots for renewed conservative fealty within the party. And as one historian of the period observed: "Each successive wave of grassroots activism would move the definition of movement conservatism further to the right, like a ratchet. A 1964 conservative activist would seem like a comparative moderate by the late '70s."[12]

In the wake of the Watergate scandal and the resignation of Richard Nixon, many moderate Republican candidates were defeated for Congress in 1974 and 1976, which produced large Democratic majorities in both the House and Senate and also moved the GOP farther to the right. The enactment of the Voting Rights Act in 1965 effectively enfranchised black voters throughout the South, setting in motion a regional realignment in which conservative white voters shifted partisan loyalties toward the Republicans and away from the Democrats. Over time, the House Republican Conference would take on an increasingly southern cast, which reinforced the aforementioned rightward shift.

The Republicans' electoral setbacks during the 1970s also created incentives for innovation.[13] Elected chair of the Republican National Committee in 1977, former Senator Bill Brock transformed the party's national donor base and otherwise used new direct mail techniques to energize and extend its activist base. The party effort was reinforced by outside conservative organizers such as Richard Viguerie, who pioneered the use of targeted advertising techniques to mobilize conservatives across the country. During the 1970s and 1980s, right-leaning think tanks, such as the American Enterprise Institute, the Heritage Foundation, and the Cato Institute, increasingly served as incubators of conservative policy ideas. Of particular importance was the emergence of supply-side economics. Popularized by conservative economists such as

Jude Wanniski, Robert Mundell, and Arthur Laffer, the supply-side argument was that reductions in marginal tax rates would provide such incentives for investment and economic growth that revenue losses would be substantially reduced or even eliminated, which in turn would alleviate any increases in the size of the federal budget deficit. As a rhetorical tactic for politicians, the theory helped unify Republicans nationally around a platform centering on tax cuts and significant reductions in the scope of government.

In July 1979, for example, House Republican leaders whipped their rank-and-file members about tax reduction as a party priority. "Will you join the Republican leadership in cosponsoring the [party tax package] when it is introduced on August 1?" GOP leaders asked their colleagues. "The leadership urges all Republicans to cosponsor this important measure," they continued.[14] The proposal was unlikely to be scheduled by Democratic leaders and primarily served as a party messaging device. But in response to the whip call, nearly 60 percent of House Republicans responded in the affirmative and another 20 percent were undecided but clearly open to persuasion. Only five members answered as no or leaning no. To be sure, the list of tax-cut advocates included staunch conservatives such as Philip Crane (R-IL), Richard Cheney (R-WY), and Dan Quayle (R-IN), as well as prominent moderates such as Pete McCloskey (R-CA), Benjamin Gilman (R-NY), and John Porter (R-IL).

In 1980, the conservative Ronald Reagan was elected president, Republicans assumed majority control of the Senate, and although still in the minority, the size of the House GOP Conference grew from 157 to 192. Fully embracing the supply-side mantra, Reagan helped push through the largest tax cut in American history, substantial increases in defense expenditures, significant spending reductions on the domestic side, and a range of other conservative initiatives. By the end of the Reagan administration, US tax policy had been transformed, with marginal rates now falling to the lowest levels since before the Great Depression.[15] As federal revenues declined as a percentage of gross domestic product, the previous rounds of spending reductions proved insufficient to close the deficit gap, and the national debt nearly tripled to $2.8 trillion. The Reagan Revolution, it should be emphasized, also solidified the coalition within movement conservatism between free-market advocates and the religious right, and the influence of religious conservatives within the Republican base grew especially pronounced in the late 1980s and early 1990s following the presidential run of the televangelist Pat Robertson.[16] Still, at the heart of the Reagan agenda was the effort to use tax reductions as leverage to substantially decrease the scope of government. As Reagan himself put it during the

1980 presidential debates: "[My opponent] tells us that first we've got to reduce spending before we can reduce taxes. Well, if you've got a kid that's extravagant, you can lecture him all you want to about his extravagance. Or you can cut his allowance and achieve the same end much quicker."[17]

The aforementioned "ratchet" associated with movement conservatism continued to tighten into the 1990s and 2000s, as right-leaning insurgents such as Newt Gingrich, Tom DeLay (R-TX), Eric Cantor, and Paul Ryan entered the leadership and confronted for themselves the practical exigencies of governing. The result invariably was disenchantment within their base of activists, donors, and organizations concerned about what these outside actors viewed as the progressive drift of American institutions. From this perspective, the complaints of contemporary Tea Party activists about Republican congressional leaders in the 2010s are a continuation of trends that began with analogous dissention on the right during the 1980s and 1990s.

Michel and Gingrich

The rise of movement conservatism, in conjunction with the presidencies of Ronald Reagan and George H. W. Bush, provided the backdrop for the institutional leadership of Republican Bob Michel in the House. Elected by chamber Republicans as their minority leader in 1980, Michel was a staunch conservative and a fierce partisan. He was also a pragmatist who believed that, ultimately, the passage of legislation was critical to conducting the people's business. In the race for leader, Michel's main challenger was the flamboyant Guy Vander Jagt (R-MI), who for twenty years had chaired the National Republican Congressional Campaign Committee. Michel's prepared comments for the Republican Conference session that would choose between the two men highlighted the Illinoisan's signature characteristics:

> I'll be the first to concede that [Vander Jagt] is one of our premier orators on our side [but] it's going to take more than biblical and poetic quotations to get any Democrat to vote for any part of President Elect Reagan's program. . . . Are you looking for a fighter or a preacher as your leader . . . our bottom line has got to be, how do we get the Reagan program enacted? As your leader, I intend to be out there on the front lines as his lieutenant, leading the charge as a good soldier. Conversely, when we have our leadership meetings with the President you can count on my fighting just as hard to see

that your individual and collective views are communicated to the Commander in Chief.[18]

Throughout Michel's fourteen years (1981–1994) as Republican Leader in the House, the Democrats had organizational control of the chamber, with majorities that ranged in size from 243 to 268. And for twelve of those years, there was a fellow Republican in the White House. According to the most authoritative account, thirty-seven pieces of legislation that passed during the Reagan administration can be characterized as "major" enactments.[19] Included were the historically important tax and spending cuts of 1981, to be sure, but also various deficit reduction packages that would follow, an extension of the Voting Rights Act, landmark immigration reforms, and so on. During the George H. W. Bush administration, the list of major enactments includes the 1990 Budget Enforcement Act, to which we will shortly return, the Americans with Disabilities Act, an important child care package, and significant environmental legislation. In the presence of large Democratic majorities in the House, the vast majority of these enactments necessarily had the support of numerical majorities within both congressional parties. Indeed, of the major bills adopted during this era, roughly two-thirds were supported by majorities on both sides of the aisle in the House and Senate, and another 13 percent were supported by both Democratic and Republican majorities in one or the other chamber.[20]

As minority leader during these years, Michel's core task was to work with the Reagan and Bush administrations, as well as other GOP leaders, to maximize internal party support for presidential initiatives, but also—and this is key—to reach across the aisle and secure the Democratic crossover votes necessary to pass legislation in a chamber controlled by the partisan opposition. Michel described his hopes in January 1981:

I should like to feel . . . that when the really big issues of great importance are considered in this House, there will be many occasions when partisanship will be laid aside and a significant number of you [Democrats] will be so persuaded by our logic, good sense and compelling arguments that you will actually vote with us. You do have it within in your power, in this House, to give life and breath to the new President-Elect's proposals, modify them slightly or drastically, or to kill any one of them outright. I simply want to pledge to you Members of the Majority my desire as the Republican Leader to work with you in the best interests of the American people.[21]

Perhaps the most important House roll call of the decade was the motion on the previous question on the rule for consideration of the Reagan economic program in June 1981. House Republican leaders sought to defeat the motion, which would allow them to propose a substitute procedure necessary for the Reagan cuts to be considered on the floor. Every Republican voted against the motion, but the GOP still needed to pick up about two dozen Democratic supporters to defeat it and thereby bring the critical Republican budget alternative before the House. Michel's role was to work with White House staff, House Republican Whip Trent Lott (R-MS), and Deputy Whip Tom Loeffler (R-TX) to convince conservative Democrats like Loeffler's fellow Texan, Charles Stenholm, to break with their party and support the Reagan administration.[22] They were successful, an alternative procedure was adopted, and the GOP budget cuts passed the chamber. "My most exhilarating days were those during the first Reagan administration," Michel later recalled. "We had only 192 members, but we enacted his program. And we had those issues, one after another, about seven votes in a row, I think, where we won by three or four votes. Now, that was satisfying. You'd go home at night and say, 'Well, I did the Lord's work today (laughs).'"[23] As Michel was a self-described lieutenant to successive Republican presidents, then, the political context in the House required that he regularly work across the aisle with pivotal Democrats.

Newt Gingrich, in contrast, was elected to the House in 1978 from a suburban Atlanta district that in many ways was a microcosm of political and demographic changes that were sweeping the South and that, over the next two decades, would form the bedrock of the modern Republican Party. The details of Gingrich's remarkable rise have been recounted elsewhere, but the highlights are worth recalling.[24] From his first days in the chamber, Gingrich focused on building a Republican House majority centered on conservative values, with observers as diverse as journalist David Broder and the direct mail wizard Richard Viguerie describing him as a right-wing visionary.[25] In 1982, along with other junior Republicans, Gingrich formed the Conservative Opportunity Society as an incubator of reform ideas. Together the group regularly took to the floor to lambast Democratic leaders as corrupt, which eventually led to a series of conflicts with Speaker Thomas P. "Tip" O'Neill (D-MA). In 1986, Gingrich accepted the chairmanship of GOPAC, an outside political organization aimed at building a farm team of Republican candidates for state and national office. During 1987–1989, Gingrich turned his fire on Democrat Jim Wright of Texas, who became House Speaker following the retirement of O'Neill. The effort was partially responsible for a finding by the House Ethics Committee that Wright may have violated House rules, which in turn led to the Speaker's resignation in 1989.

After House GOP Whip Richard Cheney (R-WY) resigned in 1989 to become secretary of defense, the assurgent Gingrich ran to replace him as the second-ranking Republican leader in the chamber, and he prevailed by a single vote over Michel's preferred candidate, a moderate. In a letter to a constituent, Michel explained his skepticism toward Gingrich's whip candidacy: "I simply said that Newt had catapulted to the second ranking leadership position without any experience in having to deal with all the problems a leader has to deal with, not only with the Congress, but in his own party and by his own admission, he has said quite publicly that he has a lot to learn. I have heard him say privately: 'Yes, as a leader, I guess I have to be more responsible.'"[26]

In 1990, Gingrich broke with Michel and President Bush over the latter's decision to compromise with congressional Democrats on tax increases, which produced an embarrassing defeat for the administration. Then, in 1993, with Democrat Bill Clinton in the White House and support for Gingrich's tactics and movement conservatism surging among GOP activists, Michel announced his retirement as party leader and was replaced by Gingrich. The following year, Republicans won a historic electoral victory, became the House majority for the first time in four decades, and over the next few years with Gingrich as Speaker attempted to advance a strongly conservative agenda.

Among many, the standard view is that Michel was an old-school kind of Republican, pragmatic, an institutional loyalist who loved the House and enjoyed friendships and collaborations across the aisle. Gingrich, in contrast, was often derided as a bomb-thrower, a guerrilla warrior, an extremist. As a result of his tactics, so the argument goes, norms of civility within the House quickly atrophied, and as Gingrich allies began to win election to the Senate, intense partisan infighting came to characterize that side of the Capitol as well.[27] Indeed, scholars and journalists often relate the corrosive partisanship and lack of comity that they believe defines the twenty-first-century Congress back to the aforementioned juxtaposition between a congenial Bob Michel and a discordant Newt Gingrich.

At best, that narrative is incomplete. For one, both members were firm conservatives who in important ways reflected the rise of movement conservatism as a political force within the Republican Party. Table 11.1 provides summary evidence. The first two columns denote the quintile of the House Republican Conference in which each member fell, relying on their DW-NOMINATE ideological scores and ranging from (1) the most moderate

Table 11.1 Ideological ratings of Michel and Gingrich, 1979–1994

Congress	Ideological Quintile (DW-NOMINATE, first dimension)		American Conservative Union Rating	
	Michel	Gingrich	Michel	Gingrich
96th (1979–1980)	4	3	81.5	82.5
97th (1981–1982)	4	3	84	89
98th (1983–1984)	4	3	81.5	84.5
99th (1985–1986)	3	3	86	81
100th (1987–1988)	3	3	89	98
101st (1989–1990)	3	3	80	87
102nd (1991–1992)	3	3	88	100
103rd (1993–1994)	2	3	90	98

quintile to (5) the most conservative. The last two columns include the roll call ratings of Michel and Gingrich produced by the American Conservative Union (ACU), a long-standing and respected organization that has been associated with movement conservatism for many decades.

As you can see, Michel was more ideologically conservative than Gingrich during the late 1970s and early 1980s, while Gingrich's record was the more conservative during the late 1980s and early 1990s. Based on the DW-NOMINATE measure, for instance, Michel fell in the fourth ideological quintile (only one quintile was more conservative) from 1979–1984, while during these years Gingrich was in the third quintile, which of course included the GOP Conference median. From 1985–1992, both of them were in quintile three, and during 1993–1994, Michel's DW-NOMINATE values were in the relatively moderate second quintile, with Gingrich remaining in the third quintile. The voting scores compiled by the ACU may be more useful for pinpointing shifts over time.[28] For 1979–1986, the ACU ratings of Michel and Gingrich indicate no clear trend. Some years Michel is rated more highly, while for others Gingrich gets the nod. But from 1987 onward, Gingrich clearly is more closely associated with the priorities of the ACU. Both members are rated positively by the organization, but the Georgian is rated on average nearly ten points higher. Taken together, the two indicators suggest that over the decade of the 1980s Gingrich moved to Michel's ideological right and that 1987 constituted a turning point of sorts.

In part, the timing of Gingrich's shift reflected the speakership of Jim Wright. Compared to Tip O'Neill, Wright was more aggressively partisan and more inclined to push his procedural prerogatives to the limit. As mentioned, Gingrich's ascension to the leadership was facilitated by his successful campaign to end Wright's speakership. But Michel also was no fan of Wright's hardball tactics, and he fully participated in House Republican efforts to expose that behavior, including a well-publicized GOP walkout in fall 1988. Gingrich's growing alignment with conservative elements probably should be viewed from the perspective of his leadership role with GOPAC. Founded by former Delaware Governor Pierre S. Dupont in 1978, GOPAC is a 527 organization aimed at recruiting and training Republican candidates at the state and local levels, with an eye toward strengthening the party's farm team for elections to Congress. Gingrich chaired the group from 1986 until May 1995. As chair, he traveled the country, speaking to conservative groups and prospective GOP candidates, orchestrated the production of audiotapes and other instructional materials that encouraged grassroots Republicans to adopt an aggressively conservative approach, and to refer to Democrats using so-called contrast words such as "betray," "corrupt," "decay," and "pathetic."[29] Gingrich's burgeoning association with movement conservatism within the chamber, in other words, was closely related to his outside leadership role among right-leaning donors and grassroots activists.

Years later, in an interview, Gingrich was asked whether Michel treated him well when they were both in the leadership:

It's better than that. I mean, Michel, I tried once or twice, I got out of bounds, and he jumped on me, and he was right. I mean, I am the Whip to the Leader, I'm not the co-leader. And we worked together reasonably well. And I think he was a little bit uncomfortable but he was a professional and you know this was the conference's choice. And he protected me some against the White House and sort of communicated, "Look, you've got to deal with Gingrich." . . . It made for an integrated team. And then frankly we got to the budget negotiations of '90 and it all blew up.[30]

Indeed, additional insight on the evolving relationships among Michel, Gingrich, and movement conservatism can be gleaned from the aforementioned vote in October 1990 on an historically important budget accord struck by the Bush administration and congressional Democrats.

"Read My Lips" (Or Not)

In 1989, there was substantial pressure in political Washington to alter federal budgetary priorities. Projected deficits were high, concerns about rising interest rates were widespread, and a sequester (across-the-board spending cuts) associated with the Gramm–Rudman–Hollings law would be implemented by the fall unless major changes were made. With the executive branch under GOP control and large Democratic majorities on Capitol Hill, it was clear that some mix of spending cuts and revenue changes would be necessary to pass legislation and secure a presidential signature. One key factor, however, was President George H. W. Bush's campaign pledge the previous year never to raise taxes. In accepting the GOP presidential nomination in August 1988, Bush had emphasized, "Read my lips: no new taxes," and the promise almost immediately became the only memorable sound bite from the speech.

Taking the lead for the administration, Office of Management and Budget Director Richard Darman urged junior lawmakers to pressure their leaders for high-level talks, but in the absence of signals that the Republicans might accept tax hikes, Democrats balked. Remarked House Speaker Thomas Foley (D-WA): "The first action has to be taken by the president. . . . First the president then with us."[31] The twin prospects of economic upheaval and sequestration, however, induced the administration and congressional leaders to begin bipartisan discussions about the deficit in spring 1990, negotiations that would continue through the fall. At first, little progress was made, but on June 26 Bush and Foley agreed in principle that tax increases and entitlement reforms would be on the table. Bush's strategic decision to accept the possibility of tax hikes generated intense opposition within the House Republican Conference. In mid-July, House Republicans passed a resolution in opposition to tax increases aimed at deficit reduction and instead urged significant spending cuts. Although the GOP Conference vote was private, participants claimed that the resolution passed by a margin of two-to-one. As the conservative Richard Armey (R-TX) commented: "Today we sent a message to congressional Democrats that if they want to raise taxes, they can do it without us."[32]

At this point, Gingrich was aligned with Bush and Michel on the matter. On July 20, for example, the *Washington Post* reported that he told Democratic negotiators of his willingness to "sponsor and support" a deficit reduction package that included tax increases.[33] The day after the House Republican Conference adopted its antitax resolution, Gingrich explained the move to Democratic negotiators as a response to recent statements by Senate Majority Leader George Mitchell (D-ME) that any reductions in capital gains taxes must be coupled with tax increases for the wealthy.[34] As Foley later recalled:

> Our instinct was always to work with Bob Michel, but Newt Gingrich could be very beguiling when he wanted to be. He would come over early and sit down. Maybe Bob Michel was due to come to the meeting, but hadn't arrived yet, and so we were just sitting and chatting, Dick Gephardt, Dave Bonior, Vic Fazio. There would be some staff there. All of a sudden Newt would say, "you know, we could work this deal out. We could do this and we could do that, and if you did this, and we did that, we would be glad to support that." Well, before you knew it, you were negotiating with the Minority Whip outside the presence of the Minority Leader, and you'd have to stop yourself and say, "Whoa, you can't start making commitments here, it's Bob Michel's job to decide what the Republican line is going to be. If we can reach an agreement, we're going to have to reach it with Michel." Gingrich was not all oppositional and contrary. Every once in a while he would put his negotiating hat on and he would want to do business. At that time, you had to be careful that you always were insuring that Bob Michel was in the room.[35]

Fearing that the impasse would doom efforts to avoid sequestration, the negotiators, after returning from the August recess, moved their discussions offsite to the officer's club at nearby Andrews Air Force Base. On September 17, a core group of eight people took the lead to hammer out a final bargain. Included in those discussions were Senate Majority Leader Mitchell, Senate GOP Minority Leader Robert Dole (R-KS), House Speaker Foley, House Majority Leader Richard Gephardt (D-MO), and Bob Michel. The administration negotiators were Darman, Bush Chief of Staff John Sununu, and Treasury Secretary Nicholas Brady. Newt Gingrich was not present. Within the House, Tom DeLay and other conservatives began wearing yellow buttons that read, "Junk the Summit."[36] Just hours before the feared sequesters were to be implemented, the core negotiators arrived at a bipartisan accord that included a mix of spending cuts and revenue-raisers acceptable to the Bush White House and congressional Democratic leaders. Both Dole and Michel also supported the bargain, which was formally unveiled at a Rose Garden press event.

At that point, Gingrich announced his opposition to the bipartisan compromise. As Bush recalled: "I met with all of the Republican leaders, all the Democratic leaders. . . . The plan was we were all going to walk out into the Rose Garden and announce the deal. Newt was right there. Got ready to go out into the Rose Garden, and I said, 'Where's Gingrich?' Went up to Capitol Hill. He was here a minute ago. Went up there and started lobbying against the thing."[37] Gingrich's recollections of the session, not surprisingly, were a little different:

And we're now sitting there with the President and he makes his pitch, and the Secretary of Treasury makes his pitch. And then they start with, I guess, Senator Dole who was the leader at that point. And they go around from the most senior, Bob Michel, and so I'm the last guy. And when they get to me, I just say, "You know I can't do it, this breaks your word, it is a huge mistake and I won't do it." And so CNN, which was the only news channel at that time, has this split screen and so does CSPAN, and you have all the Republican leaders and the President walking into the Rose Garden and me walking out of the front door.[38]

Michel's memory fell somewhere between the two and has the ring of truth:

We had to go out to Andrews Air Force Base. . . . Of course, the big thing out of all that was while Newt Gingrich was participating in some of the dialogue, he was certainly not one to give into his point of view to even the president. . . . But he really didn't openly express outright opposition during that particular time. The thing that caught me unaware [Michel laughed] was when we were at the

White House . . . after the president made his pitch. . . . It was quite obvious as the end of the meeting, he was not going to sign off to the president's point of view. . . . [This] had quite an effect on the membership [because] it showed a split in our ranks.[39]

Regardless, after Gingrich returned to the Capitol that day he met with members of the House Republican whip organization, informing them of the break and that he would not be personally lobbying in favor of adoption.

In gathering votes for the budget agreement, GOP leaders were forced to proceed without the party whip. On October 1, they began polling rank-and-file Republicans about whether they would vote for the budget resolution that would implement the summit agreement. The whip sheets used for the count emphasized that Bush and Michel both urged votes in favor of the resolution, and the regular whip apparatus was used—for example, results were to be returned to the office of the whip by the close of business on October 1.[40] The initial count was 7 yes, 16 leaning yes, 55 undecided, 30 leaning no, 52 no, and 16 who were nonresponsive in some fashion. Although the administration, Michel, and other mainstream Republicans were furiously lobbying for passage, by midmorning on October 3 there had been only limited movement: now 9 members were reported as a solid yes, 17 were leaning that way, 50 were undecided, 31 were leaning no, 60 were no, and the number of nonresponders had dropped to 9. Bush appealed for public support via a prime-time television address. On the House floor, Foley and Michel both urged adoption. Argued Michel: "I wish there were a better way of doing it. . . . We have to accept it as a whole, as it provides the only bipartisan basis for attacking the deficit problem."[41]

When the House roll call occurred around 1 A.M. on October 5, the budget resolution went down in defeat 179–254, with the Democrats voting 108–149 and the Republicans 71–105. Based on the last draft of the Republican whip count, all 26 of the members who had been listed as yes or leaning yes ended up voting that way. In the end, 31 of the 50 undecided Republicans also voted affirmatively with Michel, as did 8 of the members initially recorded as leaning no and 3 who had been solidly no. But 23 of the leaning no (74.2 percent) and 57 of the no (95 percent) responders stayed that way on the roll call, as did two-thirds of the members who were nonresponsive throughout the whip process.

Tables 11.2 and 11.3 provide information about which Republicans broke which way during the lobbying endgame that week. The tables denote support for the budget resolution at the whip and roll call stages by six factors: region;

Table 11.2 Percentage of House Republican whip responses on the 1990 budget summit agreement, selected district and member characteristics

		Y/LY	U	N/LN	Other
Region	NE	20.0	20.0	50.0	10.0
	MW/ Plains	14.6	33.3	47.9	4.2
	South	21.1	26.3	52.6	0
	Border	0	60.0	40.0	0
	West	7.5	25.0	60.0	7.5
District-level pres vote	Closer to R average	14.8	26.9	53.0	5.4
	Closer to D average	14.8	37.0	44.4	3.7
Seniority	Fresh	11.8	29.4	58.8	0
	2/5 terms	11.8	25.8	58.1	4.3
	>5 terms	19.7	31.8	40.9	7.6
Extended leadership	Yes	12.9	33.3	46.2	7.5
	No	16.9	22.9	57.8	2.4
Whip network	Yes	13.2	29.0	52.6	5.3
	No	15.2	28.3	51.5	5.1
Ideological quintile (least to most conservative)	1	25.0	30.6	30.6	13.9
	2	15.8	36.8	42.1	5.3
	3	15.2	36.4	45.5	3.0
	4	13.9	30.6	52.8	2.8
	5	3.0	6.1	90.1	0

percentage of the two-party vote cast within the relevant district for Democratic presidential candidate Michael Dukakis in 1988; seniority within the chamber; whether a member was part of the extended party leadership; whether the member was part of the whip organization; and ideology. To simplify the table, district-level presidential vote is dichotomized into two categories: whether a lawmaker is from a district where presidential voting in 1988 was closer to the average for GOP members or closer to the average for Democrats. Membership in the extended leadership includes the top party posts (e.g., minority leader, minority whip, Conference chair), but also the various leadership committees that both parties had come to use by the 1980s and 1990s. And a member's ideological inclinations are captured by the DW-NOMINATE quintile among Republicans, ranging from least (1) to most (5) conservative.

Table 11.2 summarizes the distribution of Bush/Michel support on the last draft of the whip count taken just days before the vote. There are some differences by region, with northeastern and southern Republicans more likely to be yes or leaning yes (Y/LY), the few border-state members disproportionately likely to be undecided (U), and most western Republicans falling in the category for no and leaning no (N/LN). Members from districts where recent presidential voting patterns were closer to the Republican average were somewhat more likely to be opposed, while those from districts closer to the average for the other party had a greater share in the undecided column, but the differences here are not particularly large. Seniority is associated with leadership support at the whip stage: more-senior members tended to be Y/LY and less likely to be N/LN. Membership in the extended leadership is also connected to leadership support, but not by very much. Involvement in the whip network has no effect, which comes as no surprise given Gingrich's highly public defection on the question at hand. And there is a clear ideological cast to the initial positions members took on the budget summit, with opposition strongly rising the more ideologically conservative the lawmaker.

Along those lines, Table 11.3 summarizes the relationship between these six factors and the votes that Republicans cast on the floor, differentiating among members who were undecided and N/LN at the whip stage. Since every Republican who pledged support for the Bush/Michel position ended up voting that way, and the number of nonresponders was small, only the undecided and N/LN categories are included in the table. Not surprisingly, the likelihood of a yes vote was much higher for initially undecided members than it was for members in the N/LN column across all elements of the Republican Conference. Still, among undecideds, the prevalence of yes votes

Table 11.3. Percentage voting "yes" among House Republicans whipped as undecided or opposed, 1990 budget summit agreement

		U	N/LN
Region	NE	62.5	20.0
	MW/Plains	81.3	4.4
	South	40.0	10.0
	Border	50.0	0
	West	60	16.7
District-level pres vote	Closer to R average	60.0	11.4
	Closer to D average	70.0	16.7
Seniority	Fresh	40	0
	2–5 terms	66.7	13.0
	>5 terms	61.9	14.8
Extended leadership	Yes	67.7	14.0
	No	52.6	10.4
Whip network	Yes	72.7	10.0
	No	59.0	12.7
Ideological quintile (least to most conservative)	1	63.6	18.2
	2	71.4	18.8
	3	75.0	13.3
	4	45.5	10.5
	5	0	6.7

was nearly twice as high for midwestern members than it was for Republicans hailing from southern states, and for the initial opponents, leadership support was particularly low for southern and border-state representatives. Roll call support for the bipartisan agreement was greater for Republicans from districts where presidential voting patterns were closer to the average for the other party. Seniority continued to matter. Controlling for the initial position, freshmen Republicans were substantially less likely to switch to leadership support on the vote. Participation in the extended leadership or the whip network seemed to improve the Bush/Michel success rate among initially undecided Republicans. And when we focus on the votes of initially undecided or opposing members, the relationship between the ideological measure and roll call behavior is particularly strong. Among the members who reported indecision during the whip process, for example, the percentage of yes votes on the floor ranged from 45.5 percent to a high of 75 percent for quintiles 1–4 (albeit with some drop-off for the ideological moderates of quintile 1). For the most conservative quintile, in contrast, proleadership votes were rare to nonexistent, regardless of the whipped position.[42]

In the end, most Republicans split with the Bush administration and the bipartisan congressional leadership and voted instead with Gingrich and the consensus position of movement conservatives. Michel chalked up the defeat to the conflict between ideas and practicalities: "You can talk all you want about Big ideas and New ideas and the Big picture. But if you don't put together the legislative means to get from here to there, all your rhetoric and all your Big ideas aren't going to win a single victory. We just weren't able to put together the logistics of victory on the budget vote, and because we couldn't, we lost."[43] On the Democratic side of the aisle, members watched the insurrection unfold among Republicans. There was considerable skepticism among liberal Democrats about the package due to the proposed spending cuts for domestic programs. Although Speaker Foley and other Democratic leaders had been confident that they could retain the support of their copartisans, as Republican after Republican voted no, support for the accord also collapsed among chamber Democrats, who like their minority counterparts ended up voting disproportionately against the budget resolution.

The remarks of party conservatives on the floor during consideration of the agreement indicate that their desire to reduce the scope of the federal government more than countervailed any concerns about sequestration or other consequences of defeating the bipartisan agreement. Bush, argued Gingrich, "should order a sequester. This would result in something approximating a nominal spending freeze. Then, he should challenge Congress to reorder spending priorities."[44] Asked about the tradeoff between passing the budget or forcing sequestration, Richard Armey responded: "I'll take sequestration. . . . Sequestration hurts the government, and this package hurts the American people and their economy."[45]

Following the House defeat of the budget accord, Congress passed a short-term continuing resolution aimed at keeping the government running. An angry President Bush vetoed the measure and demanded passage of a full budget plan, and portions of the federal government began to close. The Democratic-controlled House attempted to override the veto but fell short. At this point, House and Senate leaders met to devise another budget package, with the House Republican leadership now excluded because of the obvious divisions within their ranks. Another direct consequence of the GOP infighting was a reduction in the bargaining leverage of the Bush administration and Republican leaders in the Senate as the new wave of negotiations unfolded. Indeed, when the negotiators released a revised budget resolution on October 9, the result was even less favorable to the administration. According to party whip counts on the second version, both Michel and Gingrich were now opposed, and both voted no when the measure reached the floor and passed along mostly party lines. New continuing resolutions were passed and signed to avert a shutdown. Then, a reconciliation bill implementing the structure of the newly passed budget resolution was stitched together in just three weeks, and Bush signed it into law on November 5. That measure, known as the Budget Enforcement Act of 1990, became one of the most consequential budgetary measures of the post–World War II period and helped usher in dramatic reductions in the deficit and a booming economy during the late 1990s. Once again, the reconciliation measure passed the House along party lines, with Michel and forty-six other Republicans voting in favor of the legislation. Gingrich and the vast conservative majority of the GOP Conference voted no.

By all accounts, the process leading up to enactment of the Budget Enforcement Act included stunning reversals for President Bush and the bipartisan congressional leadership. It marked the full emergence of Newt Gingrich as the titular leader of GOP conservatives in Congress, as well as the willingness—even the eagerness—of the most conservative elements of the House Republican Conference to go to extreme lengths to leverage concessions aimed at reducing the scope of government. Moreover, the conservatives for the first time exhibited a willingness to use such tactics even in the face of significant pressure from their own leaders to do otherwise. As such, the 1990 budget fight can be viewed as a turning point of sorts in the recent history of the Republican Party in Congress.

The entire experience, it could be argued, left Bob Michel shaken. In accepting yet another term as leader, Michel told the Republican Conference on December 3, 1990: "Let me get right to the point. First, I know there are rumors that this is my last term. . . . The reports of my political demise are greatly exaggerated." He admitted that he had not yet made up his mind about running for reelection in 1992 but promised his colleagues that he intended "to take charge," not serve simply as a "caretaker" leader. He expressed "deep concerns" when "we make this Republican Conference a battleground where we spend our time swiping at each other, at the President, or at members of our Administration." He launched into a strong defense of President Bush and warned against voting against the administration: "The really important distinction for House Republicans is not the one between the branches, but the one between the two major political parties." In an obvious reference to the ideologues in the room, he advised: "If you want to debate fine points of political philosophy, then I would suggest arguing with the latest Socialist addition to the Democratic Caucus, Bernie Sanders." Leader Michel explicitly rejected what he called the paradigm of "guerilla warfare," preferring "the second paradigm, which is working constructively to enact our legislative program." And at the end, Michel told the Conference: "The job of Leader isn't all it's cracked up to be."[46] He would retire four years later, having tired of his regular battles with his more conservative colleagues in the Republican Conference.

Before considering the aftermath, we need to highlight what precisely was at the heart of the leadership dilemma confronting Michel and Bush. There was widespread unity among Republicans of all stripes about the importance of holding the line on taxes and securing significant cuts in domestic spending to reduce the deficit. Indeed, for the first half of 1990, Bush and Michel signaled little flexibility on the "Read my lips: no new taxes" pledge, and only when fiscal calamity appeared imminent did President Bush agree to consider tax hikes. Moreover, there is nothing inherent in strongly held views that precludes compromise aimed at securing the best possible outcome, whatever these views might be. Why, then, would the most conservative elements of the Republican Conference embrace tactical intransigence, when endorsing the bipartisan accord might have moved public policy toward their preferences?

The answer lies in the representational relationships that lawmakers have with important political actors outside the House and Senate chambers, especially the activist base and the voters at home. For citizens, ideology can serve as a heuristic, or a simplifying device for making sense of a complex political world. For members of Congress, ideological moorings can likewise help them interpret complex policy and political information and thereby make up their minds about how to vote. But for our elected representatives, the positions they take and the votes they cast are best viewed as strategies aimed at satisfying the outside actors critical to securing reelection. As political scientists like Richard Fenno and John Kingdon have demonstrated, the explanations that members construct to frame their positions and votes before constituents, activists, and influential donors matter as much or more than the choices themselves.[47] This is why Republican leaders and lawmakers who depend on grassroots conservative support have such difficulty selling compromise. The institutional arrangements and political divisions that make compromise necessary are difficult to explain. And for conservative activists who want to significantly roll back government and are deeply skeptical about elites of all stripes, the potential costs of tactical intransigence—government shutdowns, across-the-board cuts, breaches of the debt limit, and the like—often seem well worth the risk. The absence of analogous forces on the Democratic side of the aisle makes the leadership dilemma that results distinctly Republican.

Biting the Distasteful Bullet

Since 2011, as congressional Republicans became regularly embroiled in intraparty squabbles, and with party conservatives periodically using obstructionist tactics to leverage policy concessions, longtime observers of Washington politics noticed the obvious similarities with the events of fall 1990. In November 2012, for example, as the Congress once again approached a fiscal cliff of sorts, several Washington research centers and think tanks organized a forum on Capitol Hill that reunited many of the primary negotiators from 1990.[48] When Gingrich challenged former Massachusetts Governor Mitt Romney for the Republican presidential nomination in 2012, Romney supporter John Sununu tried to make the 1990 revolt a campaign issue during the New Hampshire primary.[49] And as Gingrich emerged as a major presidential contender that cycle, the renowned journalist Bob Woodward resurrected interview notes with Gingrich about the events of 1990, including telephone calls he had received from former House conservatives then serving in the Bush administration (Vice President Dan Quayle and Defense Secretary Richard Cheney), in which they signaled tacit approval for Gingrich's defection.[50] In 2014, the John F. Kennedy Library gave its annual Profile in Courage Award to George H. W. Bush for taking "a principled stand" and "risking his career" during the 1990 showdown.[51]

The events of that fall marked an important and enduring transition in the internal factional politics of the House Republican Conference and within the GOP more generally. From the 1990s onward, elements of the Conference most directly linked to movement conservatism periodically emphasized doctrinal purity over tactical compromise and the practical exigencies of governing within a federal system characterized by separate institutions sharing power. Much of this factional infighting occurred behind the scenes, within the Republican Conference, and often surfaced on the whip counts that party leaders conducted before bringing major legislation to the floor. The remarkable unity on party votes exhibited by House Republicans during the 1990s and 2000s, in other words, often masked considerable internal conflict over policy and tactics. At critical junctures, the Republican leadership dilemma surfaced into public view.

During 1995–1996, for example, the new Republican majority in Congress, with Gingrich now serving as Speaker, forced a showdown with President Bill Clinton over spending and the budget, leading to a partial shutdown of the federal government that proved publicly disadvantageous to the Republicans and provided Clinton with a major polling boost. As Gingrich recognized the public relations costs of the closure and attempted to strike a bargain with congressional Democrats and the administration, conservatives within the GOP Conference greatly complicated these efforts.[52] Concerned that Gingrich had mismanaged their relationship with the administration, several conservative leaders in 1998 attempted an unsuccessful coup against the Speaker, who in turn resigned under pressure later that year. In a nutshell, Gingrich was the next casualty, after Michel, of his party's leadership dilemma.

During the late 1990s, the remarkable unity of House Republicans on floor roll calls masked significant factional differences within the party. The whip counts conducted by Tom DeLay, House GOP whip from 1995 to 2002, regularly showed that a dozen or more moderates were undecided or opposed to party priorities prior to major floor votes. But DeLay's counts also routinely indicated substantial opposition from party conservatives concerned that their leaders were compromising too much with centrists. During the 106th Congress (1999–2001), for example, conservative firebrand Tom Coburn (R-OK) led a revolt on the floor against the Republican leadership's management of the appropriations process in order to leverage more significant spending reductions.[53]

In 2003, with DeLay now serving as House majority leader and Dennis Hastert (R-IL) in the speakership, the GOP administration of George W. Bush sought to pass legislation creating a new Medicare prescription drug benefit, in part to inoculate the party against Democratic charges that they were unfriendly to seniors concerned about health care costs. Once again, conservatives within the House Republican Conference rebelled against their own leadership and a GOP president, and when the bill was brought to the floor, DeLay and Hastert lacked the votes to prevail. Republican leaders were forced to hold the standard fifteen-minute vote open for three hours as they attempted to strong-arm recalcitrant conservatives like Nick Smith (R-MI) and James DeMint (R-SC) into voting yes.[54]

In 2008, with the United States in the throes of a financial crisis unprecedented in the modern era, the Bush administration sought a deal with Democratic House and Senate majorities for legislation to bail out the industry and forestall what many feared was a global economic crisis. Conservatives within the House Republican Study Group staged yet another revolt, seeking a free-market alternative to a nascent plan from the Treasury Department. Although Bush lobbied for adoption, personally telephoning every Republican in the large Texas delegation, the legislation was defeated on the floor with GOP conservatives taking the lead in opposition. As stock prices plummeted and fear spread throughout the financial sector, Bush and congressional leaders brought a revised measure to the floor that passed with most conservative Republicans voting no.

As grassroots opposition to the bailout and the newly adopted Affordable Care Act emerged across the country, including the assurgent Tea Party movement, Republicans won majority control of the House in the 2010 midterm elections. In 2011, GOP House Speaker John Boehner and the Democratic administration of President Barack Obama neared agreement on a budget that would include critical provisions to raise the limit on the federal debt. Conservatives within the House Republican Conference bolted, and for a time the negotiations imploded. With a default looming and financial markets in flux, Obama and the bipartisan congressional leadership struck a bargain to avoid default. The measure was adopted, but sixty-six GOP conservatives voted no.

In 2013, conservative Republicans in the House and Senate again attempted to leverage policy concessions from the Obama administration by blocking passage of compromise legislation to fund the federal government. The result was a sixteen-day government shutdown. Outside groups like Freedom Works and other Tea Party–affiliated organizations generated grassroots pressure on Republican lawmakers not to compromise and to instead use the shutdown as leverage in a game of brinkmanship with Democrats. In the end, Speaker Boehner and other Republican leaders decided that the conservatives' strategy had failed, and they embraced a compromise that largely reflected the preferences of the administration. While the top GOP leadership, including Boehner, all supported the legislation, 144 Republican conservatives voted no.

Two years later, facing the prospects of more budgetary negotiations with the Obama administration and another potential government shutdown, a faction of conservative House Republicans known as the Freedom Caucus all but forced the resignation of Boehner as Speaker. Boehner had begun his House career as a top lieutenant to Gingrich and a fervent conservative, but the most right-leaning portions of the GOP Conference had come to view him as insufficiently willing to hold the line over conservative principles. Importantly, just the year before, Majority Leader Eric Cantor, who had begun his own House career as a conservative firebrand close to DeLay, had been defeated in a primary by a Tea Party–backed challenger.

Following Boehner's decision to step down, Paul Ryan was selected as Speaker. Like his predecessors, Ryan as party leader regularly confronted factional infighting within the Republican Conference, with the most conservative elements refusing to compromise on major issues. As usual, much of the internal strife occurred before legislation was brought to the floor and concerned tactics and the ideological purity of party proposals. Such intraparty conflict greatly complicated GOP efforts to pass legislation to repeal the Affordable Care Act during the first year of the Donald Trump administration, as well as adoption of major tax legislation that was a central Republican priority.

I could go on, but you get the drift. The Republican leadership dilemma is an enduring feature of congressional politics, dating back at least to the relationship between Bob Michel and Newt Gingrich in the late 1980s and early 1990s. The dilemma is rooted in the nature of movement conservatism as a social and political force and thus is not wholly or even primarily a consequence of internal congressional politics. Unlike its Democratic counterpart, the modern Republican Party is held together by shared ideological and doctrinal beliefs, and maintaining that coalition creates incentives for many members to embrace firm, often unyielding positions. Ideological infighting also breaks out within the Democratic Party, of course, but Democrats have always been more oriented internally toward interest-group politics and logrolling. As many scholars have observed, in recent decades there has been nothing akin to movement conservatism on the Democratic side of the aisle, and it greatly complicates the ability of GOP leaders to strike the bargains necessary to govern. Such cross-pressure is particularly daunting when the party is in the majority and thus responsible for advancing appropriations bills, debt limit increases, and other must-pass bills, or when the party controls the White House and thus shares responsibility for governing with a copartisan chief executive.

Bottom line? The leadership dilemma that took form during the 1990 budget deliberations is now deeply rooted in Republican politics and unlikely to recede anytime soon. As Bob Michel observed as early as 1973: "We have our differences in the Party, among our own members and with the White House, but when you're elected to a leadership position you've got to put it all together for a party stance or position. . . . It requires swallowing hard sometimes—turning the other cheek more than you'd like—eating a good deal of crow—and biting the distasteful bullet."[55]

Notes

1. Christopher S. Parker and Matthew A. Barreto, *Change They Can't Believe In* (Princeton: Princeton University Press, 2013).
2. Thomas E. Mann and Norman J. Ornstein, *It's Even Worse Than It Looks: How the American Constitutional System Collided with the New Politics of Extremism* (New York: Basic Books, 2012).
3. Dana Milbank, "In the House's Dark Hour, Speaker Paul Ryan Offers a Glimpse of Hope," *Washington Post*, October 29, 2015.
4. Gary W. Cox and Mathew D. McCubbins, *Setting the Agenda* (New York: Cambridge University Press, 2005).
5. David W. Rohde, *Parties and Leaders in the Postreform House* (Chicago: University of Chicago Press, 1991); John H. Aldrich, *Why Parties? The Origin and Transformation of Political Parties in America* (Chicago: University of Chicago Press, 2011).
6. The DW-NOMINATE values used in this chapter encompass roll call data from the 1st through the 113th Congresses and were downloaded from the Voteview archive maintained by Keith Poole at the University of Georgia (legacy.voteview.com). Based on the roll call votes of lawmakers, the NOMINATE algorithm provides for each member in each two-year Congress of service a numerical score that ranges from −1 (very liberal) to +1 (very conservative), with scores near zero reflecting various degrees of ideological moderation. Figure 11.1 illustrates changes over time by party in the distribution of members over the NOMINATE range (first dimension) using intervals of 0.1.
7. Matt Grossmann and David A. Hopkins, *Asymmetric Politics* (New York: Oxford University Press, 2015). For related treatments, see also Jacob S. Hacker and Paul Pierson, *Off Center* (New Haven, CT: Yale University Press, 2005); David Karol, *Party*

Position Change in American Politics: Coalition Management (New York: Cambridge University Press, 2009); and Kathleen Bawn et al., "A Theory of Political Parties: Groups, Policy Demands, and Nominations in American Politics," *Perspectives on Politics* 10 (September 2012): 571–597.

8. Based on survey data from the Pew Research Center, for instance, Republican identifiers are nearly twice as likely as Democrats to prioritize ideological purity over moderation and compromise during the governing process. See Grossmann and Hopkins, *Asymmetric Politics*, 130.

9. Grossmann and Hopkins, *Asymmetric Politics*, chaps. 2–3.

10. RHM Papers, Speech and Trip File, f. March 19, 1987, "In Praise of Compromise," American Bar Association Leadership Institute.

11. For a discussion of the role played by movement conservatism in the growth of party polarization since the 1970s, see Barbara Sinclair, *Party Wars: Polarization and the Politics of National Policy Making* (Norman: University of Oklahoma Press, 2006), chap. 2.

12. Geoffrey Kabaservice, *Rule and Ruin* (New York: Oxford University Press, 2012), 351.

13. Nelson W. Polsby, *Consequences of Party Reform* (New York: Oxford University Press, 1983), 86.

14. RHM Papers, Leadership Series, Box 3, f. Whip Polls (7/17/79–9/3/80).

15. For a comprehensive description of the 1980s budget battles, see Joseph White and Aaron Wildavsky, *The Deficit and the Public Interest* (Berkeley: University of California Press, 1989).

16. On the rise of religious conservatives in American politics and the linkages to partisan polarization, consult Geoffrey Layman, *The Great Divide* (New York: Columbia University Press, 2001).

17. Sebastian Mallaby, "Don't Feed the Beast," *Washington Post*, May 8, 2006.

18. RHM Papers, Leadership Series, Box 2, f. Leadership Contests 1980 (3).

19. David R. Mayhew, *Divided We Govern* (New Haven: Yale University Press, 1991).

20. Mayhew, *Divided We Govern*, 122.

21. RHM Papers, Speech and Trip File, f. January 5, 1981.

22. C. Lawrence Evans, *The Whips: Building Party Coalitions in Congress* (Ann Arbor: University of Michigan Press, 2018), chap. 6.

23. Fred W. Beuttler interview, September 6, 2007, RHM Papers, Post-Congressional Series, f. Subjects: Interviews (2).

24. See especially William F. Connelly, Jr., and John J. Pitney, Jr., *Congress' Permanent Minority? Republicans in the U.S. House* (Lanham, MD: Rowman & Littlefield, 1994); and also C. Lawrence Evans and Walter J. Oleszek, *Congress under Fire* (Boston: Houghton Mifflin, 1997), chap. 2.

25. David S. Broder, *Changing the Guard* (New York: Simon & Schuster, 1980). Broder's chapter about the early Gingrich is particularly striking. But see also the sections on Gingrich in John M. Barry, *The Ambition and the Power* (New York: Penguin Books, 1990).

26. RHM to Ernest Angelo, Jr., June 14, 1989, RHM, Personal, f. 1989, N-P.

27. Mann and Ornstein, *It's Even Worse Than It Looks*. For an exploration of Gingrich's impact on the Senate, consult Sean Theriault, *The Gingrich Senators: The Roots of Partisan Warfare in Congress* (New York: Oxford University Press, 2013).

28. By design, DW-NOMINATE scores are constructed to follow a linear trend and this constraint flattens out Congress-to-Congress movements in a member's ideological measure. For nearly fifty years, the ACU has scored approximately twenty roll calls per year as especially germane to movement conservatism. Like DW-NOMINATE values, interest group ratings also have their limitations. For instance, groups tend to pick votes to score in order to maximize the difference between their congressional supporters and opponents, and also to create variance among the members seeking their support. This "artificial extremism" can limit the value of interest group scores as an indicator of member preferences. Still, the continuity of the ACU policy agenda and the relatively large number of votes it scores make these ratings a valuable indicator of a lawmaker's orientation toward movement conservatism. James M. Snyder, Jr., "Artificial Extremism in Interest Group Ratings," *Legislative Studies Quarterly* 17 (August 1992): 319–345.

29. Michael Oreskes, "Political Memo: For G.O.P. Arsenal, 133 Words to Fire," *New York Times*, September 9, 1990; Laura C. Stotz, "Becoming a Majority: GOPAC, the Republican Party, and Innovation at the Grass-roots," unpublished honors thesis, The College of William and Mary, 1989.

30. Newt Gingrich Transcript, Conversations with Bill Kristol, November 31, 2014, conversationswithbillkristol.org/transcript/newt-gingrich-transcript/#presidents.

31. "Budget Adopted after Long Battle," *CQ Almanac 1990*, 46th ed. (Washington, DC: Congressional Quarterly, 1991), 111–166.

32. Pamela Fessler, "Summit Talks Go in Circles as Partisan Tensions Rise," *CQ Weekly*, July 21, 1990, 2276–2278.

33. John E. Yang, "Rep. Gingrich 'Prepared' to Back Increase in Taxes," *Washington Post*, July 20, 1990.

34. Yang, "Rep. Gingrich 'Prepared' to Back Increase in Taxes."

35. Jeffrey R. Biggs and Thomas S. Foley, *Honor in the House: Speaker Tom Foley* (Pullman: Washington State University Press, 1999), 147.

36. "Budget Adopted after Long Battle," 111–166.

37. Bob Woodward, "In His Debut in Washington's Power Struggles, Gingrich Threw a Bomb," *Washington Post*, December 24, 2011.

38. Newt Gingrich Transcript, Conversations with Bill Kristol, November 31, 2014.

39. Fred W. Beuttler interview with RHM, October 5, 2007, RHM, Post-Congressional, Subjects, Interviews (3).

40. Information related to House Republican whipping of the 1990 summit agreement and related proposals is from calculations by the author based on materials in the Newt Gingrich Papers, Box 1983, folders 2 and 10, Special Collections, Ingram Library, University of West Georgia, Carrollton, Georgia.

41. "Budget Adopted after Long Battle."

42. The six member and district factors included in the tables are, of course, related to one another. In Tables 11.2 and 11.3, relationships are presented in cross-tabular form for descriptive reasons, and also because several of the indicators, especially member ideology, are endogenous to other factors. When multivariate analyses are conducted of support for the budget agreement at the whip and roll call stages, three factors stand out—ideology, seniority, and membership in the extended leadership. More concretely, two probit regressions were conducted, one for whipped position and the other for the

vote. For whipped position, the dependent variable took the value of one if a member reported as Y/LY, zero if the report was undecided or N/LN, and nonresponders were dropped. For the vote regression, the dependent variable was one for yes votes and zero for no, with only members reporting as undecided or N/LN included in the analysis. For both regressions, the explanatory variables included first-dimension DW-NOMINATE, the district-level presidential vote in 1988, number of terms, and indicator variables for participation in the extended leadership and party whip networks. Using two-sided tests, in both regressions only the ideology score achieved statistical significance. However, since our expectations about the relationships captured in Tables 11.2 and 11.3 are all signed, one-tailed tests are appropriate here. With one-tailed tests, the coefficient for chamber seniority also achieves significance at the 0.1 level in both regressions. And for the vote regression, the coefficients for participation in the extended leadership are also statistically significant and in the expected direction when one-tailed tests are used. Finally, if the dependent variable for whip position is allowed to take on three values (Y/LY, undecided, or N/LN) instead of two, and ordered probit is relied on as the estimator, the results resemble the aforementioned dichotomized version, but here the parameter estimate for presidential voting at the district level is also statistically significant with a one-tailed test.

43. Remarks to the American Bakers Association, RHM Papers, Speech and Trip File, f. October 8, 1990.

44. *Congressional Record*, October 4, 1990, 27673.

45. "Budget Adopted after Long Battle," 111–166.

46. RHM Papers, Speech and Trip File, f. Acceptance Speech/Leader Election, December 3, 1990.

47. Richard F. Fenno, Jr., *Home Style* (Boston: Little, Brown, 1978); John W. Kingdon, *Congressmen's Voting Decisions* (New York: HarperCollins, 1973).

48. "Looking Back to Move Forward: The 1990 Budget Summit Revisited," George Mason University, Centers on the Public Service and Department of Public and International Affairs, November 2012. Other sponsors included the Bipartisan Policy Center and Deloitte Consulting.

49. Trip Gabriel, "Sununu Disputes Gingrich Account of Tax Fight," The Caucus: The Politics and Government Blog of the Times, *New York Times*, December 12, 2011.

50. Woodward, "In His Debut in Washington's Power Struggles, Gingrich Threw a Bomb."

51. "2014 JFK Profile in Courage Award," May 4, 2014, at www.jfklibrary.org/Events-and -Awards/Profile-in-Courage-Award/Award-Recipients/2014-George-HW-Bush.aspx.

52. Glenn Kessler, "Lessons from the Great Government Shutdown of 1995–96," *Washington Post*, February 25, 2011.

53. Evans, *The Whips*, chap. 8.

54. Charles Babington, "Ethics Panel Rebukes DeLay," *Washington Post*, October 1, 2004, A01.

55. RHM Papers, Speech and Trip File, f. January 3, 1973, Nomination of Les Arends for Republican Whip.

CHAPTER 12

A "LESS PLEASANT" ELECTION

Bob Michel and the 1982 Congressional Midterms

Robert David Johnson

In early September 1982, one of the nation's leading political reporters, the *Washington Post*'s David Broder, traveled to Peoria. His task: profiling the House race between Republican Leader Robert Michel and his Democratic challenger, G. Douglas Stephens. With 60 percent of the district's territory, and 45 percent of its voters, new to him, Michel confessed that "it's a lot less pleasant" on the campaign trail than he was accustomed to.

Redistricting was not Michel's only problem. President Ronald Reagan's economic policies had failed to return prosperity to central Illinois, and voters were blaming the incumbent, given his prominence in Congress. The recession particularly harmed the district's largest employer, Caterpillar, especially after White House policies blocked a proposed contract with the Soviet Union. Michel worried that "that darn thing just won't go down. There are people who believe that all 8,000 of the Cat layoffs around here resulted from that decision—instead of the collapse of their international and domestic markets." As Broder recognized, Michel's experience showed how "the vexations of being both a congressman and a congressional leader are unending."[1]

Michel ultimately survived the election—but by only 3.25 percent, or 6,125 votes, the narrowest margin of any during his thirty-eight years in Congress. The 1982 campaign was a "transitional and transformational" event in Michel's career and in the political history of the 18th District.[2] The race also provided a case study in a House leader torn between national and local interests, at least when representing a district that the opposition party had a chance of winning. And the Michel–Stephens contest showed how competitive House elections changed in the early 1980s, with an increased emphasis on fundraising and modern-style messaging and campaigning.

A perfect storm of issues threatened Michel. He faced a gifted challenger in Stephens, who had never held office. Michel staffers "pegged him immediately as a serious candidate"—a "camera-ready candidate" with labor backing.[3] The unemployment rate in Peoria, the district's largest city, soared to 15.1 percent. Diplomatic disputes, job losses, and an eventual strike involving Caterpillar fortified what one observer termed the district's "general angst" about the economy.[4] Other large employers also suffered: local Pabst and Hiram-Walker plants closed, while the Fiat-Allis plant experienced substantial layoffs. Michel's support for Social Security indexing exposed him to attacks in a year when Democrats pressed the issue nationally. Beyond these specific matters lay a general sense that Michel had prioritized the interests of Reagan and Republican donors over those of Peoria.[5] Michel was torn by three, not necessarily mutually compatible, goals: to serve his constituents; to safeguard the interests of his GOP colleagues in Congress; and to advance the Reagan administration's goals.[6]

A World War II veteran and former congressional aide, Michel's most difficult congressional race before 1982 had come in his first contest (1956), when he narrowly captured a four-candidate primary and then bested a strong Democratic opponent, Fred Allen.[7] The district, which included only six counties, anchored by Peoria, was solidly Republican, last having elected a Democrat in 1914—and then only because a third-party candidate siphoned votes away from the GOP nominee. The district expanded a bit to the south in 1972, taking in Cass, Schuyler, and Brown Counties. Its electorate seemed to unequivocally accept how the Republican's experience and increased power in Washington would benefit Peoria.[8]

The congressman himself eschewed district politics. "Michel's campaigns over the years have been," recalled his 1982 campaign treasurer, Bob Strodel, to "make the rounds, speak to the folks, and get reelected."[9] His DC focus allowed Michel to advance at an "unheard of" rate, as his successor, Ray LaHood, recalled, and he soon became a major player on Capitol Hill.[10] His progress culminated in his election as minority whip in 1974 and then Republican Leader in 1980.[11]

The 1980 elections dramatically enhanced Michel's power. The congressman, as expected, defeated a state senator from rural Menard County by nearly 25 points. Ronald Reagan overwhelmingly was elected president on a platform of sweeping conservative change. In a surprise, Republicans seized control of the US Senate and gained thirty-four seats in the House. Michel then helped to construct a working coalition of House Republicans and conservative Democrats that pushed through much of Reagan's economic agenda. Reflecting on Reagan's first eighteen months in 1982, Michel rejoiced: "It's been a pleasure being down there (in Washington) because we're winning a few."[12]

Even in the headiest days of 1981, however, some staffers expressed concern that Reagan's program was playing poorly politically. Democrats, Michel aides worried, were effectively appealing to "emotion" and could inflict lasting "damage" on the Reagan program.[13] Discussing "supply-side economics in the abstract" seemed to play into the Democrats' hands. "We talk about bankers, businessmen, brokers and industrialists," Michel press secretary (and later chief of staff) Mike Johnson noted, "but we assume it's not necessary to explain much more authoritatively why those investments are important and what they can do" for everyone.[14]

The 1980–1982 recession disproportionately affected the industrial Midwest, thereby threatening Caterpillar. (At one point, 45 percent of the households in the tri-county area— Peoria, Tazewell, and Woodford Counties—were economically dependent on Caterpillar.[15]) As Caterpillar faced intense competition from Japanese and German firms, the State Department in July 1981 approved the company's request to sell one hundred mechanical pipelayers, a $40 million deal, to the Soviet Union. Caterpillar overcame Pentagon skepticism that the pipelayers, intended for a 3,600-mile natural gas pipeline from Siberia to Western Europe, also could be used for military purposes.[16]

As Michel concentrated on national politics, a political problem emerged at home. The state lost two of its twenty-four House seats after the 1980 Census, and the Illinois General Assembly, with one chamber controlled by each party, failed to agree on a map. A three-judge panel then chose the Democratic map, drawn by the future Illinois Speaker Mike Madigan, which collapsed four Republican-held districts into two.[17]

What one GOP congressman deemed the map's "diabolical cleverness" manifested itself in major changes to each of the central Illinois districts.[18] Madigan most obviously targeted the Springfield-area 20th District; incumbent Republican Paul Findley's sympathy for the Palestinians had made him a controversial figure, and he had shown some political weakness in 1980.[19] (When he saw the specifics of the new map, Findley bluntly observed: "That means trouble."[20]) Central Illinois seats held by GOP Representatives Tom Railsback and Dan Crane also shifted considerably.[21] With every district surrounding his radically altered, Michel also faced a dramatically different 18th District. As the longtime holder of a safe seat, he had not adapted to the altered nature of House elections in the mid- and late 1970s, a real problem because he now needed to introduce himself to tens of thousands of new voters.[22] "We were not equipped to conduct a campaign of that nature," Mike Johnson recalled. Michel hadn't experienced a tough race since 1956; until 1980, he had never spent more than $61,000 on a campaign.[23]

In contrast to its traditional focus on Peoria and contiguous counties, the new 18th District sprawled to Peoria's south and west; only four whole counties (Tazewell, Mason, Cass, and Brown) remained from the district that reelected Michel in 1980. Mapmakers divided Michel's base, Peoria County, retaining Peoria and Peoria Heights but assigning most of the rural areas to Railsback's 17th District. The new district lacked major highways, and blanketing it with advertisements would require spending money in four television markets—Peoria, Quincy, Decatur, and Springfield.[24]

Though no longer a safe seat for Michel, the district continued to lean Republican.[25] One of the additions (heavily Republican Woodford County) improved Michel's position. At the district's southern fringe, mapmakers seeking to weaken Paul Findley gave to the 18th District part of Sangamon County, which had a strong GOP county organization.[26] This move, however, also boosted the number of public employees in the district, extending it into the suburbs of Springfield, whose reputation from state politics embodied a very different sort of public service than that associated with Michel.[27]

At the district's southeastern tip, mapmakers added most of blue-collar Macon County. The county traditionally had formed the western edge of eastern Illinois congressional districts, so Decatur media had paid scant attention to Michel or the 18th District. Home to Archer Daniels Midland, and located around 75 miles from Peoria, it had shown a willingness to vote Democratic in competitive races. It was also the only area of the district where economic conditions were even worse than in Peoria; unemployment in Decatur was 18 percent.

Finally, the new maps extended the district all the way to the Illinois–Iowa–Missouri border, adding parts of three counties to Peoria's southwest. Rural, heavily agricultural McDonough and Hancock Counties leaned Republican. More troubling for Michel was a portion of Fulton County, previously part of Railsback's 17th District. Fulton was heavily Democratic, populated by retired or out-of-work coal miners; by the early 1980s, most of the strip mines had closed. International Harvester had once been the county's largest employer, resulting in a heavy union presence. During his sixteen years in the House, Railsback had only one tight congressional race, in 1966, when he lost Fulton County by 12 points.[28] See also Figure 12.1.

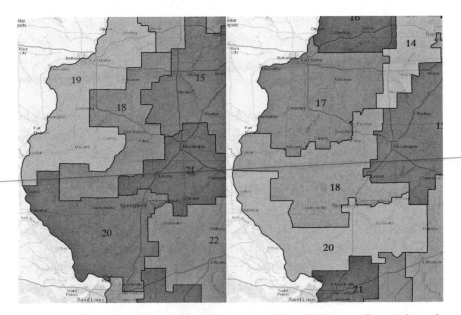

Figure 12.1 These maps show the transformation of the 18th District from its boundaries from the 1972, 1974, 1976, 1978, and 1980 elections (*left*) to the district that Michel confronted in 1982.
Sources: Author-created from Jeffrey B. Lewis, Brandon DeVine, Lincoln Pitcher, and Kenneth C. Martis, Digital Boundary Definitions of United States Congressional Districts, 1789–2012; github.com/JeffreyBLewis/congressional-district-boundaries/blob/master/Illinois_93_to_97.geojson; github.com/JeffreyBLewis/congressional-district-boundaries/blob/master/Illinois_98_to_102.geojson], 2013; cdmaps.polisci.ucla.edu.

Former Peoria County GOP Chairperson (and future Michel staffer) MaryAlice Erickson was overseas in 1981; after learning of the court decision, she asked a visitor to bring her a copy of the new map. When she inspected it, she immediately remarked: "Oh my gosh, Bob Michel is in trouble."[29] Michel privately conceded that "we got the tar beat out of us in redistricting"; it was, he lamented, a "raw deal."[30]

Despite the new district lines, no Democratic challenger initially wanted to "fall on his sword," as Michel advisers put it.[31] Timing helped Michel, since the redistricting decision came down on November 23, 1981, less than a month before the filing deadline for the first-in-the-nation March primary. A few Democrats, such as State Representative Gerald Bradley, considered running; so too did local attorney G. Douglas Stephens. Born and raised in Peoria, Stephens grew up poor; neither of his parents attended college, though he and three of his siblings did. He helped pay his way through school by working in construction. His progress through college and law school received occasional mention in the local labor press.[32]

After graduating from law school, Stephens started handling workers' compensation cases from the United Auto Workers, which had around 20,000 local members. Stephens's father, who died in 1977, was business agent of the Teamsters local, and in December 1981, a union friend of his father's called, urging the son to enter politics. "What did you have in mind?" Stephens asked. The reply: run against Michel. Stephens thought about it but demurred, knowing the reputation of the man nicknamed "Unbeatable Bob."[33]

Then national and international events intervened. In early December, Caterpillar obtained a permit to double its sale to the Soviet Union—to two hundred pipelayers, at $90 million. That news mitigated the effect of Caterpillar's laying off 2,100 of its 67,700 workers. Then, on December 28, in an announcement made public by Michel's office, the State Department revoked Caterpillar's permits: the Reagan administration had imposed sanctions on the Soviet Union following imposition of martial law in Poland. (The contract went to Caterpillar's major competitor, Japan-based Komatsu.) Privately, the Michel campaign recognized the problems caused by a Soviet trade embargo. "Where I come from," Michel wrote Secretary of State Alexander Haig in early 1982, people "cannot be expected to support a policy that hurts them while allowing our allies to benefit economically."[34]

Publicly, however, Michel defended Reagan's decision. "The president has laid it on the line," Michel observed. "We want to make absolutely sure we get the message across to the Soviet Union. That's the president's decision."[35] He downplayed the decision's effects, noting that "even if we had the pipeline contracts," they "would have affected only 2 to 3 percent of Caterpillar's total business." But back home, the announcement raised concerns, as one retail executive put it, about whether Michel "could have been more forceful" in resisting the president. Other constituents wondered why the congressman had not used the power that he often referenced to help out Peoria's workers.[36]

This kind of confrontational approach, however, would have been out of character for Michel. The congressman was, aide Mike Johnson recalled, "out of the old school of politics." Loyal to the president and intensely patriotic, he was reluctant to distance himself from Reagan on any issue touching on foreign policy or national security concerns.[37]

Michel's decision "incensed" Stephens; the Democrat believed that the congressman had put "his role as the leader of the [House] Republican Party ahead of the needs of his district." So Stephens reconsidered his decision not to run. By this point, however, the ballot deadline had passed. Gerald Bradley likewise showed interest in the race as the political climate grew more favorable, but the outgoing state representative lived just outside the district and seemed like a weak candidate. Though Bradley offered to bow out, Stephens argued that a competitive primary—even with two write-ins—could generate some useful publicity for him as a first-time candidate. He also was quite confident he would win the primary.[38] Stephens prevailed by more than 50 percent, 2,778 to 847 votes.[39] (He carried Peoria County 89 percent to 9 percent, with the remaining votes going to a third write-in candidate, Robert Cassady.) One Republican consulting firm termed it "impressive" that Stephens had received 1,500 votes in Peoria alone, given the technical difficulties of casting a write-in vote under Illinois law.[40]

In many parts of the country, launching a congressional campaign through a write-in primary bid might have seemed futile. But political observers in central Illinois could easily recall the 1964 contest in what was then the 19th District, due west of Peoria. After missing the filing deadline, Democrat Gale Schisler decided to challenge the first-term congressman Robert McLoskey. Schisler tallied 1,951 votes as a write-in, enough to get on the ballot. Echoing themes that would reappear in 1982, the Democrat's campaign portrayed McLoskey as out of touch for having voted for a congressional pay raise. Aided by Lyndon Johnson's landslide victory, Schisler narrowly prevailed, although he held the seat only for one term.[41]

Veteran Illinois political reporter Bernie Schoenburg recalled Stephens as a "cutting edge type of candidate," a much different sort of opponent than Michel had faced previously. Stephens was a "very effective communicator," former Michel aide Mike Johnson observed. He was well attuned to his audience, a compelling articulator of populist sentiments.[42] The challenger relentlessly linked Michel to the national GOP's economic policy; he "played perfectly" to the national environment. Michel, by contrast, was more of a throwback candidate; at one campaign appearance, before the local Kiwanis Club, he broke into song.[43]

Although the redrawn district had a significant labor cohort, its voters were not stereotypical liberals—most had lived in the Peoria area for many years, in some instances for generations, and had come to know and like Michel. On social and even some economic issues, they were open to conservative positions.[44] (The head of the United Auto Workers local estimated that 80 percent of his members cast ballots for Reagan in 1980.[45]) Stephens, however, was well suited to appeal to these voters. Beyond his personal ties to local union members, he was a prolife Catholic; he also was a gun owner and was pro–Second Amendment.[46]

Stephens maintained that an upset victory in Peoria would show that Reaganomics had been "dealt a serious blow." (Union leaders were responsive: as MaryAlice Erickson recalled, "They couldn't vote against Reagan, so they voted against Michel."[47]) Populism was central to Stephens's message: "I come from the average man's roots," and "it's time we had a fighter on our side in Congress."[48] He claimed that Michel had done little for the district despite being "one of the most powerful men in Washington, D.C."[49]

As Adam Clymer of the *New York Times* noted, it soon became clear that Michel's race would combine the "key elements of redistricting and recession" that would dominate the 1982 midterm elections.[50] Nonetheless, Michel remained the clear favorite. His twenty-six years of incumbency gave him a stature that Stephens, who remained little-known in the district, lacked.[51] At least three of the counties added to the district (Morgan, Sangamon, and Woodford) seemed likely to vote strongly Republican in the fall. A postprimary poll taken by the Michel campaign showed the incumbent leading, 53 to 33 percent.[52]

After the primary, Illinois political operative and Sangamon County native Paul Krell signed on as Stephens's campaign manager. He spent a few days traveling around the district, speaking to voters, before taking the job; upon his return, he told Stephens: "We can make this a close race." A tireless worker, Krell presided over a small number of paid staffers and a larger group of volunteers. Stephens himself spent between sixteen and eighteen hours a day on the campaign trail; in the car between appearances, he would phone potential donors, beef up on issues, or write speeches. He aggressively campaigned at local county fairs, some of which hadn't seen Michel for years—if at all, in the new counties for the district.[53] "We ate our share of corn dogs and funnel cakes," recalled James Grandone, who managed Stephens's primary campaign before coordinating media relations in the general election.[54] Nonetheless, his campaign showed its structural limitations. During a campaign appearance at the Menard County Fair, one concessionaire asked, "Are you guys the health inspectors?" Neither the candidate nor the aide who joined him wore a campaign button or carried campaign literature.[55]

Stephens was noticeably weaker than Michel in one critical respect: fund raising. Some funding initially came in through the Democratic Congressional Campaign Committee, thanks to Rahm Emanuel, then an aide for Tony Coelho (D-CA). But it soon dried up, upon orders of House Speaker

Tip O'Neill (D-MA). O'Neill later told Stephens that he acted to uphold "the ideals of your Democratic Party and mine." The Speaker said that he could work with Michel constructively, unlike his potential replacements, such as Trent Lott (R-MS) or even Newt Gingrich (R-GA).[56]

After O'Neill's move, as Stephens recalled, it was an "uphill battle" to raise money, and the campaign had to rely on low-dollar efforts. In one particularly notable instance, the candidate and Paul Krell received a visit from five members of the Electricians Union local. Having worked with volunteers, they raised $3,400 between them. To Stephens, the donation, and the effort behind it, "breathed new life into the campaign."[57] The campaign also employed its share of gimmicks, like a "dollar-a-dance" event among Peoria union members: women lined up to dance with Stephens, men with his wife, Sherry, and each donated $1 to the campaign.[58]

These sums could not come close to Michel's. As of July 1, Michel had around $250,000 in his campaign war chest; he raised $130,000 in April, May, and June alone. Stephens, by contrast, had only $4,000 to spend and had raised only around $30,000 for the campaign.[59]

Michel would need this fundraising advantage. On June 18, Reagan broadened the sanctions to target foreign companies using technology licensed by US companies that had continued to trade with the Soviet Union. (The European Union formally protested the decision.)[60] The move, which signaled that Caterpillar would not regain access to the Soviet market anytime soon, coincided with a series of economic blows to the company. By summer 1982, Caterpillar had laid off 16,500 workers nationwide, with 7,700 of that total coming from the Peoria area.[61] In the first half of 1982, Caterpillar's foreign sales (more than half of its business) dropped by 19 percent, while sales overall were down 40 percent from 1981. A company spokesperson conceded that "encouraging signs" of recovery did not exist.[62] As the Caterpillar layoffs continued, the Peoria-area unemployment rate surged; by the end of July it was 15.9 percent.[63]

Mike Johnson noted that Michel's office needed to "hurry" to get out a response, and—at a minimum—the congressman "must pull out all of the stops to get some of those defense contracts for Cat[erpillar]." But Johnson cautioned that a decision to support congressional Democrats' efforts to overturn the sanctions "should be founded on a conviction that sanctions and embargoes are wrong, from both a domestic and an international perspective." He worried that Michel would need to justify any "decision to interfere on a quasi-foreign policy issue" on "more than a quasi-political need basis."[64]

The congressman agreed, framing his opposition to Reagan's move in broader terms, even if local politics were his primary motivation. Michel joined other prominent Illinois Republicans (Senator Charles Percy and House members Paul Findley and Lynn Martin) and executives from Caterpillar, Fiat-Allis, General Electric, International Harvester, and John Deere in an emergency meeting with National Security Advisor William Clark, Commerce Secretary Malcolm Baldridge, and Undersecretary of State James Buckley. The group recommended a "continued reassessment" of the sanctions, doubting they would temper Soviet behavior. The campaign also made clear that Michel would support any congressional effort to repeal them—fully aware, of course, that the GOP-controlled Senate was very unlikely to pass such legislation.[65]

In late July, one local reporter captured the conventional wisdom about how Peoria's political climate had changed. "A little over a year ago," the *Jacksonville Journal Courier*'s Bill Kilby wrote, "anyone suggesting that Congressman Robert Michel . . . was vulnerable to a 'tough' run for re-election would have been accused of dreaming. Apparently, the world has changed."[66] Polling showed Michel's once-overwhelming lead (20 points after the primary) diminishing. In June, a Cooper Associates poll (conducted for a liberal interest group) found "an interesting mix of what would normally be called liberal and conservative viewpoints." The survey detected strong support for a congressman focusing on local issues, protecting Social Security, and reducing the defense budget. A slight majority also favored a nuclear freeze with the Soviet Union. In a trial heat, the poll showed Michel ahead by only nine points, 42–33 percent. The two candidates were statistically tied (30–29 percent) in the western portion of the district, and Stephens led among independents, with heavy numbers of undecided voters.[67]

An early August poll for Michel likewise suggested that he still had work to do. His name recognition was surprisingly poor for a longtime incumbent; fewer than half of the electorate could identify him as the district's congressman. The campaign outlined a goal of winning with 60 percent of the vote—a margin that it came nowhere near meeting.[68] Michel forces, a campaign self-study later admitted, also "had almost no background material on Stephens." They had no particular sense, for instance, of what positions Stephens had taken before the campaign on the Equal Rights Amendment, gun control, or abortion.[69]

Amid the polling news, Michel reassigned his administrative assistant, John Schad, to campaign chair and also opened a Peoria headquarters for the first time since the early 1960s.[70] Yet the campaign still seemed slow to get into gear. MaryAlice Erickson dropped by the downtown Peoria campaign office in August, only to find it mostly unstaffed, with unpacked boxes. Schad conceded that Michel might "have a bit more of a challenge" than usual but remained optimistic about the congressman's chances. The campaign, Erickson astutely recognized, was too DC centered, which also ensured that scheduling decisions prioritized Michel's legislative needs over the political demands at home.[71]

Michel initially relied on traditional campaign practices that seemed more appropriate to the 18th District of the 1960s or 1970s. The campaign invested heavily in generic billboards—twenty-nine locations around the district, at a cost of $4,546 per month.[72] Early Michel television ads were equally ill-suited to the tough environment. One ad opened with singing about "that old pride we used to have" and promised, without specificity, that Republicans are "turning America around." Another positioned Michel "in a position to fight for agriculture"—even as he conceded that "we need to do more." A third projected optimism, claiming that the "worst is behind us" and that central Illinois will "bounce back stronger than ever."[73]

These messages contradicted the campaign's own data, which found district voters were very pessimistic about the local economy—92 percent believed (not without reason) that Peoria had more layoffs than the country as a whole. The upbeat portrayals, a 1983 campaign self-study conceded, failed to capture the shift toward an "angry, cynical electorate"; the ads' "pleasant jingles" thus "grated" voters and made Michel seem out of touch. The ads also described the candidate as "Republican leader," as if voters would, on their own, see the leadership position as an asset, despite Stephens's message that the congressman cared more about his duties in Washington than people back home.[74] See also Figure 12.2.

On the trail in late summer, Michel claimed to be "running around like a freshman congressman." When the circus was in town, he even rode an elephant, symbol of the Republican Party, through downtown Peoria.[75] Still, at times, he seemed to be campaigning as if his reelection were assured. In late August, he made his first campaign trip to one of the new additions to the district, Hancock County, around 100 miles southwest of Peoria. Seemingly confirming Stephens's portrayal of him as too deferential to Reagan, Michel described his and the president's philosophies as "compatible." It was "happy days for me to be able to work with him," the congressman asserted. He conceded that some aspects of the administration's policies—especially restrictions on trade with the Soviets—might harm some voters in the district. But, he added, Reagan had to consider the national interest and

Figure 12.2 Michel campaigns for reelection, Peoria, Illinois, September 2, 1982
Source: RHM Papers, Audiovisual Series, Still Photographs, September 2, 1982.

whether the embargo might serve as leverage to prevent further repression in Poland. In a politically unfortunate line, the Republican Leader told constituents that he was "too small to know if that is possible."[76]

To Michel, defending how his status as party leader helped his constituents seemed absurd—the benefits were obvious. Stephens, by contrast, had no trouble portraying Michel's leadership position as a detriment. Michel, he charged, had pushed into law programs that "may be good for Washington and big business but are not good for the people of the 18th District."[77] Michel's "world has been Washington," and when "the policies of this administration hurt this district, you don't hear Bob Michel's voice raised in protest. He may have power, but it's not being used for our good."[78] For good measure, Stephens resurrected the populist charge used so effectively by the last successful Illinois write-in congressional candidate, Gale Schisler, and criticized Michel for having (along with all other House leaders) voted in favor of a 1979 congressional pay-raise measure.

If Michel (not entirely unreasonably) recoiled at Stephens's populist attacks, their success came as less of a surprise to Michel's aides. In a May 1982 memo, Mike Johnson conceded that "there is a good deal that

Republicans can do and ought to be doing in regard to communicating our position and influencing the public perception of Republican positions and Republicans as individuals." In the end, "if the public doesn't understand it, they ain't going to like it, and if they don't like it they ain't going to accept it whether it's good for them or not." Republicans, Johnson recognized, especially needed to counter the impression that they cared only about the rich.[79] "This race was just the sort of race that Republicans won in 1980 when they surprised longtime Democratic incumbents," according to Michel's postelection self-study. "The more prestigious the national position those incumbents held, the more likely we had been to succeed in 1980."[80]

As often occurs with populist campaigns, Stephens mostly avoided specific policy positions. He opposed a balanced budget amendment, criticized members of Congress for accepting a pay raise, and endorsed the social safety net. When pressed for a concrete idea to get the unemployed back to work, he cited an odd proposal to allow unemployed Illinoisans to search for welfare fraud, with a promise that they would be allowed to retain a portion of the misbegotten funds they had uncovered. The Democratic nominee "got away with murder without being specific," Mike Johnson asserted, in part because the Michel campaign lacked sufficient opposition research to challenge him. The local media, meanwhile, played up the horse-race angle, especially when faced with the novelty of a legitimate challenger to Michel.[81]

Sometimes, Stephens's vagueness reflected the district's mind-set. "Michel spoke farm very well," one of his aides recalled. "It was his second language."[82] But in 1982, an economic downturn in rural America spurred Democratic strength, even though neither the Democrats nor farmers suddenly sympathetic to the opposition party offered a clear sense of what policies would restore agricultural prosperity. During campaign appearances, Michel encountered what one reporter deemed "the now-familiar farmer's lament—'high interest rates and low prices.'"[83] Jack Goetze, whose debt on his 800-acre farm skyrocketed during the early 1980s, compared the economic situation to the Great Depression. Stephens's rhetoric resonated with him; while Goetze lacked any suggestions on how to address the problems, he concluded that "Bob Michel has become real complacent until this election." Based on conversations with his customers, the owner of a Pekin fertilizer company agreed that "Bob Michel is in trouble." Local farmers, it seemed, "blame him for not doing a little more" in the House.[84]

There were, moreover, two high-profile issues in which Stephens did adopt clear positions and in which the tension between Michel's leadership position and the incumbent's political needs worked to the challenger's advantage: Social Security and a nuclear freeze with the Soviet Union.

Social Security was the subject of Stephens's most powerful TV ad. In 1983, the two parties would eventually compromise, creating a commission to address the program's long-term funding. But the question remained politically alive in 1981 and 1982, and Michel dutifully defended the Reagan administration's suspicion of the welfare state. Embracing calls for indexing Social Security payments, Michel remarked on the House floor that many recipients were "pretty well-heeled." Stephens used the video (in violation of C-SPAN rules) in what even Michel staffers conceded was a "pretty effective ad."[85] It opened with the narrator asserting that Michel believed some Social Security recipients should see their funding cut. The ad then moved on to Michel's quote, repeated multiple times, before concluding: "That's why the National Council on Senior Citizens gave Michel a zero rating. Send Doug Stephens to Congress. He'll remember where he comes from."[86] Social Security worked well for Democrats in House races around the country; Representative Claude Pepper (D-FL) became the party's face on the issue.

On foreign policy issues, similar to many Democrats in competitive House races, Stephens championed a nuclear freeze with the Soviet Union.[87] The Democrat chastised Michel for having "consistently opposed meaningful efforts to halt the massive nuclear weapons build-up."[88] "The real issue," he maintained, "is whether America is prepared for peace."[89] Stephens even suggested that "it is *not* necessary for the U.S. to retain our position as #1" in nuclear arms.[90]

Stephens's campaign conducted no issue-related polling and therefore had no idea how many people in the district shared these beliefs.[91] But while these views probably would have caused problems in the GOP-leaning district a decade or two before, by 1982 central Illinois—like much of the upper Midwest—was open to a critique of the Cold War consensus. Michel got a taste of this opinion shift when he used his newsletter to solicit feedback on the freeze. Nearly 20,000 constituents responded. By nearly two-to-one margins, the respondents believed the United States was spending too much money on defense. A similar supermajority endorsed a nuclear freeze.[92] Little surprise, then, that Michel's claims that Stephens considered it acceptable for the United States to be militarily inferior fell flat.[93] Nonetheless, as with Social Security, Michel stood by Reagan: "Any freeze proposal based on the false idea that the United States is currently engaged in something termed an 'arms race,'" he said on the House floor, "is worthless because it is not based in reality."[94]

On Social Security and especially the nuclear freeze, Michel functioned as a principled legislative leader—placing the party's interests and fidelity to his own beliefs ahead of his short-term political needs. "It's a dual role," Michel noted in an August interview, discussing the tensions between tending to the 18th District's concerns and serving as Republican Leader. "On each decision, it makes you look at things from two perspectives—your own district's and the President's. But I walked into the job with my eyes open. When you are the leader, you have to be able to take the heat."[95]

As the congressional session continued through September into early October, Stephens monopolized local campaigning and the media coverage it generated—which campaign manager Paul Krell recognized was the major benefit from outside campaign appearances.[96] Visits from potential Democratic presidential candidates, including former Vice President Walter Mondale, Senator John Glenn of Ohio, and Senator Alan Cranston of California, heightened the focus on Stephens.[97] They also, Krell noted, helped "to convince people that 'Unbeatable Bob' is beatable."[98]

Two of these appearances particularly stood out. Arizona Democratic Congressman Mo Udall, a favorite of national liberals who had come up just short in a string of primaries to Jimmy Carter in 1976, joined Stephens and one hundred workers who had been laid off from the Pabst brewery in Peoria Heights. At a roundtable organized by the local Teamsters leadership, Udall blamed Reagan's policies for increases in national unemployment—and tied Michel to Reagan. "I like Bob Michel," Udall noted, "and am sympathetic with the box he's in as the chief [House] supporter of Reaganomics. But Reagan is wrong."[99] The Udall visit showed why Stephens was such a formidable challenger. In contrast to a generic Democrat, Stephens had a personal connection to the Pabst plant: his father had worked as a truck driver at the plant for twenty-eight years, and his brother had worked there for twenty years until the plant closed.[100]

For Stephens, the most significant outside visit came from Senator Ted Kennedy (D-MA). The campaign focused on a key battleground in the race, Tazewell County, home to a significant number of Caterpillar workers.[101] The Kennedy rally occurred at the county seat in Pekin; five hundred people attended. "The eyes of the nation are on this congressional district," the veteran senator proclaimed. "You can be sure Doug Stephens would never support an economic program that is going to try to solve the problems of inflation by putting millions of people out of work."[102] At the conclusion, attendees surged to be able to speak to—or even just touch—Kennedy. The

Massachusetts senator and Stephens then took Kennedy's plane to Springfield, where a subsequent event raised money for state Democrats.[103]

Stephens continued to use Michel's leadership position as a cudgel against the incumbent. Michel was "punishing the people of the 18th District" by "representing Washington" instead of their interests. The challenger also criticized Michel for failing to use his influence to block the "foolish sanctions" that had "crippled" local industry, especially Caterpillar. As one local reporter noted, Stephens effectively used "Michel's name as synonymous with the administration."[104]

Into this atmosphere came more bad news from Caterpillar. The company lost more than $100 million in the third quarter of 1982, its first negative quarter in more than forty years. Then, on October 1, what *New York Times* correspondent Winston Williams wrote "was never supposed to happen in this prosperous company town" did in fact occur: the company's 22,000 workers went out on strike, protesting Caterpillar's demand for reductions in paid holiday and vacation time, as well as a scaling back in promised cost-of-living increases.[105] Michel staffers privately lamented that the move left an "enormous number" of blue-collar workers feeling "the pinch of a tough economy."[106] By contrast, as one aide recalled, the Stephens campaign had the "luxury of volunteers because there were so many people being laid off"; not only did laid-off union members work on Stephens's behalf but also their sons and daughters.[107]

By this point in the campaign, Stephens recalled, his effort "took on a life of its own, a momentum of its own."[108] In mid-October, the statewide Democratic ticket joined him for a 3,000-person Sunday afternoon rally. Held at Peoria City Court House, with heavy union participation, especially from striking Caterpillar workers, the rally used a theme of "Export Reagan–Michel, Not Jobs." Stephens, introduced as a "giant-killer," received the warmest reaction of the day; attendees waved signs reading "HELP CATERPILLAR, NOT KOMATSU (LOCAL 947)." The challenger's keynote address attacked Michel and Republican Governor Jim Thompson for staying in office too long. A Michel campaign observer who attended the rally conceded its effective organization and noted how Stephens was the event's "favorite son."[109]

In the final weeks of the campaign, Michel's media team, Rick Daniels and Fred Roberts, started producing much sharper TV advertising.[110] New spots dismissed Michel's opponent as a "union lawyer" or a "young labor lawyer."[111] (Stephens consistently denied the claim—"I work strictly for people," he said—but the portrayal hurt the Democrat in some of the district's rural counties.[112]) Michel ads increasingly linked Stephens to Jimmy

Carter and the "liberal, big union financed wing of the Democratic Party," on which the Republican blamed the economic downturn. ("Some of you may have noticed a shift in Congressman Michel's campaign strategy. The happy jingles are gone," Stephens responded.[113]) Ads highlighted how Michel and the president parted "company on the Soviet pipeline because the people working at Caterpillar and Fiat-Allis and the businesses that depend on them must not be forced to bear the entire burden of U.S. foreign policy."[114]

The campaign also started rebuffing some of Stephens's most effective lines of attack. Of the Democrat's complaints about his leadership position, Michel cut an ad noting that his status as Republican Leader "means we can solve local problems more easily"—by "lighting a fire" under the bureaucracy.[115] An accompanying television ad featured photos of public works projects from around the district, with the tagline "Let's re-elect a congressman who knows how to work for us."[116] The incumbent also strongly pushed back on Stephens's claims (which, to be fair, were widely shared) that he had not done enough to aid Caterpillar. In a high-profile speech on the House floor, he contended that the sanctions had not tempered Soviet behavior. "We have to be smart enough to change course when the course we are on does no good." The congressman argued that the sanctions only harmed US business, since foreign competitors would sell to the Soviets in any case. "I represent the needs of the workers in Peoria," Michel asserted. After Michel's remarks, the House narrowly approved (209–197) a bill sponsored by Paul Findley to repeal the sanctions within ninety days. But the measure had no chance in the Senate.[117]

The two campaigns' disparity in financial resources helped Michel get this message to voters—and to respond, even if indirectly, to Stephens's attacks.[118] For the five weeks before Election Day, the Michel campaign spent $15,000 weekly on radio advertisements, with spots running on twenty-four stations, including several outside the district's boundaries whose listening area included some of the district's fringe areas. Television expenditures, meanwhile, increased as Election Day drew near. The campaign placed ads on eight area television stations, from five different markets, with a budget rising from $20,266 to $31,275 in the week before the vote. Around two-fifths of the TV budget went to stations in Peoria; the remainder financed ads on stations in Champaign, Springfield, Decatur, and Quincy.[119] Stephens, by contrast, only had enough funds to run TV ads in the Peoria market.[120] For the campaign, Michel raised $687,875; his Democratic challenger managed only $166,928.[121]

The closing days of the campaign featured two high-profile events. The first seemed to benefit Michel; the second clearly helped Stephens. On

October 20, Ronald Reagan came to Peoria to rally with Michel and conservative favorites Pat Boone and Charlton Heston.[122] (Stephens denounced the event as a "Hollywood extravaganza," and around 200 laid-off workers, college students, and peace activists protested the president.[123]) Five thousand people paid between $5 and $15 to attend, raising $30,000 for Michel, providing a boost, as local Republicans had hoped, for the incumbent in the polls. Reagan hailed Michel as a "terrific captain for House Republicans." The president admitted that the sanctions were "not popular with Peoria or Bob Michel. But a president sometimes has to make decisions that are painful to even his best friends." Nonetheless, he hinted that he might soon revisit the issue. And he made clear that "Bob has told me personally, and I might say eloquently, of the hardships of the people in his district. He understands what's going on out there."[124]

Four days later came the low point of the campaign for Michel. Throughout the summer and fall, the cash-starved Stephens had demanded debates with Michel. The congressman traditionally did not debate his opponents and tried to retain that policy in 1982. This approach, however, played into Stephens's populist attacks: "I think the bottom line is," the Democrat charged, Michel "doesn't want to discuss the issues because he can't defend his positions on the issues. He wants to reduce this to a media, personality campaign."[125] By early October, the Michel campaign had concluded—probably correctly—that "we had to do it," since "there would be more political fallout" from refusing to debate.[126]

Michel agreed to only one debate, at Peoria television station WEEK. It was, aide Mike Johnson recalled, "an absolute utter disaster." During debate prep, Michel was unresponsive to suggestions from staffers to better focus his approach.[127] In the debate, Michel's tone was off-putting; he came across as too arrogant and seemed dismissive of the idea that anyone could accept Stephens's "magic" proposals.[128] Angered by Stephens bringing notes to the podium, he interrupted both the moderator and his opponent; political analysts Michael Barone and Grant Ujifusa deemed his loss of temper a "performance that almost suggested panic and belied the image of a calm, competent leadership he was trying to project."[129]

As Election Day neared, Michel attacked the Stephens effort in increasingly harsh terms. "The Stephens campaign has taken the attitude that the end justifies the means," Michel charged in an address at the Peoria Ad Club. "Elections must be decided on substance, not the sideshows and shell games we have seen." Michel again complained about the debate, claiming that Stephens had violated the rules by using notes.[130] "I still don't know much about where my opponent stands on a vast array of issues," the congressman asserted.[131]

Michel generally closed out his public campaigning on the eve of the final vote. On Election Day itself, he would typically cast his ballot and then remain at home for the rest of the day. In 1982, however, he sensed a need to depart from tradition. After they voted, he told his wife that they needed to prepare themselves for the possibility that he might lose. Before that happened, he maintained, he needed to spend Election Day reaching out for more votes. So he visited several nursing homes, as well as a community event, and kept campaigning right up until the polls closed.[132]

The returns showed a significant shift to Democrats throughout central Illinois. In one of the year's biggest upsets, a young legal aid attorney, Lane Evans, captured the 17th District, to Peoria's northwest, after an ultraconservative state senator had unseated Republican incumbent Tom Railsback in the primary. To the south, the 20th District featured the year's fourth-closest House election, as Democrat Dick Durbin unseated incumbent Paul Findley by slightly more than 1,000 votes. After the election, Durbin called Stephens to thank him for preventing Michel from coming to Findley's assistance.[133]

As the 18th District returns rolled in, the results clearly were tighter than Michel's final polling had predicted. Stephens easily carried Fulton County, as well as three smaller counties to Peoria's south, and held down Michel's margins in the new, GOP-leaning western counties. As expected, Michel won the Springfield suburbs, though not by an overwhelming margin (1,410 votes), and he easily carried GOP-heavy Woodford County. Stephens prevailed in Macon County, but by a narrower-than-expected 212 votes.

In the end, the two key counties were the district's most populous ones—Peoria and Tazewell. To win, Stephens needed to carry both. Instead, while Michel's margin in both was narrower than any of his previous thirteen races, the incumbent prevailed. He carried Peoria County by 1,067 votes (out of more than 51,000 cast) and Tazewell County by 264 votes (out of more than 47,000 cast). That translated to a 6,125-vote margin overall. Among the parts of the district he had represented between 1972 and 1982, Michel won by only 408 votes.[134] See also Figure 12.3.

At around midnight, Michel delivered his victory speech, thanking his longtime supporters who had stuck with him through difficult times. But he also reached out to organized labor, expressing appreciation for union workers who had voted for him and hoping the time had come "to heal the wounds."[135]

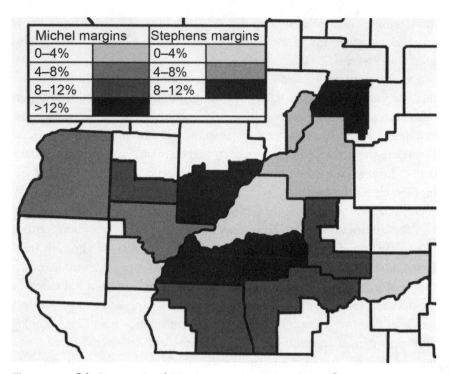

Michel margins		Stephens margins	
0–4%		0–4%	
4–8%		4–8%	
8–12%		8–12%	
>12%			

Figure 12.3 18th Congressional District county vote margins, 1982
Source: Wikimedia Commons, commons.wikimedia.org/wiki/File:Map_of_Illinois_counties.svg.

Stephens made his final appearance of the campaign around an hour later, at Peoria's Italian American Club, amid chants of "Doug in '84!"[136]

Michel privately admitted that he hoped "we never have another cliff-hanger" like this "tough election," which fundamentally changed his approach to his office.[137] He boosted his staff, hiring two former Illinois state legislators, Ray LaHood and Craig Findley, to oversee district offices (LaHood in Peoria, Findley in Jacksonville). "Our job," LaHood recalled, "was to show people that Bob Michel was interested in the district."[138] In general, as a Michel staffer noted in 1983, "the need exists to 'humanize, personalize and localize' our national leader to the 'folks' in the home district. Washington is one world. Peoria and other communities in the 18th District are a different world totally."[139] The new hires enhanced Michel's image as someone who cared about the 18th District, to which Michel returned on weekends, even when Congress was in session, far more regularly.

After 1982, Michel kept a full-time campaign office open, even during off years.[140] He also changed his approach to campaigning. In 1984, he did far more appearances in counties throughout the district. The campaign focused more on grassroots efforts and targeted mailings and dramatically increased fundraising. In this respect, MaryAlice Erickson noted, 1982 was "kind of a turnover in terms of how we do politics now."[141]

The congressman also made sure he wouldn't be caught off-guard in redistricting, as he had been after the 1981 court decision. Following the 1990 census, he delegated his aide (and eventual successor) Ray LaHood to lobby the legislature in Springfield. The new redistricting restored all of Peoria County to the district—and removed Stephens's strongest county, Fulton.[142]

The election changed central Illinois politics; for the remainder of his tenure, Michel would be joined by two House Democrats from neighboring districts—Durbin and Evans. He worked well with Durbin, who was a "practical" politician, reflecting the traditional approach of Illinois politicians collaborating on state issues across party lines. That was less the case with Evans, a far more ideological figure, who always had a somewhat distant relationship with Michel's office.[143] Yet despite their differing approaches to their jobs, both Durbin and Evans easily won reelection. Evans even retained the support of some GOP party regulars, especially women, in the 17th District. He was "such a fine young man," they would say; many saw him as the equivalent of another son.[144]

Finally, the outcome "certainly focused his attention," Mike Johnson recalled, causing Michel to become "much more sensitive to the district." The campaign demonstrated the difficulties for a House leader—Michel was vulnerable as a stand-in for the administration, and constituents, while recognizing his value, were a little "jealous" of his spending time on national matters.[145] "I guess one of the toughest things [for me] . . . in that tough race was how little importance my own constituents attached to being leader as opposed to being an ombudsman for the district," Michel said in 1988 interview. "But it's a lesson I've learned. After eight years [as leader] I can point to projects that are coming to my district as a result of my being the leader and how we've shaped some major legislation."[146] From 1983 until his 1994 retirement, Michel efficiently minimized the tensions between his leadership, legislative, and constituent responsibilities.

Michel, however, would not be the last legislative leader to encounter these tensions; indeed, the phenomenon has become common in contemporary politics. Speaker Thomas Foley (D-WA) lost his seat in 1994 amid a Republican wave. In 2004, Tom Daschle (D-SD) became the first Senate majority leader to lose his seat in more than fifty years. Democrats aggressively targeted Mitch McConnell (R-KY) in 2008 and 2014; Republicans nearly unseated Harry Reid (D-NV) in 2010. The specifics of each of these races differed, but they shared a common theme: each legislator struggled with conflicts between his role as leader and his political needs at home. In this respect, Bob Michel's 1982 contest was a transformational event not only in his career but also in legislative politics at the national level.

Notes

1. David Broder, "Rep. Michel Fighting a Battle for Solvency and Political Survival," *Washington Post*, September 3, 1982.
2. Mike Johnson interview with author, November 20, 2017.
3. Mike Johnson interview.
4. Bernie Schoenburg interview with author, December 18, 2017.
5. "Talking Points for Senator Baker," RHM Papers, Press Series, f. Remarks and Releases: October 27, 1982; Ray LaHood interview with author, November 18, 2017.
6. R/M/S, Inc., "The Honorable Robert H. Michel Congressional Plan, April 12, 1983," RHM Papers, Campaigns and Politics, 1983, f. R/S/M Inc. Report (1–3). This plan includes a section, "1982 in Retrospect."
7. Mike Johnson interview.
8. "IL—District 16," *OurCampaigns*,www.ourcampaigns.com/RaceDetail.html?RaceID =476526.
9. Julia Malone, "In Illinois, Michel Race Epitomizes GOP Woes," *Christian Science Monitor*, September 14, 1982.
10. Ray LaHood interview.
11. Frank H. Mackaman, "Anatomy of a Congressional Leadership Race," www.dirksen center.org/leadershiprace/index.htm.
12. Malone, "In Illinois, Michel Race Epitomizes GOP Woes."
13. Mike [Johnson] to RHM, March 24, 1981, RHM Papers, Press Series, f. Memoranda, 1981–1988 (1).
14. Mike Johnson, "Memorandum for Bob," March 24, 1981, RHM Papers, Press Series, f. Memoranda, 1981–1988 (1).
15. MaryAlice Erickson interview with author, November 18, 2017.
16. "Sale by Caterpillar to Soviet Cleared," *New York Times*, July 31, 1981.
17. *In re Congressional District Reapportionment Cases*, No. 81 C 3915, slip op. (N.D. Ill. Nov. 23, 1981).
18. Robert Mackay, "The Illinois Districts," *Illinois Issues*, April 1982.
19. Bernie Schoenburg interview.
20. Paul Findley, *Speaking Out: A Congressman's Lifelong Fight against Bigotry, Famine, and War* (Chicago: Chicago Review Press, 2011), p. 240.
21. "IL District 17—R Primary," www.ourcampaigns.com/RaceDetail.html?RaceID=348 192.
22. Ray LaHood interview.
23. Mike Johnson interview.
24. Jim Nolan and Dean Brown, "Discussion Memo re Michel Campaign," April 13, 1982, RHM Papers, Campaigns and Politics, 1982, f. Consultants' Proposals.

25. Godfrey Sperling, Jr., "How Reagan's Policies Are Playing in Peoria . . . and the Rest of Illinois," *Christian Science Monitor*, May 13, 1982.

26. MaryAlice Erickson interview; Mike Johnson interview. The added part of Sangamon County did vote for Democrat Alan Dixon in the 1980 US Senate race. Steve Hahn, "Reagan Policy the Issue, Says Michel Challenger," *State Journal-Register* (Springfield, IL), July 25, 1982.

27. Ray LaHood interview.

28. Ray LaHood interview; MaryAlice Erickson interview; Mike Johnson interview.

29. MaryAlice Erickson interview.

30. Quoted in "Will It Play in Peoria?" *The PAC Manager*, August 1982, RHM Papers, Scrapbooks, Box 2, f. Clippings, 1982.

31. R/M/S, Inc., "The Honorable Robert H. Michel Congressional Plan, April 12, 1983."

32. G. Douglas Stephens interview with author, December 10, 2017.

33. Doug Stephens interview.

34. RHM to Alexander Haig, March 1, 1982, quoted in "Charge/Fact," n.d. [fall 1982], RHM Papers, Campaigns and Politics, f. Stephens (4).

35. "Caterpillar Sale Blocked," UPI, December 29, 1981.

36. Malone, "In Illinois, Michel Race Epitomizes GOP Woes."

37. Mike Johnson interview.

38. Doug Stephens interview.

39. "Illinois, 18-D Primary," 1982, www.ourcampaigns.com/RaceDetail.html?RaceID =407009.

40. Jim Nolan and Dean Brown, "Discussion Memo re Michel Campaign," April 13, 1982, RHM Papers, Campaigns and Politics, 1982, f. Consultants' Proposals.

41. Russell Lane, "State Delegation Is Demo," *Edwardsville Intelligencer*, November 4, 1964.

42. Mike Johnson interview.

43. Bernie Schoenburg interview.

44. Mike Johnson interview.

45. Rowland Evans and Robert Novak, "Blue Collars Versus GOP," *Tennessean*, October 22, 1982.

46. Doug Stephens interview.

47. MaryAlice Erickson interview.

48. Hahn, "Reagan Policy the Issue, Says Michel Challenger."

49. Stephens mailer, n.d., and Stephens print ad, *Peoria Journal-Star*, March 4, 1982, both in RHM Papers, Campaigns and Politics, 1982, f. Stephens (2).

50. Adam Clymer, "Illinois Election to Raise Curtain on 1982 Battles," *New York Times*, March 14, 1982.

51. Hahn, "Reagan Policy the Issue, Says Michel Challenger."

52. Market Opinion Research, Untitled, April 1982, RHM Papers, Campaigns and Politics, 1982, f. Miscellaneous (5). Polling related to the 1982 campaign is also located in RHM Papers, Campaigns and Politics, 1982, f. Market Opinion Research; ibid. f. Polls; ibid. f. Telephone Survey; RHM Papers, Campaigns and Politics, 1983, f. Market Opinion Research; ibid. f. Polls to Evaluate 1982 Campaign.

53. Doug Stephens interview.

54. James Grandone interview with author, June 11, 2018.

55. Hahn, "Reagan Policy the Issue, Says Michel Challenger."

56. Doug Stephens interview.
57. Doug Stephens interview.
58. Malone, "In Illinois, Michel Race Epitomizes GOP Woes."
59. Allen Abbey, "Michel in the Black, Stephens in the Red," *Peoria Star*, July 24, 1982; Hahn, "Reagan Policy the Issue, Says Michel Challenger."
60. "Europe Protests Reagan Sanctions on Pipeline Sales," *New York Times*, August 13, 1982.
61. Hahn, "Reagan Policy the Issue, Says Michel Challenger."
62. Winston Williams, "Hard Times for Caterpillar," *New York Times*, October 15, 1982.
63. "Stephens Blasts Michel, Reagan," *Pekin Times*, August 5, 1982.
64. Mike Johnson to Bob, Ralph, Bill G., Bill P., and Hyde, June 21, 1982, RHM Papers, Press Series, f. Memoranda, 1981–1988 (1).
65. Radio Actuality, June 24, 1982, RHM Papers, Press Series, f. Remarks and Releases: June 24, 1982, Trade Sanctions.
66. Bill Kilby, "Voter Response Heartens Congressional Candidate," *Jacksonville Journal Courier*, July 25, 1982.
67. Cooper Associates, "18th Congressional District Illinois: A Survey of Voter Attitudes and Opinions," June 1982, RHM Papers, Campaigns and Politics, 1982, f. Stephens (4). In worse news for Stephens, the survey found that 70 percent of the district's voters said the country should support Reagan's economic plan by giving it more time to work, and 30 percent of union members favored Michel.
68. Mike and John to Bob, Ralph, and Sharon, August 6, 1982, RHM Papers, Campaigns and Politics, 1982, f. Memoranda, 1981–1988 (1).
69. R/M/S, Inc., "The Honorable Robert H. Michel Congressional Plan, April 12, 1983."
70. Broder, "Rep. Michel Fighting a Battle for Solvency and Political Survival."
71. MaryAlice Erickson interview.
72. "The Batchelder Company," contract with "Michel for Congress," July 13, 1982, RHM Papers, Campaigns and Politics, 1982, f. Advertising.
73. Michel radio ad scripts, Roberts/Daniels/Falls & Associates, RHM Papers, Campaigns and Politics, 1982, f. Advertising.
74. R/M/S, Inc., "The Honorable Robert H. Michel Congressional Plan, April 12, 1983."
75. Malone, "In Illinois, Michel Race Epitomizes GOP Woes."
76. Elaine Hopkins, "Michel Explores Strange Territory," *Peoria Journal Star*, August 24, 1982.
77. "Stephens Challenges Michel," *Illinois Star Daily*, July 22, 1982.
78. Broder, "Rep. Michel Fighting a Battle for Solvency and Political Survival."
79. Mike Johnson to Bob Michel, "The Gingrich Memorandum," May 5, 1982, RHM Papers, Press Series, f. Memoranda, 1981–1988 (1).
80. R/M/S, Inc., "The Honorable Robert H. Michel Congressional Plan, April 12, 1983."
81. "Stephens Challenges Michel," *Illinois Star Daily*, July 22, 1982.
82. Mike Johnson interview.
83. Daniel Egler, "For Bob Michel, Re-Election No Cakewalk," *Chicago Tribune*, July 18, 1982.
84. Malone, "In Illinois, Michel Race Epitomizes GOP Woes."
85. Mike Johnson interview.
86. Bernie Schoenburg, "Reagan Called out of Touch," *Daily Pantagraph* (Bloomington, IL), October 22, 1982.

87. Douglas Walker, *Congress and the Nuclear Freeze: An Inside Look at the Politics of a Mass Movement* (Amherst: University of Massachusetts Press, 1987), 109.

88. "Doug Stephens Statement on Nuclear Weapons Freeze," Stephens for Congress press release, July 27, 1982, RHM Papers, Campaigns and Politics, 1982, f. Stephens (4).

89. Bob Sampson, "Michel Fights Freeze Efforts, Stephens Says," *Herald and Review* (Decatur, IL), July 31, 1982.

90. Philip Martz to John Schad, October 19, 1982, RHM Papers, Campaigns and Politics, 1982, f. Memoranda.

91. Doug Stephens interview.

92. RHM Papers, Press Series, f. Questionnaires: April 1982.

93. Philip Martz to John Schad, October 19, 1982, RHM Papers, Campaigns and Politics, 1982, f. Memoranda.

94. *Congressional Record*, March 30, 1982, 5345.

95. Dorothy Collin, "Rep. Bob Michel on U.S. Stage—and Playing to Peoria," *Chicago Tribune*, August 28, 1982.

96. Mike Johnson to RHM, October 13, 1982, RHM Papers, Press Series, f. Memoranda, 1981–1988 (1); Bob Sampson, "Styles Identify Top Pols," *Herald and Review* (Decatur, IL), October 20, 1982.

97. Egler, "For Bob Michel, Re-Election No Cakewalk"; George Sloan, "Mondale Blames Reaganomics for High Unemployment Rate Here," *Peoria Journal-Star*, June 14, 1982.

98. Bob Sampson, "Close Contest Likely for 'Unbeatable Bob,'" *Herald and Review* (Decatur, IL), September 13, 1982.

99. "Candidate Stephens Gets Udall's Help," *Jacksonville Courier*, September 1, 1982.

100. Doug Stephens interview.

101. MaryAlice Erickson interview.

102. Bernie Schoenburg, "500 Turn Out for Kennedy during Trip to Push Stephens," *Daily Pantagraph* (Bloomington, IL), October 14, 1982.

103. Doug Stephens interview.

104. Gary Blackburn, "Michel 'Punishing' Stephens," *Tazewell News*, September 6, 1982.

105. Winston Williams, "Hard Times for Caterpillar," *New York Times*, October 15, 1982.

106. R/M/S, Inc., "The Honorable Robert H. Michel Congressional Plan, April 12, 1983"; see also "The Michel Plan—In Retrospect, 1982."

107. James Grandone interview.

108. Doug Stephens interview.

109. Philip Martz to John Schad, October 17, 1982, RHM Papers, Campaigns and Politics, 1982, f. Memoranda.

110. MaryAlice Erickson interview.

111. "Radio ledger," RHM Papers, Campaigns and Elections, 1982: f. Roberts, Daniels, and Falls.

112. "Stephens: 'I'm Not a Union Lawyer,'" *Illinois Star Daily*, October 11, 1982.

113. G. Douglas Stephens news conference transcript, October 5, 1982, RHM Papers, Campaigns and Politics, 1982, f. Stephens (1).

114. "Radio Sixty" attached to Paul Newman to Fred Rogers and Rick Daniels, September 30, 1982, RHM Papers, Campaigns and Politics, 1982, f. Roberts, Daniels, and Falls.

115. Michel radio ad script, n.d., RHM Papers, Campaigns and Elections, 1982, f. Roberts, Daniels, and Falls.

116. Evans and Novak, "Blue Collars Versus GOP."
117. Michel press release, RHM Papers, Press Series, f. Remarks and Releases: September 28, 1982.
118. Mike Johnson interview.
119. "Television ledger," RHM Papers, Campaigns and Elections, 1982: f. Roberts, Daniels, and Falls.
120. Doug Stephens interview.
121. Michael Barone and Grant Ujifusa, *The Almanac of American Politics 1984* (Washington, DC: National Journal, 1983), 369.
122. "Remarks of Congressman Bob Michel, Peoria Civic Center," RHM Papers, Press Series, f. Remarks and Releases: October 20, 1982.
123. Karen Magnuson, "Reagan Plays Peoria," UPI, October 21, 1982.
124. Bernie Schoenburg, "President Stands Firm on Sanctions," *Daily Pantagraph* (Bloomington, IL), October 21, 1982.
125. "Stephens: 'I'm Not a Union Lawyer.'"
126. Mike Johnson interview.
127. Mike Johnson interview.
128. MaryAlice Erickson interview; Bernie Schoenburg, "E. Peoria Debate Turns Sour," *Daily Pantagraph* (Bloomington, IL), October 25, 1982.
129. Barone and Ujifusa, *The Almanac of American Politics 1984*, 368.
130. Michel press release, RHM Papers, Press Series, f. Remarks and Releases: October 28, 1982.
131. Michel, "Remarks for the Kiwanis," RHM Papers, Press Series, f. Remarks and Releases: October 21, 1982.
132. Mike Johnson interview.
133. Doug Stephens interview.
134. Doug Stephens interview.
135. "Talking Points—Victory Speech," RHM Papers, Press Series, f. Remarks and Releases: November 2, 1982.
136. Bernie Schoenburg, "Michel Claims Victory," *Daily Pantagraph* (Bloomington, IL), November 3, 1982.
137. Michel form letter, March 16, 1983, RHM Papers, Campaigns and Politics, 1983, f. Poll to Evaluate 1982 Campaign.
138. Ray LaHood interview.
139. Carole to Mike Johnson, "District Media Relations," March 8, 1983, RHM Papers, Press Series, f. Subjects: Michel Office General.
140. Ray LaHood interview.
141. MaryAlice Erickson interview.
142. Ray LaHood interview.
143. Mike Johnson interview; David Moberg, "Principles at Work: Rep. Lane Evans' Constituents Don't Always Agree with His Views, but They Keep Re-Electing Him Anyway," *Chicago Tribune*, November 29, 1993.
144. Mary Alice Erickson interview.
145. Mike Johnson interview.
146. Charles Abbott, "Bob Michel: Conservative in Philosophy, Practical in Politics," *Illinois Issues*, August/September 1988, 34.

CHAPTER 13

FROM EXPANSIONISM TO PROTECTIONISM AND BACK AGAIN

Conditional Incumbency, Disruption, and the Reimagination of Bob Michel's Representational Style

David C. W. Parker

I magine, for a moment, a brisk March day in Peoria, Illinois.

The year is 1983. Republican Minority Leader Bob Michel (R-IL) has returned to his alma mater, Bradley University, for a hastily called press conference. After more than two decades in the House, Michel is calling it a career. His last campaign in 1982 had been exhausting for him and his family, and despite having shattered his own personal fundraising record by spending nearly $700,000, he squeaked by with only 52 percent of the vote against political neophyte Doug Stephens. Michel had long hoped to steer his party to a majority in the House—a goal unlikely to materialize in the near future given Democrats had gained twenty-six seats in the midterm. Only one other member from the class of 1956 remained in the chamber with Michel, and one of his closest friends in the House—New York's Barber Conable—was retiring, too. Even if his departure would mean a vigorous and bruising leadership contest among Minority Whip Trent Lott, Conference Chair Jack Kemp, and Conservative Opportunity Society founder Newt Gingrich, it would be best for this younger generation to take the helm of a House that had become almost unrecognizable to the sixty-year-old Michel. It was time to step aside gracefully and dedicate his life to other pursuits.

This press conference never happened: Michel ran for reelection in 1984 and served another decade in the House before retiring at the conclusion of the 103rd Congress in 1995.[1] In fact, the 1982 election that nearly ended Michel's House career was an aberration: Michel's support never again dipped below 55 percent, and he never faced another serious threat from a challenger. The longevity of Michel's career after his near-demise in 1982 is nothing short of remarkable; in fact, Michel's decision to run for reelection in 1984, the difficulty Democrats faced in fielding a strong challenger after Illinois State Representative Gerald Bradley's bid that year, and Michel's ability to step aside at a time of his choosing rather than being chased out by disgruntled voters are noteworthy accomplishments and should not be underestimated. In 1982, twenty-five Republican House incumbents won reelection with less than 55 percent of the vote. Before 1994, nine of those members subsequently lost reelection, another five chose retirement rather than face a difficult reelection, and one member retired in ill health. Fewer than half of the twenty-five House Republicans who nearly lost in 1982 left the House without the specter of defeat chasing them from the chamber. Michel was one of them—with good reason.

This chapter does not tell the story of how Bob Michel won that tough race in 1982 (see chapter 12). Instead, this chapter seeks to place Michel's 1982 race into the broader context of challenging campaigns faced by incumbents nationally. It begins with a discussion of the incumbency advantage, its variability, and the unexpected disruptions even successful incumbents face throughout their careers—disruptions that often lead to defeat. It then details how Michel's 1982 midterm campaign fits a pattern of disruptions—some predictable, others less so—that threatened the continuation of Bob Michel's career in the House. Finally, it documents the lessons learned by Michel in the aftermath of 1982 and how he applied those lessons to serve his central Illinois constituents for another twelve years. Key to Michel winning reelection in 1984 and beyond was a willingness to reinvent himself as a member of Congress. Before 1982, he and his staff employed a representational style that focused on protecting an existing reelection constituency. But the 1982 reelection scare forced him to reconnect with his constituents and trust his staff to reorganize his congressional operation to respond to a new political era. He and his staff needed to be more entrepreneurial, to spend more time mending fences in the district, and to cultivate the press more effectively. "We've been functioning like a freshman or sophomore" Michel noted in 1984, suggesting that he understood the need to adapt.[2] He and his staff did so in two ways. First, they adopted a new representational style, one focused on expanding his constituency. Second, he approved, somewhat reluctantly, establishing a nearly permanent reelection campaign.

Although incumbents are the overwhelming favorites to win reelection should they choose to run, Michel's own electoral success in the wake of the 1982 campaign demonstrates that incumbency neither guarantees reelection nor means replicating the same representational style throughout a congressional career. The most successful incumbents—the ones with the most longevity in the House—learn to evolve with their districts and are attentive to the signals sent by constituents that require a reorientation of their representational styles.

The Conditional Advantage of Incumbency

Political scientists have long explored the so-called incumbency advantage and its supposed growth through the 1960s and 1970s. These scholars have used a variety of measures to determine incumbency and its advantages by treating incumbents as a collective, although these measures sometimes oversimplify. But I argue that the incumbency advantage is, quite simply, not one thing that all incumbents enjoy equally. More to the point: incumbents often need to adapt to remain in office throughout their careers.[3]

How an incumbent House member adapts one's representational style in response to electoral threats is central to retaining the confidence of the electorate over a long career. Some members of Congress never have the chance to serve more than a few terms—either because they never learn the representational lessons their elections seek to teach, or because they represent marginal districts that attract repeated high-quality challengers come election time. Other members face a few tough reelection fights early in their careers and then—having found a representational formula that works for them and their constituents—aim to replicate it throughout their career. Why change something that has been validated time and time again by the voters at the ballot box?

In his studies of members of Congress, Richard Fenno documents how members themselves choose particular representational personas and convey those personas to constituents.[4] These representational styles are closely related to how members describe the substance of the work they do on Capitol Hill and, very often, are associated closely with how members allocate their time and office resources. Personal vote advocates[5] emphasize that members accentuate attention to constituent service and casework, while Fenno claims that members of Congress are shaped not only by political context in the decision of how to represent a place but also by their life experiences. In addition, members gain constituent trust by explaining these representational choices and, to some degree, can establish the criteria by which constituents judge their performance as members of Congress. Although resources matter, so too do the tastes, proclivities, and individual talents of the member of Congress in building constituent trust and an incumbency advantage. Constituent service and the resources available to do it underpin the incumbency advantage—but so do the representational choices made by members themselves.

Value Networks in the Political Marketplace

But what happens to a successful incumbent when the magical representational formula—the perfect home style for a member and the place he represents—loses its luster? The conditionality of incumbency rests on a key idea: incumbents are akin to the successful firms analyzed by business professor Clayton Christensen in his book *Innovator's Dilemma*.[6] Incumbents, by dint of their initial election and then reelection, demonstrate a keen understanding of a political marketplace. They have identified their customers, listened to their needs, and delivered a high-quality representation product that is in demand. Evidence of their success lies in the fact that voters often opt to renew their contract every two or six years. The best companies also deliver high-quality products by responding to customer demands. They, critically, look to expand market share and grow their businesses. Incumbents often do the same. Because incumbents are risk-averse, they look for additional opportunities to dominate their electoral environment and discourage competition from emerging by continuing to listen to their existing customers. Good companies invest heavily in product development and high-quality talent. Incumbents do the same; they find ways to improve how they represent constituents so as to convert new voters while looking for the right staff to help entrench themselves favorably in the minds of voters. Good companies and incumbents succeed because they understand their respective customers and marketplaces.

The problem is that good companies, just like incumbents, can fail—and the seeds of their failure often lie in the replication of the same strategies that made them successful in the first place. The fundamental question framing Christensen's book is, Why do good companies that do everything right often fail when the marketplace changes and new technologies emerge? Why do incumbents, who are like good companies, also fail to adapt to changes in the political marketplace?

Successful firms, according to Christensen, establish value networks to maintain market dominance. These networks are "the context within which a firm identifies and responds to customers' needs, solves problems, procures input, reacts to competitors, and strives for profit."[7] The context, or shared experiences of a company, frames how it reacts to and evaluates technological challenges arising in the marketplace. Importantly, a firm's reaction is based on "its past choices of markets [which] determines its perceptions of economic value of a new technology."[8] In other words, where a firm sits at present—not only within a particular market but also in terms of the routines and procedures it developed to become successful and sustain its current success—affects how it views new technological innovations. Unfortunately, the value network that allows a firm to dominate a particular market and technological platform makes it ill-prepared to evaluate and develop new "disruptive" technologies—technologies that can compete in the marketplace where a good firm dominates market share. "Disruptive innovations," writes Christensen, "are complex because their value and application are uncertain, according to the criteria used by incumbent firms."[9]

Incumbent legislators, like incumbent firms, adopt value networks allowing them to win office and to continually win reelection. The value networks they adopt, at the same time, can make them dismissive of political disruptions—disruptions that may eventually topple them from political power in an

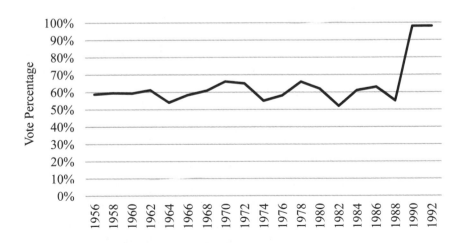

Figure 13.1 Bob Michel's career electoral performance, 1956–1992
Source: Data obtained from various editions, *America Votes* (Washington, DC: CQ Press) and *The Almanac of American Politics* (Washington, DC: National Journal).

election. It may also make it harder for them to forecast the emergence of a possible disruption and to fail to understand how that disruption could move upmarket, thereby competing successfully for elements of the incumbent's electoral coalition. Ironically, the success of past representational experiences makes it less and less likely for incumbents firmly embedded in the protectionist phase of their careers (like good companies dominating a market) to have the capability to address an unexpected and unanticipated electoral challenge led by a high-quality candidate. Often, this catches an incumbent unaware and off-guard, leading the incumbent to an electoral defeat that few predicted.

Disruptions and the Election of 1982

This is precisely the place Representative Bob Michel found himself going into the 1982 midterm election: stuck in representational patterns and relationships that had lost their luster. It almost cost Michel his career—but it didn't. Why not? How did Michel adapt to the representational challenge, and how did this adaptation allow him to continue on his leadership trajectory in the House?

Before understanding how Michel adapted to the challenge posed by the 1982 election, it is necessary to understand the nature of the disruption Michel faced going into it. Michel faced three critical challenges in 1982 that made him vulnerable but were by their nature foreseeable and (to a degree) predictable as to their effect. With President Ronald Reagan, a Republican, in the White House, congressional Republicans had to surmount history. In every midterm election save two in the post–World War II era, the president's party in the House has lost seats.[10] In fact, Michel's worst performance electorally before 1982 came in 1974, a midterm election featuring the previous Republican president, Gerald Ford, whose popularity slid when he announced his pardon of Richard Nixon. Michel received 55 percent of the votes cast that year (Figure 13.1).

The second disruption Michel faced was the 1980 decennial redistricting, which substantially altered the contours of Illinois's 18th District prior to the 1982 election. The redrawn district became larger and "remov[ed] some territory [Michel] had carried for years (Peoria suburbs, Illinois River counties) and add[ed] unfamiliar territory (suburbs of the state capital of Springfield and the factory town of Decatur)."[11] Upon seeing the new map, MaryAlice Erickson exclaimed: "Oh, my gosh. Bob Michel has a problem."[12] Erickson would become Michel's campaign manager two years later.

Although the partisan leanings of the district had not changed substantially (the old 18th gave Reagan 60 percent of the vote in 1980 compared to

58 percent as redrawn for the 1982 election), Michel had little time to get well acquainted with the new territory and his new constituents before asking them for their vote.[13]

The third disruption—unfortunately, for Michel—magnified the first two predictable ones: his ascent to minority leader combined with Ronald Reagan winning the presidency in 1980. Joining the ranks of congressional leadership requires members to navigate a tricky representational path among constituents back home. Leaders often find it difficult to travel home as often as they would like, and attention to the constituency itself is sometimes sacrificed for the greater good of the party and the goal of governance. Sometimes, the choices leaders must make put them in a difficult bind politically, especially if they are seen as advancing a program or casting a difficult vote necessary for the party but at odds with constituency views. Effective leadership demands that leaders do this occasionally. But at the end of the day, if congressional leaders cannot retain the trust of the voters back home, their constituents will send them packing. Good leadership does not exist in a representational vacuum.

Although Michel was not new to congressional leadership, having served as minority whip between 1975 and 1981, his election as minority leader at the beginning of the 97th Congress (1981–1983) came at a critical moment for the Republican Party on the heels of Reagan's landslide win over Democratic incumbent Jimmy Carter. Leader Michel's new role would severely test his skills as a coalition-builder and master legislator. Reagan's ascendancy presaged the passing of an old political regime and the arrival of a new one. The political scientist Steven Skowronek calls this the "politics of reconstruction." These political moments unleash a floodgate of political entrepreneurship and creative energies among members of the newly ascendant party. And at such moments, Skowronek contends, "the political preeminence of the presidency appears to be most naturally pronounced, [that is,] when the old regime has been discredited, when old alliances have been thrown into disarray, and when new interests have been thrust afresh upon governmental institutions."[14] In other words: the political initiative in Washington had shifted to the other end of Pennsylvania Avenue; and Michel, as minority leader with a conservative governing majority in the House, found himself expected to deliver quickly on a political program crafted by the president and his administration. This newly invigorated House minority party—the Republicans—came with "one of the most visionary and activist leadership teams of any leader before or since" peppered with "the force of personalities of [a] young Dick Cheney and a young Jack Kemp and a young Trent Lott," as well as a combative and tempestuous Newt Gingrich waiting in the wings.[15]

And Bob Michel had to manage all of them. Leadership, he once said, "requires swallowing hard sometimes [and] eating a good deal of crow."[16]

The disruptive force of Reagan's reconstruction and the challenge of Michel's position as the top Republican in the House become apparent when considering how members of Congress think about representation. Members of Congress do not view their district as an undifferentiated whole when making political decisions; rather, they think of their district as a series of concentric circles, with each circle consisting of a particular constituency with distinct interests and preference intensities.[17] The outermost circle is the geographic constituency, consisting of all the citizens living within district's political boundaries. The district as a whole may have particular interests and needs, but invariably, citizens within the district order those needs and interests differently. Citizens who voted for the member of Congress—the reelection constituency for the member—likely have different interests and needs from those who voted for the member's opponent. Similarly, a member's primary constituency (voters supporting a member in a party primary or grassroots activists who campaigned on the member's behalf) and intimates (a member's closest group of friends and political advisers) have yet another set of policy priorities and concerns to which the member ought to pay heed. In short, representation of a district is about serving multiple constituencies and multiple interests, taking those into account when each vote is cast and allocating a member's time when traveling back to the district.

Balancing these competing district interests is delicate, but as a successful incumbent winning multiple elections by large margins, it is a representational dance with which Michel was well familiar. Balancing existing interests with the new constituencies in a different 18th District with new boundaries created one fresh disruption. But perhaps the biggest complexity was the addition of two new representational circles beyond the geographic confines of the district: the White House and congressional Republicans. As a leader of a party in ascendance, Michel had additional representational responsibilities that could potentially bring him into conflict with not only his geographic constituency but also his reelection, primary, and intimate constituencies. At the same time, Michel needed to expand his constituencies within new district boundaries. The disruptive force of his new responsibilities could hardly be anticipated, creating perhaps the most fundamental threat to Michel's reelection in 1982 and beyond.

In March 1982, Michel's campaign went into the field with a poll to evaluate his political position. The results were not encouraging; his situation was precarious. Approximately one-third of respondents had no opinion concerning

Michel's job performance in Congress, and 32 percent didn't know whether they had a favorable impression of him.[18] Although only 19 percent expressed disapproval of Michel's job and 15 percent had an unfavorable impression of Michel, the high percentage of "don't know" responses should have alarmed someone who had served central Illinois in Congress for twenty-six years (see Figure 13.2). The problem, of course, is that voters without firm impressions of Michel could be persuaded more easily to support someone else by the fall. When asked whether Michel deserved reelection, only 41 percent said "yes" with nearly a third saying they would "give someone else a chance to do better." Impressions of Michel were vague, as "significant pluralities of voters [were] also unable to say whether Michel is doing a good or poor job of handling five congressional duties."[19] Clearly, the high degree of uncertainty about Michel resulted in part from the redistricting.

As 1982 progressed, the economic situation in central Illinois worsened and President Reagan's job approval began to weaken nationally (see Figure 13.3). Although the Michel campaign attempted to bolster constituent impressions of Michel by spending considerably, the campaign's internal numbers did not improve. As more and more voters found themselves able to form an impression of Michel and report an opinion on his job performance, Michel's negative numbers grew. By early October, the percentage of constituents approving of Michel's job had hardly changed from March at 47 percent, whereas the percentage expressing disapproval had climbed from 19 to 30 percent (see Figure 13.2).[20] The percentage of constituents with an unfavorable impression of Michel had nearly doubled, first from 15 percent in March to 28 percent, and again in October to 41 percent (an increase of 173 percent over eight months), indicating that someone else deserved a shot at representing Illinois's 18th District.

Despite financially overwhelming his Democratic opponent (Michel was among the top-twenty spenders in the House during the 1982 cycle), the perception existed among central Illinois voters that Michel was not doing a good job for them in Washington and that he was too focused on his job as Republican Leader at the expense of district needs.[21] Too many constituents simply didn't have a clear idea of who Michel was and what he had done, so it was relatively easy for Michel's inexperienced Democratic opponent, Doug Stephens, to turn voter frustration with crippling unemployment, the Reagan administration's unpopular economic embargo, and labor unrest at Caterpillar against Michel. This was perhaps even aided by the Michel campaign itself, which advertised Michel as the "Republican Leader"—making it easier for voters to blame their

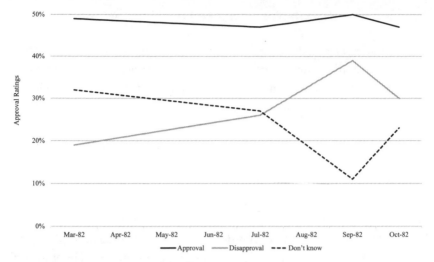

Figure 13.2 Bob Michel's job approval ratings, March–October 1982

Key: The solid black line represents respondents who approve of the job Michel is doing. The solid gray line represents those who disapprove. The dashed line shows respondents who said they did not know.

Sources: Market Opinion Research polls in RHM Papers, Campaign and Politics, 1982, Box 16, f. 1982; f. MOR 18th District Study (7/82), Analysis, f. 1982 Market Opinion Research 18th District Study (9/1982), Data; f. 1982 Market Opinion Research 18th District Study (10/1982), Data; Box 20, f. 1984 Market Opinion Research 18th District Study (1/1984), Analysis.

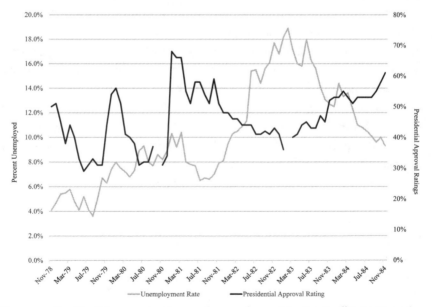

Figure 13.3 Presidential approval ratings and unemployment in Peoria, Illinois, November 1978–November 1984

Key: Gray trend line is the monthly unemployment rate for the Peoria, Illinois, Metropolitan Statistical Area as reported by the Illinois Department of Employment Security. The left axis represents percentage unemployed. The black line represents the national presidential job approval rating average by month as reported by the American Presidency Project.

Sources: Unemployment data available at: www.ides.illinois.gov/LMI/Pages/Historical_Monthly _Annual_Data.aspx. Approval ratings available at: http://www.presidency.ucsb.edu/data/pop larity.php.

congressman for their frustrations with the national Republican Party.[22] Worse still, the Reagan administration's steadfast unwillingness to budge on their economic embargo of the Soviet Union made any claims of Michel exercising considerable clout in Washington ring hollow, especially because Michel vocally criticized the administration's policy on this point. In an interview with the *Chicago Tribune* during late summer 1982, Michel refused "to run away from my president" and, while acknowledging that "the country [is] going to hell in a handbasket," he noted that he "can't be held responsible . . . just because I'm the President's leader in Congress."[23] True enough, but his constituents wanted to blame someone, and Michel was an easy target. When the voters of the 18th District went to the polls, unemployment in Peoria had reached 17.1 percent, and Reagan's approval rating nationally in the Gallup Poll had hit its lowest point of his first term (see Figure 13.3). It is perhaps a miracle that Michel won at all, let alone by 4 points over Stephens, given the interlocking political disruptions Michel faced in 1982. Michel's vulnerabilities were laid bare for an experienced challenger to exploit in 1984. Michel had work to do if he wished to continue his congressional career.

Managing Disruption and Representational Recovery

To respond to a disruption, it must be recognized. In observing members of Congress over his career, Fenno notes the propensity of members to become trapped in persistent representational patterns.[24] And why not? It's easy to presume that getting reelected repeatedly results from simply replicating what worked before; once the hearts and minds of constituents have become known, simply rinse and repeat. Bob Michel could have looked back at 1982 and concluded that nothing was wrong with how he represented his congressional district, that his electoral performance in 1982 was an aberration owing to economic and political forces outside his control.

But, to Bob Michel's credit, he escaped the trap. On election night, Bob Michel—for a few hours at least—thought that he had lost.[25] But he wasn't ready to call it a career. As MaryAlice Erickson put it, Bob Michel "still had a mission" and a role to play in politics because of his "faith."[26] He would work to restore his relationship with his central Illinois constituents, and to do so successfully, he allowed his staff the latitude to implement a series of important changes that improved public perception of his representational style. He chose to respond to the disruption rather than ignore it. He altered the value network embedded in his representational style and his congressional staff allocations.

Constituent Outreach

In thinking about how members of Congress represent their districts, political scientists often pay close attention to the representational choices made by the members. But as important as how members present themselves to constituents are the ways in which they allocate official representational resources, in particular their staffs, to represent on their behalf. What had worked since 1957 no longer did. Bob Michel and his Washington staff knew that constituent operations back in the district had to be improved. The decision was made in November to hire the Peoria native, former state legislator, and former congressional aide Ray LaHood to run the existing district office in Peoria and serve as district director. Michel also hired Craig Findley, the son of a former congressman and a former staffer to Representative Tom Railsback (R-IL), who had lost his reelection bid in 1982. Findley manned a second district office in Jacksonville, Illinois. Jacksonville, as the county seat of Morgan County, held strategic value for Michel. Findley's operation allowed the congressman to reach out to Morgan and Scott Counties, as well as Springfield's western suburbs in Sangamon County—all new to the 18th District.

Two separate analyses of Michel's congressional operations recognized the need to adapt to new representational requirements borne of the 1982 experience. The Congressional Research Service recommended that Michel "meet with more constituents" in a July 1983 memorandum. Bob Michel had never been one to come back home every weekend to the district—in fact, it was more like a weekend each month. According to District Director (and later Chief of Staff) Ray LaHood, Michel simply did not hold regular office hours to meet with constituents.[27] Instead, Michel saw his congressional responsibilities largely as going to Washington to cast votes and to work on legislation.[28] Furthermore, even if he did secure funding, it was not in Michel's nature to brag about it. "He was a man of genuine and considerable humility" said his longtime press secretary and later chief of staff, Mike Johnson.[29] "So it was kind of tough both for him to get in front of a camera and talk about how good he was and to see press releases and statements and those kind of things about what we were getting done back home. It was not something that he, through his natural instincts, would apply a lot of his time and energy to."[30] As a result, voters did not perceive Michel as working for them, and Michel did little to change that perception. To the contrary, he perceived his representational role as legislating and leading on Capitol Hill. He reminded an interviewer years later that "the people sent me here" with this charge: "'Bob, go down and cut the cost of government and get it off our back. That's all.' They didn't say, 'Give me more of this. Give me some of this. Give me this. Give me that.' Or 'What other programs can I qualify for?'"[31]

The congressman did come home more often after 1982. A comparison of district work schedules in 1982 and 1984 (both election years) shows that Michel spent at least ninety days back in Illinois in 1982 and 123 days in 1984—an increase of 37 percent.[32] Upgrading the district staff was also critical to reestablishing relations with the voters back home after Michel's near loss in 1982. It signaled the establishment of a new values network organized around new representational priorities. LaHood and Findley held regular office hours around the district, traveled the district extensively, and saw to it that problems and concerns were brought to the attention of the congressman and the Washington staff in ways they had not been before. LaHood reported that he and Findley would reach out to constituents or that they would come to them saying, "Hey, we need this project or that project funded." Once the request was made, LaHood "would communicate it to people in the leadership office who, you know, knew the appropriation process and knew who to call and then we'd tell people to submit a proposal, and then we'd send it to our staff in DC, and they'd put it in the pipeline, and it would almost always happen."[33] Up to that point, "the Peoria office was mainly geared to take care of people's immigration problems or Social Security or Medicare or veterans" problems rather than seek out and assist in the funding of district projects.[34] With careful attention to staff back in the district, Michel was able to more readily project an impression of influence and effectiveness at addressing district needs. Now his neighbors clamored for government services.

The presence of a more robust and engaged congressional staff created the potential for changing how constituents perceived Michel's representational style. Furthermore, it addressed the nettlesome issue of Michel's leadership position, which had been a millstone around his neck in 1982. The political consulting firm Research/Strategy/Management, Inc. (R/S/M), retained by Michel campaign manager MaryAlice Erickson to prepare for the 1984 reelection campaign, succinctly depicted the problem in the graphic reproduced here as Figure 13.4. Constituents once perceived that Michel gave more immediate attention to his House colleagues and the White House than he did to the concerns of the 18th District and its concerns. The goal was to flip the perceptions, making the 18th District Michel's primary and most important constituency. Findley and LaHood's work on the ground in meeting with constituents and passing on funding requests meant that the benefits of Michel's leadership position to his home district became more

To achieve that goal will require some re-ordering of priorities and a recognition of the perception in the 18th district of the Michel priorities, and the need to shift that perception.

Below is an illustration (Figure A) of how a sizeable number of constituents perceive Bob Michel and his relationship with his three constituencies. The second illustration (Fig. B) is how the constituents should perceive that relationship.

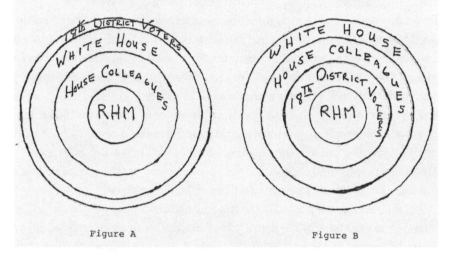

Figure A   Figure B

Figure 13.4 From perceived representational priorities to ideal representational priorities
Source: "The Honorable Robert H. Michel: Congressional Plan," R/S/M, Inc. RHM Papers, Campaigns and Politics, 1983, Box 18, f. R/S/M, Inc. Report, April 12, 1983 (1), Tab "Goals."

tangible. "One of the great advantages of being a leader," recounted Johnson, "is that it is easier for you to impact the appropriations process and get projects in the district done. . . . So we devoted much more time to that, and we were effective at it. That made a difference in terms of Bob's reputation back at home."[35] It also did not hurt that LaHood served on a number of boards himself and was active in the community, again extending Michel's presence in the district even if the Republican Leader himself could not always be home.[36] The upshot was a reorientation of the value network around Michel. Constituent needs came first and would benefit from Michel's position as Republican Leader.

Bob Michel: Your Congressman, Working for You

Michel adapted his representational style in yet another way. In addition to beefing up his district staff, he used his Washington-based staff more effectively. R/S/M recommended two key changes to office operations: better use of Michel's time when he was home, and revamping publicity and media relations efforts. Both of these tactics involved careful coordination between Michel's congressional staff and the new political operation spearheaded by campaign manager MaryAlice Erickson.

On the official side, Michel's staff organized his visits home to make a deeper and more lasting impression among the electorate. During scheduled congressional recesses prior to 1982, LaHood reports, Michel might not spend the whole time back in the district, preferring to travel elsewhere, even outside Illinois.[37] That changed. For one Easter recess, as an example, the congressman "might come back for two or three days. . . . We got him to come home a whole ten days, and we organized a lot of events around that."[38] On the campaign side, Erickson spent the first two months traveling the district, meeting with Republican Party officials, and establishing Bob Michel campaign coordinators in every county. Then as Michel came home, she would provide "a folder of every county we were going to be in that day with the names of the county chairmen and the coordinator and all the Republican office holders in that county and what we were doing, why we were going to this event, and so forth."[39] Days were full, lasting twelve or fourteen hours, and visits were carefully calibrated based upon strengths and weaknesses uncovered through a benchmark poll commissioned by Erickson early in 1983. Before 1982, the "schedule back home was haphazard, you know, someone invites him to go here, and OK, we'll go over there for 20 minutes and end up spending two hours. . . . With Craig and Ray on the ground there, we were able to manage the schedule . . . and organize each trip so that you had, for example, we would concentrate in Peoria and Pekin in one trip and another trip back would be Jacksonville and the Springfield area."[40] Bringing rigor, organization, and empirics to bear on Michel's district travels made these visits more impactful.

Scheduling visits more carefully and precisely was only half the battle in reintroducing Michel to his constituents after 1982. The other important part of the equation required revamping the press operation so that constituents knew of Michel's travels around the district. Careful examination of the press releases sent by the congressional office indicates that at least some announcing Michel's district schedule were marked "not for release, for informational purposes only" before November 1982.[41] This practice limited the visibility Michel received during his travels home as the schedule could not be published by the press in advance. After 1982, the practice changed. According to Erickson: "We always . . . got the list of all the local newspapers, and we sent out notices Bob Michel was going to be here, here, here, and here. . . . We wanted everything we possibly could get in the newspapers."[42]

Another adaptation to the representational disruptions occasioned by the 1982 election involved the local media. The *Peoria Journal Star*, the district's largest and most important paper, incurred Michel's ire. Mike Johnson, in his role of press secretary, analyzed coverage in the paper, finding that of thirty-eight stories written about the Michel–Stephens campaign, twenty-four centered on attacks about Michel's record.[43] Carole Halicki, a former television news anchor, was installed in the Peoria office as a local press secretary in May 1982 in the middle of the campaign.[44] In the spring of 1983, she wrote an important interoffice memorandum arguing strenuously to ramp up her press outreach efforts in Peoria. Fixing the amount and tone of Michel's coverage was about relationship-building, she said. Halicki, who chafed under restrictions imposed by the Washington office, wanted license to build those media contacts in the district much as LaHood and Findley had in their work. "The key to good local media relations, in my opinion," wrote Halicki, "is not measured by the number of mailings sent to them. The key is personal, one-on-one contact. Since it is not possible for the Congressman to visit the local media as often as he once did, it is necessary for a representative of the Congressman to do so."[45] This need for locally based press operations relates to the fundamental problem of serving in leadership, which the consultants at R/S/M addressed forthrightly: "Bob Michel has become a national leader and as such is getting a great deal of national news coverage. This has the effect of making him look 'National' now, maybe too important to care about the folks back home. . . . Unless the [local] press coverage is done in such a way that the constituents see local pride in the Michel leadership, that leadership has a negative value to the congressional office."[46] In outlining their recommendations to Michel and his staff, the R/S/M team agreed that Halicki should remain in Peoria, and "a regular schedule of visiting media outlets should be established just as the office hours are established, and three out of five days should be spent visiting with media in the district."[47] Not only would relations with local media outlets be better established on a more positive footing, but those efforts would serve to "localize a national leader to the folks back home."[48] This, again, signaled a shift in the values network Michel had established, even if better coordination between press in Washington and Peoria required developing

Table 13.1 Congressman Michel's official congressional press releases, 1981–1984

		National	District	Both	Misc.	Total
		Subject of Press Release				
Year		National	District	Both	Misc.	Total
1981	Percentage	63%	33%	1%	2%	100%
	Frequency	(57)	(30)	(1)	(2)	(90)
1982	Percentage	42%	45%	12%	0%	100%
	Frequency	(41)	(44)	(12)	(0)	(97)
1983	Percentage	29%	57%	10%	3%	100%
	Frequency	(53)	(104)	(19)	(5)	(181)
1984	Percentage	42%	54%	3%	1%	100%
	Frequency	(44)	(57)	(3)	(1)	(105)

Note: Coding of Official press releases issued by Congressman Michel's congressional office. Includes all releases issued in a nonelection year and January–October 31 of election years. Press releases included in the RHM Papers, Press Series, Boxes 9–15. *Source*: Data obtained from various editions, America Votes (Washington, DC: CQ Press) and The Almanac of American Politics (Washington, DC: National Journal).

new processes, clearer lines of responsibility, and some management of personalities. LaHood noted that now trips home almost always included press conferences and media availabilities, all arranged by Halicki.[49]

Apparently, this new approach created some conflict between the longtime press secretary Mike Johnson, who was based in Washington, and Halicki, as noted by the consultants.[50] Johnson expressed frustration with Halicki in a memo he penned in response to her suggestions for improving media relations in the 18th District. "There is no doubt that national news coverage has its drawbacks, but there is no way in hell that Bob is going to be able to avoid it," he wrote. "We simply have to use it to the best of our advantage. We don't need lectures on the distinctions between Mr. Michel's responsibilities as a national leader and a local Congressman. He is the leader and there is not a dam [sic] thing that can be done about that." Growing pains were evident in the establishment of a new values network moving forward after 1982.[51] This was neither an easy process nor one that happened overnight.

From "Waste, Fraud, and Abuse" to "Bringing Home the Bacon"

The changes to press operations resulted in a new way to depict how Michel's accomplishments were highlighted in press releases. Table 13.1 makes clear the difference in how Michel's press team talked about his accomplishments.[52] In 1981 and 1982, the official congressional office sent out 187 press releases. In 1983 and 1984, 286 releases were sent, an increase of 53 percent. But more important than the sheer volume of press releases is how those press releases substantively changed. I simply coded each press release as to whether the subject of the press release made mention of the district or a district-level concern or a national issue or whether the release mentioned both. In a small number of cases, if a national or local focus could not be discerned, the release was coded as miscellaneous. For example, a March 11, 1981, press release focused on President Reagan's economic package. This was coded as a national press release. An April 7, 1981, a press release discussing concerns about TWA air service to St. Louis (the nearest major airport for constituents in the southern portion of the 18th District) was coded as a district-level release. During the 97th Congress, when Michel helped shepherd Reagan's legislative agenda through Congress, only 40 percent of his office's press releases exclusively addressed specific district-level concerns or issues. In the next two years, in the lead-up to the 1984 campaign, 56 percent of press releases covered district issues or concerns. It is also notable that many of the press releases sent after 1982 were grant announcements, listing awards made by various agencies for projects back in the district. By my count, twenty-eight press releases in 1983 (15 percent) mentioned a district-level grant or award. In 1981, only ten press releases did so (11 percent).

Representational adaptation surfaced in the way Bob Michel talked about government spending. When Michel entered the House in 1957, he was interested first and foremost in government running efficiently. While a member of the Appropriations Committee, "he had been doing, as an appropriator, large amendments that cut here and there in the appropriations bill. . . . Then Bob crafted an amendment to cut a billion dollars in waste, fraud, and abuse out of the Labor HHS appropriations," recalled longtime aide Billy Pitts. "The amendment carried and it was a big win for Bob."[53] Michel earned a national reputation as a budget-cutter. As a part of his press outreach back home, Michel penned a frequent opinion column that was distributed to newspapers throughout the district. In a column written in April 1981, Michel wrote that "some people believe Congressmen operate on a philosophy that any federal money obtained for their district is well spent, regardless of how worthy the project. I don't adhere to that philosophy."[54] He continued by pointing out that the Peoria Garden Project, funded by the Community Service Act, was one such example of wasteful spending back home. Another column expressed support for "budget cuts proposed by President Ronald Reagan."[55] In both cases, Michel expressed skepticism concerning federal spending and its usefulness even when that spending came home.

As Peoria struggled with high levels of unemployment, Michel changed his tune in a column written in February 1983 titled "Government Contracts One Key to Economic Recovery in Our Area."[56] A press release one month later noted that "the Illinois Road Builders Association and the Underground Contractors Association" would honor Michel for "his efforts in passing the Surface Transportation Consistance [sic] Act" that would bring more than $1 billion to the state, including "$100 million for U.S. 51 and Peoria bypass construction as a result of an amendment sponsored by Michel."[57] Another release in April noted that "Michel was instrumental in including provisions for the funding of improvements to the Greater Peoria Airport in the legislation." In addition, staff members began to provide summaries of all grants, loans, and projects secured for the district on a regular basis. In March 1984, Michel's weekly column, this one titled "A Summary of 1983 Efforts," reported that "we helped secure more than $400 million for the 18th Congressional District in various grants, loans, and federal contracts for area business, industry, government and social service and educational programs."[58]

This type of credit-claiming activity is nearly absent from the archival record prior to 1982. LaHood confirms that, before 1982, Michel "wasn't spending his time trying to figure out how to spend money in his district. That kind of was against his philosophy in a way. . . . But after '82, and when Craig and I came on, we knew that he was in a position to make things happen and get things funded."[59] Mike Johnson does not believe the effort shifted so much as the process became more "structured."[60] If Bob Michel was uncomfortable with touting his own accomplishments in front of the cameras, his staff made sure that his efforts as leader to bring appropriations back home would be more directly and clearly communicated to the press. Only by these means could the office demonstrate the value of Michel's leadership position to the district's voters. Michel no longer touted himself as the Republican Leader who once proudly proclaimed he was the president's "handmaiden"; instead, he carefully translated his clout into projects that more directly spoke to the lives of the typical central Illinoisan.

Fenno writes about the importance of members of Congress translating their Washington work when they return home.[61] The subject and tone of Michel's press releases indicate a clear shift away from the negatives of government and spending to proclaiming their positive impact for the 18th District.

"The Michel Report," that frequent column appearing in newspapers throughout central Illinois and drafted by Mike Johnson, is an even better indicator of how Michel changed his emphasis when discussing his doings back on Capitol Hill. Of the twenty-three "Michel Reports" in 1981, nineteen addressed national topics and defended the administration, rarely making clear connections to district concerns. Or Michel explained process in great detail—which was admirable but left readers wondering how it mattered to them. His May 15 report on House passage of the Reagan budget explained the 1974 Budget Act, the process of reconciliation, and the streamlining of the appropriations process and subsequent reduction in regulation.[62] The column reads like an abstract civics lesson, making it easier to conclude that Michel was focused on Washington inside baseball.

The "Michel Report" from April 18, 1983, "Touring the District: Always a Learning Experience," showed a different side. Michel was no longer the explainer *to the district* but the supplicant who has learned *from the district.* He discussed a visit to "the United Parcel Service terminal in East Peoria where I talked with about 60 UPS drivers [and discussed] . . . the withholding on interest and dividends to the gas tax-highway improvement bill we passed last year."[63] Later, Michel recounted a lunch with retirees who brought up their concerns about Social Security and rising gas prices. In another edition, he described a drive to Fulton County, where he reported how his support for the recent gas-tax bill would bring much-needed improvements to the roads in the western part of his district. A column for August that same year began by noting that "a number of actions taken [by the House] will have an impact on West Central Illinois," including an extension of unemployment benefits—an issue on which Michel had "received a number of letters and phone calls from individuals who through no fault of their own have exhausted all of the unemployment benefits they had coming to them" despite not yet having found a job.[64] The biggest difference between the two sets of columns was the careful effort by Michel to portray his Washington work through the lens of the district's needs. Michel and his staff had heard loud and clear the need to translate Michel's clout into meaningful outcomes for constituents still hurting economically from the aftereffects of the recession.[65]

The Permanent Campaign

In terms of representational style, Michel and his staff placed more emphasis on district issues, constituent service, and credit-claiming. The other important change concerned the political operation: How would Michel respond on the campaign trail? MaryAlice Erickson, who returned to Peoria shortly after the 1982 campaign concluded, had not been home long before Bob Michel requested a meeting and offered her the job of managing his 1984 reelection campaign.[66] Erickson transformed what had been, in many respects, a low-key and amateurish effort into a full-time, professionalized political operation. Because of his long service and the heavily Republican tilt to the 18th District, Michel never felt the need to exert much effort during his reelection campaigns prior to 1982. When we spoke on the phone in 2017, I asked Erickson what problems she felt needed addressing immediately. "He'd never campaigned before. You know, [he'd] come back to the district and do what people think is a campaign. Billboards. Yard signs. Maybe go to a few meetings with the district. After all, everybody knew Bob Michel. . . . And so he didn't need to do anything."[67]

Erickson wanted that to change. She wanted him back "every weekend [he could] possibly be back," and he did return more often. She also established a stand-alone campaign headquarters, where before campaigns had been run from the kitchen table in Michel's house.[68] She hired professional consultants, Vince Breglio and Susan Bryant of R/S/M, who commissioned an extensive "baseline poll to determine where our problems were, where our strengths were, where we needed to be."[69] And, in contrast to 1982, the tagline for the campaign was "Bob Michel, He Works for You" instead of "Bob Michel, the Republican Leader."[70] The days of spending $60,000 on a reelection campaign were also over. In 1984, as in 1982, the Michel team raised in excess of $650,000. Much of the largesse went to polling and consultants, as well as covering the district with an extensive television and radio advertising campaign. The point was not only to get Michel reelected in 1984 but also to create a base of support that would endure well beyond that one campaign. "We went full bore on absolutely everything because we wanted to have this campaign re-inventing Bob Michel and lasting until he wanted to retire," explained Erickson.[71] Indeed, Erickson was horrified when, at the conclusion of the 1984 campaign, Michel wanted to shut down the political operation. "Bob, we can't do this. There is work to do every single day on your campaign, and we need to be doing this every single day, and we need that office open," Erickson said. "[Michel] reluctantly gave in. So we always kept the [campaign] office open until he retired."[72] The permanent campaign, well documented by scholars elsewhere, had come to Peoria at last, forever changing how Bob Michel would run for reelection. Michel, the evidence suggests, had moved out of the protectionist phase of his congressional career into a near-permanent expansionist phase until he decided to retire.

Representation Renewed

Did all of the effort expended to alter the way in which Michel related to his constituents and the adoption of a more professionalized, data-intensive campaign operation bear fruit? In 1984, Michel beat Gerald Bradley, a state legislator and a high-quality challenger, 61–39 percent—a margin consistent with Michel's performance in previous cycles. The skeptic can point to several key factors on the ground that were present in 1982 but now absent: The president's popularity had rebounded, the recession had receded, and the labor unrest at Caterpillar had been resolved. Returning to Figure 13.3, we see that President Reagan's approval rating nationally in November 1984 (61 percent) was at its highest point since 1981. Unemployment in the Peoria metropolitan area, which had reached nearly 19 percent in February 1983, had fallen below 10 percent by November 1984. Times were still tough but clearly improving. Furthermore, Reagan won reelection resoundingly in 1984 and repeated his strong performance in the 18th District. Perhaps Michel could have won reelection without changing his representational and campaigning styles at all.

It is hard to disentangle the factors affecting Michel's strong 1984 performance. What is certain, however, is that constituent impressions of Michel became more positive and more concrete during the 1984 campaign and after (see Figure 13.5). Michel's job-approval rating had recovered from a September 1982 low of 47 percent to 61 percent approving in September 1984.[73] More important, the congressman's favorability rating increased from 48 percent in October 1982 to 57 percent in September 1984. Fifty percent of the electorate thought Michel did a good job representing the people in the district (an 11-point increase from October 1982), and 52 and 55 percent now thought he did a good job helping and returning to the district (versus 33 and 48 percent, respectively, in July 1982). As important, perhaps, is that these improved numbers likely represented a change in constituent opinion—the percentage of voters reporting "don't know" across polling questions remained remarkably stable at about 25 percent.[74] Impressions of Michel did change, responding to the changes Michel and his staff had made relative to his image. This suggests that constituents saw these changes to Michel's representational approach and approved.

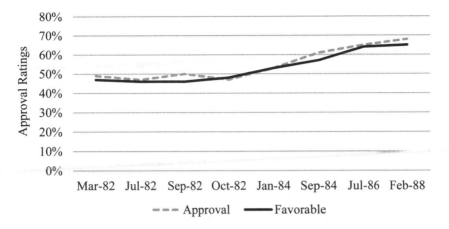

Figure 13.5 The recovery of Bob Michel's representational reputation, March 1982–February 1988

Key: The solid back line represents the percentage of respondents having a favorable impression of Michel. The dashed gray line represents the percentage of respondents approving of the job Michel is doing.

Sources: Market Opinion Research polls in RHM Papers, Campaign and Politics, 1982, Box 16, f. 1982; f. MOR 18th District Study (7/82), Analysis, f. 1982 Market Opinion Research 18th District Study (9/1982), Data; f. 1982 Market Opinion Research 18th District Study (10/1982), Data; Box 20, f. 1984 Market Opinion Research 18th District Study (1/1984), Analysis.

Comparing election returns in 1982 and 1984 is illuminating. Hancock, Fulton, Morgan, Scott, Sangamon, and Menard Counties were all added to the 18th District after the redistricting; Brown and Cass Counties, in the southern part of the district but in close proximity to the new district office run by Craig Findley, had underperformed relative to Michel's district-wide performance in 1982. In each of these eight counties, Michel saw his vote margins improve dramatically from 1982 to 1984—and in each instance, the increased margins exceeded the overall 10-point increase Michel enjoyed in 1984 over his 1982 performance. In Brown County, where Michel underperformed relative to his district-wide vote share in 1982, Michel's vote margin increased by 17.4 percentage points. In Morgan County, home to Michel's new constituent outreach office, Michel went from 54 percent of the vote to 68.1 percent of the vote—an increase of 14 points. It is yet another signpost of how a new values network adopted by Michel and his staff yielded a positive outcome among the electorate.[75]

A postelection analysis written by Susan Bryant, one of the principals at R/S/M, argued that the transformation of congressional operations in terms of constituent service and press made the difference. Bryant noted that "the district office had been a serious problem in the '82 cycle, but it was restructured early in 1983, and in fact that office operation is now among the best!"[76] On press operations, she wrote that "there was concern about the media and media relationships. . . . Simply by being more sensitive, the Michel office has eliminated much of the problem." And efforts to reach out to the new areas added to the 18th District led to those new constituents having a "firm opinion" of Michel, due to "a concentrated effort by Bob Michel himself coupled with media later in the campaign."[77] Name awareness of Michel improved from 73 percent in March 1982 to 94 percent in September 1984, with Michel's reelection numbers going from 40 percent in October 1982 to 48 percent in September 1984. Bryant summarized that "Bob went home as often as was needed, and when he was home, did the sort of traveling needed to re-cement the positive image. He was no longer the 'Leader' as Doug Stephens had tried to portray him, but rather was the good friend and Congressman, Bob Michel."[78]

Campaign Manager MaryAlice Erickson had hoped that the efforts undertaken in 1984 would leave Michel with a strong foundation to continue representing Illinois's 18th District for as long as he liked. The evidence suggests her hopes were realized. The campaign, now on permanent footing, consistently spent between $550,000 and $875,000 until Michel retired.[79] Michel's job approval and favorability ratings continued their upward climb, settling in at 68 and 65 percent, respectively, in the final poll accessible in the archival record—which was taken in February 1988.[80] Constituents also gave Michel high marks in terms of his representation of the district, helping with problems, and returning home. In February 1988, 56 percent agreed that the congressman was doing a good job representing the people of the district, 60 percent agreed he was doing a good job helping, and 67 percent thought he did a good job returning to the district. Bob Michel had survived the multiple disruptions that nearly derailed his congressional career in 1982. He survived, even prospered, because of a concerted effort to reconnect to his constituents and a political operation employing the latest and most sophisticated campaign techniques available.

Conclusion

When Bob Michel entered the House of Representatives in 1957, the political world was very different from the one he faced in 1982 when he almost lost his reelection bid. At that time, the "textbook Congress" was firmly ensconced on Capitol Hill. Committees were autonomous and represented the true centers of political power. Appropriations, in particular, was a committee where norms of bipartisanship existed. Members specialized and served apprenticeships, and the party leadership deferred to the wishes of committee chairs when bringing legislation to the floor. The ideological lines between the parties were blurred, and partisan conflict was less sharp. Members of Congress spent much of their time in Washington, returning to their districts to campaign in the fall of election years—with local party organizations playing an important and substantive role in getting out the vote. Television was still expensive and experimental, and most campaigns were conducted via leaflet and door-knocking.

By 1982, the world was very different in Washington and on the campaign trail. The political parties had become more ideologically distinctive, with the Democratic Party moving slowly leftward and the Republicans, more dramatically, lurching to the right.[81] Legislating had become more combative and negative. As well-documented by Sean Theriault and others, Newt Gingrich led a group of young conservatives to contest the Democratic majority in the House aggressively using new tactics and parliamentary tools.[82] Members began to spend less and less time in Washington forging relationships in favor of returning home more frequently to build stronger and more personal ties to constituents. At the same time, campaigns became more candidate-centered in terms of messaging and execution.[83] The medium had also moved from newspapers and flyers to radio and television, along with the hiring of specialized consultants who employed more frequent polling to aid in message development and more sophisticated voter-targeting. The value network that had allowed Michel to thrive in the House and gave him space to ascend to the top echelon of GOP leadership in the chamber had been exposed as insufficient by the multiple disruptions present in the 1982 midterm. Worse still, persisting with a value network prefaced on protectionism and the pursuit of political clout in Washington would likely have exposed Michel to a serious challenger in 1984. To survive in Washington and at home, Michel would have to respond to the weaknesses exposed by these disruptions. Michel did respond, and he transformed successfully by adopting a new values network. But why?

What is underappreciated about Bob Michel's transition is the faith he placed in his staff to help him to change his representational approach and to implement a new values network. LaHood pointed to an important aspect of Michel's prepolitical career that, perhaps, gave him the flexibility and willingness to change more than halfway through his congressional career: "Bob really respected staff because he had been a staffer. . . . Bob paid attention to his staff, and he hired good people, and then he paid attention to them. . . . We weren't just staff. We were like family."[84] Michel knew he was in trouble in 1982, and this seems to be key: he was willing to let his staff guide him during his reinvention. Mike Johnson confirmed this independently when we discussed the implementation of changes in congressional staffing and procedure post-1982: "The office management was something again that Bob let us beef up . . . and take a lot more off of his shoulders and do those kind of things. I don't think he was particularly conscious of it on a day-to-day basis, but he was very amenable to letting people that knew what they were doing do what they do best."[85] Perhaps Michel's most important asset in this transition was his fundamental humility—the same characteristic which, ironically, made it hard to tout his own accomplishments in the first place. Humility meant that he was still willing to learn and adapt—key components to responding successfully to disruptions. One characteristic common to failed firms and incumbencies is the dismissal of disruptions. Michel and his staff recognized the disruptions, embraced their importance, and made adjustments to move to an expansionist phase in Michel's congressional career.

The most important lesson that Michel's experience yields is a broader conception of the representational styles that members craft. Much of what political scientists know about the representational styles of members rests on the actions of members themselves: the speeches they make, the bills they sponsor, or the trips home they take. But as important to understanding members' representational styles are decisions and actions made by congressional staffers at home and in Washington. Bob Michel gave his staff the space and autonomy to implement key changes. Neither Michel nor his staff allowed themselves to be trapped by the demands of existing values networks.

The other key element to Michel's survival was the magnification of Michel's presence and connection to his constituencies in the 18th District through the actions and careful allocation of his staff. The best congressional staff become extensions of the member to the point where a staffer's actions are almost indistinguishable from the member him- or herself. It is no surprise that Ray LaHood himself slid relatively effortlessly into the role of successor after Michel's retirement; LaHood's job in Peoria was very much to be a physical extension of Bob Michel. I asked LaHood if, as a former staffer, there is a difference in how Capitol Hill staff alum behave as members compared to those who did not work on the Hill before serving in the House. "I do think there's a real appreciation and a real respect from a former staffer who gets to be a member" he agreed. "I mean people know the staff do the work, and the members take the credit."[86] It could be argued that because Michel served as a staff member before his election in 1956, he appreciated more than others the value of treating staff as a team, of recognizing their ability to see disruptions and offer ways to adapt. Accordingly, he was more than willing to undergo a shift in representational approach.

Michel never again faced a serious electoral threat after 1982. He and his capable staff took seriously the lessons provided by the series of disruptions they faced in 1982. They seized the opportunity to reimagine the way in which Michel would engage with, represent, and provide value to the constituents of the 18th District. Bob Michel, the former appropriator, had not just learned to love bacon—he embraced the political circumstances and realities of a new political world, very different from the one he had been socialized into when he first came to Washington as a freshman in 1957.

Notes

1. It is certainly not far-fetched to think that Michel could have chosen retirement over fighting another tough election campaign. In response to a congratulations letter from a supporter asking whether he'd run for reelection in 1984, Michel wrote in early December 1982: "It is too early to determine whether I will run in 1984. I have a lot of work to do between now and then, getting to know a new District and trying to solve some of the immense problems our district faces. I don't know of any other area in the country facing harder times than Central Illinois." See RHM to Joseph P. Donton, December 9, 1982, RHM Papers, General Series, Box 19, f. 1982.

2. Charles J. Abbot, "Bob Michel: Conservative in Philosophy, Practical in Politics," *Illinois Issues*, August/September 1988, in RHM Papers, Scrapbooks, f. Clippings 1986 through Clippings 1988 (1).

3. David R. Mayhew, *Congress: The Electoral Connection* (New Haven, CT: Yale University Press, 1974); Andrew Gelman and Gary King, "Estimating Incumbency Advantage with Bias," *American Journal of Political Science* 34, no. 4 (1990): 1142–1164; and Gary C. Jacobson, "It's Nothing Personal: The Decline of the Incumbency Advantage in US House Elections," *Journal of Politics* 27, no. 3 (2015): 861–873.

4. Richard F. Fenno, Jr., *Home Style: House Members in Their Districts* (Boston: Little, Brown, 1978).

5. Such as Bruce Cain, John Ferejohn, and Morris Fiorina, *The Personal Vote: Constituency Service and Electoral Independence* (Cambridge, MA: Harvard University Press, 1987).

6. Clayton M. Christensen, *Innovator's Dilemma: When New Technologies Cause Great Firms to Fail* (Boston: Harvard Business School Press, 1997).

7. Christensen, *Innovator's Dilemma*, 32.

8. Christensen, *Innovator's Dilemma*, 32.

9. Christensen, *Innovator's Dilemma*, 54.

10. The exceptions are 1998 and 2002, and both were held during unusual circumstances. In 1998, special prosecutor Kenneth Starr had released a salacious report of Bill Clinton's affair with Monica Lewinsky that suggested Clinton was guilty of perjury and obstruction of justice. House Republicans were quick to call for impeachment, and the electorate seemed to punish the party for its aggressive tactics in what many people deemed to be a private matter. The 2002 midterms took place fourteen months after the 9/11 attacks on the World Trade Center and the Pentagon. Republicans successfully nationalized the election, attacking Democrats as weak on national defense. In both cases, the president's party gained seats in the House. In 2002, but not 1998, the president's party also gained seats in the Senate.

11. Michael Barone and Grant Ujifusa, *The Almanac of American Politics 1984* (Washington, DC: National Journal, 1983), 367.

12. MaryAlice Erickson interview with author, September 22, 2017.

13. Michael Barone and Grant Ujifusa, *The Almanac of American Politics 1982* (Washington, DC: Barone and Company, 1981); and Barone and Ujifusa, *The Almanac of American Politics 1984*.

14. Stephen Skowronek, *The Politics Presidents Make: Leadership from John Adams to Bill Clinton* (Cambridge, MA: The Belknap Press of Harvard University Press, 1997), 295.

15. Mike Johnson interview with the author, August 13, 2017.

16. RHM Papers, Speech and Trip File, f. January 3, 1973, Nomination of Les Arends for Republican Whip.

17. Fenno, *Home Style*.

18. Market Opinion Research Illinois 18th Congressional District Study Analysis, March 1982, RHM Papers, Campaigns and Politics, Box 16, 1982, f. Market Opinion Research Illinois 18th Congressional District Study Analysis 3/82.

19. Market Opinion Research Illinois 18th Congressional District Study Analysis, March 1982, RHM Papers, Campaigns and Politics, Box 16, 1982, f. Market Opinion Research Illinois 18th Congressional District Study Analysis 3/82.

20. Market Opinion Research undertook at least four polls during 1982 for Bob Michel: one each in the months of March, July, September, and October. The analysis here is drawn from reports of those polls and a report from a baseline poll conducted by Market Opinion Research in January 1984. See Market Opinion research polls in RHM Papers, Campaign and Politics, Box 16, f. 1982; f. MOR 18th District Study (7/82), Analysis; f. 1982 Market Opinion Research 18th District Study (9/1982), Data; f. 1982 Market Opinion Research 18th District Study (10/1982), Data; Box 20, f. 1984 Market Opinion Research 18th District Study (1/1984), Analysis.

21. Barone and Ujifusa, *The Almanac of American Politics 1984*, 1331.

22. For example, see pamphlet emblazoned with the slogan "The Republican Leader Bob Michel," another pamphlet associating Michel with Reagan and reducing the cost of government, and a third noting that he's the "Top Republican in the House of Representatives." See RHM Papers, Staff Series: Pitts, Box 4, f. Campaign 1982 (2).

23. "Bob Michel on U.S. Stage," *Chicago Tribune*, August 16, 1982, RHM Papers, Campaigns and Politics, Box 16, f. 1982, Clippings (3).

24. "As constituency careers move through the expansionist stage and toward the protectionist stage, home styles tend to become more firmly established and less likely to change," writes Fenno in *Home Style*, 189.

25. Erickson interview with the author.
26. Erickson interview with the author.
27. Ray LaHood interview with the author, August 16, 2017. LaHood noted that this was unlike the practice of Congressman Tom Railsback, for whom LaHood had worked. Railsback came to Congress later, in 1966, and was a decade younger than Michel.
28. LaHood interview with the author.
29. Johnson interview with the author.
30. Johnson interview with the author.
31. Fred W. Beuttler interview with RHM, September 5, 2007, RHM Papers, Post-Congressional Series, f. Subjects: Interviews (2).
32. Days in district computed from District Work Period Schedules listing dates Michel was in the district. See RHM Papers, Campaigns and Politics, Box 16, f. 1982 and Box 19, f. 1984.
33. LaHood interview with the author.
34. LaHood interview with the author.
35. Johnson interview with the author.
36. LaHood interview with the author.
37. LaHood interview with the author.
38. LaHood interview with the author.
39. Erickson interview with the author.
40. Johnson interview with the author.
41. For example, press releases on January 15 and June 1, 1982, detailing Michel's district schedule but marked "not for release." See RHM Papers, Press Series, Box 10. Each folder contains individual press releases.
42. Erickson interview with the author.
43. Mike Johnson to RHM, "Peoria Journal Star Editorial Board," October 13, 1982, RHM Papers, Press Series, Box 1, f. Memoranda 1981–1988 (1). Michel's chief of staff during the 1982 campaign, Ralph Vinovich, wrote to the publisher of the *Peoria Journal Star* expressing frustration with their coverage of Michel. Of particular note are two sentences about their refusal to cover monies Michel had obtained for the district: "Over the years your paper has consistently either not used the press releases containing information about funds or projects the Congressman may have obtained for the district. Or if they were used, there was frequently no mention of his name in the headline or the text of the story, or it was carried very late in the article." See Ralph Vinovich to John McConnell, Publisher, *Peoria Star Journal*, December 20, 1982, RHM Papers, General Series, Box 20, f. 1982: News Media. It should be noted that not many press releases actually touted grant activity on behalf of the congressman, at least compared to releases sent after 1982.
44. RHM Papers, Press Series, Box 11, f. Remarks and Releases: May 7, 1982.
45. Carole Halicki to RHM, Ralph, Sharon, Ray, and Craig, "District Media Relations," March 15, 1987, RHM Papers, Press Series, Box 28, f. Subject: Michel Office.
46. R/S/M Inc., Campaign Evaluation Notebook, n.d., RHM Papers, Campaigns and Politics, 1982, Box 15, f. Campaign Evaluation Notebook.
47. R/S/M Inc., Campaign Evaluation Notebook.
48. Halicki to RHM, Ralph, Sharon, Ray, and Craig, "District Media Relations," March 15, 1987, RHM Papers, Press Series, Box 28, f. Subject: Michel Office.

49. LaHood interview with author.
50. RHM Papers, Speech and Trip File, f. January 3, 1973, Nomination of Les Arends for Republican Whip.
51. Mike Johnson to Carole, Ralph, Ray, and RHM, March 22, 1983, RHM Papers, Press Series, Box 28, f. Subject: Michel Office.
52. All releases obtained from the RHM Papers, Press Series, Boxes 9–15. All releases were coded from January 1981 through October 31, 1984. During election years (1982 and 1984), press releases were coded only through the end of October.
53. William "Billy" Pitts interview with the author, August 13, 2017.
54. The Michel Report, "Peoria Garden Project Is Program Gone Awry," RHM Papers, Press Series, Box 10, f. Remarks and Releases: February 4, 1981–November 9, 1981.
55. The Michel Report, "Peoria Garden Project Is Program Gone Awry,"
56. Press Release, "Government Contracts One Key to Economic Recovery in Our Area," February 14, 1983, RHM Papers, Press Series, Box 12, f. Remarks and Releases: September 21, 1982–April 29, 1983.
57. Press Release, "Illinois Republicans will present Congressman Bob Michel with the Abraham Lincoln Award Thursday, March 3 in Chicago," RHM Papers, Press Series, Box 12, f. Remarks and Releases: September 21, 1982–April 29, 1983.
58. The Michel Report, "A Summary of 1983 Efforts," March 19, 1984, RHM Papers, Project Series, 1961–1992, Box 9, f. District Project Files, Grants/Project Info, 1983–1984.
59. LaHood interview with the author.
60. Johnson interview with the author.
61. Fenno, *Home Style.*
62. The Michel Report, "House Adopts Historic Budget, but Battle Not Over," May 15, 1981, RHM Papers, Press Series, Box 10, f. Remarks and Releases: February 4, 1981–November 9, 1981.
63. The Michel Report, "Touring the District: Always a Learning Experience," April 18, 1983, RHM Papers, Press Series, Box 12, f. Remarks and Releases: September 21, 1982–April 29, 1983.
64. The Michel Report, "Help Coming for the Unemployed: House Acts on Other Issues," RHM Papers, Press Series, Box 13, f. Remarks and Releases: May 2, 1983–December 27, 1983.
65. Even though the shift is evident, political consultant and R/S/M principal Susan Bryant recommended in her post-1984 election memo to go even farther: "One suggestion I would make for change in the news media program ahead is a de-emphasis on Washington jargon in news columns and news releases. While the big dailies and their reporters understand that jargon, the local weeklies do not. So a more 'homey, corny' weekly news column would probably be better received." Susan Bryant to RHM, MaryAlice Erickson, Paul Cation, and Ray LaHood, "Review of the 1984 Campaign, What It Means for 1986," January 7, 1985, RHM Papers, Campaign and Politics Series, 1984, Box 19, f. Campaign Evaluation Memo.
66. Erickson interview with the author.
67. Erickson interview with the author.
68. Erickson interview with the author.
69. Erickson interview with the author.

70. MaryAlice Erickson, email correspondence with the author, September 23, 2017.

71. Erickson interview with the author.

72. Erickson interview with the author.

73. These data come from polls and memoranda attached to said polls located in the Campaigns and Politics Series of the RHM Papers.

74. Although in the case of helping constituents, 42 percent said they didn't know in July 1982 while only 28 percent indicated they didn't know in September 1984, which represents a considerable shift in Michel's favor. These include the polls already referenced in note 20 as well as those included in Box 20 of the series relevant to 1984. See RHM Papers, Campaigns and Elections, 1984, Box 20, Market Opinion Research. Polls were taken in January, March, August, and September 1984.

75. "Percentage of the Votes 1982 General Election" and "Percentage of Votes in the 1984 General Election," RHM Papers, Campaigns and Politics Series, 1984, Box 21, f. Vote Results.

76. Susan Bryant to RHM, MaryAlice Erickson, Paul Cation, and Ray LaHood, "Review of the 1984 Campaign, What It Means for 1986," January 7, 1985, RHM Papers, Campaign and Politics Series, 1984, Box 19, f. Campaign Evaluation Memo.

77. Susan Bryant, "Review of the 1984 Campaign, What It Means for 1986."

78. Susan Bryant, "Review of the 1984 Campaign, What It Means for 1986."

79. Amounts spent obtained from various editions of *The Almanac of American Politics*.

80. All polls are located in RHM Papers, Campaigns and Elections Series. Box 21 includes a Market Opinion Research poll from July 1985, Box 22 a study from July 1986, and Box 24 polls conducted in February, September, and October 1988. The benchmark survey conducted in February 1988 includes a summary of previous polls. See RHM Papers, Campaigns and Elections, 1988, Box 24, f. R/S/M 18th District Benchmark Survey 99/88, (2).

81. The ideological separation between the parties has reached historic highs according to DW-NOMINATE, a measure of the ideology of members of Congress based on roll call votes calculated by Keith Poole and Howard Rosenthal. See voteview.com /parties/all and Keith T. Poole and Howard Rosenthal, *Congress: A Political-Economic History of Roll Call Voting* (New York: Oxford University Press, 1997), for a discussion of the measure. See also Sean M. Theriault, *Party Polarization in Congress* (New York: Cambridge University Press, 2008); Sean M. Theriault, *The Gingrich Senators: The Roots of Partisan Warfare in Congress* (Oxford: Oxford University Press, 2013); and Thomas E. Mann and Norman J. Ornstein, *It's Even Worse Than It Looks: How the American Constitutional System Collided with the New Politics of Extremism* (New York: Basic Books, 2012).

82. Barbara Sinclair, *Party Wars: Polarization and the Politics of National Lawmaking* (Norman: University of Oklahoma Press, 2006); Theriault, *The Gingrich Senators*.

83. David C. W. Parker, *The Power of Money in Congressional Campaigns, 1880–2006* (Norman: University of Oklahoma Press, 2008).

84. LaHood interview with the author.

85. Johnson interview with the author.

86. LaHood interview with the author.

CHAPTER 14

BOB MICHEL CALLS IT QUITS

Frank H. Mackaman

I'd like to feel that as I prepare to leave the Congress, I've lived up to my parents' high ethical standard and that I'll be remembered by my constituents for representing them faithfully and well, and that nationally I will be judged as having contributed significantly to the deliberations of the House and served the institution of the Congress with honor and in an exemplary fashion.

—Robert H. Michel, October 4, 1993

I t was a matter of timing. On October 4, 1993, seventy-year-old Bob Michel announced he would not seek reelection in 1994. Thirteen months later, Republicans astounded the nation by capturing the majority in the House of Representatives, ending a forty-year drought. After thirty-eight years in the House, the longest serving Republican Leader in history quit just one election short of realizing his career-long dream. The 104th Congress would elect Newt Gingrich as its Speaker, not Bob Michel.

Years later, Michel claimed not to have had second thoughts about missing out on his fondest hope. "I don't have that all-consuming ambition, that if I didn't reach the pinnacle, like I obviously have not, then I was a failure," Michel said before confessing: "It would have been nice to have been able to at least have a majority to see what we could do. . . . It's always easy to sit on the sidelines and criticize. How would you actually have done, given the opportunity and the responsibility? I would have liked to have tested that out."[1]

Leaving Congress?

Twice before in his thirty-eight-year career, Michel thought about leaving the House. Everett McKinley Dirksen, the senior senator from Illinois and Senate minority leader, died in September 1969. Michel had grown up ten miles from Dirksen's hometown, represented Dirksen's congressional district, and considered the statesman his mentor. He called Dirksen "one of the monuments of Washington" and treasured "the privilege of knowing him, working closely with him, learning from him, and witnessing at close hand his great legislative accomplishments."[2] After a dozen years in the House, Michel thought he might have a better opportunity to replace Everett Dirksen in the Senate than achieve a position of leadership in the House of Representatives. The suddenness of the senator's death complicated the situation, however. According to Michel, it was awkward to campaign for the appointment "before the Senator's body was cold. I remember that I was so revolted at the time of all the speculation . . . as to who might succeed the Senator."[3]

Illinois politics were stacked against Michel, too. Governor Richard Ogilvie, a Republican, held the power to appoint the replacement, but Michel had been the sole member of Illinois's Republican congressional delegation to endorse Ogilvie's opponent in the 1968 primary. The die was cast, and Michel did not campaign for the appointment. The governor selected one of his own allies, Ralph Tyler Smith, Speaker of the Illinois House, for the post. Smith subsequently lost the Senate seat to Democrat Adlai Stevenson III in the 1970 special election. Disappointed but not discouraged, Michel turned his attention, in his words, "toward an extended period of service" in the House.[4]

Bob Michel waited five more years before a Republican president offered the congressman a second chance to leave Congress. As the Watergate debacle unfolded in Richard Nixon's White House, Representative H. Allen "Snuffy" Smith (R-CA) tried to persuade Bob to join the administration "to shake things up" in Nixon's congressional liaison shop. The position held some appeal for Michel, and he met with Bryce Harlow, counselor to Nixon, over lunch to talk about it. Michel did not make a commitment, however, and returned to Peoria for district events. While there, according to Michel,

Harlow called him: "Bob, the boss is going to San Clemente this weekend. Why don't we put Air Force One down in Peoria, pick up your bride, and get this thing wrapped up?" Michel replied: "Bryce, if I do that, there's no turning back. You can't do that and then tell the president 'no.'" Michel sought the counsel of Mel Laird, a former Republican congressman from Wisconsin. The two had served together on the Appropriations Committee and talked almost every day even though Laird had joined the administration as secretary of defense. Bob got Laird, who was returning from Europe, on the phone as his friend landed at Andrews Air Force Base. Laird said: "I think I know what you're calling about. I gave you the highest recommendation." He paused when Bob asked his advice and then said: "Well, Bob, you know, we had a lot of fun while we were House members. We could do our own thing pretty much, independently. We weren't beholden to anybody. Here I am, the Secretary of Defense, a pretty big job, but I'm not the boss." Bob replied: "I think I know what you're saying." Michel turned down Harlow and the president.[5]

"I Think It's a Good Time to Hang It Up"

More than twenty years later, as his career in the House neared its end, Michel found himself on the wrong side of history. A new generation replaced his friends and colleagues on both sides of the aisle. His brand of conservatism fell out of favor within his party. His style of leadership failed to meet the expectations of House Republicans relegated too long to the minority. Even his constituents demanded more of him. He tired of the job.

The generational landscape shifted under Michel's feet as he neared four decades in the House. After the 1992 elections, senior House Republicans continued to lose ground to younger party members. Of the 176 Republicans who took the oath of office in January 1993, only fourteen had served under Gerald Ford's House GOP leadership, only sixteen had served under any House Speaker before Tip O'Neill, and only thirty-two had served under any president before Reagan.[6] In other words: all but twenty-one of the Republicans had taken their seats in the House after 1978 (twenty-two years after Michel's first election—he had already served longer than anyone in history as a member of the minority party). Of Newt Gingrich, who spoke for this new generation, a senior leadership aide said at the time: "Newt is great. He's not only kicking the Democrats around, he's also serving notice to the Old Guard, pantywaist Republicans that their day is through."[7]

A shift in the nature of conservatism accompanied the generational transition. Michel's brand of conservatism had been eclipsed within the House Republican Party by the early 1990s. Billy Pitts, Michel's longtime legislative strategist, explored this theme with his boss as the two considered writing a memoir. According to Pitts, the traditional conservatives—Michel, Ford, former Minority Leader John Rhodes (R-AZ), Nixon—were not "ideological conservatives." Michel conservatives did not get wrapped up in wedge issues and social disputes. They were devoted more to "bread-and-butter, gut dollar-and-sense issues."[8] But a shift to the more rigid Republicanism of the South and West began in 1978 with the election of Gingrich from Georgia and like-minded conservatives nationwide, foreshadowing Ronald Reagan's 1980 election. Even then—with a new Republican president and a new crop of conservative Republican colleagues—Michel retained the authority within the GOP Conference to orchestrate one legislative triumph after another in a Democratic-controlled House. Regrettably for Michel, that honeymoon ended soon after 1982 as the agitators in the GOP began to question the Republican Leader's commitment to their brand of conservatism.

Michel was tormented by what he called his "curiously baseless reputation as a 'moderate' and 'compromiser.'" By every accepted means of measuring voting records, liberal or conservative, Michel scored about as conservative as any member of the Republican leadership in the House. Tellingly, he added the following to a column he wrote shortly after his retirement announcement:

> That I am not what is called a "movement" or activist ideological conservative is, of course, true, and I have had my share of criticism from the Washington-based conservative political activists and journalists. . . . But it has been my belief that true conservatism is not defined by dogmatic utterances of self-appointed ideological gurus (the real conservatives leave such thought-policing to the liberals). Conservatism—if the word is to mean anything at all—must at the very least mean adherence to political truths rooted in historical experience. Judged by that standard, my voting record over 38 years—on foreign policy, defense, and the economy—is conservative, not "moderate."[9]

Grounded in a conservatism as he defined it, Michel's style of consensus-building leadership was at odds with the confrontational tactics of the party's Young Turk wing. Bob Walker (R-PA), chief deputy whip and Gingrich ally, spoke bluntly: "We've had an attitude among many of our more senior members that because they didn't see any way out of minority status, that they found it easier to cooperate with Democrats to get a percentage of the action in the House rather than presenting alternatives."[10] The defeat of House GOP Conference Chair Jerry Lewis of California by Representative Richard Armey (R-TX) in the December 1992 leadership elections left Michel virtually isolated on a leadership team now dominated by young conservatives.[11] That isolation was compounded in January when Steve Gunderson (R-WI) and Fred Upton (R-MI), two chief deputy whips, resigned from their leadership posts. Both were seen as moderates, and their departures struck many as the result of Gingrich's maneuvering to outflank Michel.[12] *Roll Call* immediately reported that Gingrich intended to challenge Michel, although the whip later qualified it to say he would seek his party's leadership post only if Michel retired.[13]

Michel tried to remain above the fray. "The job of political leadership is not to moan about what might have been but to work for what ought to be," he said in February 1994. "The great task of political leadership is not to get caught up in factions and divisions but to transcend them and move forward."[14] But it was clear to many observers that Michel had grown tired of fighting off the increasingly combative conservatives in his Republican ranks. He realized that the Young Turks demanded a different style from their leaders. "There's a big gap between my style of leadership and my sense of values, my whole thinking process," Michel told reporters late in 1993. "[That] is giving way to a new generation, and I accept that. [That's] probably the way it ought to be. But I was really much more comfortable operating . . . [the way] we did when I first came to Congress."[15] On a personal level, Michel knew that Gingrich would challenge him for the leadership post even if Michel decided to run for another term in November 1994. The two had talked about Gingrich's plans, and although Michel believed he could rebuff the challenge, he expected "a bitter fight." "Is this good for the party, I thought. If I won, I knew it would be by a narrow margin, and I would be looking over my shoulder," Michel recalled. "Who's trying to gut me? Man, I didn't need that. I've enjoyed what I've done. I've liked doing it the way I do it. If you don't like it, get yourself another leader."[16] The fun had left the job.

No matter how toxic the Washington environment felt, Bob Michel enjoyed representing central Illinois. He often found respite in that role. He was good at it, too, and rightfully proud of the projects and funding he had procured for his constituents. But as the years marched on, he found "representing" a more demanding, and less rewarding, part of the job. When he was first elected to Congress, "the charge that the people sent me here with was, 'Bob, go down and cut the cost of government and get it off our back. That's all.' They didn't say, 'Give me more of this. Give me some of this. Give me this. Give me that.' Or 'What other programs can I qualify for?'" Michel recalled.[17] He found it harder and harder, as time marched on, to reconcile his core principles of limited government and federal thrift with his constituents' clamoring for more government benefits. Physically, the leadership duties took a toll. "I was getting up to 70," Michel remembered as an old man, "and I recognized in my own case that there were some things in which I was not as sharp as I once was, that I was slipping a bit, and better go out on a high note. . . . That's what helped me make my decision then to bow out."[18]

For myriad reasons, then, Bob Michel chose to step away. Of course, he did not expect Republicans to pick up enough seats on November 8, 1994, to win control of the House.

Reaching a Decision

"Every day I wake up and look in the mirror and say to myself, 'Today you're going to be a loser.' And after you're here for a while," the minority leader once observed, "you'll start to feel that same way. But don't let it bother you. You'll get used to it."[19] The papers of Bob Michel document a long series of retirement stories written in fits and starts by the national press. Once he became leader, seemingly every legislative reversal or evidence of some division in the House Republican ranks generated speculation that Michel would quit. Repeatedly, his office would issue a press release or grant an interview to squelch the rumor. In private correspondence, however, it seems that Michel gave renewed thought to leaving the House perhaps as many as five years before his formal announcement. The issue was a controversial bill to increase congressional pay by 51 percent—a recommendation from the Commission on Executive, Legislative, and Judicial Salaries. Reflective statements came so infrequently to Michel that this example, drawn from a February 3, 1989, journal entry, warrants its length:

> I would be remiss if I didn't recount that this past week has been one of the most difficult weeks that I've endured during my tenure in Congress and it involved the damnable way in which we attempt

to deal with the pay question with Members of Congress. I had my downers during the Watergate years when I used to hate to get up in the morning wondering what shoe would fall, but this past week knowing full well that the whole procedure is one that the public condemns and that I tried way earlier on in the process to indicate to members that you just can't play games with this issue. You are much better off taking it in reasonable amounts, right up front with a roll call vote, and then to find we're just having the wrath of God come down upon us and around us. I've rolled and tossed at night and I've gotten up early in the morning, my thoughts turn immediately to the manner in which the public is so outraged at what we're doing to ourselves. As I come to the twilight of my career here in the Congress, with certainly more years behind me than ahead of me, I don't want to go out of this job with a cloud hanging over my head but with flags flying. I don't know how the issue will finally be resolved, but I have to say that it is one of those issues that we will simply have to deal with up front, the skirmish will come this coming week and it will go on for an extended period of time because we have to resolve the differences, not only on the amount of pay, but the differences between the two houses of Congress and their view with respect to honoraria, outside income, the whole question of ethics, etc. I feel so frustrated because I want to do whatever I can for my colleagues who have been besieging me to help them get some kind of pay increase or allowance per diem for days spent away from home. In my own case, I have to satisfy the views of those folks back home.[20]

Michel's distress had already registered with his senior staff. Only six weeks before the pay-raise battle reached its climax, Bill Gavin, special assistant to the Republican Leader, wondered if his boss's heart was still in it. Although it's tempting to read too much into a single document, Gavin composed a seven-page, single-spaced memo titled "Operation Resurgence" in late November 1988 following the elections that had cost House Republicans two seats despite George H. W. Bush's White House win. Staff had met a few days before to determine how "to revitalize the leadership after a period of drift, indecision and lack of structure." The document addressed six areas of concern (attitude, direction, personnel, schedule, leadership duties, and media) and made recommendations for each. Under "Attitude," for example, Gavin wrote: "Here we must be candid: the RHM of recent years has not been on top of events *in his leadership capacity* [emphasis in the original]." Gavin expressed concern about rumors that the boss would retire or would be unwilling or unable "to meet the challenges of the brave new world of politics, a world of big, tough media, of new and often disturbing ideas, of Speakers who set their own foreign policy agenda and who savagely attack Republican presidents." If his attitude did not improve, Gavin believed that Michel would become irrelevant to the party's future:

> It is RHM's choice: does he go out with a legacy of dynamic leadership, writing a new page in the history of the Republican House leadership? Or does he go out as a good ol' boy, loved and respected, but increasingly irrelevant to the Republican future? The answer to those questions will depend on the *attitude* RHM (and, by extension, his staff) has. Do we drift for the next two or four years or do we forcefully take control of our own destiny? That is a problem of attitude and only RHM can answer it.[21]

Gavin's analysis of Michel's leadership operation proved more damning. The leadership operation going back two or three years "has lacked direction, a sense of purpose, the ability to set definite goals, assign duties and see that the goals are reached." Michel had been reacting to events rather than initiating them, his adviser reasoned. Part of the problem was Bob's collegial style, but to be effective, he had to give direction and hold people accountable. He needed to reassert his floor leadership. "Anything short of a Michel open declaration of his own vision for the session and for the Congress (not to mention 1990 and 1992) will result in the inevitable filling of the power vacuum by other Republicans."[22]

How should the Republican Leader's staff proceed? "The first big battle is to convince RHM that this radical change is needed." Gavin elaborated:

> If RHM doesn't want to change his recent leadership style, his last two or four or how many years will be drifting, purposeless and increasingly irrelevant to a new generation of Republicans in the House. With George Bush in the White House, RHM has a chance to begin anew. Unless he wants to change, nothing his staff can say will bring about the changes. But if he does want to change, his entire staff can be reinvigorated and inspired by the knowledge that RHM is going to make these last two or four or how many years full

of purpose and accomplishment and that the younger members of the House Republicans will be treated to the kind of active leadership they need and deserve.[23]

Chief of Staff Mike Johnson replied to his colleague immediately: "Our first concern has to be Bob's intent and secondly, his goals. We have to encourage Bob to delineate for us his sense of how long he wants to stay . . . and what he wants to accomplish in the next two to four years, preferably the latter."[24]

Gavin and Michel were joined by Billy Pitts, floor assistant to the Republican Leader—the three of them reiterated the points first raised by Gavin directly with Michel in memo form. They recommended that the leader use the party leadership elections in December to "set a standard that the next generation of leadership can emulate." "Nothing good can be accomplished unless you spell out to all concerned, clearly and forcefully, your vision of what the House Republicans should be doing in the 101st Congress and beyond."[25]

How did Michel respond to the challenge from his staff? He did not intend to throw in the towel quite yet. In remarks after winning reelection as Republican Leader, he told his colleagues: "I owe it to you to let you know where I think we're going in the 101st Congress." Not in 1990 or 1992, he said, but "now's the time for us as House Republicans to let Jim Wright know that this is our House, too, and we shall earn the right and the privilege to lead it into the 21st Century." His vision and the centerpiece of his legislative agenda: "true, bipartisan reform comprehensive enough to cover the waterfront from abuses of the frank to campaign finances and tough enough to stand the challenges of partisan treachery." He included several rules reforms in his platform, too, including those that would restore unlimited debate. He even offered to support the nomination of a coalition Speaker in his place on the opening day of Congress if it would "bring us closer to our goals and our dreams for this House and for the country." As his colleagues knew, Michel had spent thirty-two years in the House, all in the minority. "I wouldn't wish that on any of you," he said as he closed his remarks. "You deserve much better and together we just have to find the magic key to change all that."[26]

At first blush, it seems that Leader Michel had taken to heart his staff's warnings. But other documents in his collection reveal Michel moving ever so haltingly to a decision to retire. His campaign files shrunk markedly after 1988, perhaps signaling a winding-down; there are none of the normal records about consultants, polling, fundraising, opposition research, or district analyses as there were in his four previous races. Following congressional redistricting in 1990, he wrote privately to a dear friend: "This is my

4th time [to deal with a new district] and I'm sure it will be my last, because I've just about had it up to you-know-where with all the arguing, hemming and hawling [*sic*] and trying to take care of all the cry-babies."[27] A few months later, Barber Conable, who had retired from the House in 1984, urged Michel to keep up the good fight. At the time, House leaders were coping with the fallout from the House banking scandal and with allegations that members had used the House Post Office for nefarious purposes. Against this backdrop, Michel replied to his former colleague:

> These are indeed miserable times to be a member of the House from the standpoint of getting creamed one day after another on matters that have little to do with legislating. I wish you were back here in our midst so that I would have another crutch to lean on as I did when you were here. Sometimes you just want to throw in the sponge and begin enjoying the good life, but we're committed to another term and maybe with all the prospects for change around here, there will be a sufficient number of the good guys elected to really make a difference in the next Congress. At least we're going to give it the old college try one more time.[28]

An unguarded comment in August 1993 gave momentum to Michel's decision to retire. On Wednesday, August 11, Michel met with the editorial board of his hometown newspaper, the *Peoria Journal Star*.[29] The two-hour session followed on the heels of a key legislative battle the previous week over President Bill Clinton's sweeping tax and spending plan, which targeted rich taxpayers and increased the gasoline tax by 4.3 cents per gallon. Michel led the opposition: "The economy would be much better off if we killed the tax plan and started all over again."[30] The plan passed. Not a single Republican in the House or Senate voted for the package. It was the first time in memory that all members of a political party in Congress refused to support a major piece of legislation.

Although Michel had rallied his troops publicly to oppose the Clinton plan, he admitted in the editorial meeting, privately, that he was relieved the measure had passed. In a surprising show of frustration with his own party's unwillingness to compromise or present an alternative plan, Michel said failure of Clinton's recent efforts would have harmed the country. "As much as I opposed the bill, it would have been a devastating defeat for the president," he told the board. "To have your president so weakened, so pilloried, it tends to permeate society." As Michel explained it, if the sweeping program of tax increases and spending cuts had failed, the political fallout could have been disastrous. According to Michel, the bad feeling among Democrats, the negative effect on Clinton's presidency, and the ego boost to conservative Republicans unwilling to compromise could have ruined any chance to move forward with any deficit reduction plan. And the increasing animosity in Congress could have made the prospects for meaningful health-care reform and other major legislation less likely.

"Any number of things would tend to become unraveled," he said. "And then the debate would have become so acrimonious." He said a group of Republicans in Congress would have been overjoyed if the legislation had failed, "but they may not have been very cooperative in helping us put together something that would have been credible in its place." Michel took aim at his colleagues, describing them as probably "the most conservative and antagonistic to the other side" than at any time during his thirty-six years in Congress. Of the forty-seven freshman Republican members of the House, "seven are thoughtful moderates, and the other 40 are pretty darn hard-liners, some of them real hard-liners," Michel said. "It's eating at me," Michel volunteered. "You just shake your head."[31]

What was eating at Michel, the editorial page suggested a few days later, was his inability to do what he did best: To get opposing sides to the table, to work out differences, to forge compromises, to give a little here and get a little there and move policymaking forward. He took small pleasure in the unanimous Republican opposition to President Clinton's deficit reduction plan. "I'm more comfortable and feel much better about what I can be doing constructively to make things move," Michel told the board. That didn't happen with the deficit reduction bill, and he blamed Republicans as well as Democrats. Michel confessed that he suffered through "down days" when he felt that "you're just flapping your gums against the wind."[32]

Dean Olsen, who reported on politics for the newspaper and who had participated in the meeting, wrote a story the next day highlighting Michel's unflattering characterization of the conservatives in his own party.[33] The headline ("MICHEL GLAD BUDGET BILL APPROVED") caught the Republican Leader in a very public and embarrassing contradiction. It got an immediate rise from the Young Turks in the House. Those comments were "very disappointing to some of us," said freshman Richard W. Pombo (R-CA). Dana Rohrabacher (R-CA) added: "Those were the words of a tired leader who doesn't have the stomach for a fight."[34]

Newt Gingrich, the ringleader of the hard-liners Michel had singled out, called Michel on Friday to complain. Michel promised to issue a clarification, which he did in an interview, also on Friday, with Timothy J. Burger of *Roll Call*, the Capitol Hill newspaper. Michel explained that he intended no criticism of the Republican conservatives specifically, only of the overall political climate—a weak defense at best and one refuted a few days later in a second *Peoria Journal Star* editorial.[35] Burger pressed Michel on his own plans, noting that some on Capitol Hill speculated that Michel was preparing to step down. Michel hedged: "If there's really a chance to be maybe a participant and a constructive participant, then you feel maybe it's worthwhile." If not, Michel said, "it dampens your enthusiasm for the job." He told Burger that he would announce his reelection plans in October, two months away.[36]

Press coverage of the August 11 editorial board meeting cast a bright light on Michel's political future. News accounts preserved in his collection speculated yet again that he would retire. The *Washington Post*, for example, discovered that Michel's campaign fundraising lagged. His six-month report through June 30 showed he had raised $3,670 compared to $20,425 for the same period in 1991. His campaign balance was $142,089, down 30 percent from 1991.[37]

Michel's fans pleaded with him to stay the course. But Michel now seemed resolute. "We are mulling over our decision very seriously," he wrote to one, "and I must tell you quite frankly that had President Bush won his reelection bid I would have felt obligated to see his administration through, because I enjoyed so much working with Presidents Reagan and Bush and being their point man in the House." He added: "Things are considerably different now and sometimes I get mighty frustrated and discouraged. Also, I have, after all, served a good many years, probably longer than I should have, in view of the way a good many Americans feel about the role of a Congressman these days."[38]

Back in the district, potential Democratic opponents began to take soundings: Timothy Howard, a Peoria attorney who had spent ten years on the Peoria County Board; William Herndon, a Springfield computer consultant; Kevin Lyons, Peoria County state's attorney; and Peoria attorney Doug Stephens, Michel's opponent in 1982 and 1988. If Michel chose not to run, three stood ready to seek the Republican nomination: Ray LaHood, his chief of staff; Craig Findley, a former aide to Michel; and Judy Koehler, the unsuccessful Republican US Senate candidate in 1986.

True to his word, Michel invited reporters to his Peoria office in early fall—Monday, October 4. The ensuing thirty-minute news conference was broadcast on local television station WMBD. An emotional Michel, wearing the Combat Infantryman's Badge he earned in World War II, began his formal statement: "To our friends in the media, you'll be happy to hear that you won't have to ask me any more whether I'm running again. The answer is simply, 'No.'" Thirty-eight years in the House, eight years as a congressional staffer, and over three years in the United States Army added up to just under fifty years of public service. "That ought to be enough," Michel offered. "I think it's a good time to hang it up." Even though he thought Republicans would win big in the off-year congressional elections upcoming in 1994, "I'm not sure it will be enough to make me the Speaker." He thanked his wife, Corinne, and their family. "Yes, politics can be a noble profession," he said. "One of my constant goals in life has always been to prove to my once doubting parents that it could be so."[39]

Michel was more forthcoming in a subsequent press conference in Washington. He began by criticizing lawmakers who got elected while condemning Congress. "I never went to Congress with any view toward trashing the institution or maligning it. You've seen those who made a career of practically doing that." In contrast, his campaigns weren't "anything about revolutionizing this or changing this or that." He took criticism of Congress personally: "That hurts. Blanket charges against the Congress include us all. Have I been that bad? Have I been that rotten? I don't think so."[40] Admitting that, at times during his tenure as GOP leader, retribution against his challengers in the party may have been in order, Michel said: "That's never been my makeup. Now, that may not always be the best for a political leader sometimes, but at least that's the way I preferred to operate. It stood me well during my tenure, and that's the way I'm going to leave, under those circumstances."[41] Finally, Michel admitted, "Do I really have the same zest for the job that I once had? No."[42]

Reaction to Michel's Decision

The man poised to gain the most from Michel's retirement was generous with his praise. Newt Gingrich issued a press release immediately following his leader's announcement: "As his colleague for the past fifteen years, I have been witness to the central role Bob Michel has played in advancing both Republican and national interests," Gingrich said. "Without Bob Michel's leadership Ronald Reagan would not have passed his tax and budget cuts. Without his leadership, George Bush would not have sustained his veto strategy for four years. Indeed, little that Republican Presidents have accomplished would have been possible without Bob Michel's solid leadership."[43]

Speaker Tom Foley (D-WA) added his praise to the chorus of tributes: "While the Republican Leader and I frequently differed on the politics of government, behind the politics was a shared esteem for the institution of the Congress. I take a back seat to no one in my respect and affection for Bob, his wife Corinne, and his exceptional leadership staff." The Speaker noted that, as prevailing political philosophies changed over the years, "Bob Michel remained steadfast in his commitment to consensus in the interest of the nation and the institution of the House of Representatives. His great dignity, his constant professionalism and his instinct for decency and moderation in the face of extremes have always been proof that politics can be an ennobling profession."[44]

Michel's decision liberated the hard-edged conservative wing of the House GOP to seize the leadership reins in the House. As the *Wall Street Journal* put it, "the nihilists are routing the collaborationists." The rebellious younger generation had tired of waiting for their leader to leave and had planned to mount a challenge to him had Michel decided to stay. As if to confirm Michel's own belief: "It's time," said Representative Bill Baker, a freshman from California. "We didn't come here to watch the grass grow. We came here for change."[45]

On October 7, Gingrich announced his intention to replace Michel when House Republicans elected their new leaders, fourteen months later, in December 1994. After restating the principles of his party and the failures of the majority Democrats, Gingrich pledged "to help the American people create an opportunity society." He then paid homage to his predecessor: "We all stand on the shoulders of Bob Michel, our Leader and we know the challenges he faced. . . . As my colleague, my Leader, my mentor, and my friend, Bob Michel has taught me much about the burdens of leadership, the challenges of honest self-government and the joys and tribulations of the collegial legislative process."[46]

For Michel and Gingrich, the joys and tribulations of the legislative process played out over the last fifteen months of Michel's time in the House. The second session of the 103rd Congress commenced on January 25, 1994. Michel's last year in the House coincided with the first midterm elections during Bill Clinton's administration. According to *Congressional Quarterly*, the centerpiece of "a year of legislative setbacks and political fiascos" was the failure of President Clinton's top priority: health-care reform. Numerous other measures, some of which began the year with broad bipartisan support, fell victim to partisan disagreement, lack of time for consideration, or other problems and had to be abandoned: campaign finance, lobbying disclosure, telecommunications, and toxic waste cleanup. Veteran Democrats complained that Republican leaders had taken partisanship to a new low, *Congressional Quarterly* reported. Republicans, meanwhile, exulted in their newfound ability to stymie the Democratic majority.[47]

By October 1994, the strain between Michel and Gingrich was palpable. The understudy had paved the way for Republicans to seize the majority in the House by promoting the Contract with America. In many ways, the Contract symbolized the stark differences between the two in terms of leading, legislating, and governing. As the House Republican leadership transition drew near, the strain between the two surfaced in the press. In an interview reported on October 9, Gingrich said: "I was occasionally impatient with his style," referring to Michel in the past tense, "and he was occasionally furious at mine." Gingrich then took aim at Michel's work with Democrats: "I don't care how good a person you are. I don't care how decent you are. If you have been in the minority for 40 years, you've got a problem."[48]

In contrast, Michel said: "I didn't have to claw my way up the [leadership] ladder and stomp over people. My path to leadership came by way of being a very civil character around here and I guess being liked because I liked people." He added: "I was always very careful in my debate. I could be as partisan as others but be very careful not to overstep the ground to make it a personal thing when you're taking on somebody. . . . That tends to breed confidence among your colleagues and a respect and a camaraderie."[49]

On that score, Michel expressed reservations about his lieutenant's ability to take command: "There's a lot more responsibility to being the leader (than No. 2). . . . In that role you have to deport yourself in a manner in which you submerge the partisanship and the confrontation for the good of the country. That's what's expected of you."[50] Michel told one reporter that he had counseled Gingrich on the transition he was about to make:

In my conversations with Newt, we've discussed it very frankly. I said: "Newt, you know what you like to do and what some of your close adherents like to do. Once the total responsibility is thrust upon you, let me warn you of some of the pitfalls." He's learned a little bit of it during the course of the debate on this crime bill.[51] He told members early on that notwithstanding our being able to clean it up, he still wanted to vote against it. You can do that sometimes, but you can't do it all the time—telling everybody, "Hey folks, stick together, but I'm going to cover my backside when the final vote is cast." I always go through these things with Newt to give him a little bit of the sense of what he's going to be up against.[52]

Two months later, the 1994 midterm elections yielded a Republican-controlled House and Senate for the first time since 1955, two years before Michel was sworn in for his first term. It was a startling result on many scores. For example, Republican House candidates won 36.6 million votes nationwide, nearly nine million more than the GOP had won in 1990. That jump represented the largest midterm-to-midterm increase in one party's vote in the nation's history.[53] Had he stayed, Michel would have commanded 230 House Republican troops, an increase of fifty-two and enough to make him Speaker.

The Last Days

Not an introspective person by nature, Michel used the occasion of a meeting of the GOP Women's Federal Forum on December 8, 1994, to talk about some of the seminal events of his career in Washington. He began with the decline in the power of labor unions and continued by citing the demise of the Soviet Union, the opening to China, "the creation of more and more entitlements," the recovery and triumph of the Republican Party and the conservative movement following the Goldwater debacle in 1964, "the continuing tragedy of the continent of Africa," the civil rights movement of the 1960s, the rise of the women's movement, and, finally, the "rather painful memory" of thirty-eight uninterrupted years as a member of the minority party in Congress. He closed by offering his own political epitaph, a paraphrase of a poem by Tennyson: "Much I have seen and known. And I am part of much that I have met."[54] Yet when asked about his greatest disappointment, he replied: "It has to be that I didn't have the capacity or the wherewithal, or the knowledge, or the vision to do what Newt did to make us a majority."[55]

Robert H. Michel spent the last day of his thirty-eight years as a member of the House of Representatives on November 29, 1994. He began that Tuesday by introducing a resolution authorizing the Speaker to administer the oath of office to Steve Largent, Republican from Oklahoma, who had won a special election to fill a vacated seat. The House then handed President Clinton a rare bipartisan victory by approving a bill to implement a new global trade accord under the General Agreement on Tariffs and Trade. Michel supported the measure: "The question before us today is whether we will passively sit by and watch our destiny be shaped by other nations in the next century because we are too afraid to compete. . . . When it comes to creating jobs in a global economy, a Nation cannot sit there and contemplate its navel, twiddle its thumbs and gas about how frightened it is."[56] The bill passed, 288–146.

As the day's session neared its end, Michel introduced H. Res. 586 on behalf of the House to express thanks and appreciation for the fair and impartial manner with which Speaker Tom Foley had presided over the chamber. Michel spoke fondly of his relationship with Foley. The two had served together since 1965, "and during that time we have usually found ourselves on different sides of the issues, but we have forged a friendship for one another based on our mutual respect and love for this institution." In a surprising move, and as a sign of affection and respect, Foley then asked Michel to assume the Speaker's chair. Foley spoke of his love for the House. Michel thanked Foley for "giving me the opportunity to wield this gavel at least one time and actually sit in the chair. It was something to behold."[57]

The House adjourned at 9:10 P.M. on November 29. The second session of the 103rd Congress ended December 1 when the Senate adjourned sine die.

The consensus-builders, the solution-seekers, the pragmatic legislators are missing today. Bob Michel's imprint on history may not take the form of landmark legislative successes. Rather his legacy is one of leading a minority party with conviction, with civility, with respect for the work of a legislative body—a legacy recognized and saluted on August 8, 1994, when he received the Presidential Medal of Freedom from Bill Clinton:

> Robert Michel has served in the United States House of Representatives since 1957. That is the second longest tenure of any Republican in American history. As minority leader in the House for the last 13 years, he has served his party well, but he has also served our Nation well, choosing the pragmatic but harder course of conciliation more often than the divisive but easier course of confrontation. In the best sense he is a gentleman legislator who, in spite of the great swings in public opinion from year to year, has remained always true to the midwestern values he represents so faithfully in the House. He retires at the end of this year, generally regarded by Democrats and Republicans alike as one of the most decent and respected leaders with which any President has had the privilege to work.[58]

Notes

1. Tom Strong, "'Nice Guy' Finishes Last Session in Congress," *Peoria Journal Star*, October 9, 1994, RHM Papers, Scrapbooks, f. Clippings 1994 (1); RHM Interview conducted by One Cent Productions, LLC, October 8, 2007, RHM Papers, Post-Congressional, f. Subjects. Interviews (1).
2. RHM in *Everett McKinley Dirksen: Late a Senator from Illinois (Memorial Addresses Delivered in Congress)* (Washington, DC: US Government Printing Office, 1970), 169.
3. "Prelude to Our Race for Leader (Side B)," RHM Papers, Leadership Series, f. 96th Congress, Leadership Contests, 1980 (1).
4. "Prelude to Our Race for Leader (Side B)."
5. Fred W. Beuttler interview with RHM, September 5, 2007, RHM Papers, Post-Congressional Series, f. Subjects, Interviews (2). If Gerald Ford had won election in 1976, Michel admitted in another interview that he might have accepted an appointment as Secretary of Health, Education, and Welfare. See Shelley Epstein interview with RHM, February 1999, RHM Papers, Audiovisual Series, VHS Tapes.
6. William F. Connelly, Jr., and John J. Pitney, Jr., *Congress' Permanent Minority? Republicans in the U.S. House* (Lanham, MD: Rowman & Littlefield, 1994), 23.
7. John Podhoretz, "Newt Gingrich," *Washington Times*, August 21, 1984, RHM Papers, Scrapbooks, f. Clippings, 1984 (2).
8. "First book proposal meeting," August 19, 2003, RHM Papers, Post-Congressional Series, f. Subjects: Memoir.
9. Extension of Remarks (October 19, 1993): 25418–25419, www.gpo.gov/fdsys/pkg /GPO-CRECB-1993-pt17/pdf/GPO-CRECB-1993-pt17-7-3.pdf (Hon. Bill Emerson, "Bob Michel: A Leader and a Friend," incorporating op-ed by Robert H. Michel, "My Curiously Baseless Reputation as a Moderate and Compromiser" per *Washington Times*, October 19, 1993 ["A funny thing happened to me . . . "]).
10. Quoted in Connelly and Pitney, *Congress' Permanent Minority?* 26.
11. *Congress Daily*, October 4, 1993, RHM Papers, Personal, f. Retirement Press.
12. Charles E. Cook, "GOP House Leaders Signal New 'Take No Prisoners' Approach," *Roll Call*, January 11, 1993, RHM Papers, Scrapbooks, f. Clippings 1993 (1).
13. Timothy J. Burger, "Gingrich Prepares to Run for Leader in 1994, with Hyde and Armey Possible Contenders," *Roll Call*, January 18, 1993, RHM Papers, Scrapbooks, f. Clippings 1993 (1).
14. RHM Papers, Speech and Trip File, f. RNC Gala Leadership Breakfast, February 3, 1994.
15. Kenneth J. Cooper, "GOP Leader Michel to Retire, Opening Way for 'New Generation,'" *Washington Post*, October 5, 1993, RHM Papers, Personal, f. Retirement Press.
16. Shelley Epstein interview with RHM, February 1999, RHM Papers, Audiovisual Series, VHS Tapes.
17. Fred W. Beuttler interview with RHM, September 5, 2007, RHM Papers, Post-Congressional Series, f. Subjects: Interviews (2).
18. Brien R. Williams interview with RHM, May 24, 2007, RHM Papers, Interfile: Personal, f. 2007, Interview. Michel admitted that his hearing loss, the result of his war injuries, figured in the decision, too. See Beuttler interview with RHM, September 5, 2007.

19. Michel quoted in John Baldoni, "Bob Michel: Remembering a Politician Who Worked Both Sides of the Aisle," *Forbes*, February 18, 2017, RHM Information File, Obituary.

20. RHM Papers, Personal, f. Memoir Notes, 22–23. Michel periodically entered notes in a journal intending to write a memoir. Regrettably, he did not continue the practice.

21. Memorandum, "Operation Resurgence," November 21, 1988, RHM Papers, Press Series, f. Subjects: Michel Office General.

22. Memorandum, "Operation Resurgence."

23. Memorandum, "Operation Resurgence."

24. "Agenda Items for Meetings on Resurgence of Bob Michel," November 28, 1988, RHM Papers, Press Series, f. Subjects: Michel Office General.

25. Johnson, Pitts, Gavin to RHM, "Directions for the 101st Congress," November 29, 1988, RHM Papers, Press Series, f. Subjects: Michel Office General.

26. RHM Papers, Remarks and Releases, f. December 5, 1988.

27. RHM to Mrs. William Springer [wife of the former member], December 23, 1991, RHM Papers, Personal, f. 1991, Q–S.

28. RHM to Barber Conable, April 8, 1992, RHM Papers, Personal, f. 1992, C–D.

29. Dean Olsen, "Michel Glad Budget Bill Approved," *Peoria Journal Star*, August 12, 1993, RHM Papers, Scrapbooks, f. Clippings 1993 (2); Editorial, "Warn Us of the Next Gas Attack," *Peoria Journal Star*, September 19, 1993, RHM Papers, Scrapbooks, f. Clippings 1993 (2).

30. Michel speaking, 103rd Congress, 2nd sess., *Congressional Record*, July 26, 1993, H5076.

31. Dean Olsen, "Michel Glad Budget Bill Approved."

32. Editorial, "Message from a Statesman," *Peoria Journal Star*, August 15, 1993, RHM Papers, Scrapbooks, f. Clippings 1993 (2).

33. Olsen, "Michel Glad Budget Bill Approved."

34. Basil Talbott, "At the Crossroads," *Chicago Sun-Times*, September 12, 1993, RHM Papers, Scrapbooks, f. Clippings 1993 (2). According to Talbott, Michel regretted "gassing with the editorial board" when he "should have told the *Peoria Journal Star* to go fly a kite."

35. Editorial, "Warn Us of the Next Gas Attack."

36. Timothy J. Burger, "Bob Michel Defends Statement," *Roll Call*, August 16, 1993, RHM Papers, Scrapbooks, f. Clippings 1993 (2).

37. *Washington Post*, "Fund-Raising Lag Renews Questions on Michel's Future," August 23, 1993, RHM Papers, Scrapbooks, f. Clippings 1993 (2).

38. RHM to Beatrice Schenk, September 23, 1993, RHM Papers, Personal, f. 1993, R–S.

39. Retirement Announcement, October 4, 1993, RHM Papers, Personal, f. Retirement.

40. Associated Press, October 4, 1993, RHM Papers, Personal, f. Retirement Press; Connelly and Pitney, *Congress' Permanent Minority*, 59–60.

41. J. Jennings Moss, "Michel to Call It Quits after 37 years in House," *Washington Times*, October 5, 1993, RHM Papers, Personal, f. Retirement Press.

42. Cooper, "GOP Leader Michel to Retire." Michel said in an interview years later that a war injury that led to hearing loss also weighed in his decision: "I could tell that I was not as sharp as I was in my earlier years, and that was part of my decision." See Beuttler interview with RHM, September 5, 2007.

43. Press Release from Newt Gingrich, October 4, 1993, RHM Papers, Personal, f. Retirement.
44. Press Release from Speaker Tom Foley, October 4, 1993, RHM Papers, Personal, f. Retirement.
45. Jackie Calmes, "As Michel Leaves Top House GOP Post, Younger Generation Flexes for Fights," *Wall Street Journal*, October 5, 1993, RHM Papers, Personal, f. Retirement Press.
46. "Statement of Congressman Newt Gingrich," October 7, 1993, RHM Papers, General Series, f. 103rd Congress, First Session, Republican Conference.
47. Congressional Quarterly, *Congress and the Nation*, vol. 9, 1993–1996 (Washington, DC: Congressional Quarterly Press, 1998), 9.
48. Tom Strong, "'Nice Guy' Finishes Last Session in Congress," *Peoria Journal Star*, October 9, 1994, RHM Papers, Scrapbooks, f. Clippings 1994 (1).
49. Strong, "'Nice Guy' Finishes Last Session in Congress."
50. Strong, "'Nice Guy' Finishes Last Session in Congress."
51. The Clinton administration's crime bill triggered a fierce struggle that lasted most of 1994 and pitted conservatives who wanted stiffer punishment for criminals against liberals who wanted to emphasize crime prevention. See Congressional Quarterly, *Congress and the Nation*, 683.
52. Jefferson Robbins, "Michel Bids Farewell," *Showcase*, September 7, 1994, RHM Papers, Scrapbooks, f. Clippings 1994 (1).
53. Congressional Quarterly, *Congress and the Nation*, 9.
54. GOP Women's Federal Forum, Washington, DC, RHM Papers, Speech and Trip File, f. December 8, 1994.
55. Epstein interview with RHM, February 1999.
56. Michel speaking, Uruguay Round Agreement Act, 103rd Congress, 2nd sess., *Congressional Record*, November 29, 1994, H11498–11499.
57. Michel speaking on H. Res. 586, 103rd Congress, 2nd sess., *Congressional Record*, November 29, 1994, H11536–11537.
58. Remarks on Presenting the Presidential Medals of Freedom, August 8, 1994, *Public Papers of the Presidents*, The American Presidency Project at www.presidency.ucsb.edu /ws/index.php?pid=48956&st=&st1.

APPENDIX

REFLECTIONS

Mike Johnson

My wife, Thalia, and I went to see Bob Michel in the hospital on February 16, 2017. We knew the end—or maybe the beginning—was near for him but did not realize that he would leave us within hours.

I had known Bob for almost fifty years. It was in the years and months before he died that I came to know him best. We were able to spend more time together and talk more freely. We talked about what was going on in Washington. Actually, I would talk and he would just grimace. We also reached back into the past, his early life—the horrific fighting he went through in the Battle of the Bulge during World War II—and his early years in Congress. He reminisced about growing up in Peoria and Cubs baseball. Some days after we talked, I would do research on subjects of interest to both of us.

There was a reason for it. When his beloved wife, Corinne, died, I wrote her obituary. I talked to people she knew, recalled what I knew, and wrote it all down. I drafted and redrafted, all with tremendous affection and admiration for her. What I knew and what I learned from others were like an ink bottle from which we used to fill those classic fountain pens that somehow made it easier to turn thoughts into words. Bob liked what I wrote and startled me when he asked whether, when the time came, I would write his obituary, too.

So, I began learning about Bob what I did not know already.

I discovered much but learned little. Bob was who I had always thought he was, an exceptional human being; not a great philosopher or visionary;

not one who thirsted for fortune or fame, but a man of quiet courage and abundant character, more than I had ever seen in any one human being. It is character—that blend of virtues, values, and humanity—that defines us all. It is what made him an honorable political leader, a supreme legislator, and an extraordinary human being. His life was a model for all of those wise enough to appreciate it.

Billy Pitts, my friend and colleague on the Hill, and I have had countless conversations over time, passing judgment on how the Congress was functioning without us roaming its hallowed halls, and inevitably we would look for answers to the ponderous quandaries of the times, often asking ourselves a simple question: What would Bob do? That's "WWBD" for short.

We would sometimes come up with paths through the thicket of issues and politics based on what Michel had done in similar circumstances or what he had taught us during trying days and nights in the Capitol building's south side, where much of the work used to get done.

His blueprints, which Pitts was usually charged with turning into legislative brick and mortar, were based on a personal and political pattern of behavior Bob applied his entire career. Our colleague and Bob's successor, Ray LaHood, described the key ingredients well in his reflections. Bob listened more than he talked. He was a workhorse, not a show horse. Civility served as the cornerstone of his style of governance. He knew the difference between political principle and public policy and knew how to translate the former into the latter. He had clear objectives, exercised humble leadership, and shared both power and responsibility. He had an open mind, a big heart, an honest soul. That made him good at what he did.

When we went to see Bob that day, the obituary had been written and sent off to the family. Even though my last task for the original Republican Leader was done, I found myself next to his hospital bed, going over it in my mind, making sure it was what he wanted, making sure, as he always insisted, that the *i*'s were dotted and the *t*'s crossed.

No need really.

His life would speak for itself—like it always had and still does.

Ray LaHood

Representative Tom Railsback (R-IL) hired me as his district administrative assistant in 1977, and it must have been during the years I worked with "Rails" that I met Bob Michel. The details of that first meeting escape me now, but that in no way diminishes the impact Bob had on my life. When Tom lost the Republican primary in March 1982, I was out of work. Two months later, I was appointed to a seat in the Illinois House of Representatives only to lose the election in November. Out of work again, but Bob Michel intervened. In January 1983, I joined his staff as his district administrative assistant. In 1990, I became his chief of staff. Five years later, following Bob's retirement, I won his seat in Congress.

"Mentor" does not begin to describe Bob Michel's impact on me. In his central Illinois district, we knew him as a friendly neighbor, a devoted golfer, a spirited singer, a skilled legislator, a combat veteran, a patriot. To me, above all, he was a *teacher*. His classrooms were his office, the floor of the House, its committee rooms, and the farms and towns of the 18th District. Everywhere he went, he taught us by his example what it meant to be a public servant in the truest sense of that phrase. He came to the House every day to do the work of the people—not to engage in ideological melodramas or political vendettas. I consider myself a graduate of the Robert H. Michel School of Applied Political Arts and Sciences. Of the many lessons I learned, six stand out:

- Listening trumps talking—his first rule. I can't count the number of times Bob reminded me of his father's advice: "If you want to lead, you'd better be listening 90 percent of the time." Bob's listening was of a particular kind: earnest and respectful. He looked you in the eye. He absorbed what you had to say.
- There is no substitute for hard work. Bob prided himself on knowing his colleagues, the procedures of the House, the issues, and the needs and expectations of the folks back home. Bob was a workhorse, not a show horse, a style that won him the Republican Leader title in his contest with the more gregarious Guy Vander Jagt in December 1980.
- Civility is not weakness. And compromise is not selling out. In Bob's world, civility formed the cornerstone of governance. Quick to acknowledge that political debate in a democracy is often robust and harsh and no place for overly sensitive souls, he honored the ultimate dignity of those with whom he disagreed. I recall the remarks he delivered in 1991 at an event honoring the former Senator Howard Baker (R-TN) with the Bryce Harlow Award—Harlow, an adviser to several presidents, was well known for working with both political parties over four decades:

You know that raising the level of your voice doesn't raise the level of discussion. You know that listening with care is better than talking in sound bites and thinking in slogans. You know that peaks of uncommon progress can be reached by paths of common courtesy. Having this gift means being a knowledgeable professional—and being darned proud of it. It also means being serious without being somber, being tough without being mean, being shrewd without being devious, and being witty without being malicious. . . . It has always puzzled me that in Washington we have no public vocabulary to describe civility, which I believe is among the highest public virtues. . . . To be called "hard-nosed" or a "gut-fighter" or an "arm-twister" is in some circles the highest of praise. But civility has no similar public vocabulary.[1]

That sums up what is missing in today's politics.

- Governing differs from campaigning. In an article for *The Hill* after he retired, Bob explained: campaigns reduce issues to their simplest form; governing unravels their complexities. Campaigns define issues; governing resolves them. Campaign behavior is instinctively combative and partisan; governing might start out that way, but resolving difficult and complex problems eventually requires consensus and, yes, compromise.[2]
- Politics is neither a spectator sport nor mortal combat. Bob worked tirelessly to recruit people into politics, what he called "the noble profession." As he once put it to a group of students:

The least interesting face in a sea of faces is the face that has none of the lines of travail and triumph, failure and fortitude. I know enough about war from having experienced its steel and its fire to know that I do not want it. But on the other hand, I do not want to have it said that I lived my life like a potato in a vegetable patch with other potatoes knowing from day to day the end [as] the beginning, and waiting only to be peeled, boiled and digested.[3]

But because Bob knew war—real war, not war as it is shown in a movie or fought on the pages of a book—he refused to use macho phrases like "warfare" and "take no prisoners" when discussing politics with his staff.

He knew that the words we use often shape the political actions we take. To Bob, the harsh, personal rhetoric of ideological battles had no place in his heart, in his office, or in the House—and no place in American politics.

- Leadership, at least in the House of Representatives, is like walking a tightrope without a net. It requires balancing the ideals of the party with the complicated realities of political life. When you are in the minority, Bob advised, you learn there are three things you have to do. You have to stick to your principles. You do have to compromise. And you have to keep fighting. The temptation to abandon any of these is great. "If you've been in the minority long enough you can get to the point where you start judging issues not from the point of view of your principles but from the point of view of getting something done," Bob said. "This can lead to a gradual abandonment of principle and you wake up some fine day and find you aren't standing for anything any-more. You've become a cog in the great Congressional machine." But, he warned, "there is another, opposite, temptation. And that is to never, ever compromise, to generally accept defeat because it shows that you are not selling out. I find such a view nonsense. When you compromise in Congress, you don't compromise principle—you compromise for the *sake* of principle."[4]

When Bob passed away on February 17, 2017, I lost an inspiring teacher and a dear, dear friend.

William "Billy" Pitts, Floor Assistant to the Leader

In October 2013, at age ninety, Bob Michel spoke on the passing of former Speaker Tom Foley (D-WA) before a crowded Statuary Hall full of dignitaries including Presidents William J. Clinton and Barack Obama, as well as the bipartisan leadership of the House and Senate and members from both Houses.

As I sat in the front row, my eyes teared up when Bob spoke of me as his "right-hand man." My mind began to swirl with memories from the past forty years. I had spent endless hours working at his side, including many a late night when we found ourselves alone together reliving the day's events and pondering the future.

That brief mention by Bob in his salute to Tom Foley and to the institution of the House they both loved caught me off-guard, and my emotions swelled up inside. Bob's speech that day was one of his best, crafted in part by my friend and colleague Mike Johnson, who has a great gift with words. I had learned the art of legislating from the master. Bob was not only a man of the House but also a legislator's legislator with few peers.

The Republican Leader's characterization of how he worked with Foley struck a chord with me. I realized that the traits I had come to value and follow in my career, "faith and trust," had long ago been instilled in me by the Leader. I also realized that my work with Bob Michel had been true to my own father's creed during his forty-one years working in the House: "Work unseen, be more than you seem."

Bob Michel embraced me as part of his own family. He guided and taught me not only about the "greatest institution created by a free people" but also how to work with others with grace and civility in the struggle to find common ground. I reveled in his words about taking "great pride in knowing we had made things happen and made the House a working institution."

After Les Arends, Bob Michel was the first whip of the modern House, a House that now allowed record votes in the Committee of the Whole House, and all votes would be recorded electronically. No longer would record votes be taken by a complete call of the roll with members announcing their vote when their name was called, a process that could last forty-five minutes to an hour. Instead, members were given voting cards to use with the newly installed electronic voting stations strategically placed around the chamber. To adapt to this modern method of voting, Bob assigned his Republican colleagues to stand near the voting stations in the House chamber at the east, west, and lobby doors to make a last-minute pitch or twist an arm to line up votes.

The new minority whip operation was tested early. Organized labor had spent nearly a quarter of a century trying to enact one of their top priorities: common situs picketing. This was a controversial measure that would have permitted workers of a single construction union to shut down an entire building site. It had easily passed the House by over fifty votes during the previous Congress but was vetoed by President Gerald R. Ford in late 1975. In 1977, with President Jimmy Carter in office, the Democratic majority decided to bring the bill up just three months into the new Congress. House Republicans had to organize quickly to respond. Bob's whip operation also coordinated with outside groups, such as the builders' associations and the National Right to Work Committee. Labor and other observers in Washington were taken by surprise as the bill was defeated on a vote of 205–217. Bob taught us all an important lesson about coalition-building and about adapting his leadership to changing circumstances.

Nineteen years later, Leader Michel moved quickly to respond to President Clinton's proposed health care bill. He appointed a task force, headed by Dennis Hastert (R-IL), to develop a bipartisan health-care alternative, named "Rowland-Bilirakis" after the two primary cosponsors. With Bob's approval, I held coalition-building meetings every Monday in our office.

As reported in their book *The System: The American Way of Politics at the Breaking Point*, Haynes Johnson and David Broder wrote about our effort: "After the Clinton bill was introduced . . . Pitts" began weekly meetings with key staff directors and "lobbyists working to kill the bill. . . . They exchanged intelligence, targeted legislators for special attention. Nothing was left to chance." When Broder interviewed me regarding our coalition efforts, he wanted to characterize our weekly meetings as a "war room." I responded with a firm, "No. Absolutely not! Bob does not want us to ever use references to warfare." Our intellectual "speechwright" Bill Gavin characterized it best: "Bob Michel taught his staff, by his example, not to use these metaphors. . . . He had seen combat, firsthand, and knew that this kind of superheated rhetoric . . . demeans the service of those who engaged in actual battle and perverts politics from a way of settling differences to a way of settling scores."

Bob Michel didn't always build bipartisan coalitions to defeat legislation. Most often he employed his skills to pass measures through the House under his direction as the leader of the Republican minority. He played a crucial role in enacting President Ronald Reagan's spending reductions in 1981 by keeping the GOP Conference unified and gaining enough Democrat votes to pass the legislation. He had similar successes in passing Reagan's 1981 tax bill, his stalled crime bill, and the Tax Reform Act of 1986. In 1991, Bob Michel led the charge to enact legislation authorizing President George H. W. Bush's Desert Storm military operations against Iraq. Bush's victory was decisive, with many Democrats abandoning their party leaders while Republicans were nearly unanimous in support of the president. Leader Michel in 1993 engineered the passage through the House of President Clinton's NAFTA authorization with more Republicans than Democrats supporting the bill.

My role was always to act as a "fair and honest broker" on his behalf, working the floor, talking with key players to help understand and report back to Bob what I thought the current state of play might be, and to help in his struggle to find common ground.

Most important, throughout my time with Bob he taught me and others how to act honorably in the world of politics, a world of politics that hopefully fulfilled the will of the people. I learned my craft from someone who embodied the gold standard of public service. I learned much about character, humility, and civility and, above all, to gain the respect and trust of others in the work that I was to do.

At the end of Bob Michel's speech honoring Speaker Foley's legacy, President Clinton rose to speak and began with this: "Mr. Michel may be 90 years old, but he has the spirit of a man half his age and the wisdom of one ten times his age."

I conclude my own thoughts of the great Bob Michel by using his words to reflect my sentiment about him: "I only hope that the legislators of today, so concerned by the here and now, will feel his spirit, learn from it, and be humbled by it."

Notes

1. RHM Papers, Speech and Trip File, f. Bryce Harlow Award to Howard Baker, September 26, 1991.
2. RHM, "From Campaign to Governance," *The Hill*, contained in an email message from Mike Johnson, RHM Papers, Post-Congressional Series, f. Speeches, November 11, 2010.
3. RHM Papers, Speech and Trip File, f. "Needed: More Young Dynamic Exponents of Conservatism," St. Louis University, St. Louis, MO, May 6, 1960.
4. RHM Papers, Speech and Trip File, f. "Effective Leadership When in the Minority," Eureka College's Ronald Reagan Scholars, May 12, 1987.

ABOUT ROBERT H. MICHEL

Born in Peoria, Illinois, on March 2, 1923, Robert Henry Michel graduated from Peoria High School, the president of his class, and attended one semester at Bradley University before joining the United States Army in 1942. Wounded during the Battle of the Bulge, he was discharged in 1946, having received two Bronze Stars, a Purple Heart, and four battle stars.

Michel reenrolled at Bradley, where he met his future wife of fifty-five years, Corinne Woodruff. After graduating in 1948, Bob signed on as administrative assistant to Representative Harold H. Velde (R-IL). Upon Velde's retirement in 1956, Michel won his first term in the US House of Representatives.

One factor, above all others, defined Bob Michel's congressional service, his legacy, and his contribution to our nation's history: Republicans failed to gain the majority in the House during his thirty-eight years in Congress. His party's status as the minority party accounted for Michel's early legislative experience, his rise through the leadership ranks of the House Republicans, his leadership style and eventual challenges to that style, and ultimately to his retirement in 1995.

Minority status did not preclude political and legislative achievement, however. His central Illinois constituents elected Michel nineteen times to his seat in the House. In turn, his Republican colleagues elected him to a series of leadership posts: president of his freshman class and the only freshman appointed to the Republican Policy Committee, 1957; chairman of the National Republican Congressional Committee, 1973–1974; Republican minority whip, 1975–1981; and the longest-serving minority leader (he preferred to be called Republican Leader) in history, 1981–1995. In late 1993, Michel announced plans to retire and did not seek reelection in 1994. As luck would have it, his party won the House majority that year for the first time since 1952, and Newt Gingrich, not Michel, became Speaker.

Legislatively, Michel first made his mark on the Appropriations Committee, where he served for more than twenty years and led efforts to promote economy in government operations. The real tribute to his skill, however, occurred in 1981 during months of negotiations over President Ronald Reagan's budget and tax bills. "My most exhilarating days," Michel recalled years later, "were those during the first Reagan administration. We had only 192 members, but we enacted his program. . . . Now, that was satisfying. You'd go home at night and say, 'Well, I did the Lord's work today.'"

Michel may be most revered for something less tangible than reelections and legislative accomplishments. Speaker Tom Foley (D-WA) put it best when Michel announced his plan to retire from the House: "As prevailing political philosophies have changed over the years, Bob Michel remained steadfast in his commitment to consensus in the interest of the nation and the institution of the House of Representatives. His great dignity, his constant professionalism and his instinct for decency and moderation in the face of extremes have always been proof that politics can be an ennobling profession."

Michel's career coincided with increasing partisanship and ideological polarization in the House, with major generational and demographic changes in the membership and leadership of the House, with evolving institutional procedures, with profound changes in the balance of power between Congress and the White House, and with mounting public disillusionment with Congress's capacity to address the challenges facing the nation.

Robert Henry Michel, age ninety-three, died on February 17, 2017, nearly a dozen years after Corinne. They are survived by three sons, Scott, Bruce, and Robin; and a daughter, Laurie.

Key Dates in the Life and Career of Robert H. Michel

1923
Born March 2 in Peoria, Illinois.

1940
Graduated from Peoria High School.

1942
Enlisted in the United States Army.

1944
Wounded at Battle of the Bulge.

1946
Discharged as disabled veteran.

1946
Enrolled at Bradley University, Peoria.

1948
Graduated from Bradley University.

1948
Married Corinne Woodruff.

1949
Hired as administrative assistant to Representative Harold H. Velde (R-IL).

1956
Elected to first term in the US House of Representatives.

1958
Appointed to House Appropriations Committee.

1973
Elected chairman of the National Republican Congressional Committee.

1974
Elected House Republican minority whip.

1976
Named deputy floor leader for President Gerald R. Ford at the Republican National Convention.

1980
Named floor leader for candidate Ronald Reagan at the Republican National Convention.

1980
Elected House Republican Leader.

1981
Led House Republicans to pass the Economic Recovery Act of 1981, overcoming the Democratic majority.

1982
Defeated Democratic candidate Douglas Stephens, Michel's closest reelection bid.

1984
Named permanent chairman for the Republican National Convention.

1989
Received the Presidential Citizens Medal.

1991
Cosponsored a resolution authorizing President George H. W. Bush to use "all necessary means" to expel Saddam Hussein from Kuwait.

1994
Awarded the Presidential Medal of Freedom.

1994
Decided not to run for reelection and to retire from the House at the end of his term.

1995
Joined Hogan & Hartson as senior adviser for corporate and government affairs.

2003
Received the Congressional Distinguished Service Award.

2017
Died February 17 at the age of ninety-three in suburban Washington, DC.

BIBLIOGRAPHY

NOTE: This bibliography does not include citations to periodicals such as the *National Journal, Congressional Quarterly Weekly Report, New York Times,* or *Washington Post.*

Abramowitz, Alan I. *The Disappearing Center: Engaged Citizens, Polarization, and American Democracy.* New Haven, CT: Yale University Press, 2011.

Aldrich, John H. *Why Parties? The Origin and Transformation of Political Parties in America.* Chicago: University of Chicago Press, 2011.

Aldrich, John H., and David W. Rohde. "The Consequences of Party Organization in the House: The Role of the Majority and Minority Parties in Conditional Party Government." In *Polarized Politics: Congress and the President in a Partisan Era,* ed. Jon R. Bond and Richard Fleisher. Washington, DC: CQ Press, 2000.

Bach, Stanley, and Steven S. Smith. *Managing Uncertainty in the House of Representatives: Adaptation and Innovation in Special Rules.* Washington, DC: Brookings Institution Press, 1988.

Bacon, Donald C. "Sam Rayburn." In *The Encyclopedia of the United States Congress,* eds. Donald C. Bacon, Roger H. Davidson, and Morton Keller. New York: Simon & Schuster, 1995.

Bandura, Albert. *Social Learning Theory.* New York: General Learning Corporation, 1971.

Barone, Michael, and Grant Ujifusa. *The Almanac of American Politics 1982.* Washington, DC: Barone and Company, 1981.

———. *The Almanac of American Politics 1984.* Washington, DC: National Journal, 1983.

Barry, John B. *The Ambition and the Power.* New York: Penguin Books, 1989.

Bawn, Kathleen, Martin Cohen, David Karol, Seth Masket, Hans Noel, and John Zaller. "A Theory of Political Parties: Groups, Policy Demands, and Nominations in American Politics." *Perspectives on Politics* 10 (September 2012): 571–597.

Bessette, Joseph. *The Mild Voice of Reason: Deliberative Democracy and American National Government.* Chicago: University of Chicago Press, 1997.

Biggs, Jeffrey R., and Thomas S. Foley. *Honor in the House: Speaker Tom Foley.* Pullman: Washington State University Press, 1999.

Binder, Sarah A. *Minority Rights, Majority Rule: Partisanship and the Development of Congress.* New York: Cambridge University Press, 1997.

Black, William K. *The Best Way to Rob a Bank Is to Own One: How Corporate Executives and Politicians Looted the S&L Industry.* Austin: University of Texas Press, 2005.

Brady, David W. *Congressional Voting in a Partisan Era.* Lawrence: University Press of Kansas, 1993.

Broder, David S. *Changing the Guard.* New York: Simon & Schuster, 1980.

Cain, Bruce, John Ferejohn, and Morris Fiorina. *The Personal Vote: Constituency Service and Electoral Independence.* Cambridge, MA: Harvard University Press, 1987.

Campbell, Colton C., and Roger H. Davidson. "US Congressional Committees: Changing Legislative Workshops." In *The New Role of Parliamentary Committees,* eds. Lawrence D. Longley and Roger H. Davidson. New York: Frank Cass, 1998.

Campbell, James A. *Polarized: Making Sense of a Divided America.* Princeton: Princeton University Press, 2016.

Canon, David T. "The Institutionalization of Leadership in the United States Congress." In *New Perspectives on the House of Representatives.* 4th ed., eds. Robert L. Peabody and Nelson W. Polsby. Baltimore: Johns Hopkins University Press, 1992.

Caro, Robert A. *Means of Ascent: The Years of Lyndon Johnson.* New York: Alfred A. Knopf, 1990.

Christensen, Clayton M. *Innovator's Dilemma: When New Technologies Cause Great Firms to Fail.* Boston: Harvard Business School Press, 1997.

Clark, Jennifer Hayes. *Minority Parties in U.S. Legislatures.* Ann Arbor: University of Michigan Press, 2015.

Cleveland, James C., ed. *We Propose: A Modern Congress.* New York: McGraw-Hill, 1966.

Clift, Eleanor, and Tom Brazaitis. *War without Bloodshed: The Art of Politics.* New York: Charles Scribner's Sons, 1996.

Congress and the Nation, 1977–1980. Washington, DC: CQ Press, 1981.

Congressional Quarterly Almanac, 97th Congress, First Session, 1981, vol. 36. Washington, DC: Congressional Quarterly Inc., 1982.

Conley, Richard S. "Presidential Influence and Minority Party Liaison on Veto Overrides: New Evidence from the Ford Presidency." *American Politics Research* 30 (2002): 34–65.

Connelly, William F., Jr., and John J. Pitney, Jr. *Congress' Permanent Minority? Republicans in the U.S. House.* Lanham, MD: Rowman & Littlefield, 1994.

Cook, Timothy E. *Making Laws and Making News.* Washington, DC: Brookings Institution Press, 1989.

Cooper, Joseph, and David W. Brady. "Institutional Context and Leadership Style: The House from Cannon to Rayburn." *American Political Science Review* 75 (1981): 411–425.

Cover, Albert D., and Bruce S. Broomberg. "Baby Books and Ballots: The Impact of Congressional Mail on Constituent Opinion." *American Political Science Review* 76 (1982): 347–359.

Cox, Gary W., and Mathew D. McCubbins. *Setting the Agenda.* New York: Cambridge University Press, 2005.

CQ Almanac. Various editions. Washington, DC: CQ Press, various dates.

Currinder, Marian. *Money in the House: Campaign Funds and Congressional Party Politics.* Boulder: Westview Press, 2009.

Davidson, Roger H. "Congressional Committees as Moving Targets." *Legislative Studies Quarterly* 11 (1986): 19–33.

———. "The New Centralization on Capitol Hill." *Review of Politics* 50 (1988): 345–364.

———. "Subcommittee Government: New Channels for Policymaking." In *The New Congress,* eds. Thomas E. Mann and Norman J. Ornstein. Washington, DC: AEI Press, 1981.

———. "Two Avenues of Change: House and Senate Committee Reorganization." In *Congress Reconsidered.* 2nd ed., eds. Lawrence C. Dodd and Bruce I. Oppenheimer. Washington, DC: CQ Press, 107–133.

Davidson, Roger H., and Walter J. Oleszek. *Congress and Its Members.* 5th ed. Washington, DC: CQ Press, 1996.

Davidson, Roger H., Walter J. Oleszek, and Thomas Kephart. "One Bill, Many Committees: Multiple Referrals in the House of Representatives." *Legislative Studies Quarterly* 13 (1988): 3–28.

Deering, Christopher J. "Subcommittee Government in the U.S. House: An Analysis of Bill Management." *Legislative Studies Quarterly* 7 (1982): 533–546.

Deering, Christopher J., and Steven S. Smith. *Committees in Congress.* 3rd ed. Washington, DC: CQ Press, 1997.

Diamond, Robert A., ed. *Origins and Development of Congress.* Washington, DC: CQ Press, 1976.

Dodd, Lawrence C., and Bruce I. Oppenheimer, *Congress Reconsidered.* 8th ed. Washington, DC: CQ Press, 2005.

Dole, Bob. *One Soldier's Story.* New York: HarperCollins, 2006.

Dulaney, H. G., and Edward Hake Phillips. *Speak, Mister Speaker.* Bonham, TX: Sam Rayburn Foundation, 1978.

Evans, C. Lawrence. *Congressional Whip Count Database.* Williamsburg, VA: College of William and Mary, 2012.

———. *The Whips: Building Party Coalitions in Congress.* Ann Arbor: University of Michigan Press, 2018.

Evans, C. Lawrence, and Walter J. Oleszek. *Congress under Fire: Reform Politics and the Republican Majority.* Boston: Houghton Mifflin, 1997.

———. "The Politics of Congressional Reform: The Joint Committee on the Organization of Congress." In *Remaking Congress: Change and Stability in the 1990s,* eds. James A. Thurber and Roger H. Davidson, 73–98. Washington, DC: CQ Press, 1995.

Everett McKinley Dirksen: Late a Senator from Illinois (Memorial Addresses Delivered in Congress). Washington, DC: Government Printing Office, 1970.

Farrell, John. *Tip O'Neill and the Democratic Century*. Boston: Little, Brown, 2001.

Fenno, Richard F., Jr. *Congressmen in Committees*. Boston: Little, Brown, 1973.

———. *Home Style: House Members in Their Districts*. Glenview, IL: Scott, Foresman, 1978.

———. *Learning to Govern: An Institutional View of the 104th Congress*. Washington, DC: Brookings Institution Press, 1997.

———. *Learning to Legislate: The Senate Education of Arlen Specter*. Washington, DC: CQ Press, 1991.

———. *The Power of the Purse: Appropriations Politics in Congress*. Boston: Little, Brown, 1966.

Feulner, Edwin J., Jr. *Conservatives Stalk the House: The Story of the Republican Study Committee*. Ottawa, IL: Green Hill Publishers, 1983.

Findley, Paul. *Speaking Out: A Congressman's Lifelong Fight against Bigotry, Famine, and War*. Chicago: Chicago Review Press, 2011.

Fleming, James S. *Window on Congress: A Congressional Biography of Barber B. Conable Jr.* Rochester, NY: University of Rochester Press, 2004.

Fried, Amy, and Douglas B. Harris. "On Red Capes and Charging Bulls: How and Why Conservative Politicians and Interest Groups Promoted Public Anger." In *What Is It about Government That Americans Dislike?* eds. John R. Hibbing and Elizabeth Theiss-Morse. New York: Cambridge University Press, 2001.

Frisch, Scott A., and Sean Q Kelly. *Committee Assignments in the US House of Representatives*. Norman: University of Oklahoma Press, 2006.

———. "Dataheads: What Archivists Need to Know about Political Scientists." In *An American Political Archives Reader*, eds. Karen Dawley Paul, Glenn R. Gray, and L. Rebecca Johnson Melvin. Lanham, MD: Scarecrow Press, 2009, 401–418.

———. "Political Science and Archival Research." In *Doing Archival Research in Political Science*, eds. Scott A. Frisch, Douglas B. Harris, Sean Q Kelly, and David C. W. Parker. Amherst, NY: Cambria Press, 2012, 35–58.

———, eds. *Politics to the Extreme: American Political Institutions in the Twenty-First Century*. New York: Palgrave Macmillan, 2013.

Gains, Brian J. "Incumbency Advantage and the Personal Vote in Anglo-American Democracies." PhD dissertation, Stanford University, 1995.

Gelman, Andrew, and Gary King. "Estimating Incumbency Advantage with Bias." *American Journal of Political Science* 34, no. 4 (1990): 1142–1164.

Gely, Rafael, and Asghar Zardkoohi. "Understanding Congressional Reform: Lessons from the Seventies." *Harvard Journal on Legislation* 35 (1998): 509–535.

Gertzog, Irwin N. *Congressional Women: Their Recruitment, Integration, and Behavior*. Westport, CT: Greenwood, 1995.

Gillespie, Ed. *Winning Right: Campaign Politics and Conservative Policies*. New York: Threshold Editions, 2006.

Gilmour, John B. *Reconcilable Differences? Congress, the Budget Process, and the Deficit.* Berkeley: University of California Press, 1990.

———. *Strategic Disagreement: Stalemate in American Politics.* Pittsburgh: University of Pittsburgh Press, 1995.

Gimpel, James G. *Legislating the Revolution: The Contract with America in Its First 100 Days.* Boston: Allyn & Bacon, 1996.

Goodwin, George, Jr. *The Little Legislatures: Committees of Congress.* Amherst: University of Massachusetts Press, 1970.

Green, Matthew N. *The Speaker of the House: A Study of Leadership.* New Haven, CT: Yale University Press, 2010.

———. *Underdog Politics: The Minority Party in the U.S. House of Representatives.* New Haven, CT: Yale University Press, 2015.

Green, Matthew N., and Jeffrey Crouch. "Newt Gingrich: Strategic Political Entrepreneur." Paper presented at the 2017 Meeting of the Congress and History Conference, Washington, DC.

Green, Matthew N., and Douglas B. Harris. *Choosing the Leader: Leadership Elections in the U.S. House of Representatives.* New Haven, CT: Yale University Press, 2019.

———. "Explaining Vote Choice in the 1976 Race for House Majority Leader." Paper presented at the 2015 Midwest Political Science Association Annual Meeting.

Grossmann, Matt, and David A. Hopkins. *Asymmetric Politics.* New York: Oxford University Press, 2015.

Hacker, Jacob S., and Paul Pierson. *Off Center.* New Haven, CT: Yale University Press, 2005.

Hardeman, D. B., and Donald C. Bacon. *Rayburn: A Biography.* Austin, TX: Monthly Press, 1987.

Harris, Douglas B. "Let's Play Hardball: Congressional Partisanship in the Television Era." In *Politics to the Extreme: American Political Institutions in the Twenty-First Century,* eds. Scott A. Frisch and Sean Q Kelly. New York: Palgrave Macmillan, 2013.

———. "PanoptiCongress: Policy Deliberations in the Post-C-SPAN Congress." Paper presented at the conference on "Public Broadcasting and the Public Interest," University of Maine, Orono, 2000.

———. "Rayburn as Leader: Strategic Agency and the Textbook Congress." In *Reflections on Rayburn,* eds. James W. Riddlesperger, Jr., and Anthony Champagne. Fort Worth: Texas Christian University Press, 2018.

———. "Sack the Quarterback: The Strategies and Implications of Congressional Leadership Scandals." In *Scandal! An Interdisciplinary Approach to the Consequences, Outcomes, and Significance of Political Scandals,* eds. Alison Dagnes and Mark Sachleben. New York: Bloomsbury, 2014.

Hastert, Dennis. *Speaker: Lessons from Forty Years in Coaching and Politics.* Washington, DC: Regnery Publishing, 2004.

Herrnson, Paul S. *Party Campaigning in the 1980s.* Cambridge, MA: Harvard University Press, 1988.

Holt, Marjorie, ed. *The Case against the Reckless Congress.* Ottawa, IL: Green Hill Publishers, 1976.

Jacobson, Gary C. "Deficit-Cutting Politics and Congressional Elections." *Political Science Quarterly* 108 (1993): 375–402.

———. "It's Nothing Personal: The Decline of the Incumbency Advantage in US House Elections." *Journal of Politics* 27, no. 3 (2015): 861–873.

———. "Money and Votes Reconsidered: Congressional Elections, 1972–1982." *Public Choice* 47 (1985): 7–62.

———. "The 1994 House Elections in Perspective." In *Midterm: The Elections of 1994 in Context*, ed. Philip A. Klinkner, 1–20. Boulder: Westview Press, 1996.

Johnson, Haynes, and David Broder. *The System: The American Way of Politics at the Breaking Point*. Boston: Little, Brown, 1997.

Jones, Charles O. *The Minority Party in Congress*. Boston: Little, Brown, 1970.

———. *The Presidency in a Separated System*. 2nd ed. Washington, DC: Brookings Institution Press, 2005.

Kabaservice, Geoffrey. *Rule and Ruin*. New York: Oxford University Press, 2012.

Karol, David. *Party Position Change in American Politics: Coalition Management*. New York: Cambridge University Press, 2009.

King, Anthony. *Running Scared: Why America's Politicians Campaign Too Much and Govern Too Little*. New York: The Free Press, 1997.

King, David C. *Turf Wars: How Congressional Committees Claim Jurisdiction*. Chicago: University of Chicago Press, 1997.

Kingdon, John W. *Congressmen's Voting Decisions*. New York: HarperCollins, 1973.

Klinkner, Philip A., ed. *Midterm: The Elections of 1994 in Context*. Boulder: Westview Press, 1996.

Koempel, Michael L., and Judy Schneider. *A Retrospective of House Rules Changes since the 104th Congress*. CRS Report RL 33610. Washington, DC: Congressional Research Service, 2006.

Kolodny, Robin. *Pursuing Majorities: Congressional Campaign Committees in American Politics*. Norman: University of Oklahoma Press, 1998.

Koopman, Douglas L. *Hostile Takeover: The House Republican Party, 1981–1995*. Lanham, MD: Rowman & Littlefield, 1996.

Laird, Melvin, ed. *Republican Papers*. Garden City, NY: Anchor Books, 1968.

Layman, Geoffrey. *The Great Divide*. New York: Columbia University Press, 2001.

Lee, Frances E. *Beyond Ideology: Politics, Principles, and Partisanship in the U.S. Senate*. Chicago: University of Chicago Press, 2009.

———. *Insecure Majorities: Congress and the Perpetual Campaign*. Chicago: University of Chicago Press, 2016.

Levendusky, Matthew. *The Partisan Sort: How Liberals Became Democrats and Conservatives Became Republicans*. Chicago: University of Chicago Press, 2009.

Lind, Michael. "A Civil War by Other Means," *Foreign Affairs* 78 (September/October 1999): 123–142.

Loomis, Burdett. *The New American Politician: Ambition, Entrepreneurship, and the Changing Face of Political Life*. New York: Basic Books, 1988.

Lott, Trent. *Herding Cats: A Life in Politics*. New York: HarperCollins, 2005.

Mackaman, Frank H. "Anatomy of a Congressional Leadership Race." www.dirksen-center.org/leadershiprace/index.htm.

———. "Growing Apart: 'Civilista' Attempts to Bridge the Partisan Rift." In *Politics to the Extreme: American Political Institutions in the Twenty-First Century*, eds. Scott A. Frisch and Sean Q Kelly. New York: Palgrave Macmillan, 2013.

———. "In the Shadow of Watergate: Bob Michel Becomes a Congressional Leader." Manuscript. Pekin, IL: The Dirksen Congressional Center, 2004.

———. "Robert H. Michel: Preparing for Public Service." Manuscript. Pekin, IL: The Dirksen Congressional Center, 2017.

MacNeil, Neil. *The Forge of Democracy: The House of Representatives*. New York: David McKay Company, 1963.

Mann, Thomas E., and Norman J. Ornstein. *The Broken Branch: How Congress Is Failing America and How to Get It Back on Track*. New York: Oxford University Press, 2008.

———. *It's Even Worse Than It Looks: How the American Constitutional System Collided with the New Politics of Extremism*. New York: Basic Books, 2012.

Mayhew, David R. *Congress: The Electoral Connection*. New Haven, CT: Yale University Press, 1974.

McInnis, Mary. *We Propose: A Modern Congress*. New York: McGraw-Hill, 1966.

McSweeney, Dean, and John E. Owens, eds. *The Republican Takeover of Congress*. New York: St. Martin's Press, 1988.

Meinke, Scott R. *Leadership Organizations in the House of Representatives: Party Participation and Partisan Politics*. Ann Arbor: University of Michigan Press, 2016.

Menefee-Libey, David. *The Triumph of Campaign-Centered Politics*. London: Chatham House, 2000.

Michel, Robert H., Dick Armey, and William F. Goodling. "House Repairs: What We'll Do When We Reach the Majority." *Policy Review* (Winter 1992): 62–65.

Oleszek, Walter J. *Congressional Procedures and the Policy Process*. 5th ed. Washington, DC: CQ Press, 2001.

Owens, John E. "Taking Power? Institutional Change in the House and Senate." In *The Republican Takeover of Congress*, eds. Dean McSweeney and John E. Owens, 33–70. New York: St. Martin's Press, 1998.

Palazzolo, Daniel J. *The Speaker and the Budget: Leadership in the Post-Reform House of Representatives*. Pittsburgh: University of Pittsburgh Press, 1992.

Parker, Christopher S., and Matthew A. Barreto. *Change They Can't Believe In*. Princeton: Princeton University Press, 2013.

Parker, David C. W. *The Power of Money in Congressional Campaigns, 1880–2006*. Norman: University of Oklahoma Press, 2008.

Pearson, Kathryn. *Party Discipline in the U.S. House of Representatives*. Ann Arbor: University of Michigan Press, 2015.

Peters, Ronald M., Jr. *The American Speakership: The Office in Historical Perspective*. Baltimore: Johns Hopkins University Press, 1990.

Philipson, Evan. "Bringing Down the House: The Causes and Effects of the Decline of Personal Relationships in the U.S. House of Representatives." *CUREJ: College*

Undergraduate Research Electronic Journal (April 8, 2011). University of Pennsylvania, repository.upenn.edu/curej/141.

Polsby, Nelson W. *Consequences of Party Reform*. New York: Oxford University Press, 1983.

Poole, Keith T., and Howard Rosenthal. *Congress: A Political-Economic History of Roll Call Voting*. New York: Oxford University Press, 1997.

Rae, Nicol C. *Conservative Reformers: The Republican Freshmen and the Lessons of the 104th Congress*. Armonk, NY: M. E. Sharpe, 1998.

Ragsdale, Lyn. *Vital Statistics on the Presidency*. 4th ed. Washington, DC: CQ Press, 2014.

Reagan, Ronald. *Ronald Reagan: An American Life*. New York: Simon & Schuster, 1990.

Reiss, Edward. *The Strategic Defense Initiative*. New York: Cambridge University Press, 1992.

Rhodes, John J. *The Futile System: How to Unchain Congress and Make the System Work Again*. Garden City, NY: EPM Publications, 1976.

Riddlesperger, James W., Jr., and Anthony Champagne, eds. *Reflections on Rayburn*. Fort Worth: Texas Christian University Press, 2018.

Rieselbach, Leroy. *Congressional Reform: The Changing Modern Congress*. Washington, DC: CQ Press, 1994.

Roberts, Jason M., and Steven S. Smith. "Procedural Contexts, Party Strategy, and Conditional Party Voting in the U.S. House of Representatives." *American Journal of Political Science* 47 (2003): 305–317.

Rohde, David W. *Parties and Leaders in the Postreform House*. Chicago: University of Chicago Press, 1991.

Rubin, Ruth Bloch. *Building the Bloc: Intraparty Organization in the U.S. Congress*. New York: Cambridge University Press, 2017.

Schulze, Richard T., and John H. Rousselot, eds. *View from the Capitol Dome*. Bridgeport, CT: Caroline House Publishers, 1980.

Shepsle, Kenneth A. "Institutional Arrangements and Equilibrium in Multidimensional Voting Models." *American Journal of Political Science* 23, no. 1 (February 1979): 27–59.

Sinclair, Barbara. *Legislators, Leaders, and Lawmaking: The U.S. House of Representatives in the Postreform Era*. Baltimore: Johns Hopkins University Press, 1995.

———. *Party Wars: Polarization and the Politics of National Policy Making*. Norman: University of Oklahoma Press, 2006.

———. *Unorthodox Lawmaking: New Legislative Processes in the U.S. Congress*. 4th ed. Washington, DC: CQ Press, 2012.

Skowronek, Stephen. *The Politics Presidents Make: Leadership from John Adams to Bill Clinton*. Cambridge, MA: Belknap Press of Harvard University Press, 1997.

Smith, Steven S. *Call to Order: Floor Politics in the House and Senate*. Washington, DC: The Brookings Institution, 1989.

Snyder, James M., Jr. "Artificial Extremism in Interest Group Ratings." *Legislative Studies Quarterly* 17 (August 1992): 319–345.

Stathis, Stephen W. *Landmark Debates in Congress*. Washington, DC: CQ Press, 2007.

Steely, Mel. *The Gentleman from Georgia: The Biography of Newt Gingrich*. Macon, GA: Mercer University Press, 2000.

Stevens, Arthur G., Jr., Arthur H. Miller, and Thomas E. Mann. "Mobilization of Liberal Strength in the House, 1955–1970: The Democratic Study Group." *American Political Science Review* 68 (1974): 667–681.

Stockman, David A. *The Triumph of Politics*. New York: Harper and Row, 1986.

Stotz, Laura C. "Becoming a Majority: GOPAC, the Republican Party, and Innovation at the Grass-roots." Unpublished honors thesis. Williamsburg, VA: The College of William and Mary, 1989.

Strahan, Randall. *Leading Representatives: The Agency of Leaders in the Politics of the U.S. House*. Baltimore: Johns Hopkins University Press, 2007.

———. "Party Leadership." In *The Oxford Handbook of the American Congress*, eds. Frances E. Lee and Eric Schickler. New York: Oxford University Press, 2011, chapter 17.

Straus, Jacob R. "Electronic Voting System in the House of Representatives: History and Evolution." CRS Report for Congress. RL34366 (2008).

———. "Let's Vote: The Rise and Impact of Roll Call Votes in the Age of Electronic Voting." In *Party and Procedure in the United States Congress*, ed. Jacob R. Straus. Lanham, MD: Rowman & Littlefield, 2012.

Theriault, Sean M. *The Gingrich Senators: The Roots of Partisan Warfare in Congress*. Oxford, UK: Oxford University Press, 2013.

———. *Party Polarization in Congress*. New York: Cambridge University Press, 2008.

Truman, David B. *The Congressional Party: A Case Study*. New York: Wiley and Sons, 1959.

Walker, Douglas. *Congress and the Nuclear Freeze: An Inside Look at the Politics of a Mass Movement*. Amherst: University of Massachusetts Press, 1987.

White, Joseph, and Aaron Wildavsky. *The Deficit and the Public Interest*. Berkeley: University of California Press, 1989.

Wilson, Woodrow. *Congressional Government*. New Brunswick, NJ: Transactions Publishers, 1885 [2002].

Wolfensberger, Donald R. "A Brief History of Congressional Reform Efforts." Prepared for use by the Bipartisan Policy Center and the Woodrow Wilson Center, Washington, DC, 2013.

———. *Congress and the People: Deliberative Democracy on Trial*. Washington, DC: Woodrow Wilson Center Press, 2000.

Zelizer, Julian E. *On Capitol Hill: The Struggle to Reform Congress and Its Consequences, 1948–2000*. New York: Cambridge University Press, 2004.

CONTRIBUTORS

Colton C. Campbell is professor and chair of the Department of Security Studies at the National War College. He has worked in the offices of Senate Democratic Leader Harry Reid (D-NV), Senator Bob Graham (D-FL), and Representative Mike Thompson (D-CA). Prior to joining the National War College, he was an analyst in American national government at the Congressional Research Service and an associate professor of political science at Florida International University. He has authored or edited several books on Congress, most recently *Leadership in the U.S. Senate: Herding Cats in the Modern Era* (Routledge, 2018) and *Congress and Diaspora Politics: The Influence of Ethnic and Foreign Lobbying* (SUNY Press, 2018).

C. Lawrence Evans is the Newton Family Professor of Government at the College of William and Mary. In addition to three dozen articles and chapters in edited volumes, he is the author of three books: *The Whips: Building Party Coalitions in Congress* (University of Michigan Press, 2018); *Congress under Fire: Reform Politics and the Republican Majority* with Walter Oleszek (Houghton Mifflin, 1997); and *Leadership in Committee: A Comparative Analysis of Leadership Behavior in the U.S. Senate* (University of Michigan Press, 1991, 2001). He is also a former staff associate for Chairman Lee H. Hamilton (D-IN) on the Joint Committee on the Organization of Congress, 1992–1993; coeditor of *Legislative Studies Quarterly*, 2003–2007; and chair of the Legislative Studies Section of the American Political Science Association, 2011–2013.

Scott A. Frisch is professor and chair of political science at California State University Channel Islands. He worked in Washington for the US Department of the Treasury, as an analyst for the Office of Management and Budget, and as a legislative fellow for Senator Frank R. Lautenberg (D-NJ). He is the author or coauthor of *Committee Assignment Politics in the U.S. House of Representatives* (University of Oklahoma Press, 2006); *Jimmy Carter and the Water Wars: Presidential Influence and the Politics of Pork* (Cambria Press, 2008); and *Cheese Factories on the Moon: Why Earmarks Are Good for American Democracy* (Paradigm Publishers, 2011). His areas of expertise include Congress, public budgeting, and public policy.

Matthew N. Green is professor of politics at the Catholic University of America and an associate fellow at the Institute for Policy Research and Catholic Studies. He has written several books, articles, and book chapters about American politics. He is the author of *Underdog Politics: The Minority Party in the U.S. House of Representatives* (Yale University Press, 2015), coauthor of *Washington 101: An Introduction to the Nation's Capital* (Palgrave Macmillan, 2014), and author of *The Speaker of the House: A Study of Leadership* (Yale University Press, 2010). His most recent book is *Choosing the Leader: Leadership Elections in the U.S. House of Representatives,* coauthored with Doug Harris (Yale University Press, 2019).

Douglas B. Harris is professor of political science at Loyola University Maryland. His research on Congress, political parties, and media politics includes articles in numerous scholarly journals as well as in edited collections on congressional elections and scandals, media framing techniques, public trust in government, and archival approaches to political science inquiry. He is coauthor of *The Austin-Boston Connection: Five Decades of House Democratic Leadership, 1937–1989* (Texas A&M University Press, 2009) and coeditor of *Doing Archival Research in Political Science* (Cambria Press, 2012), *The Democratic Party: Documents Decoded,* and *The Republican Party: Documents Decoded* (both from ABC-CLIO, 2014). His most recent project is *Choosing the Leader: Leadership Elections in the U.S. House of Representatives,* coauthored with Matthew N. Green (Yale University Press, 2019).

Mike Johnson served on the White House staff of President Gerald R. Ford before moving to Congress, first as press secretary and later as chief of staff to House Republican Leader Bob Michel of Illinois for over thirteen years. He is a cofounder and member of the Board of Directors of the Congressional Institute. With Mark Strand and Jerome F. Climer, he coauthored *Surviving Inside Congress* (Perfect Paperbacks, 2009), a book originally written for new members of Congress and new staff. Johnson has served for many years as an instructor in political communications for the Legislative Studies

Institute, a graduate-level program for individuals pursuing careers in the legislative branch.

Robert David Johnson is professor of history at Brooklyn College and the CUNY Graduate Center. A specialist in congressional history, he has written seven books and edited six more on topics in US political history, US foreign relations, and contemporary US legal matters. Among them are "Ronald Reagan, Tip O'Neill, and 1980s Congressional History," in *A Companion to Ronald Reagan* (Wiley/Blackwell, 2015); *All the Way with LBJ: The 1964 Presidential Election* (Cambridge University Press, 2009); and *Congress and the Cold War* (Cambridge University Press, 2005).

Sean Q Kelly is professor of political science at California State University Channel Islands. As an American Political Science Association congressional fellow (1993–1994), he worked for the Senate Democratic Leadership in the Democratic Policy Committee as a health policy analyst. He is the author or coauthor of three books: *Committee Assignment Politics in the U.S. House of Representatives* (University of Oklahoma Press, 2006); *Jimmy Carter and the Water Wars: Presidential Influence and the Politics of Pork* (Cambria Press, 2008); and *Cheese Factories on the Moon: Why Earmarks Are Good for American Democracy* (Paradigm Publishers, 2011). He is currently working on a book focusing on the congressional appropriations process.

Ray LaHood represented the 18th District of Illinois from 1995 to 2009 in the US House of Representatives, where he served on the House Appropriations Committee and the House Intelligence Committee. He served as district administrative assistant to Congressman Tom Railsback (R-IL) before joining Bob Michel's staff in 1982. He rose to chief of staff before succeeding Michel upon Michel's retirement. President Barack Obama appointed LaHood secretary of transportation in 2009. Following a thirty-six-year career in public service, LaHood retired from his cabinet post in 2013 and joined DLA Piper as senior policy advisor. He recently published his memoir, *Seeking Bipartisanship: My Life in Politics* (Cambria Press, 2015), cowritten with Frank H. Mackaman.

Burdett A. Loomis is professor of political science at the University of Kansas. Among the most recent of his many publications are these: *Interest Group Politics* (Congressional Quarterly Press, nine editions, 1983–2015); *The Contemporary Congress* (St. Martin's, fifth editions, 1996–2005; sixth and seventh editions, Rowman & Littlefield, 2015, 2017); and *The U.S. Senate: From Deliberation to Dysfunction* (Congressional Quarterly Press, 2011). He was an American Political Science Association congressional fellow, 1975–1976. He has lectured widely for the US State Department and served as a Fulbright Distinguished Scholar in American Politics at Flinders University, Australia, 2013.

Frank H. Mackaman directs the work of The Dirksen Congressional Center, a nonpartisan, nonprofit organization. He is the editor of *Understanding Congressional Leadership* (Congressional Quarterly Press, 1981) and coauthor with Ray LaHood of his memoir, *Seeking Bipartisanship: My Life in Politics* (Cambria Press, 2015). Mackaman received his PhD in American history from the University of Missouri, Columbia. He has held adjunct appointments in political science and history at the University of Michigan, where he was director of the Gerald R. Ford Library and Museum, and Bradley University. He is a founding member and past president of the Association of Centers for the Study of Congress. A former mayor and city manager, he currently serves as an elected trustee at Illinois Central College.

Scott R. Meinke is professor of political science at Bucknell University. He is the author of *Leadership Organizations in the House of Representatives: Party Participation and Partisan Politics* (University of Michigan Press, 2016), and his research focuses on American political institutions, with an emphasis on Congress. His articles have appeared in the *Journal of Politics, Political Research Quarterly,* and *Legislative Studies Quarterly.* They include "The Changing Roles of House Party Leadership Organizations: The House Republican Policy Committee," in *Congress and the Presidency* (2014) and "Who Whips? Party Government and the House Extended Whip Network," in *American Politics Research* (2008).

Matthew S. Mendez holds a PhD in political science from the University of Southern California and is now assistant professor of political science at California State University Channel Islands. Mendez studies American politics with a focus on representation, race and ethnicity, and political behavior. "Invisible Constituents: The Presentation of Undocumented Immigrants" (2016) earned him the Best Dissertation Award from the American Political Science Association's Organized Section on Race, Ethnicity, and Politics.

Daniel J. Palazzolo is professor of political science, University of Richmond. His current research examines coalition-building in Congress in an era of partisan polarization. He was an American Political Science Association congressional fellow, 1996–1997. His publications include *Election Reform: Politics and Policy* with J. W. Ceaser (Lexington Books, 2005); *Done Deal? The Politics of the 1997 Budget Agreement* (Chatham House Publishers, 1999); and *The Speaker and the Budget: Leadership in the Post-Reform House of Representatives* (University of Pittsburgh Press, 1992).

David C. W. Parker is associate professor of political science at Montana State University. He is the author of *Battle for the Big Sky: Representation and the Politics of Place in the Race for the US Senate* (CQ Press, 2015) and *The Power of Money in Congressional Campaigns, 1880–2006* (University of Oklahoma Press, 2008), as well as articles on the consequences of divided government and how legislators employ their office expenditures to build reputations with constituents. His article "Making a Good Impression: Resource Allocations, Home Styles, and Washington Work" (with Craig Goodman) won the 2010 Alan Rosenthal Award from the American Political Science Association.

William "Billy" Pitts served Bob Michel as floor assistant to the House Republican whip and, after December 1980, as floor assistant to the Leader. In a career that spanned nearly thirty years in the House of Representatives, Pitts also served as chief of staff to the House Rules Committee, 2003–2005. He continues to consult widely on the legislative process.

Andrew J. Taylor's research focuses on American governmental institutions, particularly Congress. He has published in many journals—including the *American Journal of Political Science, Journal of Politics, Legislative Studies Quarterly, Political Research Quarterly*, and *American Politics Research*—and is the author of the books *Elephant's Edge: The Republicans as a Ruling Party* (Praeger, 2005), *The Floor in Congressional Life* (University of Michigan Press, 2012), *Congress: A Performance Appraisal* (Westview Press, 2013), and, with Toby L. Parcel, *The End of Consensus: Diversity, Neighborhoods, and the Politics of Public School Assignments* (University of North Carolina Press, 2015). In 1999–2000, he was the American Political Science Association's Steiger Congressional Fellow.

INDEX

Numbers in italics refer to pages with figures. Those followed by t refer to tables.